"*The Era of Jiang Zemin* is another t(watchers. Willy Lam's masterful stud ful, thoroughly researched, and ver) reading for anyone who wants to understand the current political scene in China today."

> ?● JOHN P. BURNS, Head, Department of Politics
> and Public Administration, University of Hong Kong

"Willy Wo-Lap Lam's work is the gold standard of Pekingology. He reads the political messages hidden amid the rhetoric and personnel shifts of Beijing, and gives us the latest on the impact of those power struggles on China's economy, military affairs, foreign affairs, and the prospects for political reform. A bracing skepticism pervades his analysis. If the unexpected should occur in China, this book will best prepare us to understand it."

> ?● ANDREW J. NATHAN, Professor of Political Science, Columbia University

"This book is quintessential Willy Lam — it is filled with an extraordinary array of information, tantalizing insights, informative analysis, and bold predictions. The author has mined all available sources and has produced a very readable account. No other study examines China of the late 1990s in such breadth or depth."

> ?● DAVID SHAMBAUGH, Director, China Policy Program and
> Professor of Political Science and International Affairs,
> George Washington University and The Brookings Institutions

"Willy Wo-Lap Lam, the dean of China watchers, has long been recognized as one of the world's most knowledgeable observers of Chinese politics. This book reveals him in top form — describing the Chinese political scene today with wit and insight, and analyzing the mounting economic and social dilemmas facing China. His extraordinary dissection of the new paramount leader, Jiang Zemin, is alone worth the price of the book for anyone interested in knowing more about China today."

> ?● JONATHAN UNGER, Director, Contemporary China Centre,
> Australian National University, and Editor, *The China Journal*

"President Jiang Zemin is about to lead China to 'Greater Glories in the 21st Century'. As the leader of an emerging superpower, Jiang has been consistently underrated. Veteran 'China Watcher' Willy Lam has put together a gripping story of Jiang, with a lot of interesting anecdotes and personal insights but also backed by extensive research. Timely and up-to-date, this is the kind of book that will appeal to both general readers and specialists."

                                     ✌ JOHN WONG, Research Director,
East Asian Institute, National University of Singapore

"In a graphic account of politics in Beijing in the era of Jiang Zemin that is based on unique access to Chinese sources, Willy Lam provides Western readers with an unrivalled analysis of how Jiang prevailed over his rivals and of the problems that arise from the limitations of his political vision."

                           ✌ MICHAEL YAHUDA, Professor of International Relations,
London School of Economics and Political Science

The ERA of

Jiang Zemin

江澤民

WILLY WO-LAP LAM

PRENTICE HALL

Singapore   New York   London   Toronto   Sydney   Mexico City

Published in 1999 by
Prentice Hall
Simon & Schuster (Asia) Pte Ltd
317 Alexandra Road
#04-01 IKEA Building
Singapore 159965

Prentice Hall, Simon & Schuster offices in Asia: *Bangkok, Beijing,
Hong Kong, Jakarta, Kuala Lumpur, Manila, New Delhi, Seoul,
Singapore, Taipei, Tokyo*

Cover photographs: New China News Agency

Printed in Singapore

5 4 3 2 1
03 02 01 00 99

ISBN 0-13-083701-6

Simon & Schuster (Asia) Pte Ltd, *Singapore*
Prentice Hall, Inc., *Upper Saddle River, New Jersey*
Prentice Hall Europe, *London*
Prentice Hall Canada Inc., *Toronto*
Prentice Hall of Australia Pty Limited, *Sydney*
Prentice Hall Hispanoamericana, S.A., *Mexico*

For
Grace

About the Author

WILLY WO-LAP LAM is a recognised authority on China. A journalist, author and researcher with more than 20 years' experience, Mr Lam has published extensively on areas including the Chinese Communist party, economic and political reform, the People's Liberation Army, and China-Taiwan and China-Hong Kong relations.

A Beijing correspondent from 1986 until the Tiananmen Square crackdown, Mr Lam is Associate Editor and China Editor of Hong Kong's *South China Morning Post*.

Mr Lam's views on China and Hong Kong are frequently sought and cited by global media such as CNN and the Voice of America (US); BBC, ITN and Channel 4 (UK); TVB, ATV and RTHK (Hong Kong); NHK (Japan); TCS (Singapore); major international news wires and *Reference Material*, an internal news source for Chinese cadres.

A Hong Kong native, Mr Lam is a graduate of the University of Hong Kong and the University of Minnesota. He is the author of three books including *China after Deng Xiaoping* (1995), which has been translated into Chinese and Japanese.

Contents

Acknowledgements

Times change. The voice of the people will be heard. The Chinese Communist Party leadership can hardly say that the principles embodied in these two sentences are products of the "bourgeois liberal West". The imperative of being in sync with the zeitgeist underpins Marx's dialectical materialism. And "people power" was first advocated by the ancient philosopher Mencius, Confucius' disciple.

For reasons that will be explained in this book, however, the Jiang Zemin administration has yet to fulfil its pledges on economic and political reform. As US President Bill Clinton repeatedly pointed out, Jiang and company needed to be on the "right side of history". Chronicling President Jiang's policies and exploits, however, has proven to be a very rewarding experience for this author in the past decade.

Hong Kong being such a pressure-cooker society, writing a book of this magnitude is no easy task. The ordeal has been sweetened by help and comradeship offered by various friends and institutions. This book has benefited immensely from the international perspective I gained while taking up a fellowship at the Media Studies Center of the Freedom Forum at New York City in early 1997. Part of the research was done during a fellowship at the Asia Research Centre of Murdoch University, Perth, Australia in 1996. I must thank these two esteemed institutions for their extraordinary hospitality.

I am very grateful to the management of the *South China Morning Post* for generous support of this project. Individual segments of this book have made use of material from articles that I wrote for the *Post*; such material has been rewritten or updated. Special thanks are due Editor Jonathan Fenby for his advice and encouragement. My colleagues at the *SCMP* China desk, Daniel Kwan, Vivien Pik-kwan Chan and Chan Yee-hon, have provided invaluable assistance. Other colleagues who have been especially helpful with this endeavour include Kevin Kwong, Dick Lau, Joseph Leung, Glenn Schloss, Gracia Wong and Chris Yeung. I have continued to benefit from the advice of former *Post* editor Phillip Crawley and former China editor David Chen.

Andrew Lynch provided much-needed help with the copy-editing and general trouble-shooting. Peter Welton and Oliver Chou, in addition to a host of experts and scholars, read through parts of the manuscript and offered perceptive suggestions. I have received top-class advice from Prof Frankie Leung of California. Thanks are particularly due the staff of Prentice Hall/Simon & Schuster, Chiang Yew Kee, Ang Lee Ming, Christine Chua Poi Kian, Stephen Troth, and Henry Leung for expert production and marketing work, as well as overall assistance.

I owe much to the following friends and China-watching colleagues for tea and sympathy, patronage and free lunches, tasteful jokes and timely tips, and much more: John Ashton, Au-yeung Kwan, Prof Richard Baum, Richard Bernstein, Alice Bishop, Prof John Burns, Daniel Burstein, Dr Francis Casey, Prof Thomas Chan Man-hung, Prof Anita Chan, Timothy Chan Tak-yue, Ying Chan, Chao Ke-Lu, Prof Chen Ke-kun, Prof Chen Ku-ying, Ching Cheong, Bibi Cheung, Prof Peter Cheung, Tai Ming Cheung, Jane Ciabattori, Prof Jerome Cohen, Prof Maurice Copithorne, John Corbett, Terry Cormier, Prof Joseph Cheng Yu-shek, Dr Andrei Denissov, Monica Faulkner, John Dolfin, Prof Edward Friedman, Victor K. Fung, John Gittings, Brad Glosserman, David Hale, He Yiwen, Andy Ho, Ho Pin, John Hoffman, Citi Hung Ching-tin, Kalina Ip, Dr Rock Yanshi Jin, Prof Brian Job, John Kamm, Prof Kuan Hsin-chi, Dinah Lee Kung, Geri Kunstadter, Carol Lai Pui-yee, Dr David C. Lam, Godfrey Lam, Sam Lam, Prof Diana Lary, Prof Lau Siu-kai, Johnny Lau Yui-siu, Dr Lee Cho-kay, Dr W. H. Leung, Li Kwok-keung, Prof Paul Lin, Dr Lawrence B. Lindsey, Damin Liu, Dr Lo Chi-kin, Paul Loong, Pauline Loong, Bette Bao Lord, Lu Keng, John Lantry, Prof Bernard Luk, Man Cheuk-fei, Nancy Maynard, Jeanne Moore, Mou Chi-wang, Robin Munro, Ross Munro, Yoshihisa Murayama, Prof Mineo Nakajima, Prof Andy Nathan, Edith Nee, Dr Robert Oxnam, Tom Polin, Norio Saitoh, Prof Orville Schell, Prof Ian Scott, Peter Seidlitz, Prof David Shamburgh, Shen Hongfei, Anthony So, Dan Southerland, Cisca Spencer, Karen Sutter, Dr Michael Swaine, Prof Akio Takahara, Prof James Tang, Anne Thurston, Prof Daniel & Lois Tretiak, Bill Triplett, Patrick Tse, T.L. Tsim, Jing Ulrich, Carmen van Kerckhove, Nury Vittachi, Prof Ezra Vogel, Wang Chi, Chris Wells, Prof Byron Weng, Dr Alfred Wilhelm, Fanny Wong, Prof Wong Siu-lun, Prof Wong Yiu-chung, Prof Wu Guoguang, Prof Wu Xiaoying, Prof Yan Jiaqi, Yang Lujun, Joseph Yau Sai-man, Dr Ti-Sheng Young, Dr Zhang Jian, Jing Zhang, and Zhang Weiguo.

For understandable — though regrettable — reasons, I cannot acknowledge the help given me by a number of friends in China, some of whom I have known for more than two decades. I am glad to report that quite a few have successfully "dived into the sea of business" and are prospering. I must also thank those who have bought my books in the past. I hope I have not let them down.

I am much indebted to my dearest wife Grace for spiritual support, and much else. And I look forward to spending more time with our splendid children, Michelle Ching-wen and Julian Wen-chung, after this tome is published. My fifth book won't appear until the next millennium.

Willy Wo-Lap Lam
Hong Kong, November 1998

Introduction: Can Jiang Zemin Lead China to Greater Glories in the 21st Century?

CRACKS IN THE SUPERSTAR'S ARMOUR

Enter the Era of Jiang Zemin

The year 1997 was a landmark for Jiang Zemin. He presided over the historic July 1 Hong Kong handover. The Chinese economy grew by 8.8 per cent while inflation dipped to two per cent. The president shoved aside long-standing enemies Qiao Shi and Liu Huaqing at the 15th Chinese Communist Party (CCP) Congress in September. A month later, the 71-year-old head of the Shanghai Faction achieved the long-sought-after stature of world statesman by holding a historic summit with US President Bill Clinton at the White House.

By mid-1998, Jiang had served nine years as party General Secretary, longer than the combined tenures of illustrious predecessors Hu Yaobang and Zhao Ziyang. More significantly, the Jiangsu-born, Jiaotong University-educated politician proved to all that he was no Hua Guofeng, the hapless *apparatchik* elevated to the dragon throne by Mao Zedong in 1976, only to be edged aside by Deng Xiaoping two years later.

It was a credit to Jiang's Machiavellian skills that he was pretty much the only Chinese politician with no worries about being stabbed in the back. From the mid-1980s onwards, Jiang was helped along by legendary luck. From 1995, most of the party elders — who gave nightmares to his predecessors Hu Yaobang and Zhao Ziyang — either died or became seriously indisposed. Cadres of Jiang's generation or seniority — Zhu Rongji, Li Peng, Li Ruihuan and former National People's Congress chairman Qiao — were not in a position to challenge him. Equally important, Jiang, who had never been a professional soldier, was able to ensure that the People's Liberation Army top brass would toe the line of "the party leadership with comrade Jiang Zemin as its core".

Almost more than any other cadre in post-1949 politics, Jiang was from the mid-1990s onward, well placed to stamp his mark on China — and history. The era of Jiang Zemin began in the second half of 1995, when Deng Xiaoping's health nosedived and the helmsman was no longer in a position to rein him in.

For reasons including residual boycotts over the June 4, 1989 crackdown, it was not until Jiang's trip to the US, Canada and Mexico in late 1997 that the West was able to assess him closely. And the media-savvy president took advantage of the limelight to project his personality fully. During his eight-day swing through the US, he played guitar, sang karaoke, debated with Clinton and harangued "anti-Chinese" students at Harvard University. With the signing of the joint statement at the White House — dubbed the "virtual Fourth Sino-American communique" by some Chinese diplomats — bilateral ties were substantially returned to pre-1989 levels.[1]

More importantly, Jiang scored a hit with different sectors of the American population by appearing to be more tolerant to different voices than expected of the leader of a monolithic Communist regime. He stressed that the opportunity to experience US politics at first hand was an eye-opener. "In the US, I have had concrete experience of American democracy — much more concrete than can be gleaned from books," he said at Harvard. When asked about the protests, he said he had heard the discordant voices but that "my only method is to ensure that my voice is louder than theirs".[2]

Jiang's Style of Governance

Jiang was in one sense China's first modern president thanks to his ability to manipulate the media — and the full arsenal of public relations and mass psychology weaponry — to his advantage. On nightly TV newscasts, the neo-authoritarian chieftain was seen handing gifts to poor peasants in hamlets in Shaanxi Province or patting the backs of soldiers guarding the remote Russian border. During a trip to the Philippines in 1996, he crooned Elvis Presley love songs with President Fidel Ramos in Manila Bay. Top guests including key US congressmen were often invited to barbecues in Chairman Mao's famed swimming pool compound in the Zhongnanhai party headquarters. The highlight of those evenings was the inevitable karaoke sessions with the polyglot host.[3]

Yet the pitfalls of Jiang-style leadership emerged soon after he took over Zhongnanhai in late June 1989. While his aides worked overtime to guarantee the president's over-saturated media exposure, he was no problem-solver. No Clinton-style "policy wonk", Jiang seemed to lack an interest in or knack for the complexities of economic and social issues. The 1997 US tour, though successful in many respects, illustrated to the full the shortcomings of both the content and style of his statecraft.

Firstly, Jiang was so enamoured of special effects and grandiose gestures that pomp and circumstance often got in the way of substance. This was evident during his tenure as electronics minister and party secretary of Shanghai in the 1980s. Jiang failed to distinguish himself in these positions. When both Jiang and Zhu Rongji served in Shanghai in the mid-1980s, one factor behind their rivalry was that Jiang was given to grandstanding while Zhu wanted to get things done. Most Shanghainese would attribute notable achievements such as the opening up of the Pudong zone to Zhu, not Jiang.

The president's approach to governance was marked by a penchant for Mao-style "mass movements" and cliquishness. Problems were often handled not through building up viable or scientific procedures and institutions but through whipping up the enthusiasm of the masses. Somewhat like the Great Helmsman, Jiang had a tendency to bend the rules — even changing the roles and functions of offices and their staff — to suit his purposes. He moved heaven and earth to nurture the Shanghai Faction into the CCP's biggest clique. Policy was at times seen through the prism of a cluster of advisers from the East China metropolis.

Jiang's preparations for his 1997 US tour smacked of many of Mao's excesses. Starting mid-year, anti-American books were removed from the shelves and America-bashing academics told to lie low at international conferences. General decision-making practically ground to a halt by August, when the best brains of China in the fields of diplomacy, military affairs, economic policy, and foreign trade burned the midnight oil writing position papers for the president. Leading the pack were trusted aides from Shanghai including Zeng Qinghong and Wang Huning. Apart from preparations for the 15th Party Congress, all matters — including the incipient currency crisis in Thailand and Indonesia — were put on the back burner. In the week before the departure on October 26, Jiang began to sleep an hour or so earlier each day — in an attempt to adjust to the time difference.[4]

Jiang was so mesmerised by the global limelight he sometimes went overboard. On returning to Beijing in early November, he insisted on representing China at the summit of the Association of Southeast Asian Nations in Malaysia later that month. Then premier Li Peng, who was still head of the party's Leading Group on Foreign Affairs, had been scheduled to attend. Jiang's lust for international exposure raised eyebrows because in the Chinese context, the position of state president or head of state was largely ceremonial.[5]

Jiang then visited Canada and Mexico in late November and early December. Chinks in his armour became obvious when he addressed staff at the Chinese Embassy in Ottawa. "In the US, it was so *noisy*, but here, everything is *calm*," he said, saying the two italicised words in English. This footage, televised on CCTV in China, had a devastating effect. "Why is he showing off his English to fellow Chinese?" said a Beijing cadre. "He should be back in China tending to growing problems of the economy." A few days later, Jiang plunged into the choppy seas of Cancun, Mexico, despite the fact that local authorities had raised a black flag to warn off swimmers. The president, however, was keen to show off his physical prowess much the same way that Mao braved the Yangtze River in 1966. He swam for just 10 minutes, most of the time supported by two burly bodyguards.[6] While he won marks from foreign correspondents, such showmanship backfired among his conservative audience back home.

CHINA'S MULTITUDINOUS — AND EVER-GROWING — PROBLEMS

Jiang Zemin Versus Deng Xiaoping

To put Jiang in better perspective, it is useful to compare him with politicians such as Deng Xiaoping and the latter's disciples Hu Yaobang and Zhao Ziyang. If either Hu or Zhao had shepherded China down the road to modernisation, the country would have taken a more "bourgeois-liberal", Westernised path. While being committed Marxists, the Dengists were more single-minded in their quest for fast-paced development — and integration with international norms.[7]

At least in the eyes of Jiang and like-minded cadres such as Li Peng and Zhu Rongji, the Dengists' development strategy had the following flaws. In pursuing double-digit growth, Deng and his associates had brought about dislocation in the economy such as hyperinflation. Moreover, the patriarch's "favouritism" towards the coast and his doctrine of "letting one group of Chinese get rich ahead of the others" had engendered a sizeable gap between east and west China and between the haves and have-nots.[8]

Equally important, the Dengists had neglected spiritual civilisation — or traditional Chinese and Marxist values — in the course of market reforms. Jiang liked to quote Deng's *mea culpa* of 1989, that "the biggest mistake in the past 10 years of reform is the neglect of [ideological] education". Some of Jiang's followers went so far as to insinuate that the Dengists' utilitarian creed would spawn corruption. They claimed that Zhao had condoned if not coined the slogan "corruption is inevitable at the preliminary stage of socialism".[9] While some of Deng's young turks had long traded Confucius and Marx for Adam Smith and Milton Friedman, Jiang wanted a revival of aspects of orthodox Marxism and traditional mores.

Coinciding with the patriarch's incapacitation in mid-1995, Jiang and company masterminded an elaborate de-Dengification movement. This was despite the fact that if only to boost his legitimacy and status as Deng's successor, Jiang also manoeuvred to have Deng Thought enshrined in the party constitution. China-watchers have called the "isms" and policies associated with Jiang and colleagues such as former premier Li Peng and Premier Zhu Rongji "neo-conservatism with Chinese characteristics". As will be seen in the later chapters, so-called Jiang Zemin Theory contained large doses of Maoism.[10]

In a nutshell, neo-conservatives believed that market reforms had to be tempered with state guidance, what they euphemistically called "macroeconomic adjustments and controls". Recentralisation also served the additional purpose of reining in centrifugalism, or regional cadres undermining central authority. The Jiang leadership was committed to one version of Mao-style egalitarianism: narrowing the coast-hinterland gap and ensuring that all Chinese be lifted out of the poverty line by 2000 or thereabouts.[11]

While Jiang seemed at times to be toadying up to the Americans, he sponsored a far more nationalistic line than the Dengists. And while seeming to follow elements of the "pro-US policy" of Deng, the president made it clear that China would go its own way. Pleas of Zhao Ziyang and such "all-out Westernisers" as dissident intellectuals Yan Jiaqi and Fang Lizhi notwithstanding, there would be no headlong rush towards Western-style modernisation — in both economics and politics. The post-Deng administration would bide its time, going by the body clock of the Middle Kingdom. As the official China News Service put it: "China will go about the open-door policy by sticking to its own time-table." Or as Li Peng reportedly said in reaction to the shock therapy tried out in Russia and Eastern Europe in the early 1990s: "Moscow may want to do it in a few months. China can afford to do it in 10 years or more."[12]

Jiang was probably luckier than his predecessors. After the gunshots at Tiananmen Square, society became depoliticised. Chinese would remain quiescent lambs so long as the standard of living kept rising. In another sense, however, the pressure on Jiang was growing by the day as time was running out for the CCP to come up with a magic formula to extend its mandate of heaven. Deng drew the right lesson from the demise of the Soviet Union by putting economic construction before ideology. By early 1998, Jiang had yet to offer a distinct body of beliefs and policies he could call his own. No visionary strategist, the president and collaborators such as Premier Zhu could only patch together titbits of the teachings of Mao, Deng and other Communist-Chinese titans: Maoist nationalism and egalitarianism, a somewhat watered-down version of Deng's market reforms, and conservative patriarch Chen Yun's Puritanism and "macro-economic adjustments and controls".[13]

The Karaoke Singer Faces the Music

To a large extent, Jiang was following the hackneyed path of the East-Asiatic model: Confucianist, paternalistic rule coupled with a centrally-supervised application of market economics. Even before the Asian financial crisis blew away the myths of "Asian values", however, it had become highly doubtful whether a Singaporean, Indonesian or South Korean approach could eradicate China's age-old ills.

In terms of China's millennium-long history, Jiang's flashy efforts at one-upmanship whether at the handover ceremony in Hong Kong or in the

Rose Garden of the White House, were mere blips on the screen. The important question is: had Jiang and company made any headway in cracking China's problems, which had accumulated with stunning ferocity since Tiananmen Square, when reform had in many areas been frozen?

The most visible threat to political stability — and Jiang's position — in the late-1990s was unemployment. Including the superfluous hands in the countryside, more than 200 million Chinese were jobless or underemployed. In the northeast rustbelt, railway officials were given standing orders to stop Beijing-bound trains if they saw hordes of workers trying to board them. The reason: the authorities wanted to prevent ugly demonstrations in the capital. As former vice-mayor of Beijing Jin Renqing put it: "Every time that jobless workers go to Tiananmen Square, we have a political problem on our hands." Jiang recognised that urban and rural unemployment was a time bomb. "If we do not come up with timely and effective methods to resolve [the problem], social stability will be jeopardised," he said.[14]

Hardly a day passed in 1997 and 1998 without the media devoting saturation coverage to new re-employment programmes or new aid packages for the unemployed. The full force of censorship was deployed to prevent the press from reporting bombings and other quasi-terrorist acts by the disgruntled and the dispossessed. Yet the jobless issue, while explosive, was but the tip of the iceberg. On the economic front, the Jiang leadership had repeatedly dragged its feet in restructuring state-owned enterprises (SOEs). The leadership's failure to bite the bullet meant precious funds kept being pumped into dinosaur concerns even as the non-state and private firms — the most efficient generators of products and jobs — suffered discriminatory policies in securing loans and other resources (see Chapter 8).[15]

Then there was the new lease of life given to the Leninist political apparatus. One of the clichés repeated in every Chinese Politics 101 or Chinese Economics 101 course on Western campuses was that economic reform had reached a dead end because no commensurate steps were taken in political liberalisation. Yet Jiang was determined as ever to hold the fort of orthodoxy. This was despite the fact that unemployment and other socio-economic problems would have been much less inflammatory had there been quasi-democratic channels for the oppressed and the disadvantaged to air their grievances. Owing to the ban on press coverage and on unofficial trade unions, there was no way in which the leadership could persuade the people to bear short-term pain for long-term gain.

Ultimately, however, the issue was not Jiang's peculiar personality, ideology or statecraft; it was the survival instinct of an ossified and frightened cadre. The CCP had become such an anachronism in the last few years of the 20th century that a slight relaxation of the "dictatorship of the proletariat" could have disastrous consequences. To sustain party power, Jiang had no choice but to buttress its control over the army, the banks and enterprises.

CAN JIANG'S NEO-CONSERVATISM REVIVE CHINA'S FORTUNES?

As China's would-be helmsman, the president had to answer the question first posed by the spunky *World Economic Herald*, whose closure on Jiang's orders when he was party secretary of Shanghai marked the beginning of the irrational turn of events that climaxed in the Tiananmen Square massacre. It was the issue of *qiuzhi* ("membership of the global community"). Liberal scholars writing in the paper in the mid-1980s asked the overwhelming question: Yes, it is inevitable that, sooner or later, China will become strong and powerful. But does the world's most populous country deserve a place in the sun? What has it done for world civilisation?[16]

Jiang's speech-writers came up with some stock answers. As the president put it in late 1997, the party and government's goal was to build up by mid-21st century "a socialist, modernised country that is rich, strong, democratic and civilised". While romancing the US media on his American tour, Jiang waxed lyrical about developing "a scientific socialist culture ... that is geared to the needs of modernisation". On other occasions, Jiang committed Beijing to "a strategy of rejuvenating China through science and education". "We shall follow the strategy of 'using science and technology to revive the nation,'" he told a group of scientists in late 1997. "We must bring to new heights the superior moral tradition of ancient times as well as the revolutionary tradition. We must diligently create an advanced spiritual civilisation through imbibing all the superior moral achievements of mankind."[17]

This book will look at how Jiang went about tackling these mind-boggling tasks by examining his policies, personality and statecraft. The beliefs and exploits of other key players such as Zhu Rongji, Li Peng, Wu Bangguo, Qiao Shi and Tian Jiyun will also be discussed. There are chapters and sections on the political system and political reform; the reform of SOEs; the People's Liberation Army, whose nominal head is Jiang; relations between central authorities and the regions; and developments in the run-up to and after the pivotal 15th Party Congress. A chapter is devoted to projections of future developments through gauging the impact of ideology, nationalism, Hong Kong and the mushrooming civil society. The epilogue will examine the meteoric rise of Premier Zhu and China's intriguing response to the Asian financial crisis of 1997 and 1998. For reasons of space and cohesiveness, foreign policy angles, apart from those touching Hong Kong and Taiwan, are not explored in detail.

The book covers events up to mid-1998, including the confirmation of Zhu Rongji as premier and Zhu's initiatives in economic and governmental reform. The author is convinced that this juncture is a good cut-off point because while Jiang's term as party General Secretary runs into 2002, much of what we know about him — his ability and idiosyncrasies — has already come to the fore.

As Beijing braced for the unpredictable new world of the 21st century, the one figure it should study carefully was the late Soviet president Leonid Brezhnev, who presided over the longest period of stagnation in the history of the global communist movement. In early 1998, even as the leadership declared China a "safe haven" from the Southeast Asian currency turmoil, the Chinese mind-set was like an amphitheatre, where the agents of change battled with a fixation on its Stalinist past.

By mid-1998, there were signs that the Jiang-Zhu team was willing to take early steps on a wide range of reforms. Market forces were given a bigger role in some economic sectors even as issues including direct elections at county level were being discussed by the president's think tanks. Yet, viewed with the perspective of momentous events such as the fall of the Suharto dynasty in Indonesia, it was by no means certain whether these moves would not be too little, too late.

New forces inside and outside the party were waiting in the wings. New ideas were beckoning. Many observers were placing their bets on Zhu who, despite sharing many of the traits of Jiang-style neo-conservatism, might be willing to try bolder measures to overhaul the system during his five-year premiership (1998–2003). Many of the economic tsar's young turks were technocrats with ample exposure to Hong Kong and the West. Moreover, real change could come at the 16th Party Congress in 2002, when politicians in their 40s and early 50s must spin out novel visions of the future to win the nation's acquiescence. There might also be exciting input into the system by non-party elements including the new class of entrepreneurs and professionals. However, the main problem for Jiang — and all Chinese — was that neither the world nor China was standing still. Even assuming that a white knight were to wake the Chinese Beauty from slumbers in some Brezhnevian castle, the nation would be hard-pressed to make up for lost time. But this is the subject for another book.

The Era of Jiang Zemin:
2 The Making of a Helmsman

INTRODUCTION: THE TRAITS OF
A STRONGMAN

Mao Zedong created heaven and earth; Deng Xiaoping changed the course of heaven and earth," according to a popular assessment of Communist-Chinese titans. "Jiang Zemin waxes eloquent about heaven; he has lots to say about the earth." Another saying went like this: "Under Mao, we *xiaxiang* [went and lived among the peasants]; under Deng, we *xiahai* [dived into the sea of business]; under Jiang, we *xiagang* [lost our jobs]."[1]

Are these appraisals of President Jiang Zemin fair? In the eyes of former *People's Daily* editor Wu Guoguang, Jiang's statecraft was neither Maoist nor Dengist. "Jiang resembles Mao but he is no Mao; he resembles Deng but he is no Deng," said Wu. "The president is consumed by con- tradictions."[2] By mid-1998, Jiang, 72, had already served nine years as party General Secretary, longer than the com- bined reign of his two precedessors, Hu Yaobang and Zhao Ziyang. However, Jiang watchers were hard put to pin down the traits of the "Jiang era". Indeed, the president, party boss and chairman of the Central Military Commission could not be credited with that many original, outstanding ideas or policies.

Future historians could perhaps characterise the years 1989 to 1998 as an interregnum, a prolonged period of hesitation and gestation. The country was recovering from the June 4 massacre. Jiang was building up his power base and trying to knock out his enemies. It was true that large numbers of cadres and non-party intellectuals wanted to move the country forward — and in the direction of reform. Yet Jiang, whose obsession was stability, was reluctant to take risks. In the meantime, old problems such as the state-owned enterprises (SOEs) and unemployment kept piling up. With political reform put on hold, it became that much harder for the Chinese Communist Party (CCP) to make its case to the people — or to persuade the masses to make relatively short-term sacrifices for the sake of long-term gain.

Instead of devoting his time and resources to hacking out new paths, Jiang gave observers the impression of a muddle-through artist. Yet while the president was largely successful in wriggling out of difficult situations, he failed to adequately address the ever more pressing demands on the economic and political fronts. By 1998, individuals and groupings in and out of the party had put forward an array of blueprints for the future. Which direction the CCP leadership would take remained uncertain. The one thing that was clear was that Jiang and company could no longer afford to drift along in currents that were picking up speed by the day. The consensus among Beijing analysts was that if Jiang did not turn a new leaf in the early part of the five-year term he secured at the 15th Party Congress of September 1997, the momentum could go to another party faction — even a non-CCP political entity.[3]

Taking another perspective, however, it could be argued that Jiang was the right man at the right time. After all, the people deserve the leaders they get. In whatever country, the calibre, moral fibre, and world-view of the supremo reflect the economic and educational level of the populace. Jiang's lack of "progressive" ideas matched the backward conditions of his country. It was true that urban intellectuals in the mid-1990s were dissatisfied with the president's apparent dearth of gravitas and vision. However, it might be that Hu and Zhao — whose stature had increased immensely after their death and ouster respectively — were too "advanced" for China. They came before their time.

This much could be said for the president. When he first came to power in late June 1989, practically all observers in China and abroad called him a new Hua Guofeng, that is, a transient figure like the party chairman ousted by Deng. But Jiang confounded his critics. From 1989 to the mid-1990s, the president successfully consolidated his own power and that of his Shanghai Faction. Moreover, China's global position having improved, Jiang was better able to counter the "peaceful evolution conspiracies" of unnamed foreign forces.

The tragedy for China was that Jiang's consuming interest was little more than maintaining the status quo — and his power base. His priorities included preserving the supremacy of the CCP and the dominant role of the "wholly people's owned sector" in the economy. Market reforms were often rolled back when they were seen to threaten the basis of party rule. Jiang's strategy for interaction with the West harked back to the famous motto of the Qing Dynasty minister Zhang Zhidong: "Chinese learning for the essence; Western learning for the applications." In other words, Jiang only wanted the technology and management skills; Western culture and democratic ideals would be barred from corrupting Chinese minds.[4]

The party boss failed to articulate a clear strategy to meet the challenges of the 21st century. Deng had nudged China's centre of gravity towards the future: hence the pro-market, pro-West bias of most of his policies. With Jiang, it was a series of zigzags. Some moments, Jiang moved the ship of state on to a leftwards course by embracing conservative, Maoist ideals. Other times, including the run-up to the 15th congress, he seemed to give his reluctant blessing to reformist, market-oriented gameplans. Overall, however, Jiang came across less as a helmsman charting bold courses than a fire-fighter scrambling to keep disasters at bay.

This chapter will look at Jiang the political animal and his Machiavellian statecraft. The preoccupation, philosophy and economic policy of the president will be thoroughly analysed. The concluding section will be devoted to an assessment of his achievements and shortcomings.

JIANG ZEMIN'S PERSONALITY AND STATECRAFT

Jiang the Political Animal

For a clue to Jiang Zemin's character, historians or psychologists need not look further than the now-famous picture of the president combing his hair before Spanish monarch Juan Carlos during a public function in Madrid in May 1996. The photograph was splashed on the front pages of all Spanish newspapers — in addition to receiving wide coverage in the international press. The Chinese were so furious that then Foreign Minister Qian Qichen cancelled a meeting with the local media. The episode, however, was revealing. Firstly, Jiang was obsessed with appearances. Secondly, he liked to project a self-confidence that was close to cockiness.[5]

While Jiang liked to tell people that he hailed from northern Jiangsu province, not Shanghai, he had a typical *haipai* (literally "ocean-style", figuratively "Shanghai-style") personality. *Haipai* traits include an expansive, outward-going style bordering on the unctuous; an ability to handle oneself to good advantage in public arenas; a soft spot for lavish ceremonies and big feasts; and a concern with public relations effects rather than substance. A polyglot, Jiang lost no opportunity in demonstrating his skill in languages and dialects including English, Russian, Romanian, Japanese, and Cantonese. He also liked to show off his knowledge of classic Chinese poetry — as well as aphorisms and proverbs in Chinese, Russian and Romanian.[6]

Jiang was a man for all seasons — particularly behind the microphone. He sang songs on both serious and jovial occasions. While discussing the anniversary of World War Two with a group of deputies to the 1995 National People's Congress, Jiang could not help humming a few songs popularised by the Red Army. During the Asia-Pacific Economic Cooperation meeting in Manila a year later, Jiang made international headlines singing golden oldies — including Elvis Presley's *Love Me Tender* — with President Fidel Ramos.[7]

Karaoke singing was a popular form of entertainment that the party chief put out for VIP visitors, including US Congressmen. Sometimes the merrymaking took place in his office close to Mao's old swimming pool. Jiang, however, also had a taste for the classics, ranging from Peking opera to Mozart, Beethoven and Schubert. Immediately after Deng's death, Jiang reportedly consoled himself with Tang Dynasty poetry and lots of Mozart.[8]

Behind his bonhomie was a mastery of the art of winning friends and influencing people. More often than not, Jiang was able to earn the grudging acceptance of political foes or cadres who dismissed him as a lightweight. He always rewarded those who had done him a favour. Sometimes, his largesse extended to adversaries about to go into retirement — perhaps to make sure they would just lie low. Part of his apparent popularity in the People's Liberation Army stemmed from the frequency with which he had raised the salaries of soldiers and promoted senior officers.[9]

Jiang's loyalty to members of his inner circle — the so-called Shanghai Faction — was legendary. This was particularly so for Wang Daohan, 83 (in 1998), the former Shanghai mayor who played a big role in Jiang's elevation. According to insiders, Jiang would often drop by Wang's house in

Beijing. Once in the summer of 1996, he waited for nearly two hours for Wang to return. Just before Wang went on a trip to the US the same year, Jiang called up a member of Wang's party to ensure that the old man's schedule would include plenty of rest. In early 1997, Jiang convened a high-level meeting to discuss Taiwan in the guesthouse where Wang was staying because the elder had not been feeling too well. Such important conferences were normally held behind the high walls of the Zhongnanhai party headquarters near the Forbidden City in Beijing.[10]

Jiang demonstrated remarkable camaraderie with long-time advisers from Shanghai, many of whom had not brought their families with them to the capital. On festivals or weekends, aides including Vice-President of the Chinese Academy of Social Sciences Liu Ji, 63, and political scientist Wang Huning, 43, were often asked to dine at the Jiang household. Choice Shanghainese cuisine was featured. The president never forgot to send presents on his cronies' birthdays. Many of the latter framed pictures taken with the president and displayed them in their offices to impress friends and clients.[11]

The sons and daughters of his former patrons were always well taken care of. Take the case of Jiang's "favours" for the associates and offspring of Gu Mu, the vice-premier who was his superior and patron at the National Import and Export Commission. Soon after his elevation to power in 1989, Jiang promoted Gu's long-time secretary, Hu Guangbao, as a deputy director of the party Central Committee's General Office. One of Gu's sons-in-law was made a vice-governor of a medium-sized province in the mid-1990s.[12]

In the spring of 1996, Beijing and Shenzhen were abuzz with a story of how Jiang had allegedly offered protection to one of Gu's children. After a function one evening, the driver of the wife of a senior Shenzhen official got into an altercation with the driver of another big shot. A fistfight followed. When the cadre's spouse tried to intervene, she was manhandled. It turned out the other limousine belonged to one of Gu's sons.

According to one version of the story reported in the Hong Kong media, the Shenzhen official's protests went all the way to Jiang's office. A month later, a person who identified himself as "General Secretary Jiang" called the official's wife to "clear up the matter". His first question was: "Was the limo you were using that evening an official car?" She said yes. "But isn't it against cadre regulations for spouses to use municipal vehicles after office hours and for their own purposes?" the caller continued. The official's wife was nonplussed. But she got the message that given his antagonist's power-ful patron in Beijing, there was no way her husband could do anything.[13]

But Jiang could be spiteful to his foes, particularly those who had lost influence. He lacked the magnanimity of a Hu Yaobang. The harsh treat-ment meted out to the secretary of ousted party chief Zhao Ziyang, Bao Tong, was said to be "retribution" for the latter's failure to respond to efforts by Jiang to curry favour with Zhao in the 1980s.[14]

Jiang was also cold to foreigners who used to know him as either the Shanghai mayor or as a mid-ranking official at the Ministry of Electronics — but who failed to pay homage to him after his elevation to the Dragon Throne. This was the fate of a Hong Kong businessman who wined and dined Jiang when the latter was based in Shanghai. Upon seeing Jiang on a social function in the early 1990s, the same businessman thought he needed not stand on ceremony — and tried to engage the president in small talk. Jiang humoured him for a minute or so and then bitterly scolded his aides for letting the executive get near him.[15]

The Obsession with Power

Jiang watchers have spotted similarities between his Machiavellian ap-proach to grabbing and wielding power and that of Mao. The Great Helms-man, a bookworm and expert on ancient Chinese history, was an authority on the rise and fall of dynastic monarchs. While Jiang, an electrical engi-neer, had no scholarly pretensions, he instructed close aides such as Zeng Qinghong and Wang Huning to make detailed studies of the "power pro-file" of historical figures. Jiang was said to be particularly interested in "Truman-like super-achievers" — officials with humble origins and medio-cre track records who proved the pundits wrong.

Jiang was at pains to point out the importance of leadership cores. "Each leadership must have a core," he said in early 1995. "Chairman Mao was the core of the first-generation leadership, and comrade Xiaoping the core of the second generation." He added while there might be different appraisals of the stature of the three "core" figures, such a position was needed to preserve the sanctity and authority of any leadership group. The president went on to admonish cadres to remain in unison with the party leadership "no matter what happens".[16]

Jiang's difficulty lay in the fact that to rule such a complex country as China effectively, he had to become a helmsman with the authority of

Deng. However, he was neither Deng nor Mao. And the time for helmsmen was past. Thus Jiang went through a series of manoeuvres to keep in power. These machinations had an adverse impact on the quality of his administration — and his record in the history books.

To understand Jiang's Machiavellian ways, it is important to bear in mind his narrow political base in late June 1989. When he first ascended the Peacock Throne, he had few "mountain strongholds" to rely upon. Apart from Shanghai, the power base he could count on was the Ministries of Machine-Building and Electronics, where he served more than 10 years. Jiang was particularly close to the machine-building minister in the 1970s, Zhou Jiannan, who died in 1995. The president was partly responsible for the meteoric rise of Zhou's son, Zhou Xiaochuan, who became vice-governor of the People's Bank of China in the mid-1990s.[17]

Jiang also had links with the powerful automobile industry, having served in the First Automobile Plant in Changchun upon his return from the USSR in 1956. Among members of the "automobile mafia" who saw their political fortunes rise under Jiang's tenure were Vice-Premier Li Lanqing; head of the Taiwan Affairs Office Wang Zhaoguo; and the former party chief of Shenzhen Li Youwei.[18]

However, even after his promotion to the Politburo in 1987, Jiang was seen as a lightweight. He was looked down upon by Zhao Ziyang's people right until the June 4 crackdown. Upon becoming General Secretary, he was also snubbed by the Beijing Faction led by then party secretary of Beijing Chen Xitong. However, Jiang soon proved to be a skilful manipulator. He built up his Shanghai Faction into a formidable redoubt (see following section).

Jiang's *savoir faire* manifested itself most clearly in his handling of the party elders, including Deng Xiaoping. In the early 1990s, the president managed a delicate balancing act by currying favour with the Chief Architect of Reform and humouring conservative party veterans. This tested Jiang's skills to the limit — and almost cost him Deng's support. As a protest against Jiang's lack of interest in his reforms, Deng went to southern China to begin his *nanxun* ("imperial tour") without bothering to tell the president.[19]

With the death of Chen Yun and Deng Xiaoping nearly incapable in 1995, Jiang knew he would be spared the ordeal of Hu Yaobang or Zhao Ziyang — that is, having his fate controlled by the veterans. He listened to the advice of aides such as Wang Huning in maintaining party unity by

appearing to continue his veneration of the first-generation revolutionaries
— and taking care of their children. Most of Deng's children either kept
their government posts or were allowed to go into business.[20]

The only known conflicts that took place between Jiang and members
of the "first family" involved Deng Rong and Deng Zhifang in 1995. In
January that year, Ms Deng gave an interview to the *New York Times* in
which she hinted her father might welcome a revaluation of the June 4
massacre. After that, Jiang ordered her to keep her mouth shut. Deng
Zhifang briefly ran into trouble when his business associate Zhou Beifang
was arrested in the spring of 1995. The younger Deng was reportedly let off
the hook after a few months' investigation.[21]

Jiang was generally successful in building bridges to left and right.
Given his neo-conservative credentials, the president had in many arenas a
common language with the leftists, or remnant Maoists. Jiang's connivance
with the shenanigans of Maoist ideologue Deng Liqun — including the
latter's attack against Deng — was well known (see Chapter 6).

Moreover, Jiang tried to repair ties with the followers of Hu Yaobang,
including the so-called Communist Youth League Faction. In 1992,
the president caused a stir when he visited Hu's grave in Jiangxi province.
On that occasion, Hu's wife was grateful that Jiang graced the tomb
with his calligraphy eulogising Hu. Jiang saw to it that Hu's son, Hu Deping,
fared well, first as a cadre in the United Front Department and later as a
vice-chairman of the All-China Federation of Industry and Commerce.[22]
A large number of former league stalwarts still held major positions up to
the mid-1990s. They included Politburo Standing Committee member Hu
Jintao, Electronics Minister Hu Qili, Taiwan Affairs Office chief Wang
Zhaoguo, and vice-chief of the United Front Department Wan Shaofen.

The Rise of the Shanghai Faction

The rise of the *Shanghaibang* or Shanghai Faction was one of the most
significant political developments after Tiananmen Square. The Shanghai
clique might perhaps never become as powerful as the Gang of Four — all
of whom had a Shanghai connection — at its height in the early 1970s.
However, by early 1998, Jiang's *Shanghaibang* had eclipsed all other power
blocs of the day. It certainly had more clout than, for example, Deng's
Sichuan clique, those generals who hailed from the southwestern province
such as Yang Shangkun, Yang Baibing and Zhang Aiping.

Firstly, the *Shanghaibang* accounted for the staying power of Jiang. Members helped Jiang win friends and, more importantly, edge out enemies. The following episode concerning Zhao Ziyang illustrates in full the near-diabolical cunning of faction affiliates. In January 1997, not long after it became apparent that Deng was on his death bed, Jiang's staff dispatched an order to upgrade medical care for the former party general secretary. An essential element was that the health of Zhao, then 77, must be "preserved for at least three years".[23]

Given the enmity between Jiang and Zhao, why the solicitude? As a party insider put it, the president was confident that Deng's demise would not lead to a repeat of the 1989 events, which were precipitated by Hu Yaobang's death on April 15 of that year. "However, Jiang knows that the death of Zhao, who has suffered from lung problems in the past few years, could herald thunder and lightning," the source said. "Like Hu, he is seen as a victim of the party's Byzantine in-fighting. There is still strong respect of Zhao for supporting the students." He added that Jiang reckoned he needed two to three more years to consolidate power — and he could not risk any bombshells. The idea behind the "protect Zhao scheme" came from members of the inner circle of the Shanghai Faction, who were Jiang's eyes and ears — and brain.[24]

Who are the members of the Shanghai Faction?

Jiang owed his rise to a solid cadre of loyal, slick operators with the can-do savvy and cosmopolitan exposure of China's premier commercial city. Among the veterans, the most important adviser was Wang Daohan, the former Shanghai mayor. Among the younger generation, prominent affiliates included cadres in their late 50s to early 60s: Zeng Qinghong, Zeng Peiyan, Wu Bangguo, Huang Ju, and Xu Kuangdi.[25]

Wang was nominally based in Shanghai but since 1995, he had been spending more time in the capital. Thanks to his career in the Shanghai underground in the 1940s, Wang enjoyed excellent relations with party elders, as well as retired generals such as Zhang Aiping. One of Wang's masterstrokes was to think of ways to "oblige" Deng in 1992 to relieve the powers of two Jiang opponents, former president Yang Shangkun and General Yang Baibing. Wang's advice was reportedly for Jiang to secure the help of a Deng son as well as General Wang Ruilin, Deng's *aide-de-camp*.[26]

After Deng's death, Wang persuaded Jiang to cement ties with veterans such as Bo Yibo, Peng Zhen (who died in May 1997), Song Renqiong, Wan Li and Song Ping. As Wang saw it, if the elders were on the president's side, it would be difficult for his top foe, then NPC chief Qiao Shi, to stage a challenge.

Zeng Qinghong, 59, was Jiang's confidant, ideas man, public relations specialist, and troubleshooter rolled into one. A vice-party secretary in Shanghai who served under Jiang in the mid-1980s, Zeng was the only person Jiang brought with him to Beijing. The neo-conservative technocrat swiftly became Head of the General Office and Head of the Jiang Zemin Office. Zeng had inherited the political connections of his father, Zeng Shan, a former minister, and his mother, Long March veteran Deng Liujin. A respected "older sister", Deng helped Jiang smooth his relations with various mountain strongholds in the party. Among his most brilliant ideas was for Jiang to isolate the remnant Zhao Faction while building a bridge to the so-called Communist Youth League Faction, or followers of the late Hu Yaobang.[27]

Jiang's other alter ego was Zeng Peiyan, the economic guru and policy wonk. (Zeng and Zeng Qinghong were known as the two Zengs.) Until his promotion at the Ninth NPC (see Chapter 8), Zeng's official positions were Vice-Minister of State Planning and Vice-Secretary General of the Leading Group on Finance and Economics (LGFE). However, Zeng's main job was Jiang's principal economic adviser. The former counsellor at the Chinese Embassy in Washington accompanied Jiang on most trips abroad. While Zeng spoke good English and knew Western economics well, his views tended to be conservative.[28]

Two other senior members of the Shanghai Faction were Wu Bangguo and Huang Ju, who became Politburo members in 1992 and 1994 respectively. A youthful-looking 57-year-old former party chief of Shanghai, Wu was Jiang's candidate for premier. He cut his teeth as a technology cadre and was put in charge of Shanghai's industry and economy before moving to Beijing in 1994 to be vice-premier designate in charge of SOEs. Wu lacked a track record, but he was picked for his nimbleness of mind and relatively liberal ideas.[29]

Huang Ju, 60, went up the hierarchy largely on account of his ability to curry favour with superiors, particularly Jiang and Zhu. The Shanghai mayor, who became party boss and Politburo member in 1994, was particularly expert at massaging Zhu's ego. In the early 1990s, Huang embarrassed Zhu when, in a municipal meeting, the then vice-mayor compared the party boss to a flower — and the lesser officials, including himself — as cow dung. In New York in 1993 on official business, the first thing Huang did was to have dinner with one of Jiang's sons then based in the US.[30]

While Huang was good at carrying out orders, he was not credited with any new ideas, particularly reform-oriented ones. His only "original" contribution was a relatively efficient job-placement programme for unemployed workers in Shanghai. By early 1997, however, there were reports Jiang wanted to appoint him as head of the Central Committee's Commission for Political and Legal Affairs or the Central Commission for Disciplinary Inspection.[31]

Then there was the younger generation of *Shanghaibang* affiliates. Xu Kuangdi, then 57, succeeded Huang Ju as mayor in 1994. The constant bickering between the two had detracted from the achievement of Xu, a technocrat par excellence who was close to Zhu Rongji. Xu was an eloquent speaker who did a lot for Shanghai during frequent road shows to the US. Fluent in English, Xu was popular with foreign businessmen and diplomats. By early 1998, he was tipped for a major ministerial posting in Beijing.[32]

Then there was the academic-turned-cadre Wang Huning, who became one of Jiang's most influential political advisers in late 1994. In spite of his inexperience as a cadre, the political science and legal scholar became a gifted strategist. He coined Jiang's favourite rallying cry: "talk more about politics". Wang also crafted a multi-pronged gameplan for Jiang to tighten his grip on the PLA (see Chapter 4).

Apart from these big names, about 30 cadres from Shanghai had by 1995 taken the "helicopter ride" to Beijing. Typically, a Jiang associate who used to be chief or vice-chief of a municipal department was made the head or vice-head of a ministry or national department. Large numbers of Shanghai cadres were also parachuted into other provinces and cities. Moreover, the Shanghai municipal Organisation Department was grooming technocrats and experts in the areas of economics, finance and technology — and "exporting" them to Beijing and other provinces. The department's "export target" for the year 2000 was 100 "internationally known experts", 3,000 senior specialists, and a 10,000-strong "back-up team" of technocrats. Corresponding figures for the year 2010 were 150, 6,000 and 20,000.[33]

Manoeuvres in late 1996

In the second half of 1996, Jiang was closing in for the kill. It was the turn of "third-generation" *Shanghaibang* cadres to hit the big time in the capital. Said a Beijing source in the winter of 1996: "The president recently looked at the dossiers of around 20 young turks in party and government units in Shanghai. These rising stars, who are in their 40s, are tipped to move into key slots in Beijing next year."[34]

Third-generation Shanghai cadres referred to relatively young officials, many of whom had worked for "second generation" stalwarts such as Wu Bangguo and Huang Ju. "It's like an assembly line," the source added. "First, members at the top — the party secretary and mayor, or their deputies — go to Beijing. Then functionaries at department-head levels are inducted into the premier echelon in Shanghai. Soon, secretary-generals, bureau chiefs and heads of municipal districts get ready for their step up the ladder." Some of the third- and fourth-generation Shanghai Faction members were protégés of Wu Bangguo, Huang Ju or Xu Kuangdi rather than first-generation potentates such as Jiang Zemin or Zhu Rongji.[35]

The signal of another scramble for power came in November 1996, when Vice-Mayor Hua Jianmin was transferred to Beijing to become deputy to Zeng Peiyan at the Leading Group on Finance and Economics. As was usual with Shanghai Faction-related promotions, the new job for Hua was not announced publicly. Final arrangements were also made for vice-party secretary Chen Zhili, a Jiang protégé and expert on ideology and propaganda, to be appointed party boss at the State Education Commission in Beijing.[36]

To make way for the possible Beijing transfer of Huang Ju and Xu Kuangdi, Shanghai cadres Chen Liangyu and Feng Guoqin were made vice-mayors. Chen, 50, a protégé of Huang Ju, was given the slot of First Vice-Mayor. He was a long-term vice-party secretary of Shanghai as well as the head of the city's prosperous Huangpu District. Chen was regarded as a possible new party secretary or mayor. In addition, two rising stars were tipped to go up. They were the head of the party committee of the Pudong Zone, Zhou Yupeng, and the Secretary-General of the Shanghai party committee, Song Yiqiao.[37]

Zhou Yupeng, a former secretary-general of the Shanghai party committee, was a protégé of Wu Bangguo. In the early 1990s, he was sent for a year's training in administration at an American university. In early 1996,

Zhou was appointed head of the Pudong Work Committee, the party's master cell in the zone. Managers in Pudong pointed out that Zhou had since eclipsed Vice-Mayor Zhao Qizheng, who was theoretically the zone's senior administrator. They said Zhou was a candidate for vice-mayor or vice-party secretary of Shanghai.[38]

Other technocrats tipped for elevation included Song Yiqiao, a protégé of Huang Ju. The political fortune of several academics and think tank members were expected to rise. They included Li Junru, who was transferred to the Policy Research Office of the Central Committee (PROCC) with Wang Huning. Li had been a specialist in Deng Thought at the Shanghai branch of the Chinese Academy of Social Sciences. Other young turks such as Wang Zhan, who headed the municipal government's Economic Development Research Centre, were expected to earn promotions to senior Beijing posts.[39]

Offshoot of the Shanghai Faction: The Zhu Rongji Clique
Zhu's cronies and think tanks

To understand fully the nature of the Jiang cabal, it is instructive to look at the so-called Zhu Rongji offshoot of the Shanghai Faction. While some scholars consider Premier Zhu a member of the Shanghai Clique, the economic tsar and his followers actually formed a different political entity. This was despite the fact that quite a few Shanghai-related cadres such as Xu Kuangdi could belong to both the Shanghai Faction and the Zhu Rongji Clique.

Like Jiang's followers, a large number of Zhu's associates and underlings had worked in Shanghai or were picked by Zhu because they had excelled in Shanghai positions. These included People's Bank of China Governor Dai Xianglong, former PBoC vice-governor Zhu Xiaohua, and former Guizhou vice-governor Lou Jiwei. However, the economic tsar also recruited talents from different State Council units — as well as large numbers of graduates from American and foreign universities. This made Zhu less liable to accusations of factionalism.[40]

The bulk of the members of the Zhu Faction were technocrats, mostly with backgrounds in engineering and finance. Compared with Jiang's men, Zhu's associates were much less interested in ideology. Like the economic tsar himself, his underlings studiously avoided going on the record on political issues. This relatively low-profile approach also made them less susceptible to be accused of seeking power.

Zhu's Machiavellianism manifested itself most clearly in his predilection for hiring — and maintaining good relationships — with the princelings. The vice-premier played a role in the rising political fortune of at least three offspring of senior cadres: PBoC vice-governors Chen Yuan and Zhou Xiaochuan; and the former head of the Construction Bank, Wang Qishan.[41] In general, however, Zhu came across as an exemplar of the ideal *fumuguan* ("parent-like cadre") once championed by his illustrious fellow Hunan native, Mao Zedong. His commitment to fighting corruption was evident in this famous saying: "Make available 100 coffins for the graft-takers and the big-time scoundrels who screw up the people. Just in case, prepare one coffin for myself — if I get gunned down in the battle with the crooks."[42]

Zhu Rongji's special appeal

The following story illustrates well Zhu's appeal — as well as his problematic relationship with Jiang and the powers-that-be. Zhu, who did not bat an eyelid when savaging ministers and firing governors, shed tears while watching a play in Beijing in December 1996. The drama, performed by the Shanghai Youth Troupe, was about Shang Yang (390–338 BC), the legendary reformer in the era of the Warring States. A fire-spitting exponent of tough laws, centralisation of power, and the abolition of the privilege of nobility, Shang laid down Draconian but effective codes and administrative systems which made possible the aggrandisement of the Qin Kingdom.[43]

Shang's strict statutes and holier-than-thou approach, however, later ran foul of his emperor — and the latter's corrupt and scheming aides. China's first and best-loved reformer was arrested and convicted by his own laws. He was tortured to death and his body dismembered. While Zhu's star was rising high in 1997, similarities between the then vice-premier and the Qin Dynasty minister ran deep. Each tried to retool a universe given to the rule of personality by sponsoring stringent laws and practices that do not recognise nepotism or special privileges. At least for Shang Yang, however, the rule of law tottered before the wanton might of feudal potentates.[44]

Premier Zhu was vulnerable because of his flimsy power base and his famous temper. During the economic rectification campaign of 1993–1996, the economic tsar offended some of the most powerful blocs in the country: state entrepreneurs, regional warlords and PLA generals. Even the official New China News Agency biography cited his *mea culpa*: "It's true that my criticisms [of officials] were often too severe. This is not good."[45]

In the course of his reform, Zhu had to make many a compromise with reality: toning down market mechanisms or suing for compromise with this or that power bloc. Most of all, however, the economic tsar had to seek patrons and backers. Perhaps with Shang Yang in mind, he realised that, ironically, the protection of well-placed personages was indispensable to the success of his crusade against the rule of personality. After all, the meteoric rise of the former Shanghai mayor was due to the largesse of Deng. From 1996 onwards, Zhu had to build bridges to conservative party elders such as Song Ping. In 1997, the latter returned the favour by backing his bid for premier.[46]

Referring to his reputation as a rightist or bourgeois-liberal cadre in the 1950s, the neo-Maoist veterans began calling Zhu a "likeable rightist". In spite of his brilliance and determination, Zhu might be trapped in a Shang Yang-style dilemma. His reforms risked being overwhelmed by opposition if they were seen as wrecking the system and hurting the vested interests of power blocs. Yet if Zhu were to mend fences with elements of the *ancien regime* and soft-pedal the changes, he would barely be scratching the surface (see also Chapter 8).

Philosophy of the *Shanghaibang*

What are the traits of Shanghai Faction affiliates? They all had impressive academic credentials. Many were college professors before turning to politics such as Wu Bangguo, Xu Kuangdi, and Chen Zhili. Truly "red and expert", they satisfied Jiang's requirements about "paying attention to and talking about politics".[47]

Shanghaibang members were pragmatic, opportunistic neo-conservatives. Ideologically, they were pro-establishment, in that they believed in the perpetuation of CCP one-party dictatorship. However, their faith in Jiang and the glorious role of Shanghai and the CCP were also tied to their own self-interest and advancement. In economics, they believed in juggling cautious market experiments with a regime of recentralisation. At the same time, they had ample exposure to the West and they could be good joint-venture partners.[48]

Shanghaibang affiliates were slick operators. They could quickly trim their sails to meet the political requirements of the day. It was not for nothing they were dubbed the Wind Faction — that is bending with the prevailing wind of the day. They looked at policy through the prism of Machiavellianism: be it black or white, a policy was good if it enhanced the power of the faction.

Shanghai cadres were fastest to respond to calls by Beijing to demonstrate their loyalty to the *zhongyang*. While responding to the "talk politics" slogan, Vice-Mayor Chen Liangyu almost went overboard with his oath of fealty. "There are some time-honoured sayings that we should not only talk about but frequently repeat," he said. "We should repeat them time and again till we have attained the level of Communism. If not, we can easily get out of line." What were some of these fantastic sayings? Dog-eared Maoist teachings such as making a "clean break" with privatisation and fighting the sugar-coated bullets of capitalism.[49]

Take, for example, Wang Huning's view of corruption. In his much-noted 1995 book *A Political Life*, Wang took a cogent look at graft. In his view, corruption had "graduated" from low quantity, low quality, low level, and superficial to high quantity, high quality, high level and deep-rooted. Yet the thrust of his argument — and advice for Jiang — was that fighting corruption would enhance the president's popularity and grip on power. The corollary was that if combating graft would invite political problems, Jiang should call a halt to it — as he did concerning the Chen Xitong affair (see following section) at least in the 1995–1997 period.[50]

Likewise, Wang Daohan's views on combating graft were opportunistic. In 1997, the former Shanghai mayor asked Jiang to boost "the degree of force" in clamping down on corruption, again with a view to building up his prestige. As Wang put it: "Mao was famous for building up the country; Deng for improving the economy and people's livelihood. And Jiang should be remembered as the cadre who has promoted clean government." After Deng's death, however, Wang Daohan and other Jiang aides counselled the president not to move against the patriarch's relatives, some of whom had been accused of having made dubious economic deals. The reason: turning against Deng's kin would invite criticism that Jiang had betrayed Deng's cause.[51]

The Shanghai Faction was adept at making tactical retreats to avert danger or to buy time. Comrades still based in Shanghai were anxious to shed the image that they had benefited from special treatment sanctioned by Jiang or Zhu. Such cadres were vociferous about the fact they would play the *zhonghua* [Chinese] and not just the Shanghai card. "Shanghai is the Shanghai of the entire nation," Huang Ju said during the 1995 NPC. "The whole country has supported Shanghai; and Shanghai must provide service to the entire country."[52] According to Wu Bangguo, "Shanghai must under any circumstances be humble and cautious." "This is the idea of General Secretary Jiang," he said. "It is better to just go ahead with some matters and not talk about them." Wu said this principle had a significant bearing on Shanghai's relationship with the entire country.[53]

Throughout the Chen Xitong affair, Shanghai Faction affiliates kept a low profile — so as not to be seen as gloating over the defeat of Chen's Beijing clique. Huang Ju cautioned his subordinates against adopting an "over-exuberant" attitude over Chen's demise. "You must not air your views, not be more gung-ho than the others, and not make yourself too conspicuous," he said. Huang indicated the most important thing was to run Shanghai well. "We must not add trouble to comrade Zemin, so that he can concentrate on affairs of state," Huang reportedly said.[54]

In economics, Shanghai Faction affiliates tried to strike a balance between the requirements of the market and state power. Take Xu Kuangdi, who had the ear of both Jiang and Zhu. Xu started his career in academia, becoming a professor of engineering and vice-president at the Shanghai Industry University. He spent two years working at a big Swiss factory in the mid-1980s. Xu caught Zhu's eye when they were travelling on a delegation to Europe in 1990. When Zhu asked Xu whether he was interested in the position of head of the municipal planning bureau, Xu said traditional planning was not his cup of tea. To which Zhu replied: "That's exactly my idea — to recruit somebody who dislikes planning to head the planning bureau."[55]

Shanghaibang affiliates, however, were no Zhaoists. They largely went along with the neo-conservative, recentralisation-oriented policies of Zhu Rongji (see Chapter 6). The prospects of their going overboard in market experiments were slim. Zeng Peiyan worked closely with Zhu in licking together a long-term programme of macro-level adjustments and controls. By late 1996, when the three-year-old austerity programme seemed to have succeeded, Zeng laid down strict instructions that a programme of "adequately tight money policy" be continued in the foreseeable future.[56]

The *Shanghaibang* under Siege

A case of gloating too soon

One of the worst sins of politics is gloating too soon. Particularly in the Chinese context, the flaunting of superlatives exposes a lack of gravitas that can spawn new enemies even as existing animosities are exacerbated. Despite extra caution, *Shanghaibang* affiliates often failed to hide their glee as they took the helicopter ride to the top. On these occasions, they precipitated a wave of jealousy — and made foes across the nation.

A case in point was the announcement of yet another special deal for Shanghai and Pudong a couple of weeks before the Fifth Central Committee Plenum of 1995. The unveiling of 18 "super-special" policies in investment and other areas — which would further widen the gap between Shanghai and the hinterland — came as the party was mulling ways and means to narrow the east-west discrepancy.[57]

Jiang and his *Shanghaibang* colleagues should perhaps have drawn the right lesson from the Fourth Central Committee Plenum of October 1994. That session saw the promotion of Wu Bangguo, already a Politburo member, to the party Secretariat, and Huang Ju to the Politburo. Many Central Committee representatives from the central and western areas openly expressed dissent. At that juncture and later, the regional officials also praised two other Politburo Standing Committee members for not forming their own factions. Then vice-premier Zhu Rongji was eulogised for not favouring his former associates. The same was said of Li Ruihuan for not granting special favours for cronies in his former power base of Tianjin.[58]

Some commentators argued that the *Shanghaibang* could prove to be Jiang's undoing. Deng, for example, was much more discreet about hoisting the *Sichuanbang* flag. It is, after all, a taboo in Chinese politics for any cadre to blatantly build up a clique. Mao warned against factionalism when he issued one caveat after another on the phenomenon of "mountain strongholds". Deng laid down the touchstone about the "five lakes and four seas" in 1992, meaning there should be no favouritism or factionalism in the promotion of officials.[59]

Jiang, of course, was aware of the taboo — and at times he made efforts to dismiss claims he was propagating a Shanghai Faction. "In the past months, many cadres have talked about a Shanghai Faction and that I am the head of it," he said in early 1995. "This is without foundation. I was not born in Shanghai. It's true that I worked there. But so did many senior party officials. Can you also call them members of the Shanghai Faction?" Jiang cited cadres including Qian Qichen and Qiao Shi.[60]

The president denied "rumours" about factionalism again in mid-1996. "Disregard talk about a so-called Shanghai Faction," he said in an internal speech. "I am not a native of Shanghai. I come from Jiangsu." Jiang said when he first started working in Shanghai in 1986, he was disparaged as a "northern Jiangsu pig" by veteran cadres.[61] The president also made light of stories he had favoured Shanghai in terms of its share of national resources. "It was comrade Xiaoping who initiated the idea of making Shanghai the national pacesetter of reform," he said in late 1995. "Deng said he regretted not having made Shanghai a special economic zone [in the early 1980s] and that the central authorities must make up for lost time by giving Shanghai favourable policies."[62]

By 1997 the *Shanghaibang* had tried some damage control by fostering a more benign image. Consider, for example, the conversation that took place between Wang Daohan and Wang Yuanhua, a scholar and former propaganda chief of Shanghai noted for his liberal tendencies. Beijing sources said Wang called on the academic at home and asked him his views on the cultural scene. The latter said frankly that the party had exerted too tight a control on ideology, the media and the arts. The senior Jiang adviser expressed concurrence and offered to pass on his views to the *zhongyang*. This episode was widely circulated among Beijing's political circles.[63]

Anti-*Shanghaibang* sentiments

Underneath the surface of calm, grievances had piled up against individual *Shanghaibang* leaders. Take Zeng Qinghong, perhaps the most exposed Jiang protégé. The head of the Jiang Office was accused by officials in central party and government units of "unconstitutional power grabbing".[64] Both the Central Committee General Office and the Jiang Zemin Office had taken over decision-making powers in areas such as internal security, economic policy, party organisation and ideology and propaganda (see following section). In theory, these two units should be "secretariat-type" outfits whose duties did not go beyond coordination and logistical support. However, they had taken on policy-making roles. And they were outside the purview of supervisory and disciplinary units in either the party or government.[65]

In late 1995, Beijing was awash with rumours that Zeng had been hurt by allegations against a relative, a mid-ranking official in a cultural unit of the central government. The kin, also surnamed Zeng, was reportedly under investigation for sexual harassment of two budding starlets. The innuendo was that Zeng had offered shelter to the cadre.[66]

Other juicy reports also came to light concerning how Jiang's men had clashed with State Council bureaucrats loyal to Li Peng or Zhu Rongji. Economics guru Zeng Peiyan and his one-time deputy at the Leading Group on Finance and Economics (LGFE), Huang Qifan, reportedly had run-ins with ministers and department heads in the central government. The confrontations were over enterprise reform, the extent of the tight money policy and the contents of economic laws. However, they had as much to do with turf as with concrete differences in policy.[67]

Perhaps because of their lack of popularity — and power struggle with other factions — a few Shanghai cadres promoted to Beijing in 1994 and 1995 were transferred back to the city. Huang Qifan, a Wu Bangguo protégé and former vice-chief of the Pudong Zone who came to the LGFE in late 1994, had to beat a retreat after less than a year. He was named a Vice-Secretary General of the Shanghai party committee in June 1995.[68]

Similarly, the vice-head of the Propaganda Department, Gong Xinhan and the vice-chief editor of the *People's Daily*, Zhou Ruijin, returned to Shanghai in early 1996 after about two years in the capital. The official reason was that Gong had returned to Shanghai to nurse an unknown ailment. However, the real reason was his lack of advancement in the department. Zhou returned to Shanghai to look after the *People's Daily*'s East China edition. A relatively forward-looking journalist who had supported Deng's reforms when he was the No. 2 at Shanghai's *Liberation Daily*, Zhou was at first expected to liberalise the party mouthpiece.[69]

A number of Shanghai cadres and scholars retained by Jiang were not sure whether they could make a go of their Beijing venture. Social scientists Wang Huning and Li Junru had not given up their Shanghai positions. A few of Jiang's aides still resided in the quarters attached to the Beijing office of the Shanghai municipal party committee — an indication they did not consider Beijing their home.[70]

Veteran party observers pointed out the *Shanghaibang* could never really win over their colleagues because even ordinary members of the nomenclature were disturbed by the machinations of Jiang's aides. While factionalism had always been integral to Communist-party politics, few cliques had been as single-mindedly devoted to amassing power. By way of contrast, the observers cited the Communist Youth League Faction and Zhao's market-oriented disciples. Members of these two groups came from much more diverse backgrounds in terms of experience, ideals and geographical distribution. More importantly, apart from helping their boss maintain power, the followers of Hu and Zhao seemed to be concerned with causes such as economic and political liberalisation. For Jiang's men, however, power was the be-all and end-all of statecraft.[71]

Test Case: Jiang Zemin Versus the Beijing Faction

The saga of how the president vanquished the Beijing Faction yielded insights galore on Jiang-style Machiavellianism. Led by the redoubtable Chen Xitong, the Beijing municipal machinery was a bastion of anti-Jiang sentiment until Chen's arrest in April 1995 in the wake of the exposure of perhaps the largest corruption scandal in Communist-Chinese history. Jiang had thus accomplished what Mao said he could not do in the 1960s. Beijing Faction members were political descendants of the party's City Construction Department in the early 1950s; they would never allow "outsiders" into senior positions in the party-and-government establishment. This led Mao to say that "you can't poke a needle" into *Beijingbang* ramparts. Influential elders and cadres who had close association with the Beijing clique included Deng Xiaoping, the late Peng Zhen, Wan Li, and Li Ruihuan.[72]

Much has been written about how Jiang made use of the monkey business perpetrated by Chen and his underlings such as Vice-Mayor Wang Baosen as a pretext to unravel the Beijing gang. Less well documented is that the president had exercised a high degree of patience and tact. First of all, Jiang hid his anger well. Chen did not even deign to camouflage his disdain for Jiang the day the latter came to Beijing from Shanghai. The Beijing supremo, who thought he did a lot for the party by crushing the "student rebels" in 1989, also had little respect for other members of the Shanghai Faction. Jiang bided his time. After all, the Beijing Faction was close to Deng Xiaoping, whose kin reportedly had numerous business dealings with clique members.[73]

By late 1994, however, Deng's health had deteriorated and it was time to strike. The first volley was the disgrace of the patriarch of the mammoth Capital Iron and Steel Corporation (Shougang), Zhou Guanwu, and the arrest of his son Zhou Beifang. Zhou senior was a long-time crony of Deng and Zhou Beifang was a business partner of Deng's son Deng Zhifang. This was followed by the suicide of Wang Baosen and the disgrace of Chen. Both before and after Chen's fall, Jiang worked hard to cobble a united front with other factions led by Qiao Shi and Li Peng; the then premier had more than tangential links with members of the *Beijingbang*. Even more important, Jiang let the other cliques share the spoils of victory.

Politburo member and head of the Central Commission for Disciplinary Inspection, Wei Jianxing, succeeded Chen as party boss. Wei was a card-carrying member of Qiao's legal and security establishment. Jin Renqing, a vice-head of the State Planning Commission who had ties with Li Peng and Zhu Rongji, became Executive Vice-Mayor. And then premier Li's alter ego, Luo Gan, was made concurrently head of the municipal planning committee. Jiang resisted suggestions from some of his advisers to move Shanghai party secretary Huang Ju to Beijing to replace Chen.[74]

The president also made a superb job of extending an olive branch to his former enemies. After destroying Chen, Jiang saw that he had asserted his authority and broken the back of the *Beijingbang*. Now was the time to show his magnanimity. The conqueror lost no time in reassuring Chen's cronies that, as a Chinese proverb put it, he would not "hit the dog which is already down in the river". Close associates of Chen such as then mayor Li Qiyan and then vice-mayor Zhang Baifa were allowed to keep their jobs. Both Jiang and Wei Jianxing reiterated the imperative of maintaining political stability in the capital — and raising the morale of its cadres.[75]

It was not until mid-1996 that Jiang made the final move to take control of the capital. Fujian party secretary Jia Qinglin was made acting mayor. The understanding was that Jia would later become party secretary. Jia was not a member of the Shanghai Faction. However, his association with Jiang went back decades. Both worked in different units of the Machine-Building Ministry in the late 1970s and early 1980s. In the 1960s, they were together at the No. 1 Automobile Plant at Changchun in the northeast. Jia was reportedly the best man at Jiang's wedding. Within China itself, however, Jia's relationship with Jiang was not well recognised. If Jiang had promoted a Shanghai Faction member to the capital, he might have sown more seeds of dissent.[76]

Manifestations of Machiavellianism

For all his jovial appearances — particularly when talking to foreign guests

— Jiang was a ruthless power-grabber. He revived the quintessentially Maoist tradition of power struggle. While the Great Helmsman moved heaven and earth to topple opponents such as Wang Ming, Liu Shaoqi, Deng Xiaoping and Lin Biao, Jiang waged gory battles to unseat his four major foes: Yang Shangkun, Yang Baibing, Chen Xitong and Qiao Shi. By contrast, Jiang's predecessors as party chief, Hu Yaobang and Zhao Ziyang, largely stayed away from Mao-style back-stabbing.[77]

Jiang's concept of power

Somewhat like Mao Zedong, Jiang had an all-or-nothing concept of power: he wanted a finger in every pie. By mid-1998, after nine years on the job, the president's tentacles had extended into most areas of the party, government and army. While Jiang still could not aspire to having Deng's authority, the would-be helmsman arguably had more territory under control than even the patriarch.

Deng was far from omnipotent. He had a decisive say in many policy areas thanks to his status as the chief strategist of reform and his solid control over the army. However, the patriarch had to share power with the other party elders, in particular the late Chen Yun, Li Xiannian and Wang Zhen. It was Chen and Li — and their protégés such as Li Peng and Yao Yilin — who controlled the economy, in particular, financial policy. Deng also could not penetrate the legal and security establishment, the preserve of Peng Zhen.[78]

In the early 1990s, the president moved quickly to boost his influence in various mountain strongholds. He let Zhu Rongji have the run of the economy for two reasons. Jiang knew he lacked expertise in this area; and he wanted Zhu as a scapegoat should things go wrong. Moreover, the party boss retained control over the Leading Group on Finance and Economics, the nation's highest organ on economic decision-making. Jiang must have been proudest with his exploits in the People's Liberation Army, his weakest link (see Chapter 4). He was able to promote not only military officers friendly to himself but also civilians to top positions. For example, his former secretary Jia Ting'an became a Vice-Director of the General Office of the Central Military Commission in 1995.[79]

By the mid-1990s, the only area where Jiang was seriously outflanked was the legal and security establishment, which was under the influence of Qiao Shi. Even though Qiao became NPC chairman in 1993, his portfolio in the Politburo Standing Committee remained security. Moreover, his protégés dominated the field. They included the head of the Commission for Political and Legal Affairs (CPLA) and the CCDI, Ren Jianxin and Wei Jianxing respectively. The then head of the Ministry of State Security, Jia Chunwang, was also close to Qiao.[80]

In 1996, Jiang tried to take control of the Ministry of State Security through the back door. While the ministry was, in theory, a unit of the central government, it had always reported to the shadowy CPLA. At a Politburo meeting in late 1996, Jiang proposed that the ministry be put under the direct control of the State Council. Jiang said the move would boost accountability of the unit. He went on to recommend that Vice-Premier Li Lanqing look after the ministry's operations. As of mid-1998, the issue had not been settled. Jiang had the support of a number of Politburo colleagues for this power move. The ministry had long been criticised, particularly by central government units and local administrations, for being a law unto itself.[81] However, the forced retirement of Qiao Shi at the 15th Party Congress in September 1997 would open the way for Jiang to penetrate the security apparatus (see Chapter 7).

New organisations to seize power

Much of the criticism against neo-conservative economic theory had focused on the recentralisation policies of "Great Rectifier" Zhu Rongji and other State Council bureaucrats. However, in the area of the centralisation of political powers, Jiang went further than Zhu ever did in the financial field.

Compared with forebears such as Hu and Zhao — and indeed Deng — Jiang had a better appreciation for the dynamics of organisation. We need only look at how Jiang — and the *Shanghaibang* — strengthened the Central Committee General Office (CCGO), to the extent it became a chief operating centre for the entire country. Under Zeng Qinghong, the CCGO expanded from less than 100 people under Zhao Ziyang to nearly 300. Top cadres at the CCGO practically absorbed — and took over the functions — of the Central Committee Secretariat.[82] These duties included making policy and issuing top-level party documents and controlling the paper flow between headquarters and other CCP organs.

The office also took on KGB-like functions. In early 1995, Jiang established a top-level Security and Investigative Group (SIG) within the CCGO to check on the loyalty of senior cadres. Beijing sources said the investigative group served as an internal security watchdog to prevent high-level cadres from committing acts detrimental to the interests of the "third-generation leadership with comrade Zemin as its core".[83]

The SIG was headed by Zeng Qinghong. The deputy was the CCGO Vice-Director Hu Guangbao, another former Shanghai official. Apart from administering loyalty checks, the KGB-like unit looked into the "Marxist purity" of selected cadres, as well as their administrative probity and personal integrity. Officials' dealings with foreigners and groups with links to "bourgeois-liberal" and dissident elements would also be thoroughly examined.[84]

By mid-1996, there were signs that the CCGO had taken over some military functions as well. For example, Zeng recruited a number of retired army officers into the SIG. The Central Committee office was also "meddling" with decision-making on aspects of military affairs that should properly be the prerogative of the Central Military Commission, according to sources. This led to the intense dissatisfaction of members of the top brass including Generals Zhang Zhen and Zhang Wannian.[85]

Of particular significance was Jiang's decision to expand the functions of many leading groups within the Central Committee. This went against the principle of the separation of party and government as well as the streamlining of the bureaucracy. Take for instance, the Leading Group on Finance and Economics. It practically lapsed into dormancy in the first two years after the June 4 massacre. Until Jiang's special tutelage, it swelled from a small, advisory committee to a policy-setting and, in some instances, policy-implementing department with sections for macro-economics, planning, industry, and agriculture.[86]

In late 1995, Jiang set up *zhongxinzu* ("core groups") within the party leaderships of regional administrations so as to better promote loyalty to the *zhongyang* — and to himself. The groups were established within many provincial and municipal party committees to ensure that the instructions of party headquarters would be obeyed in their entirety. They were also formed in top central and regional organs of the PLA and People's Armed Police. *Zhongxinzu* became a handy vehicle for Jiang to install protégés and informants in civilian and military departments.

"While a typical core group is made up of the party secretary and vice-party secretaries of a provincial or a military unit, it includes 'plenipotentiaries' who answer directly to the Jiang Zemin Office," a source said.[87]

In 1996, an important function of the core groups was to implement the propaganda crusade for studying Jiang's "talk more about politics" credo. Many of the special sessions held by party and army units to study Jiang's teachings were conducted by the core groups.

Mechanisms to extract professions of loyalty

Apart from institution building, Jiang and his personal office were adept at improving mechanisms for top-down interaction to promote central authority and loyalty to the president. Jiang, together with such neo-conservatives as Zhu Rongji, reinstated the Maoist practice of the "responsibility system" for regional cadres. Starting in the mid-1990s, party secretaries, governors and mayors were again given quotas for tasks including grain production, helping the poor, and nabbing criminals (see Chapter 3).

Of more direct relevance for Jiang-style Machiavellianism was how to extract protestations of loyalty. The most important of these was the revival of the practice of *biaotai*, or the public airing of views, in support of a *zhongyang* policy or personality. The *biaotai* ritual was used exhaustively — and disastrously — by Chairman Mao. In the early days after toppling Hua Guofeng, Deng also resorted to the *biaotai* mechanism to ensure that central and local cadres support new institutions and slogans such as "practice is the sole criterion of truth".[88]

As Deng's health nosedived, Jiang obliged regional and army officers to profess loyalty to himself. In late 1994 and early 1995, CCP committees in each province and main city held meetings to discuss the political requirements of the "new era", a euphemism for the post-Deng order. Under instructions from the Central Committee General Office, the party secretary chairing such sessions asked senior cadres to *biaotai* on the need to profess "absolute allegiance to the leadership collective with comrade Zemin as its core". Each cadre was also asked to give his opinion on the need for regional administrations to sacrifice local economic advantages in the interest of the "overall national situation".[89]

After the *biaotai* rounds, the party bosses read out Central Committee documents on the imperative of maintaining the utmost unison with the *zhongyang*, particularly in the face of unexpected incidents in the "new era". A party source said that, taking the cue from the party whips and current central documents, most participants in such meetings used similar language to show their enthusiastic support for the Jiang leadership. They insisted that should a conflict occur between the interests of Beijing and those of the localities, they would unhesitatingly toe the *zhongyang's* line. "Many cadres employ the metaphor that the whole country is a like a game of chess and every move taken must advance the overall interest," the source said. Transcripts of these *biaotai* sessions, which were recorded in detail by confidential secretaries, were sent to the CCGO and the Jiang Office.[90]

Jiang ordered another series of *biaotai* sessions after promulgating his "politics first" dictum in late 1995. The *People's Daily* ran a sampling of the views expressed by regional cadres in January 1996. The paper claimed that there was a "unanimity of views" among local chieftains that "the more the country goes about its reform and open-door policy, the more attention should be paid to politics — and the country should further raise its guard against the loss of political direction".[91]

Judging from the list of those who had given positive views, however, it was obvious that support for Jiang was not exactly overwhelming. Protestations of loyalty came from Shanghai, Beijing, Fujian, Shanxi and Hebei. For example, Shanxi leaders said putting the utmost stress on politics was "the long-standing conviction of three generations of leadership cores", a reference to Mao, Deng and Jiang.[92] Analysts pointed out that excessive use of the *biaotai* mechanism could backfire. It betrayed a sense of insecurity on the part of a "leadership core" which was in constant need of reaffirmation.

The best illustration of a maladroit *biaotai* could be the one made by Wang Ruilin soon after Deng's death. The occasion was an enlarged Politburo committee meeting in April 1997. Wang, an *aide-de-camp* of Deng, vouched three times for the fact that it was the patriarch who had ensured Jiang's supremacy. Party sources said the conclave was called by Jiang to give an account of the post-Deng situation. Apparently to dampen the jockeying for position that had intensified, Jiang became uncharacteristically humble. He hinted it was wrong to assume that he had schemed to get the positions he was holding, such as party chief, head of state, and commander-in-chief.

"When I was asked to take up the position of party general secretary, I thought there must be other cadres who had more ability or greater seniority," Jiang reportedly said to the Politburo meeting. Whereupon General Wang said: "General Secretary, you are being too self-deprecating. We all know it was the patriarch who made the arrangement." Wang came up with similar protestations when Jiang went on to say he had not sought for himself the position of state president and CMC chairman. Particularly with reference to the CMC position, Wang claimed that it was a "brilliant strategic move" by Deng to name Jiang chairman, a position that had not been given the two previous party chiefs, Hu Yaobang and Zhao Ziyang. According to insiders, this fairly ostentatious, well-orchestrated duet between Wang and Jiang only exposed the president's unsure grip on power.[93]

The Personality Cult and Propaganda Crusades
The quasi-Maoist personality cult

In many ways a private, self-effacing person, Deng Xiaoping was uncomfortable with excessive publicity. This, together with his animosity towards Mao-style personality cults, was the reason behind his long-standing order not to erect a personality cult. Jiang, however, needed to see himself on prime time TV every night and on the front page of newspapers every day because he lacked the spontaneous authority commanded by Deng.

It would, of course, be unfair to compare Jiang's strategy with that of the German propagandist Joseph Goebbels, whose famous aphorism was that "lies repeated 1,000 times become truths". However, Jiang probably made use of modern studies in mass psychology. Saturation coverage of himself sent the message to the masses — and his enemies — that he was in charge. That it might turn people off did not matter; the overexposure could condition people in their subconscious that it was futile to look for an alternative. Moreover, at least as much as Mao, Jiang's adrenaline flowed faster when he knew he was in the limelight.

At times of course, Jiang was careful not to go too far. For example, in the summer of 1996, the Jiang Office drastically contained the scope of his 70th birthday celebration on August 17. Since early that year, Jiang's supporters, including a number of politicians who had recently crossed over to his camp, had said they wanted to hold a lavish birthday party. These loyalists wanted to play up the fact Jiang was in good health, and that he could serve as supreme party leader well into the 21st century. The president eventually heeded the point that birthday parties were taboo in the Communist-Chinese tradition. Neither Mao nor Deng held such celebrations.[94]

Self-restraint, however, was hardly Jiang's strong suit. It would also have contravened his expansive, *haipai* ("Shanghai-style") personality. The president's cult-building activities reached a crescendo in mid-1996. Every night, the first two to three minutes of the 7 pm CCTV news were devoted to Jiang's exploits. This cult was particularly evident in the army, which had in Mao's days been a grotesque vehicle for hero and leader worship.[95]

On August 1, 1996, every PLA unit was told to hang out scrolls of calligraphy bearing the instructions on army building issued by Mao, Deng and Jiang. This was despite a long-standing injunction against highlighting individual leaders through portraits or calligraphy. In the week before and after the leadership conference at the Beidaihe seaside resort, CCTV ran lengthy reports on Jiang's visits to PLA bases across the country. The footage, each at least five minutes long, was the lead news of the day. The publicity stunt had the soldiers looking awestruck by the larger-than-life CMC chairman. "Chairman Jiang was bursting with energy when he visited us," one soldier said. "We must firmly remember the spirit of Chairman Jiang's instructions."[96]

As is so often with Communist-Chinese propaganda, Jiang's past was re-written. One best-selling book, *The Saga of the People's Republic of China*, romanticised the time Jiang spent in the Soviet Union in the 1950s. The tome had it that "the factory girls were smitten with this Chinese college graduate who did not smoke or drink. They took pictures with Jiang after work". Even though Jiang had a remarkably lacklustre career as minister of electronics in the early 1980s, he was later said to have laid the foundation for China's hi-tech development, including the beginnings of Star Wars strategies.[97]

Jiang might be faulted for lack of originality. His self-conscious copying of Mao looked somewhat stilted in the eyes of intellectuals. A case in point was the pose he adopted while taking a picture with the PLA units that had participated in a drill off the Yellow Sea in October 1995 to frighten Taiwan. That picture recalled a similar photo of Mao in the late 1950s. This lack of authenticity informed an intriguing trip that he made to Henan in June 1996. The entire journey, including the way he handled himself with local officials and farmers, was choreographed with reference to Mao's Henan tour in 1957. Then, the chairman gave approval to the first people's commune. The same gauche public relations was behind a front page *People's Daily* picture published in November 1996 of a red scarf-clad and smiling Jiang in Guizhou surrounded by a crowd of clapping schoolchildren similarly dressed. This was reminiscent of a 1959 photo of Mao making a return to his hometown in Hunan.[98]

The other first-generation titan that Jiang modelled himself on was the revered Zhou Enlai — perhaps the most people-oriented Communist-Chinese leader. Zhou was given particularly high marks for his interaction with intellectuals — writers, singers, dancers and so forth. Jiang showed off Zhou-like touches when he sent floral baskets, cakes, inscriptions, and telegrams to mark the birthdays, deaths and special anniversaries of artistic personalities. In 1995 and 1996, recipients of his special favour included movie star Bai Yang, the late essayist Zhou Zhiqing, writer Bing Xin, and painter Zhou Yizhan.[99]

Jiang's efforts at self-lionisation bordered on vulgarity in mid-1995 when he commissioned "royal painter" Li Qi to do a picture of himself mixing with the masses. Li had done most of the Communist-Chinese elite including Mao and Deng. Rhapsodied the painter: "I shall try to capture in paint not only the charm of the great general secretary, but also the harmony comrade Zemin shares with ordinary Chinese people."[100]

This apparent lack of good taste manifested itself when Jiang's handlers encouraged regional chiefs to spew the superlatives in praising the president. This was the case with then Jiangxi party boss Wu Guanzheng, generally regarded as a liberal. In late 1995, Wu went so far as to subtly compare Jiang to an emperor. While responding to the rallying cry to study Jiang's "talk more about politics" credo, Wu called upon regional cadres to show more concern for the party centre with Jiang as the "core". The Jiangxi party boss cited a couplet from a well-known poem by Song Dynasty literary giant Fan Zhongyan: "Perched on top of temples and halls, we worry about the people; based at the far end of oceans and lakes, we worry about the emperor."[101]

Policy on Propaganda and the Media

The media as Jiang's mouthpiece

Much more than Hu Yaobang, Zhao Ziyang and even Deng Xiaoping, Jiang shared the Maoist viewpoint that the party must have a tight grip over the pen. The media must be firmly in the hands of "trustworthy Marxists who are loyal to the party", Jiang liked to say. In another context, he pointed out that party papers, radio and television stations must be run by good politicians. "We must let politicians run newspapers," he said.[102]

Jiang's views on the media and propaganda were made clear during his landmark visit to the *People's Daily* in September 1996. "The party's media enterprise is integral to its well-being," he said. "The work of the media is ideological and political work — on which the future and fate of the party and country lie." As a foremost task of media workers, Jiang cited toeing the line of the *zhongyang* and maintaining socio-political stability.[103] Or as the leftist director of the *People's Daily*, Shao Huaze, put it: "Journalists should increase their capacity to distinguish between political rights and wrongs. There must be no ambiguity over the crucial principles of the party's leadership over the media and the role of the media as the mouthpiece of the party."[104]

However, it is important to note that the president was not just after traditional, "Communist-style" control. Much more so than his predecessors, he was adept at using the press and television to his own advantage. Thus, the propaganda-related requirements of the party became equated with those of his own.

Jiang's grip on the media became more evident in 1995 — when Deng was dying and he saw the need to score a knock-out blow to enemies such as Qiao Shi. The president issued a series of statements such as "newspapers must not waver in the slightest on the principle of the party spirit".[105] Moreover, editors and other propagandists must "guide the entire party towards showing concern for, protecting and obeying the overall situation". Then came the homilies on "talking more about politics". In internal briefings, Jiang and his publicists made it beyond doubt that shibboleths such as "the overall situation" and the "party spirit" could be reduced to one thing: showing obeisance to the party central authorities "with comrade Zemin as its core".[106]

Jiang was very conscious about his image in the foreign media. The president only gave interviews about once every two to three months — and most often, only to selected media such as CNN. However, he always made sure that his spin doctors had total control. For example, questions had to be submitted in advance, and no follow-up questions were allowed. In mid-1996, he blamed unnamed foreign media for suggesting that his emphasis on "talking more about politics" showed he was a leftist. "Some newspapers and magazines outside China have distorted the facts to claim that China has returned to the past practice of taking class struggle as the key link," he said.[107]

As the power struggle intensified in 1996 and 1997, Jiang was particularly concerned about his image in the Hong Kong, Taiwan and US press. In internal meetings, he fumed about Beijing's lack of control over the Chinese-language services provided by the likes of Voice of America, Radio Free Asia, the BBC and French Radio. For example, in a closed-door speech,

Jiang took exception to commentaries on an America-based radio service that he was inferior to Mao and Deng.[108]

Measures to muzzle the press

Let a hundred flowers wilt! That was the key message of the landmark "Resolution on the Construction of Spiritual Civilisation", which was passed at the sixth Central Committee plenum in October 1996 (see following section). The resolution indicated that macro-level controls and adjustments would be applied to culture and the media.

As propaganda chief Ding Guan'gen saw it, the rightful calling of the arts and the media was to "resolutely develop the leitmotif of patriotism, collectivism and socialism; and to combat the influence of corrupt and decadent thoughts".[109] While Ding also went through the motion of ticking off the old ideals of "letting a hundred flowers bloom", the authorities made it clear anything smacking of bourgeois liberalisation would not be tolerated. Another big no-no was "negative reporting", or dwelling on the dark side of society. This area not only covered scandals involving senior cadres or labour unrest but apparently innocuous, apolitical topics such as casualties from fires and floods — or even the fact that schoolchildren were burdened with too much homework. Embarrassing historical subjects such as the Cultural Revolution also became taboo.[110]

To trim the potential poisonous weeds, the number of newspapers, magazines, publications and TV stations was cut down. Starting in 1995, the State Press and Publications Administration stopped issuing licences for new newspapers and publishing houses. From mid-1996, Beijing announced plans to cut thousands of print and electronic media. For example, in-house newspapers and magazines run by party and government departments would be slashed. In late 1996, then vice-premier Zhu Rongji ordered the closure of dozens of publications sponsored by the state banking system. In the first half of 1997, 1.16 million copies of 3,400 books were seized. The illegal volumes ranged from pornography to those with "misguided" political views. Particularly targeted were the nation's 3,500-odd TV stations, which were deemed too numerous for a developing country. The commissars claimed China had twice the number of TV facilities in the US.[111]

Not surprisingly, more complicated reasons than frugality and avoidance of duplication were behind the closure of many media outlets. Among the most notable magazines axed in the mid-1990s was *Oriental,* a semi-private monthly journal for intellectuals. In mid-1996, *Oriental* ran foul of the commissars by running a special issue commemorating the Cultural Revolution. It also featured pieces that advocated "thought liberation" and praised the free-market reforms and the "East European experience". Foremost among books that were banned was *The Wrath of Heaven* of 1997, a fictional account of the corrupt empire of disgraced Beijing party boss Chen Xitong.[112]

What media analysts found especially disturbing about Jiang's tough regime were signs of the militarisation of Beijing's policy towards culture and the media. The analysts recalled how, during the end of the Cultural Revolution, PLA officers were stationed in newspapers and broadcast units to ensure the latter's ideological rectitude. For example, General Chi Haotian ran the *People's Daily* during the tail-end of the Revolution. The last paragraph of the "Resolution on Spiritual Civilisation" urged the PLA and the PAP to "go to the forefront" in the construction of Marxist values. This recalled statements by Deng and Jiang that the PLA and the PAP should form a "great wall of steel" to protect the party's prerogatives.[113]

JIANG ZEMIN'S PHILOSOPHY AND POLICIES
Promoting Stability and Muddling Through

The key word for Jiang was stability: maintaining a balance among the disparate forces in society and the party so that there would not be a direct challenge to his ruling elite. As *People's Daily* commentator Ren Zhongping (a collective pen name representing the views of the Jiang Office) put it in 1996: "Politics is the ability to mediate between — and ride — the contradictions and clashes of various [types of] realities."[114] The balancing of contradictory forces one against the other precluded upheavals; however, it also militated against radical, thorough-going changes. Jiang was dead-set against the kind of shock therapy approach proposed by Russian and East European economists — or the young advisers to Zhao Ziyang.

The clearest message that Jiang gave out was the Theory of the Twelve Relationships, which formed the basis of his speech to the Fifth Plenum of the 14th Central Committee in September 1995. Maintaining the 12 relationships was the key to that Chinese political goal that goes back the centuries: *changzhi jiu'an* ("long reign and perennial stability"). After all, in the mid-1950s, Mao had put forward the Eight Relationships as the *ne plus ultra* of statecraft.[115]

The 12 arenas where an optimal balance should be sustained were: the relationship between reform, development and stability; that between speed and efficiency; economic development on the one hand, and considerations of population, resources and the environment on the other; the relationship between the primary, secondary and tertiary sectors of the economy; that between the eastern and western parts of the country; the balance between market mechanisms and macro-level adjustments and controls; that between the state-owned sector and other economic sectors; the relationship between the state, enterprises and individuals in the distribution of income; that between expanding the open-door policy and the principle of self-sufficiency; the balance between the *zhongyang* ("central authorities") and localities; the relationship between national defence construction and economic development; that between material and spiritual civilisations.

Of these 12 relationships, perhaps the most important was the one between reform, development and stability. It was the issue that the president had most often addressed since 1989. Jiang upheld Deng's instructions issued soon after the June 4 crackdown: "Stability is the over-riding task of the nation." While reform and development were important, they must be subsumed under the task of maintaining stability. The difference between Jiang and Deng was that the patriarch had proposed his "stability above all else" theory to quell the residual unrest of the post-Tiananmen Square period. By the time Deng went on his *nanxun* ("imperial tour of the south"), his emphasis had shifted to reform and development.[116]

Jiang, however, carried the "stability *über alles*" goal into the end of the 1990s. "Without a stable political and social environment, nothing can be done and it will be difficult to accomplish any plan no matter how good it is," he said at the fifth plenum. The theme was repeated on other occasions. "Development is the goal; reform is the moving force; and stability is the premise," Jiang said at a press conference while visiting Germany in July 1995. "If we depart from political stability, reform, the open door, and economic construction will bear no fruit." Likewise, the president pointed out in a speech on Labour Day in 1995 that the nation must "push forward reform and development in the midst of stability".[117]

To maintain stability, Jiang avoided taking sides — or taking the dilemma by the horns and going full throttle in the direction he thought best for the nation. His admirers might call it a policy of strategic ambiguity.

And the public relations professionals would refer to it as a Deng-style "both hands be tough" policy — meaning he would implement one side of the argument as vigorously as the other. For most observers, however, this meant lapsing into an "on the one hand, and on the other" mode of lack of resolve and direction. The country had become too complex — and the leadership too weak — for Jiang to rule in favour of one political orientation or programme of action. This policy was geared towards muddling through difficult times — and it proved to be largely successful in prolonging his reign. Contradictions were minimised but long-term solutions remained illusory.

Take, for example, the polarisation of income between rich and poor — or the wealth gap between the coast and the heartland. Mao was a clear-cut advocate of egalitarianism. Deng coined the lasting slogan: "Let one part of the population get rich first." Moreover, the late patriarch unabashedly favoured the coastal rim over the hinterland. Jiang could only take a "balanced" approach by saying that on the one hand, one sector of the population such as inhabitants of the coastal rim could get rich first; however, he went on to say this could only be predicated upon the premise of common prosperity in the not too distant future. Thus, the nation should do all it could to shorten the gap between the haves and have-nots; and between east and west.[118]

This was how the party chief put it while meeting members of the Guangdong delegation to the National People's Congress in 1995: "On the one hand, we implement the policy of letting one part of the people — and some regions in the country — get rich first; on the other, we effectively prevent unfair distribution [of wealth] and ensure the eventual goal of common prosperity for all the people."[119] Not surprisingly, Beijing's policy in this regard was contradictory. *Fupin* ("help the poor regions") was elevated to a top priority; yet the most favourable policies and the bulk of resources were still funnelled towards Shanghai and the eastern coast (see Chapter 5).

The same ambiguity informed his policy towards the SOEs (see later section). On the one hand, the president was anxious to stop the red ink flowing at the moribund enterprises. On the other, he had to satisfy the workers, the "vanguard of the proletariat" and basic supporters of the regime. Thus Jiang's call for a continuation of Deng's market reforms was hedged with guarantees for the welfare of the proletariat. "Only when there is a general improvement in the living standard of workers can reform and economic development have popular support," he said in 1996.[120] On another occasion he pronounced: "We must wholeheartedly rely on the working class. We must have political guarantees of the status of workers as masters of enterprises." More reform-minded leaders such as Deng, Zhao Ziyang or Hu Yaobang were, of course, aware of the need to at least pay lip service to the plight of workers. Yet they usually left it to second-tier leaders such as the heads of the official trade union to dole out the palliatives.[121]

On numerous issues, too, Jiang walked the tightrope of the conflicting demands of various sectors of society. On the relationship between Beijing and the regions, Jiang went through the motions of saluting the fact that, as a result of the devolution of powers in the past 15 years of reform, the "enthusiasm of localities" had been fully developed. Yet it was apparent his own sympathies laid with recentralisation. "The phenomenon of orders and prohibitions [by the *zhongyang*] not being carried out has increased," he said. "We will not allow local or departmental interests to jeopardise national interests."[122]

Jiang adopted the "both hands be tough" policy towards contentious issues such as balancing material pursuit and Marxist values. In his Fifth Plenum speech, Jiang said: "On the one hand, we must concentrate our resources on developing the economy and building up material civilisation; on the other, we must earnestly strengthen socialist spiritual civilisation." A much less "pro-Western" politician than either Deng or Zhao, Jiang put caveats galore on learning from the West. "On the one hand, we must boldly absorb all the beneficial things abroad," he said. "On the other, we must insist upon developing our superior tradition and self-consciously combat various corrupt things from abroad."[123]

"Talk More about Politics"

If the first cornerstone of Jiang-style politics was muddling through while preserving a balance of disparate forces, the second pillar was a partial restitution of Maoist norms. Particularly at times when the Jiang team felt unsure of its hold, the centre of gravity was nudged towards the left. Nowhere was this born-again, late-20th century Maoism more evident than in the slogan "talk more about politics" that the Jiang Office started popularising in late 1995. Regardless of the spin that Jiang and others put on this shibboleth, the point was that the president was reviving Mao's infamous

"politics in command" ethos: everything, including economic consideration, must be subsumed to the politically correct line from the *zhongyang*.

Many interpretations were put on Jiang's most well-known battlecry.
On one level, it was an order that cadres should spend more time studying
the Marxist classics as well as the *zhongyang*'s instructions. Moreover, officials had to have a clean work style and be responsive to the needs of the
masses. In an essay on "talking politics" that was released in mid-1996, Jiang
urged cadres to ensure that they had the right "political orientation, political standpoint, political discipline, political discrimination power, and political sensitivity".[124]

On another level, however, this politics-first requirement meant cadres
had to boost their ability to read the weathervane perched on top of the
Zhongnanhai party headquarters. For cynics, this was nothing more than a
call for either *ruzhong* ("Confucian-style loyalty") or opportunism — to
trim the sails according to the wind blowing through Zhongnanhai. As
Head of the Organisation Department and Shandong Faction affiliate
Zhang Quanjing put it, "to talk about politics is to insist on the correct
political direction as laid down by the party centre with Jiang Zemin as its
core".[125]

At yet another level, "talk more about politics" meant the ability to
discern the truth according to the rigid rules of Marxism-Leninism as
understood by Jiang. When the president talked about the 12 relationships
in his Fifth Plenum speech, there was a modicum of tolerance in some
areas. For example, cadres were encouraged to use both market mechanisms and macro-level controls; they were also allowed to develop both the
public and the private sectors. Jiang's "talk more about politics" credo,
however, would make no room for diversity.

To make sure that cadres were talking about the right kinds of politics
and that they would not fall into ideological traps, Jiang laid down the law
of the so-called Seven Differentials in early 1995. This was an exercise in
hair-splitting aimed at drawing the line between "pure upon pure"
Marxism-Maoism on the one hand, and manifestations of adulterated
Marxism or bourgeois liberalisation on the other.[126]

In a kind of Seven Commandments with Chinese characteristics, Jiang
asked cadres to tell the difference between seven sets of concepts, which
shared disturbing levels of grey areas. First and foremost, Marxism must
not be confused with anti-Marxism or pseudo-Marxism. The other six
areas were: the socialist economy where public ownership was the mainstay

and where different sectors could co-exist, versus private ownership; socialist democracy versus Western parliamentary democracy; dialectical materialism versus *weixinzhuyi xing'ershangxue* ("subjectivist metaphysics"); socialism versus feudalism and the corrupt attributes of capitalism; learning
"advanced things" from the West versus blind worship of the West; a civilised, healthy lifestyle versus a negative, decadent lifestyle.[127]

The subtle art of "political sensitivity and political discrimination
power" was illustrated when Jiang drew the line between "learning from the
West" and "all-out Westernisation". "When we are learning from and copying the good things of capitalist countries, we must not belittle ourselves,"
he said at an internal meeting in 1996. "We must not lose confidence in
socialism. We are not backward in all areas. However, if, in the course of
learning from foreign countries, we think that we are no good through and
through, this becomes a blind worship of things from abroad."[128]

As much as the Four Cardinal Principles, Jiang's Seven Differentials
amounted to a sword of Damocles hanging over reform. The chasm between Jiang and Deng was obvious. After all, "talking more about politics"
was the antithesis of Deng's famed goodbye to politics, which was embodied in the line of the Third Plenum of the 11th Central Committee — that
economics had become the core of party work.[129]

Jiang's insistence on doctrinal purity was also a revival of the so-called
Theory of Surnames: that a policy can only be pursued if it is "surnamed
socialist" or if it does not smack of "capitalist decadence". Deng was a major
opponent of such nihilistic formalism. Note his time-honoured "theory of
the black and white cats" as well as the *nanxun* concept of "staying away
from controversies". The gist of the theory of avoiding controversies was:
regardless of its "surname", a policy should be pursued if it brought about
concrete benefits to the economy. The latter were summarised by Deng as
the "three advantages" or "three favourables": raising productivity; boosting
the people's standard of living; and elevating the comprehensive strength of
the nation.[130]

Jiang's efforts to deny that his "politics first" persuasion and the Seven
Differentials were a negation of reform were futile. Shortly after the "talk
more about politics" slogan was unveiled in late 1995, it came in for heavy
flak from the party's moderate faction and from international opinion.
None other than Jiang's principal patron, former Shanghai mayor Wang
Daohan, advised the president to tone down the rhetoric. No wonder that
in his essay in the official journal *Qiushi*, Jiang went out of his way to flag

his Dengist or reformist credentials. He pointed out there was no going back to the old-style "politics in command" because the "most important politics was socialist modernisation". "When we ask leading cadres to talk about politics, it will never affect economic development," he claimed.[131]

Preserving and Rejuvenating the CCP

A corollary of "politics *über alles*" is the CCP *über alles*. Jiang's attitude towards the CCP was different from that of Zhao Ziyang — or the "liberal persona" of Deng Xiaoping. Both leaders had reservations about further boosting the powers of the CCP, which had at least in a few areas become a millstone round the neck of reform. One major achievement of the 13th Party Congress of 1987 was the "separation of party and government", which saw the partial truncation of the functions and powers of party cells. Moreover, soon after coming back to power in late 1978, Deng had breathed word about the abolition of party cells in certain government departments.[132]

For Jiang, there was no question that the CCP's powers should be further boosted, that things would fall apart without a quasi-totalitarian party. In a mid-1995 speech, the General Secretary said goals such as national independence and prosperity could "only be achieved based on the struggle of all the people under the leadership of the CCP". Talk that the CCP had become obsolete was sacrilegious. "The party's leading position was formed by history and is generally acknowledged by the people nationwide," he said. "The party's links with the masses are as close as flesh and blood."[133]

How could the CCP withstand the new challenges of the times? First of all, stay united and banish wild thoughts. As Jiang protégé Zeng Qinghong said in early 1995: "The key is to unite our thoughts and safeguard the authority of the *zhongyang*."[134] Secondly, the president was convinced that through "self-construction" and self-renewal, the CCP could remain fit for the 21st century. This was his homily for the 74th birthday of the party in 1995: "To better develop the function of the party as the leadership core, the CCP must under new circumstances ceaselessly strengthen its self-construction. It must diligently raise its level in administration and in leadership qualities."[135]

Jiang's formula for giving back the right stuff to the party had the elitism of both Confucianism and Leninism. Harking back to first-generation revolutionaries such as Mao and former president Liu Shaoqi, Jiang lay a lot of store by *xiushen*: building up the virtues of individual party members. Compared with Liu, who authored the classic *Building Up the Virtues of Communist Party Members*, however, Jiang's definition of Marxist morality was narrower and more sanctimonious.

"Don't go to nightclubs and high-class ballrooms," was one of Jiang's admonitions to the party rank and file. In his talk at the Fifth Plenum, Jiang gave top billing to Mao's instructions about withstanding the "sugar-coated bullets" of capitalism. He cited the chairman's lionisation of Lei Feng and Norman Bethune — the Canadian doctor noted for his total self-abnegation and devotion to the revolution. Speaking like a Confucian monk, Jiang intoned: "All levels of leaders should have self-respect. They should exercise self-scrutiny and self-encouragement, and give themselves [early] warnings." Nightclubs were a definite no-no for senior cadres, Jiang said, "even though the masses could go there".[136]

After marathon scandals in early 1995 involving the so-called Beijing mafia, Jiang upped the ante in his purification campaign. "Cadres who lead corrupt lives and fool around with women will not be promoted," Jiang said after the Chen Xitong affair. He also instructed that cadres who wanted to keep their jobs must not suffer from five weaknesses: love of fame, hunger for power, money, women, and using *guanxi* ("human relationships") for immoral gain.[137] In 1996 and 1997, central and regional administrations also promulgated a host of regulations against corruption.

Jiang did not believe in modernising the CCP or the *dangxing* ("the nature of the party") through erecting "Western-style" checks and balances. His approach to building up virtues and combating corruption amounted to a genuflexion to *weixinzhuyi xing'ershangxue*. Like Mao, Jiang believed that the most important thing was to mould — and remould — one's worldview so that a kind of revolutionary, Lei Feng-like spirit could be nurtured. And then by sheer force of moral influence, one's friends and associates would be shepherded down the path of righteousness. As the party chief put it: "The force of doing good through setting an example is infinite."[138]

In numerous speeches, the president dwelled long and hard on the "spiritual state" of a cadre: he must have a lofty spiritual station before ever laying claim to the Communist hall of fame. "If a man wants to achieve something, he must have an elevated spiritual state," he told students at the National Defence University in 1995. "We transform our subjective world even as we go about transforming the objective world."[139]

The Campaign on Spiritual Civilisation

The *jingshen wenming* or spiritual civilisation campaign was on a limited —
and much less brutal — scale a replay of Mao's Great Proletarian Cultural
Revolution. Chairman Mao ordered the Red Guards to bombard the headquarters of a party hierarchy that he thought had been corrupted or otherwise succumbed to the siren song of Khrushchev-style revisionism. For
Jiang, there was the need to undo the damage done by market reforms.
"Under the conditions of reform and the open door, the corrupt thoughts
and culture of capitalism will necessarily creep in," he said at a meeting of
the Central Commission for Disciplinary Inspection in 1995. The party
chief pointed out that the infiltration of capitalism, coupled with the residual influence of feudalism, had spawned "money worship, extreme individualism, and corrupt lifestyles". "We must assiduously promote the traditional virtues of the Chinese race in aiding the poor and the disadvantaged,
helping each other and maintaining neighbourly love," he said.[140]

The Sixth Plenum of the Central Committee of October 1996 passed
the long-awaited "Resolution on the Construction of Socialist Spiritual
Civilisation". It affirmed Jiang's slogan of "talking more about politics; paying more attention to studying [the Marxist canon]; and putting emphasis
on righteousness". Party members were urged to establish "the correct
worldview, personal philosophy and value system". The usual deference was
made to the "three isms": socialism, patriotism and collectivism. Chinese
would be turned into "socialist citizens who have ideals, morality, culture
and discipline".[141]

The *jingshen wenming* movement testified to Jiang's belief in his ability
to "transform the subjective worldview" of cadres and citizens. Ideological
and political work (IPW) specialists, as well as teachers, artists and writers
would be transformed into "engineers of the human soul". The resolution
carried the implicit criticism that such of Deng's lieutenants as Hu Yaobang
and Zhao Ziyang failed to adopt the "both hands be tough" policy. The
document said that in some regions and departments, "the phenomenon of
neglecting ideological education and neglecting spiritual civilisation has
still not been resolved".

The plenum legitimised and institutionalised more controls on people's spiritual life beyond existing strictures such as a ban on new publications and controls over the Internet. "Macro-level adjustments and controls" should be strengthened over the news and publications arena, which
would conform strictly to "the nature of the party". A Guiding Committee

for the Construction of Spiritual Civilisation, headed by Ding Guan'gen, was set up in 1997 to enforce the Draconian measures.[142]

Apart from the orthodox teachings of Marx, Mao and Deng, Jiang would like to reinstate "the traditional cultural quintessence of the motherland" so as to boost the content of the "correct" type of spiritual civilisation. There was a revival of lores ranging from Confucianism to Beijing Opera. The spiritual civilisation campaign would also be strictly tied to the crusade on nationalism that was the rage in China in the mid-1990s (see following section).

Not surprisingly, the resolution did not mention the need to fight "leftism". This was despite the fact that at the Politburo meeting and the leadership conference at Beidaihe just before the plenum, moderate cadres such as Qiao Shi had revived Deng's dictum given during the *nanxun*: "While the party should continue to combat rightism, its major task is fighting leftism." For the party's liberals, there were fears that excessive stress on spiritual civilisation would bring back Maoism.[143]

Jiang's revision of Deng's "economics first" dictum was obvious. As he put it in a 1997 talk: "The history of human society has shown that a people must not be materially poor; nor should they be spiritually poor."[144] However, many of Deng's most famous teachings, such as "poverty is not socialism" and "to get rich is glorious", referred only to material wealth. Both the *jingshen wenming* document and other Jiang speeches stressed that "at no time should we sacrifice spiritual civilisation in return for temporary economic development".

The Goal of Nationalism

Reviving the splendour that was China

The entire ideological programme of Jiang had a strongly nationalistic — and at times xenophobic — element. While nationalism will be discussed in detail in Chapter 5, it is important to point out that it was a vital premise of "long reign and perennial stability". At a time when few Chinese — particularly those under 45 — were interested in Marxism-Leninism, Jiang staked a claim to protecting China from foreign "infiltration", maintaining its independence and developing Chinese civilisation to new heights.

In May 1995, the media released a long tract by Jiang on the development of national arts and spirit. This was to coincide with the 53rd anniversary of Mao's famous Yan'an Talk on Literature and the Arts. "The Chinese people are a great people who have 5,000 years of splendid history, culture and traditions," Jiang wrote. He decried the "great danger" that, if the Chinese were to give up such lores, China would become "a vassal of foreign, particularly Western, culture".[145]

A key goal of the propagation of *jingshen wenming* was to combat "peaceful evolution", or the "conspiracy" of the Western world to turn China into a spineless, second-rate capitalist realm. "We must prevent and obliterate the spread of cultural rubbish," said the Sixth Plenum resolution. "We must counter and sabotage the plots of hostile forces to promote Westernisation and to sow dissent [in Chinese society]." Again, while talking to a meeting of Chinese writers and artists in late 1996, Jiang hoisted the flag of nationalism. "Our country must be independent," he said. "And it must be independent not just in politics and economics but also in thought and culture."[146]

Jiang lavished tremendous resources on the commemoration of major historical events to drum up nationalism. Particularly notable were the 50th anniversary of the end of World War II (1995) and the 60th anniversary of the "triumph" of the Long March (1996). On the later occasion, Jiang pledged the CCP would pull out all the stops to ensure China's continued "independence and self-reliance". "We must consider the fundamental interests of all the Chinese people and the Chinese race as towering above everything," he said.[147]

As with many other of his policies, Jiang's appeals to nationalism were geared towards raising his own stature. Campaigns of patriotism and nationalism were not only waged to guarantee China's independence from foreign influence; they were linked to efforts to promote the "renaissance of the entire Chinese race".[148] While Jiang appeared in the eyes of many Chinese as a lightweight thinker and flaccid policymaker, he made himself out as no less than the saviour of the Chinese civilisation. Like Generalissimo Chiang Kai-shek and Chairman Mao, Jiang laid claim to being the embodiment of the *guohun*, or the country's soul.

Taiwan, Hong Kong and US policy

Given the difficulty the Jiang leadership faced in scoring points on domestic issues, the president was hopeful that he could boost the party's legitimacy and his own stature through some triumph in reunification — and foreign — policy. Jiang's eight-point initiative on Taiwan, announced in January 1995, amounted to the most original policy that the president had ever come up with. Results of the olive branch, however, were disappointing. Most domestic factions did not think highly of it. Worse still, Taiwan President Lee Teng-hui interpreted Jiang's overture as a sign of weakness and proceeded to visit the US in May that year. Cross-strait relations deteriorated into a series of war games in late 1995 and early 1996 (see Chapter 4).

By early 1997, of course, Jiang had salvaged some lost political capital through diplomatic gains over Taiwan such as persuading South Africa to switch recognition to the People's Republic. Taipei also suffered other setbacks in the international arena, for example, a cut-off in further supplies of armaments from France and the Netherlands. In internal meetings, some Jiang aides were predicting confidently that Taiwan would be "liberated" by the second decade of the new century. The president drew satisfaction from the fact that opinion polls seemed to support his administration's handling of Taiwan, including the use of quasi-military tactics.[149]

Hong Kong became an emblem of the CCP's success in leading the nation to repel imperialism and to accomplish unification. As Jiang put it in the New Year's message for 1997: the handover meant "the washing away of more than 100 years of national humiliation". "It shows the struggle waged by the Chinese people for national reunification has scored a major success," he said. The president's July 1 speech at the Workers' Stadium highlighted the "three revelations of recent history". The gist of these lessons from history was: "The liberation of the people and [the building up of] national strength are predicated upon the leadership of an advanced political party and [the people] being armed with scientific theory."[150]

Given Deng Xiaoping's demise, Jiang was able to take the full credit for the patriarch's "one country, two systems" invention. Celebrations and media coverage in Beijing in late June and early July played up the contribution of the Jiang leadership to the unification process. A commentary by the semi-official China News Service eulogised the president and his followers for "inheriting, bringing forward and implementing" the Hong Kong strategy of Mao and Deng. Army officers expressing their trust in the probity of the PLA Hong Kong Garrison invariably cited Jiang's instructions on "building an army that passes muster politically".[151]

At the same time, Jiang adroitly exploited China's enhanced global position — and Chinese citizens' desire for a better international image — to push a tougher foreign policy. Both the CCP and the Jiang leadership seemed to have scored points by "standing up to the Americans". The psychology implicit in the bestseller of 1996 — *China Can Say No* — allowed Beijing to claim that under Jiang's tutelage, Chinese could walk tall on the world stage. The leadership was clever in lumping together the post-Tiananmen Square boycott (which was caused by the CCP's mistakes) and anti-Chinese fusillades fired by Washington over the trade deficit and the intellectual property rights issue (where the blame could be pinned on foreigners). Likewise, Jiang and company tarred with the same brush condemnations of Beijing on human rights issues — which some Chinese might applaud — and US Congressmen disparaging Beijing as a venue for the 2000 Olympic Games.[152]

Jiang was largely successful in using the two Sino-US summits in 1997 and 1998 to enhance China's global stature — and to bolster his own image. Through convincing Washington to restore bilateral ties to pre-1989 levels, the president was able to show the hawks — including PLA generals — that he had done the right thing in persevering with Deng Xiaoping's so-called "pro-American policy".[153] The concrete benefits he brought back, particularly in the areas of trade and hi-tech transfer, would help to buttress his argument that he had improved relations with the world's only superpower without giving up the demands of nationalism.

The longer-term effects of rapprochement with the US, however, could be to further undermine the status of Marxism, socialism and patriotism in the hearts of Chinese. Because of the reduction of tension and the concessions Beijing had made in opening up its market, 1998 witnessed a semi-deluge of American products, including videos and computer software. College students were fast jettisoning ideologically stilted reading material for Chinese translations of text-books used on American campuses. The craze surrounding the film *Titanic* was illustrative of the popularity of American culture. Jiang himself heaped praise on the blockbuster. The president claimed he was interested in the movie primarily because of what it said about capitalist mores.[154] Yet the increasing Americanisation of Chinese popular culture could undermine on-going campaigns about nationalism.

Jiang's Populism and Efforts to Woo the Masses

The image of the *fumuguan*

Jiang Zemin hoped to gain support in the one area where the Dengists seemed to have neglected: the welfare of the masses. While critics had accused Jiang of minding only the interests of his Shanghai Faction, he made himself out to be the champion of the common man, whose cradle-to-grave benefits used to be taken care of by the socialist state.

Jiang's public relations experts wanted to present him as the time-honoured *fumuguan* ("parent-like official"). Playing his "man of the masses" persona to the hilt, Jiang simplified socialism or communism to the minimum: an egalitarian society where the masses — in particular the working class — are king, and where there is a safety net for everybody. He told his working-class audiences that there would be no new-fangled experiments with market reforms if they were to shortchange the benefits of the masses. "Caring about the masses in things big and small; doing everything for the masses," Jiang said while visiting Zhangjiakou in 1995. "This is the superior tradition of the party."[155]

In the mid-1990s, Jiang fired off a volley of assurances to the masses. "Only when there is a general improvement in the living standard of workers, farmers and intellectuals can our reform and economic development have popular support and get its motivation," he said in March 1996. "Modernisation must first benefit the average man." "Common prosperity is the fundamental principle of socialism and must never be shaken," Jiang liked to say.[156] There was a celebration in particular of the contribution and status of workers. The president's efforts to woo the working class could be because among the various sectors, only labourers could pose a frontal challenge to the regime.

Jiang's message was there would be no sacrifice of their position in the headlong dash towards modernisation. "We must wholeheartedly rely on the working class," he said in the May Day celebration in 1995. "This [principle] must not be shaken at any time and under any circumstances." "The working class are the masters of the country and masters of enterprises," he said while touring Shaanxi and Gansu. "When we bring about reform and the socialist market economy, we must resolutely and wholeheartedly rely on the working class."[157]

The great *fupin* campaign

In 1987 and 1988, enemies of Zhao Ziyang used photos and TV footage of him teeing off at exclusive golf courses to attack the "bourgeois-liberal" party chief. On the other hand, Jiang was frequently seen on national TV visiting mountainous villages in remote provinces or the urban poor. On such visits, he showered the families he visited with gifts of food, cotton-quilt blankets, electrical appliances, and even red packets containing cash.[158]

"Leading officials at all levels should feel uneasy when large numbers of people cannot get enough to eat and wear, and many regions still suffer natural disasters," he said while inspecting Shaanxi and Gansu in late 1995. "Party members and well-off families should bear in mind that tens of millions of people are still living under the poverty line, and should carry forward the spirit of common prosperity." "If they see impoverished people, officials should have the feeling of 'not being able to sleep'," he added. Just before Chinese New Year of 1997, Jiang visited destitute families on the outskirts of Beijing. He told a laid-off worker that while she was suffering hardship, "we can see the bright future of socialism".[159]

Unlike his predecessors, Jiang came up with a solid *fupin* ("help the poor") programme to try to lift all the destitute above the poverty line by the year 2000 (see Chapter 5). The administration claimed that China's poor had already declined from 80 million in 1994 to 65 million by 1996. Relief funds jumped 55 per cent to 8.5 billion yuan in 1997. Richer provinces and cities, mostly those along the coast, were given orders to pour aid or development projects into the hinterland.[160]

As with everything else, what propelled Jiang to action was the fear of instability — the spectre of the millennial, dynastic peasant uprising. "Solving the problem of shelter and food for our peasants in the villages affects the long-term balance and stability of our economic and social development," Jiang said while touring eastern China in September. "This is not just an economic problem but a political one."[161] Unlike Zhao — or Deng, for that matter — Jiang would not expose himself to charges that he was being callous towards the have-nots.

In the mid-1990s, Jiang gave orders to all regional party secretaries, governors and mayors to "personally grasp the *fupin* crusade". "They must organise the task forces, map out solutions and set up model units to tackle the poverty issue," he said while touring the hilly regions of Guizhou and

Guangxi. Cadres of all levels should make as many trips to factories and farms — particularly impoverished ones in faraway places — as possible.[162]

How successful the programme to woo the workers and farmers was became a matter of controversy. There were horror stories of administrations in the remote provinces holding up funds from the *zhongyang* as well as from the rich provinces — and using them to buy stocks and shares. However, Jiang pulled off a largely convincing public relations campaign. The party chief could at least parry charges from leftists that he had forsaken Mao's teachings about giving a fair shake to the proletariats.

Science and Technology as National Saviour

Given Beijing's anxiety to ban the "objectionable" websites, it did not look as though Jiang was an enthusiastic fan of the information age or other futuristic gadgets. However, the one Jiang idea that seemed most modernistic was his stress on science and technology. It is important to note, of course, that science was first cited as a way out for the country during the 1919 May Fourth Movement. At that point, the students said China could be rescued from the threat of imperialist powers through Mr *Cai* ("Science") and Mr *De* ("Democracy").[163]

Mr *De* was pretty much strangled by Jiang. The party chief, however, was a fervent believer in the formula: socialism plus science and technology equals modernisation. In other words, the 1919-vintage goal of *fuqiang* ("prosperity and strength") could be attained without going through the "Western" path of democratisation. Jiang cited a Deng instruction of 1986 on the same subject: "Our national power will be augmented immensely through reform, modern science and technology, and putting emphasis on politics." Or as the party chief put it in late 1997, priority must be put on developing the "technological quality" of the entire race.[164] In the military sphere, the former minister of electronics was a prime advocate of "modern, electronic, three-dimensional warfare".

In mid-1995, Jiang kicked off a massive propaganda campaign on "the strategy of reviving the nation through science and technology". As Jiang put it in a national conference a year later: "The intimate synthesis of socialism with modern science and technology will have a major and far-reaching significance for speeding up the construction of Chinese modernisation."[165]

Indeed, for Jiang and other neo-conservative leaders, it was as though science and technology were the civilian versions of the PLA and the PAP in fulfilling the role of a Great Wall of Steel to protect the party. Jiang indicated at a high-level seminar on the subject in mid-1996 that the marriage of socialism and technology would be the best way of developing Deng's concept that "science and technology are the primary productive force". "In light of both the international and domestic situation, implementing Deng's theory is a pressing and arduous task in China's socialist modernisation drive," he said.[166]

Jiang also called for a movement to popularise science and technology. Mindful of the fact that many scientists in the modern era were advocates of democracy — astrophysicist Fang Lizhi comes to mind — there would be close links between science and technology on the one hand, and "patriotism" and party supervision on the other. Inevitably, the science-and-technology drive was politicised. Apart from shoring up the regime, science would be a key weapon in building up "spiritual civilisation". "We must strengthen the party's leadership of science and technology work," the president said. "We must propagate a large corps of technology personnel who possess both morality and ability." By "morality" Jiang meant Marxist ideals.[167]

The heads of party committees and governments of all levels had to personally take up the task of scientific and technological development. Jiang called upon various levels of party and governments to "ceaselessly promote and enthusiastically support" various types of superior technological talents.[168] Top scientists were invited to give lectures at Zhongnanhai. Under Beijing's directions, cadres of large and medium cities began studying computers. There was, however, fear that excessive political zeal might nip in the bud initiative and imagination, the soul of science.

JIANG ZEMIN'S ECONOMIC STRATEGY

President Jiang and other economic policymakers such as Zhu Rongji and Li Peng were basically men of the 1950s. Their formative years were spent studying Stalinist economics; both Jiang and Li had experience working in Soviet factories. Economic tsar Zhu was an admirer of Yugoslavian and Hungarian reform. However, that did not turn him off state-planning — just rigid state planning.

Jiang's strategy for the economy was not complicated. He would push economic development and reform so long as the predominant role of the state sector — and the party leadership — was not jeopardised. To preserve CCP rule and political stability, the president subscribed to the late conservative patriarch Chen Yun's slogan "without sufficient grain production, there will be chaos". The private sector could only be a "supplement" to the state sector. Doubts were raised, however, as to whether such a gameplan could tackle the increasingly complex nature of the Chinese economy.

While Jiang sanctioned slightly more radical reforms in late 1997 and 1998 (see Chapters 7 and 8), the premise remained the same: economic liberalisation must not be at the expense of the socialist system. "The goal of the reform of the economic structure is to build up a socialist market economy, not a capitalist economy," the party chief said in 1995. He added that in the course of reform, the state-owned economy could only be improved and strengthened, and must "absolutely not" be curtailed.[169]

The "East Asian Strategy"

Jiang wanted a mixture of the market economy and centralised control. For the president and fellow neo-conservatives such as Zhu Rongji, the East Asian development model was the answer to the search for the "Golden Mean". In countries and areas such as Japan, South Korea, Singapore and Taiwan, there was a co-existence of paternalistic, heavy-handed state control — or at least guidance — and a body of business practices according to "international norms".[170] The neo-conservatives' faith in the East Asian approach did not seem to be substantially shaken by the Asian financial crisis that began mid-1997 (see Chapter 8).

Jiang, who started his career in state-owned enterprises (SOEs), wanted to copy the experience of the Japanese *zaibatsus* and South Korean *chaebols*. These concerns worked in close association with the government and were instrumental in the economic take-off of their countries. The party chief's belief was reinforced after a tour of South Korea in November 1995. Upon returning home, he reportedly gave instructions to the Ministry of Foreign Affairs and Ministry of Foreign Trade and Economic Cooperation to study South Korean development plans from the 1960s. Jiang also expressed an interest in "learning from the Japanese example" while meeting a senior delegation from the Mitsubishi Corporation in 1996.[171]

One of the centrepieces of Jiang's economic policy was developing about 1,000 key enterprises. "Look at the US economy," the president said in an internal meeting in late 1995. "Its scale is so big; and yet its prosperity is mainly predicated upon 500-odd multinationals. In Japan and South Korea, about 10 major multinationals are throwing their weight around. So we must promote the concept of 'grabbing hold of the key minority' [for fast development]." He added in an economic strategy session in 1997 that the country should rely mainly on large SOEs and *jituangongsi* (conglomerates) for "economic development, industrialisation, and raising the quality of the whole economy".[172]

By mid-1996, Jiang had masterminded a rush to build up *jituangongsi à la* Japan and South Korea. Cadres of each province, city, and in some instances, even towns, were given directives and targets for the formation of conglomerates. In prosperous areas, each city must have at least one such corporation, defined as having assets of more than 60 million yuan. Many local cadres just went through the motions and satisfied the "quota" by claiming that one or two of their more successful village and township enterprises (VTEs) had become *jituangongsi*. In other instances, so-called conglomerates were loose umbrella companies whose components had no organic relationship with each other.[173]

The Imbroglio of State-owned Enterprises

As a trained engineer who spent the first couple of decades of his career in factories, Jiang was keenly aware of the SOEs' predicament. While inspecting industrial plants during a regional tour in late 1995, Jiang expressed his anxiety in poignant terms. "How can we afford to drag on?" he asked. "Should we just sit and wait for another opportunity for reform to arrive? This is impossible. Five, seven years later, much of the equipment [of SOEs] will have been written off as obsolete junk. We must have a sense of urgency. We must be bolder. It won't do if we do not bear some risks."[174]

Yet Jiang was unwilling and unable to cut the Gordian knot. Firstly, he was dead set against structural changes that smacked of privatisation. "That some SOEs lack vigour has nothing to do with the ownership system," he indicated in 1995. The president claimed the crucial problems had to do with internal enterprise mechanisms; the "exterior environment" of a socialist system in transition; and the "residual problems of history". "These problems can be completely solved through deepening reforms," he said. He cited separation of government and enterprise; improving management and the supervision of state assets; establishing a social security system; and removing the excessive social burdens borne by enterprises.[175]

Particular attention was given to the reform of internal management, what the neo-conservatives called "building up a modern enterprise mechanism". "SOEs must change their management and operation mechanisms so as to become legal persons and [full] entities in the marketplace," Jiang said in 1995. "They must operate with autonomy and be financially self-sufficient. They must seek their self-development and exercise self-restraint."[176]

Structural changes such as tinkering with the ownership of SOEs were frowned upon because of fear of the adulteration of the state sector and runaway unemployment. In an internal speech in late 1995, the party chief reaffirmed the four principles of reform laid down at a party plenum in 1993: "clarifying" the property rights or ownership issues; ascertaining the powers and responsibilities [of managers and other staff]; separation of government and enterprise; and scientific management. Jiang faulted liberal cadres and managers for merely concentrating on overhauling the ownership of SOEs.[177]

At least in the eyes of free-marketeers, Jiang displayed extreme caution even with respect to *pochan*, or bankruptcies, which was introduced as a cure-all for sick SOEs as early as 1985.[178] The president indicated that this measure could only be tried out on a large scale after the establishment of a social security system. Jiang backed Zhu Rongji on the fact that as far as possible, Chinese-style mergers — a robust enterprise absorbing one on the brink of collapse — should be preferred to *pochan*. In 1996, Beijing offered 200 billion yuan in the way of incentives for healthy enterprises to merge with sick ones.[179]

In late 1995 and early 1996, the neo-conservatives settled on the formula for tinkering with SOEs: "taking a tight grip over large-scale enterprises, and setting the small SOEs free". Official propagandists again attributed the "breakthrough" to Jiang.[180] As was typical with the president, it was a clever, stop-gap measure aimed at muddling through. Under this schema, far-reaching structural changes could be tried out in all small-scale and some medium-sized SOEs. However, the large SOEs — the so-called pillars of the socialist system — would stay in the hands of the party and government. As we shall see in Chapters 6 and 7, the premise of state control would not be significantly affected by shareholding experiments unveiled at the 15th Party Congress.

In many instances, "taking a tight grip" actually meant more central-government attention and funds. First 300, and later 1,000, selected SOEs would benefit from priority government assistance. During an inspection trip to Shanghai in May 1996, the president gave instructions to the banking system to give special aid to the 300 enterprises. Jiang reportedly dwelled on the importance of "improving the relations between banks and enterprises".[181]

Jiang's excuse for directing more resources to large-scale enterprises was to improve their "exterior environment" — and help them shed the baggage of history. It also meshed with the neo-conservatives' agenda for building Chinese-style *zaibatsus*. Yet the decision to back up SOEs with hefty loans reeked again of the politicisation of economic policy. It would minimise social disruptions and ensure the longevity of the socialist system. By early 1998, there was no evidence that the Jiang leadership's decision to throw good money after bad had raised the productivity of SOEs.[182]

The Political Angle of Jiang's Reforms

Jiang's approach to the SOEs can be better gauged if we appreciate the fact that apart from the profit-and-loss calculus, the president relied on Mao's "spiritual yardsticks" to right the wrongs. For example, Jiang subscribed to the Maoist concept that if you have an ideologically correct understanding of a problem, the solution becomes much easier. Thus Jiang said on the issue of SOEs: "The whole party should try to analyse the situation of SOEs in a correct and all-rounded manner, taking both their merits and problems into consideration." Implicit in the president's injunction was that Chinese should not view SOEs from the narrow perspective of dollars and cents.[183]

One of Jiang's arguments was that if the entire people adopted a Maoist-style, "the-fool-moves-the-mountain" attitude, SOEs could be salvaged. After touring a number of basket-case enterprises in the northeast in mid-1995, Jiang saluted the following "spiritual values" among the workers: boldness in exploration and in creativity; ability to forge ahead in spite of difficulties; plain living and hard struggle; giving priority to the "overall situation" of the nation; restraining oneself and serving the public; ceaselessly working for the glory of the nation. "If we insist upon developing such a lofty spirit, difficulties can be overcome and miracles can be created," Jiang claimed.[184]

At a time when the nation was consumed by the mentality of "looking at everything with only money in mind", the party general secretary gave the impression that he believed a couple of well-delivered quasi-Maoist incantations could do the trick. As he put it on another inspection tour of factories: "SOEs must be rendered productive; and they can totally be made good. The entire party and the country must from top to bottom uphold this determination and confidence."[185]

While in the political sector, Jiang spent a lot of effort propagating "trustworthy Marxists" to guard the faith; he also championed a new breed of "superior entrepreneurs dedicated to rendering SOEs well". Jiang termed the process of discovering and training managerially savvy and ideologically committed cadre-managers "entrepreneurial engineering".[186] The president was apparently oblivious of the fact that in the West and much of Asia, the market was the only force that did the picking — and the training.

That Jiang had to some extent politicised Beijing's SOE policy was not surprising given his upbringing and outlook. The party chief was known to have given special favours to the factories to which he was sentimentally attached. Take, for example, the Shanghai Yi Min Foodstuffs Co., where Jiang worked as a vice-director for two years in the early 1950s. By the early 1990s, Yi Min had fallen upon hard times due to factors including too many retirees on its payroll. In a meeting in early 1994 with then Shanghai party boss Wu Bangguo, Jiang reportedly said, "You must not let it fall," adding that the municipality had to take "active measures" to bail it out. Why? It was a matter of face — and feudalism. Beijing's top leaders considered it *de rigueur* that institutions, factories and farms where they had worked be seen as model units.[187]

Restrictions on Private and Foreign Capital

Jiang had reservations galore about the private sector, including foreign capital. In his seminal talk to Shanghai entrepreneurs in mid-1995, he toed the traditional line that *getihu* ("individual"), private and foreign enterprises could only be a "supplement" to the public domain. Moreover, non-public sectors must be subjected to "correct guidance, strengthened supervision and management by law". The only concession he was willing to make was that while the public sector must enjoy overall predominance in the country, there might be exceptions in certain areas and product lines.[188]

Like other senior cadres who went through the Tiananmen Square crisis, Jiang was convinced that private entrepreneurs were by nature sympathetic to the democracy movement — and quite a number of the 1989 radicals had gone into business to harness their "revolutionary capital". Jiang seemed equally suspicious of private bosses in the countryside, the owners of village and township enterprises (VTEs). Both Jiang and then premier Li Peng flew into a rage when liberal Politburo member Tian Jiyun wrote an inscription to a rural industry newspaper on the fact that "VTEs are the future of Chinese agriculture".[189]

China reached the high point of the absorption of foreign capital during Jiang's tenure. However, the president was partly to blame for mixing questions of nationalism with investments and commerce. This was despite the fact that both his sons — one American- and the other German-trained — were in the mid-1990s making headway as private entrepreneurs in Shanghai. In his introduction to an early 1995 book on foreign investment, Jiang warned against China losing its economic independence in the face of the onslaught of overseas cash. The spectre of China becoming a "vassal" of the neo-colonialist economic powers was raised. "From beginning to end, the initiative in using foreign capital must be kept in our hands," he said.[190]

After all, in his Theory of the Twelve Relationships (see earlier section), Jiang had put emphasis on the principle of self-sufficiency. "We must handle well the relationship between expanding the open-door policy and hacking out our own path," he said. "Our point of departure must be reliance on our own resources and ability." Numerous statements similar to Jiang's cropped up in the media in 1995 and 1996, causing grave concern among multinationals. It was typical of the president that, to allay the fears of foreign investors, he pulled back his rhetoric and authorised the *People's Daily* to run commentaries affirming that the open-door policy was a "long-standing national policy".[191]

As discussed in Chapter 8, the Jiang administration's attitude towards private capital changed fairly dramatically in 1998. Under the whiplash of the Asian financial crisis — and in view of the worsening performance of SOEs — non-state-owned firms including foreign-owned companies were seen as the most efficient sector of the economy. Instructions were given to banks to provide more loans to private enterprises.[192] This, however, illustrates another deep-seated problem of Jiang-style statecraft: passively reacting to events rather than initiating policy to stay on top of fast-changing socio-economic realities.

Policy on the Agrarian Sector

Jiang was gung-ho about the prospects of Chinese agriculture. And at least so far as official statistics were concerned, the figures had borne him out. In spite of periodic flooding, China enjoyed bumper harvests through the mid-1990s. Jiang therefore felt confident in slamming Western officials and economists for spreading the "conspiracy theory" that there would be a grain shortage in China in the next century.[193] He reiterated Beijing's confidence in finding a terminal solution to the agrarian problem.

Yet Jiang, whose portfolios before 1989 had all been concerned with industry, had minimal personal experience in the countryside. The party chief did not offer any new solution to the farming problem. He largely stuck to old formulae: the late party elder Chen Yun's slogan of "taking grain as the key link", plus a high degree of recollectivisation.

Reviving the Chen Yun line

Jiang's policy towards agriculture was conservative: for strategic reasons, China must never depend on imported grain. As the president put it in 1996: "Self-sufficiency in grain concerns the strategic issue of whether China can maintain and strengthen its independence in international competition."[194] He supported Chen's well-known caveat that "without sufficient grain production, there will be chaos". As Jiang indicated in 1996: "Agriculture, particularly grain production, must absolutely not be curtailed; it must be grasped tightly from beginning to end."[195] The problem of feeding 1.2 billion mouths could only be solved by the Chinese people themselves.

Somewhat similar to the large SOEs, Jiang was willing to give the sector hefty subsidies. "If we do not give it emphasis and protection, agriculture easily falls into a disadvantaged position in a market economy because of reasons including comparative advantage," he said during a provincial tour in mid-1996. "We must constantly and repeatedly talk about the importance of highly valuing agriculture and strengthening agriculture." Or as he put it while touring Jiangxi Province in mid-1995: "Agriculture has both natural and market risks; it is a vulnerable type of production. And we must boost the status of agriculture."[196]

The trend of recollectivisation, which began in the late 1980s and early 1990s, was exacerbated under Jiang. The party chief called it a dual approach, or "double-tiered management system". The household-based contract responsibility system (HCRS) would be retained. However, private initiative would be synthesised with collective efforts. "Production and management on an adequately large scale" should be encouraged in areas with the prerequisites — and where farmers were receptive, the president indicated. "The point of departure must be local reality," he emphasised. "We must respect the wishes and creativity of farmers. We can adopt different formats; there is no need to strain for uniformity."[197]

There seemed little doubt, however, that Jiang's sympathy was with the collective approach. He called the HCRS the "first breakthrough" in agrarian reform. The second step was what he termed the *shehuihua* ("socialisation") of production, developing production on a comparatively large scale. The party chief urged large agrarian provinces such as Henan to integrate farm production with processing, transportation, and marketing. He expressed confidence that the "comprehensive utilisation of farm produce" should result in "the comprehensive economic returns of agriculture".[198]

The integration of economic and political goals

China was not the only country to put agriculture on the level of strategic importance — and to subsidise the agrarian sector. Developed nations such as the US and Japan came to mind. The more important question was: did China's agrarian policy make for productivity through giving more incentive to farmers? Could it live up to Jiang's billing of liberating "the vast enthusiasm and creativity hidden within farmers?"[199] For a "politics *über alles*" president, however, it was quite inevitable that his agrarian measures were linked with the requirements of the CCP. Agricultural policy also became a means to ensure the party's hold on power — and to enforce the "democratic proletarian dictatorship".

From a public administration angle, the "governor responsibility system" of grain production — whereby each head of province must meet quotas laid down by Beijing — was a means of reining in the freedoms of various "warlords". For example, autonomy by the coastal provinces, including Guangdong, to import rice and other material was curtailed. As Jiang put it in an internal meeting: "It will not do for leaders of coastal provinces to put the responsibility of increasing grain yield on hinterland provinces. It is not China's way for grain production to decrease in the wake of economic advancement."[200]

Jiang's agrarian programme was tied to the "rural socialist education campaign" to strengthen grassroots party cells. In agriculture as in other arenas, the party chief took the "both hands be tough" approach: spiritual civilisation must be boosted along with economic production. "We must strengthen the power of the collective economy," the party chief said during his tour of Henan in 1996. "And we must strengthen the construction of rural grassroots organisations." He went on to underscore the importance of propagating "politically qualified and incorrupt experts" to become members of the rural leadership, particularly, the party secretaries of villages.[201]

Obviously, the collective approach to agriculture would make for party power. The household-based responsibility system had since the early 1980s led to the disintegration of party cells if not party authority. The breakdown of collectives had also given an opener to underground religious and political organisations to expand their memberships. Jiang's worries were made clear in an introduction to a book on ideological education for farmers. "We must educate the masses of peasants to be concerned with the collective," he said. "They must develop the collectivist spirit of helping each other; being friendly with each other; and seeking pleasure in helping others."[202] It is difficult to imagine Deng or his market-oriented disciples saying similar things.

A fair deal for farmers?

In spite of the growing popularity of opinion polls in the cities, few attempts were made to gauge the feelings of the farmers. Were they satisfied during the Jiang era? The answer seemed to be no. Except for the successful rural entrepreneurs, the gripes of the peasants were palpable. Particularly impoverished were the large number of migrant labourers to the cities, mostly folk from the central and western areas.

This was despite a commitment by Jiang to boost central investments and other support to the agrarian provinces. "At the end of the day, we must not let those [cadres and people] who are engaged in agriculture become losers," the president said in 1996. "We must let everybody feel they have something worth fighting for." On another occasion, the party chief called upon "all professions and trades in the nation to firmly establish the concept of supporting agriculture".[203]

Even though the grain procurement price had been raised almost yearly through the 1990s, farmers still felt disadvantaged. The reasons were simple. In locales with the necessary endowments or transport links, farmers would take home more by concentrating on cash crops or commercial activities — not grain production. Moreover, the phenomenon of local governments paying farmers IOUs had returned by the early 1990s. This was despite the fact that the Agriculture Bank had issued special funds for the procurement of produce. For example, in late 1996, many county governments were not paying farmers for two main reasons. One was that the local adminstrations were so poor they had to use all available funds for the salaries of civil servants, militiamen, police and teachers. The other was that the cadres used the money to speculate in the stock market. Many victims of the stocks crash of late 1996 were regional cadres.[204]

Not surprisingly, Jiang's agrarian policy had met with opposition. Even such a pro-establishment theoretician as economist Hu Angang indicated the country could afford to import more grain. He pointed out that the goal of self-sufficiency in grain could be lowered from 98 per cent to 95 per cent.[205] While Hu was hardly advocating a big change, his view echoed those liberal economists who thought the priority given grain was a reflection of an autarkist mentality.

Jiang's agrarian policy was also subjected to indirect fire from the "opposition" parliamentary faction headed by then NPC chairman Qiao Shi and his deputy, Tian Jiyun. While touring the provinces, the two leaders revived the Zhao-era concept of devolving more powers to farming households. "The direction of agriculture development must still be 'to each [area] according to its own characteristics,'" Qiao said during the 1996 NPC. The head of the moderate faction urged the nation to look at the big picture in farming policy. "We must go for multi-genre production and management," he added.[206]

AN ASSESSMENT OF JIANG ZEMIN

Apart from Hong Kong's re-absorption, the year 1997 was feted by the Jiang leadership for one other reason: the 20th anniversary of Deng Xiaoping's legendary comeback from disgrace. The celebration, however, masked a Machiavellianism with Chinese characteristics. It would provide the justification for Jiang, 71 at the time, to stay in power for at least one decade.

The reasoning went like this. The patriarch was in his early seventies when he went about the difficult business of righting the wrongs of the

Gang of Four — and launching perhaps humanity's biggest reform project. As a social scientist who advised Jiang put it, life began at 73 for the Chief Architect of Reform. "Most of what we know about Deng Xiaoping Thought was spelt out when the patriarch was nearing 80," he said. "He was 88 when he delivered his *nanxun* homily on accelerated reform." The academic claimed that western politicians and Sinologists had complained unjustly about the vacuousness of Jiang's ideas and policies. "Just wait and see what the core of the third-generation leadership will do in the coming 10 years or so," he said.[207]

By the time the 15th Party Congress opened, Jiang had already been top dog for more than eight years — longer than two terms for a US president. While his spin-doctors would have us believe that the would-be helmsman would open up a new heaven and earth during his third term of 1997–2002, it is worthwhile to make an assessment of his achievements and aberrations during the pivotal years of 1989 to 1998.

Hu Yaobang was best remembered for rectifying the mistakes of the Cultural Revolution — and for "discovering" that Marxism could not solve all the problems of today. Zhao Ziyang was praised for his market reforms and political liberalisation. Some of Jiang's supporters hoped he would be noted for "attainments" including the Hong Kong handover, the "peace initiative" towards Taiwan, fighting corruption, abolishing the special privileges of the *gaoganzidi*, and promoting balanced, non-inflationary growth in the economy.

In the eyes of objective observers, however, the credit for the Hong Kong handover should go to Deng, the inventor of the "one country, two systems" formula. Zhu Rongji, not Jiang, deserved praise for steady economic growth beginning 1993. By early 1998, there was very little to show with regards to Taiwan, the anti-graft campaign, or reining in the princelings.

The truth was that Jiang spent so much time consolidating his power base he had little left to attend to real policy. His biggest "achievement" was keeping the CCP — and his own clique — in power. While this in itself was not without significance, the bulk of the Chinese populace would hardly give a thumbs-up to the president's record.

Moreover, as the above sections have demonstrated, Jiang suffered from a dearth of ideas, what dissident intellectual Zhang Weiguo called "political imagination". The president failed to emerge from the shadow of Mao and Deng. "In his optical spectrum, there are only two bands: Mao-style politics or Deng-style politics," Zhang wrote. Jiang's conservatism could be traced to Mao, his dynamism to Deng.[208] Efforts by Jiang's commissars to close the Chinese mind were reminiscent of the late chairman's paranoia about the outside world. As we shall see in Chapter 7, the reforms he introduced in 1997 had their roots in Deng and such of the latter's lieutenants as Hu and Zhao. Notwithstanding the information revolution in the 1990s — and his own emphasis on science and technology — Jiang did not do enough to keep up with the times.

Too Much Politics and Too Little Action

Much fun has been made of Jiang's name, literally "the River Benefiting the People". Some unkind wags said it was the flooding throughout the 1990s which made possible the accumulation of Jiang's power. Yet the former Shanghai party boss was famous for another kind of watery quality: his oily, unctious personality and philosophy of life. You could not pin Jiang down on anything specific. This might have been good for backroom politics. But was it any way to lead the nation?

It was of course true that, taking the historical perspective, the quality of decisive, charismatic leadership had declined from one generation to another. For all his faults and disasters, Mao never minced his words. A noted flaw in Deng's character was his duplicity. His "two hands be equally tough" approach meant he could never go whole hog with reform; liberalisation was often tempered with the Four Cardinal Principles of orthodox Marxism. Jiang had in a sense inherited Deng's ambivalence. In terms of policy formulation and implementation, however, the president was even less decisive. There was no distinctive drift of policy. Jiang's needs to conciliate most factions — and points of views — in the party also contributed to the rudderless feeling of his statecraft.[209]

It is useful to examine once again perhaps Jiang's most celebrated slogan: "Talk more about politics." By early 1997, the amorphousness — actually the meaninglessness — of this shibboleth had become obvious to all. Firstly, there was vociferous criticism that the politics-above-all credo spelt a return to Maoism. This sentiment was widespread not only among liberal intellectuals but also the nomenclature. When they were drafting a new in-house motto in the spring of 1996, senior cadres in the People's Bank of China originally settled on this rallying cry: "Talk more about politics; emphasise reform; put stress on law and discipline; aim for efficiency; raise the level of service." However, there were fears that the top billing given politics might scare away investors. In the final version, reform was given pride of place.[210]

Even Jiang himself had to fend off accusations that the slogan was a revival of the Maoist "politics in command". In April 1996, the president instructed the *People's Daily* to run a commentary on the fact that the battlecry was not meant to supersede or counter Deng's teaching that "economic development is the core of the party work". "Talking more about politics," the newspaper said, was mainly to "provide a forceful guarantee for economic construction and social development". It added that there would be no going back to the "old road of talking empty politics".[211]

Thanks to the slogan's vacuity, different factions had a field day putting self-serving glosses on it. In a May 1996 commentary, the *Liberation Army Daily* interpreted "laying stress on politics" to mean mobilising the bulk of the nation's resources for defence — and giving pride of place to the troops, "the most devoted and trusted offspring of the motherland". And in January 1997, the *Shenzhen Special Zone Daily* ran a commentary on the fact that "talking more about politics" was equivalent to "giving priority to the interests of the people". In the context of the quasi-capitalist zone, of course, this meant the authorities providing the people with opportunities to get rich quick.[212]

Jiang's credibility problem was compounded by the fact that he tried to please every faction, social sector or constituency. Unlike politicians with more character or commitment such as Hu Yaobang, Zhao Ziyang or Zhu Rongji, Jiang wanted to build bridges to all and sundry. The inevitable result was that he ended up alienating a number of power blocs and social groupings. For example, reformers faulted him for turning back the clock on liberalisation. And leftists, or remnant Maoists, blamed him for continuing with Deng's experiments.

Take, for example, Jiang's treatment of SOEs and workers, perhaps the single most serious challenge to stability. As discussed in an earlier section, the party chief promised that no reforms would be undertaken if they hurt labour interests. This stance aroused criticism from reformers, who said his administration had dragged its feet on SOE restructuring. The president's tough tactics against wild-cat trade unions, on the other hand, invited attacks from labour groups in and out of the country.[213]

By 1996 and 1997, however, Jiang had no choice but to heed the advice of his own aides: that unless the SOEs were overhauled, the entire economy might collapse. To lay the theoretical groundwork for smashing the iron rice bowl, official commissars and commentators began saying that workers should be treated as what they really were, that is, "paid or contract employees" or even "commodities". Members of Jiang's think tanks proposed revising the party and state constitutions, which still identified workers as "masters of factories" and "masters of the state". In the eyes of leftists, however, it was wrong to regard labourers, even retired ones, as "baggage" that the SOEs must shed to raise efficiency. The Maoists privately accused Jiang of selling out the proletariats.[214]

Jiang's Track Record in Political Reform
Is populism enough?

At least on the surface, Jiang revelled in the Maoist touches of populism. The president seemed to have struck a right chord when he suggested that in their zeal to expedite reform, the likes of Deng and Zhao had neglected the common man. In their anxiety to "seize the day" and to "storm the fortress" of reform, the radical reformers failed to take into full consideration the possibly disastrous fall-out of their experiments.

As sociologist and futurologist Wang Shan saw it, Jiang's "politics first" call basically meant "paying more attention to the social consequences of reform and allied policies" — and preventing these consequences from upsetting the ship of state. As Jiang put it in 1995: "Only when we talk politics can we adequately handle the relationships among different interest groupings, arouse the enthusiasm of various sectors to the largest extent — and to correctly guide, protect and develop this enthusiasm."[215]

Partisans of the ideals of the 1950s would perhaps give Jiang credit for reviving the "serve the people" credo of Mao — which remained important in a country of 1.3 billion people that lacked natural resources. Yet it was obvious that Jiang's "populism" was a reflection of his anxiety to preserve political stability through deflecting if not defusing the gripes of workers and farmers. It had nothing to do with democracy. Even Jiang supporters might concede that when it came to the real thing — honouring "people power" and letting the people take part in politics — the president tended to drag his feet.[216]

Jiang's approach to political reform is treated in detail in Chapter 3. It is useful to point out here that the party chief saw as his primary avocation the salvation of the CCP. What is more, he considered one-party dictatorship a "superior attribute" of the nation. "At this trans-century historical juncture, wherein lies China's advantage vis-a-vis other countries?" Jiang asked in late 1996. "China's superiority is its political superiority, the political authority of the CCP leadership collective."[217]

The president cleaved to the time-honoured line that Western-style democracy was not for China. "In the development of democracy in our country, the point of departure must be our national conditions," he said. "The nature, content, form and system of democracy [in China] must bear the characteristics of our country."[218] The point of this tautological statement was that Western democratic ideals were not suitable for China. Jiang upheld Deng's dictum that the "Western-style multi-party system" was "too foreign" for the Middle Kingdom. Jiang seemed oblivious to the charge that Chairman Mao and other "first-generation revolutionaries" had also tried to forcedly transplant an alien set of values to Chinese soil. That philosophy was Marxism-Leninism.

Similar to his stance on economic reform, Jiang was hardly interested in overhauling the political system. He was mildly concerned about improving administrative efficiency. Thus in his speech to the national conference on the soft sciences in mid-1995, the president cited the old ideal of "scientific decision-making". Jiang, however, did not even mention "democratic decision-making".[219] And no wonder. The party chief could often be seen on TV talking to and even consulting local cadres and impoverished peasants. In the high councils of the party and government, however, Jiang had ears only for members of his own clique.

Lack of a systematic approach

Jiang was a pre-modern politician to the extent that he did not believe in systems. By contrast, in the hiatus of political reform in the late 1970s and early 1980s, Deng upheld the importance of building institutions and systems including a retirement age for cadres and the separation of party and government. Jiang realised, of course, that a systematic approach to government could spell an end to special privilege — including that of the CCP and his own faction.

Jiang did, however, make a qualified concession with regard to legal institutions, the idea that modernisation must be built on the premises of laws and due process. He seemed to acquiesce in attempts by then NPC chief Qiao Shi to build up a legal system, including some form of "legal supervision" of the executive branch of government (see Chapters 3 and 6).

Jiang also went along with Qiao's fast-paced programme of law-making. And in his own area of the army, the Central Military Commission chairman rushed through scores of new laws on matters ranging from army finances to mobilisation of civilians.[220]

In internal speeches in early 1996, Jiang raised the slogan of *yifazhiguo*, or "using laws to run the country". This was deemed to be an "important principle on how the party and government should run the country". There was, however, quite a chasm between the concepts of "using laws to run the country" and ruling by law, on the one hand, and rule of law, on the other. The "Western" ideal of rule of law means everybody is equal before the law — and that the law towers above the government and other political institutions.

Jiang's thinking, however, was that the laws would be a reflection and substantiation of the party's will and its strategy for solving socio-economic problems. As the president pointed out in 1996: "Under the leadership of the party, the broad masses of cadres and people take part in managing the country in accordance with the constitution and the law."[221] Translation: the party was more important than the law. Moreover, Beijing took a utilitarian attitude towards law-making and implementation. Laws deemed prejudicial to one-party dictatorship might not be enacted or enforced. Other statutes would be introduced apparently to improve China's image overseas. For example, the Law on Criminal Procedures of 1996, which did away with "counter-revolutionary crimes", was meant to pacify the international human rights community.[222]

At the same time, Jiang went about reviving the quasi-Confucian ideal of "running the country on the basis of morality". Such other early leaders as Mao and Liu Shaoqi, of course, also had visions of cadres with superior virtues. As a veteran Jiang watcher put it: "Comrade Zemin's statecraft relies mainly on the building up of morality; it is supplemented by rule by law." The observer added that in terms of the political structure, the president relied primarily on a group of virtuous cadres and secondarily on democratic institutions. And in fighting corruption, Jiang looked first at the "self-discipline and morality" of cadres and secondarily at "social supervision".[223]

In spite of the call for streamlining the party and government apparatus, Jiang created a plethora of new departments and units to meet the political needs of the day. Far from a reflection of a respect for institutions, this urge to open one new office after another showed up the ad hoc, fire-fighting nature of Jiang's approach to governance.

Take, for example, the "core groups" that Jiang created in early 1995 to enforce loyalty in central and regional units. Such groups were formed within major party, government, and PLA cells. Later that year, the president established yet another *modus operandi* — Guiding Committees for the Construction of Socialist Spiritual Civilisation (GCCSSC) — to help propagate "socialist ethics" and patriotic values all over China. The committees supervised ideological study sessions on Jiang-style politics. The big question: if the core groups and other existing indoctrination units had been effective, there would have been no need for the GCCSSCs.[224]

Political elitism and the anti-corruption campaign

Jiang's failure to construct viable or lasting institutions and systems — plus his emphasis on the crypto-Confucian value of "morality" — inevitably led to a Chinese-style elitism. This was evident in the party chief's dependence on the offspring of senior cadres as well as the Shanghai Faction.

It was ironic that Jiang was initially opposed to the rise of the gang of princelings. At least according to the publicists, the president used his political muscle to ensure that the princelings enjoyed no advantage at the 14th Party Congress of 1992. Jiang's views changed after he had taken part in the crusade to catch "China's Gorbachevs and Yeltsins", or traitors. Sources close to the Jiang camp said the president was soon persuaded that for reasons including self-preservation, the descendants of "first-generation revolutionaries" were least likely to become turncoats. "Jiang has instructed that if there are 150 or so offspring of party elders working at high levels, the purity of the party can be preserved," the sources said.[225] This was, of course, a return to the theory of the revolutionary bloodline first put forward by orthodox elders such as the late vice-president Wang Zhen.

The single most important factor affecting the quality of cadres, however, was unchecked corruption. Given Jiang's emphasis on the party as the be-all and end-all of politics, it was a stinging indictment of his record that the cadres' level of morality kept going down. Jiang's shortfall in this area was pathetic given the opportunities he had missed: with the eradication of graft, Jiang could have succeeded in putting his "populism" to good use — and gained a place in the CCP pantheon.

The president himself admitted in early 1997 that combating graft would be a "task over a long period". "At the moment, the party is facing a severe situation in the fight against corruption," he said in a conference on party discipline. "We face a heavy burden in rectifying party style."[226] As a retired cadre put it, because of the pervasiveness of graft, a thorough-going movement against the plague would bring down the house of Chinese Communism. The cadre quoted the note of defiance sounded by disgraced Beijing party boss Chen Xitong soon after his arrest in April 1995. "It is true that I may have to take moral responsibility for corruption in the Beijing municipality," Chen reportedly said. "But who is to take responsibility for corruption in the entire CCP?" The arrow was pointed Jiang's way.[227]

In more ways than one, Chen was right. Jiang could not take the risk of rocking the boat. Soon after the Capital Iron and Steel Works (Shougang) scandal broke, Wei Jianxing reportedly suggested to Jiang that he took advantage of the situation to deal a death blow to corruption. "Shouldn't we emulate Chairman Mao in the 1950s and chop off the heads of a dozen-odd big tigers?" Wei asked. After pondering a while, Jiang reportedly replied: "Our top priority remains maintaining stability. Today, few people have the chairman's authority." Translation: going the distance in fighting graft would affect cadres whose support Jiang needed to stay on top.[228]

Moreover, Jiang had political motives galore not to press graft charges against the elite, particularly the princelings. In mid-1995, at least two of Deng's relatives were briefly questioned by Beijing security personnel with respect to alleged "economic matters" as well as "suspicious relationships with foreign countries". For a time, the pair reportedly had to apply for permission from the Central Committee General Office before they could leave Beijing or the country. A few months later, however, Jiang made it clear he would not touch the families of "first-generation revolutionaries" irrespective of their involvement in corruption or other misdemeanours. Beijing sources said Jiang had followed this advice from a top Shanghai-based adviser: "Use Deng's stature and theory to build up your position; but do not do anything to the relatives because this would invite a backlash from Deng loyalists."[229]

Jiang's Track Record in Economic Reform

The Chinese economy was doing relatively well in the years after the Tiananmen Square crackdown. Yet the prominent figures in this period were Deng Xiaoping and Zhu Rongji. Deng brought about a new wave of reform — and inflationary, undisciplined growth — with his historic *nanxun* talks in early 1992. And Zhu tidied up the problems and engendered a soft landing through his three-year programme of "macro-level controls and adjustments".

There were two reasons why Jiang could not have played a big role in the economy — particularly market reforms. Firstly, the party chief had drawn perhaps the right lesson from Zhao Ziyang's disastrous brush with hyper-inflation in 1988: a badly handled economy could cause the top dog his job. Almost from day one, Jiang let Li Peng and later Zhu run the economy. While he retained the position of head of the Leading Group on Finance and Economics, Jiang was in a position to let Li, and in particular Zhu, become the scapegoat for major mishaps in the finance, industry or agriculture sectors.

Moreover, Jiang was careful to ensure that market reforms did not threaten either the socialist nature of the country or social stability. The president lacked the determination of Deng or such of his disciples as Zhao Ziyang or Tian Jiyun to "storm the fortresses" of reform. A reform policy that required substantial sacrifice on the part of the people such as unemployment would be too risky for Jiang. Moreover, the authority of the CCP had been eroded. It could be suicidal for party leaders to ask the people to tighten their belts for some long-term ideals.

Jiang frequently re-oriented the country back to a concern with ideology whenever there was a danger of market forces getting out of hand. As conservative theorist Wang Guiqin put it succinctly in late 1995: "Economics cannot be a substitute for politics; economic construction requires a political guarantee."[230] Indeed, Jiang and his advisers often saw economic development through the prism of politics. Other times, economics became the handmaiden of ideological requirements. This explained why the president could never become a qualified economic policymaker.

For example, Jiang's concern with upholding self-sufficiency and thwarting "neo-colonialism" had a deep impact on his definition of the open-door policy. "On the one hand, we must assiduously study and borrow the scientific knowledge and experience in the Western market economy," he said in late 1995. "On the other, we must produce something that is uniquely based on our national conditions and the practical [requirements] of our economic development."[231] Less ideologically inclined leaders would have just plunged into revving up production or making money without such hair-splitting.

Consider also Beijing's dispute with the Americans over intellectual property rights (IPR). In the eyes of the Jiang team, the Sino-American row was much more than a question of market accessibility or dollars and cents. For cadres including then Minister of Foreign Trade and Economic Cooperation Wu Yi, Washington's IPR crusade masked a "neo-imperialist" plot to infiltrate China's culture and to expedite its "peaceful evolution" to capitalism.[232]

Political considerations also played sizeable roles in areas ranging from which factories should get government loans to which areas should enjoy preferential policies. Not surprisingly, Jiang focused the development dollars on the Shanghai-Pudong area, his power base. Since the early 1990s, Shanghai and the Yangtze River Estuary had displaced Guangdong as the national pacesetter. Vice-Premier Wu Bangguo disclosed that Jiang had always had a soft spot for Shanghai. "General Secretary Jiang Zemin has always had great expectations of Shanghai leading the country in improving SOEs," Wu told NPC delegates in 1996.[233] Analysts said there might be some similarity between Jiang's predilection for Shanghai and Chen Yun's affinity for the city. The latter believed that while Shenzhen had gone too far down the capitalist road, Shanghai could still be turned into a "socialist economic zone".

By early 1997, Jiang had received flak from many of Deng's comrades-in-arms for departing from the patriarch's "economics first" persuasion. Party elders who had faulted Jiang included Yang Shangkun, Bo Yibo, Wan Li and the late Peng Zhen. They had particular objections to Jiang's oft-repeated point that China "must not at any time sacrifice spiritual civilisation for temporary economic benefits".[234]

After Deng's death, Jiang had redoubled his claims to be the patriarch's anointed successor. Yet the president seldom honoured what to many was the core of Deng's teachings: fighting "leftism" and weaning economic work away from Maoist-style ideological obsessions. It was not until 1996 that the president openly saluted Deng's instructions on the separation of economics and politics. While touring Shanghai in May 1996, Jiang revived a key credo of the *nanxun* talks: that any policy could be pursued if it brought about the "threefold benefits" of boosting productivity; raising the living standard of the people; and increasing the comprehensive strength of the nation. However, unlike his own leftist slogans, Jiang did not ask the media to play up this Dengist rallying cry.[235] And it was only after the 15th Party Congress of 1997 that the theory of the "threefold benefits" or "three favourables" was fully rehabilitated.

In the final analysis, Jiang's economic policy had to be judged by concrete results. It was true that China's economic team had in the mid-1990s avoided the worst excesses of free marketeers such as Zhao Ziyang. Jiang's cautiousness, however, was a poor recipe to crack age-old problems such as SOEs. Even worse was his tendency to substitute hard work and risk-taking with appeals to hackneyed spiritual ideals. "It is true that SOEs have problems," Jiang said in 1995. "Yet they also have advantages and potentials". "If the leaders [of enterprises] and the masses are of one heart and mind, and if they are united in their struggle, SOEs can entirely be rendered well," he added. "We must look on the bright side."[236]

Jiang Zemin's Position in History

Jiang as the "equal" of Mao and Deng

Jiang was determined to leave his mark in history as an equal of Mao or Deng. As preparations for the 15th Party Congress hotted up in early 1997, the president made bold moves to substantiate his claim to be helmsman and philosopher-king. In speeches in early 1997 to his inner circle, Jiang issued this instruction on what to do with Deng's legacy: "We must not treat Deng Thought as though every sentence was gospel truth."[237]

Jiang was, of course, taking the cue from Deng's 1979 campaign against the "whateverism" of Hua Guofeng, Mao's chosen successor. Chairman Hua enraged party liberals by swearing that "whatever Chairman Mao said and did was correct". Deng's obliteration of the "whateverist" creed led to the Thought Liberation Movement of the late 1970s — and his own coronation as the Chief Architect of Reform. Jiang's motive in knocking Deng off the pedestal was the same. It was no accident that the hottest book in Beijing in late 1996 — *Having a Heart-to-heart Talk with the General Secretary* — dwelled on areas where Jiang was said to have gone beyond the patriarch.

Commissioned by Jiang protégé Liu Ji, the tome suggested that Jiang had tackled "subjects that have not been covered by Deng Thought". "Historical change is accelerating," the book said. "New situations and new questions appear ceaselessly. Based on comrade Deng Xiaoping's teachings, we must study new situations and solve new problems." The big question for Jiang was whether he could measure up to the expectations of "going one better than Deng".[238]

According to sources close to the Jiang Office, the president's advisers were focusing on four areas where he could claim to have scored well. The first one was the economy. The public relations specialists were arguing that thanks to "macro-level adjustments and controls", the Jiang leadership had brought about a soft-landing in the economy. Dislocations common to the Deng era, such as hyperinflation and wild fluctuations in growth, had been straightened out.

Official economists said the goal of "medium-level prosperity" — a standard of living halfway between that of the First World and the developing world — could be reached by 2020. In the mid-1980s, Deng had put forward the objective of crossing this threshold by 2040 at the earliest. While Jiang admitted that SOEs were still encumbered with difficulties, he pointed to new triumphs that could be attained by the 500 to 1,000 enterprise groupings that Beijing would nurture in the Ninth Five-Year Plan period. The hope was that a group of globally competitive conglomerates would spearhead the turn-around of the entire state sector.

Moreover, Jiang claimed credit for stopping the polarisation of income between rich and poor — and that between coastal and hinterland residents. Going by official statistics at least, the save-the-poor campaign was successful. Jiang's corrective to Deng's theory in the area of "common prosperity" was obvious. "Our goal is the eventual common prosperity of the entire people," Jiang said at a *fupin* conference in early 1997. "Poverty is not socialism. Yet the phenomenon of one part of the population getting rich and another part of the population staying perennially poor is also not socialism."[239] This was an obvious dig at Deng, who coined the famous "poverty is not socialism" line in the early 1980s.

Secondly, as a result of Jiang's "both hands be tough" policy, spiritual civilisation, or socialist ethics, had not been ignored. Jiang's propagandists had, in internal papers, cited Deng as admitting in 1989 that he had made a mistake in neglecting ideological education over the previous decade. As a result of Jiang's orthodox crusade, Beijing had made headway in propagating a novel generation of "new socialist men" — model citizens "with ideals, morality, culture and discipline".

Thirdly, Jiang was by late 1997 laying out a road map to help China meet the challenges of the 21st century. It highlighted the marked advance of Chinese science, technology and weaponry, which were poised to take off on a sound economic base. Under this schema, Jiang indicated China could achieve the *fuqiang* ("prosperity and strength") goal of the 1919 May Fourth Movement without going through "Western-style" democratisation.

Fourth, and most significantly, would be Jiang's vision of a Greater China: synergy between the mainland, Hong Kong and Taiwan. Even though reunification with Taiwan remained illusory on the surface, the president believed this could be achieved by around 2020. Apart from forging symbiotic economic links, socio-political integration between the three places could set the stage for a "Greater Chinese Civilisation". This would represent a leap forward beyond Deng's conception of "one country, two systems", according to sources close to the Jiang Office.[240]

Doubts about Jiang's philosophy and statecraft

Yet tough questions were being asked about the four goals. Could the enterprise groupings Jiang was nurturing remain free from the kind of nepotism and corruption that tainted quite a few of the early state corporations? Until Jiang agreed to a clear-cut separation of politics and business, abuses such as well-connected enterprises having priority access to state loans could hardly be curtailed. Even more disturbing questions loomed over Hong Kong and Taiwan. While three-way trading links were sure to surge, what about the more ambitious vision of a Greater Chinese Civilisation?

It is important to note that Jiang had never given up the Four Cardinal Principles of Marxism — and a cold-blooded approach to wielding power. His ideological straitjacket and "talk more about politics" shibboleth had led to a blight of new areas including the arts and the sciences. Could invention and creativity, not to mention world-class culture, flourish in a climate of inhibition and Machiavellianism?

During his *nanxun*, Deng made a memorable assessment of the economic retrenchment programme that Li Peng oversaw from 1988 to 1991. He gave grudging acknowledgement to the fact that the austerity regime had steadied the economy. However, Deng indicated, this was only a minor achievement compared to the patriarch's own goal of "crossing a new threshold once every three years". As the patriarch put it in the *nanxun* instructions: the three-year retrenchment programme was "an attainment in [bringing about] stability. Yet it was not an achievement in reform and development".[241]

In the same way that former premier Li had reined in the economy, Jiang and Zhu managed largely to maintain a kind of superficial calm in the socio-economic arena. But there were many catches. Firstly, underlying contradictions were put off, not solved. In spite of the willingness of younger members of the Jiang team such as Wu Bangguo to experiment with ownership changes and other thorough-going measures, the basic problem of inefficiency in socialist enterprises remained unresolved. Jiang and company had yet to come up with ideas and policies to enable the country to excel in the Asia-Pacific century.

Worse still, particularly in ideology and political reform, Jiang presided over an alarming retrogression. Largely because of the freeze in the political structure, corruption became ever more malignant. While official statistics seemed to show that the income gap between the haves and have-nots had narrowed, the prevalent feeling among the populace was that society had become more unjust. Frustrations about the inequality of opportunity was behind the bombing incidents in 1997 and 1998 in cities ranging from Beijing to Guangzhou (see Chapters 3 and 6).

Had Jiang led his country into a Brezhnev era with Chinese character-istics? Both former Soviet president Leonid Brezhnev and Jiang posited as their highest priority the maintenance of stability. Both paid the following big price in trying to achieve this goal: the dearth of initiative and the roll-back of reform. In 1997 and 1998, there were signs that the more liberal among Jiang's advisers were urging the president to take bolder steps in reform. Yet despite some tentative steps in the direction of change such as curtailing the state sector, it was uncertain whether he was willing to make a clean break with the past (see Chapters 7 and 8).

Of course, China and the world in the late 1990s were different from the USSR in the 1970s. The globe was getting much smaller — and the cross-wires and interlinkages even among dissimilar communities grew denser by the day. Even given Jiang's straitjacket of ideological control, citizens in at least the large cities were bombarded daily with thunderous sounds and kaleidoscopic sights. The information superhighways and new modes of thinking were speeding away. More and more Chinese were hop-ping on the futuristic bandwagon of the 21st century. And no matter how often Jiang talked about politics, the president would be left behind if he refused to overhaul his fast-obsolescing worldview and statecraft.

Political Reform: 3 The Administrative Malaise and Prospects for Liberalisation

INTRODUCTION: THE QUANDARY OF POLITICAL CHANGE

In his eulogy at Deng Xiaoping's funeral, President Jiang Zemin delivered an hour-long speech on how to continue the patriarch's reforms. He pointed out that the "reform of the political structure and other systems would be deepened". However, apart from "running the country according to law", the president did not say much about how political liberalisation would be carried out.

Yet Jiang's passing mention of political reform was enough for his spin doctors to declare that a phenomenal change was in the offing. One quasi-official news agency and a few pro-Chinese papers in Hong Kong claimed that Jiang wanted liberalisation of the political structure to be his legacy. The reasoning was that while Mao built the New China, and Deng worked on economic reform, Jiang would be remembered for political reform.[1]

However, by early 1998, there was no indication that the Jiang administration would develop initiatives started by the likes of ousted party chiefs Hu Yaobang or Zhao Ziyang. These included, for example, the separation of party and government, which was the theme of the 13th

Chinese Communist Party (CCP) Congress of 1987. At the start of the National People's Congress (NPC) days after Deng's death, parliamentary spokesman Zhou Jue cited Deng-style political reform, saying it was a major component of the Deng legacy. Yet Zhou was careful to point out that for Deng, political reform was "aimed at developing socialist democracy, improving the socialist legal system, invigorating the party and government, getting rid of bureaucracy, and bringing the initiatives of the people into play".[2] There was no mention of even rudimentary endeavours such as rendering decision-making more scientific and democratic.

Jiang, by nature more conservative than Deng or Zhao, largely followed the prescription of the patriarch for preventing China from going the way of the Soviet bloc: to concentrate more power in the party, meaning propagating an elite corps of "trustworthy Marxists" — and to ensure that the party had tighter control over the government, the army and the business world.[3]

Steps were taken to invest central party organs with more power. Owing to the slow pace of political reform, however, the party and government structure showed signs of being top-heavy and unwieldy. Decades-old problems such as the rule of personality, nepotism, and corruption resurfaced with a vengeance. Attempts by the Jiang leadership to revamp the bureaucracy and improve the quality of cadres remained dubious. Slightly more substantial results, however, were scored by relatively liberal cadres such as Qiao Shi in boosting the powers of the National People's Congress. This chapter will also assess the implications of village-level elections and other embryonic exercises in "mass democracy".

By and large, however, the picture was one of administrative malaise against the backdrop of a stagnation in political liberalisation. The shortfalls of the Jiang administration became even more obvious given China's development into a "class-based society" with sectors such as farmers and workers clamouring for their rightful share of the pie. The aspirations of the "new classes" will be examined. The conclusion will look at possible developments of the political structure in the new century.

RECENTRALISATION OF POWERS IN THE PARTY LEADERSHIP

Beginning in the early 1990s, centralisation of power in the CCP's top echelons manifested itself in different arenas. The most obvious instance was the multiple positions that Jiang held. There was also the principle of "cross lead-ership", the fact that a senior cadre could hold concurrent positions in the party, government, the legislature and even the Chinese People's Political Consultative Conference (CPPCC). Consider also the infamous tract put out by a group of princelings in 1991 on the fact that to survive, the CCP must boost control not only over the army and administration but also the fi-nances and the economy.[4] During the period under survey, 1994–1998, Jiang exacerbated this tendency in even more disturbing ways.

All Power to the Top

Jiang Zemin retooled the power structure of the party for two reasons: to continue the Deng doctrine about recentralising power; and to grab more authority for himself. Supreme power was vested with the seven-member Politburo Standing Committee (PSC), which met almost on a weekly basis. Such age-old institutions as the Politburo and the Central Committee Sec-retariat became less important. The Politburo, for example, often met just once every six weeks or so. Jiang's decision to sideline the full Politburo had much to do with the fact that he already had problems controlling the PSC.[5] For example, from 1994 to 1997, Jiang often encountered challenges from Qiao Shi, Li Ruihuan and General Liu Huaqing (see Chapter 6).

The Central Committee Secretariat was originally intended as a high-level policy-making and implementation organ for the party. Yet as long as he could get away with it, Jiang moved many of the Secretariat's functions to his Jiang Zemin Office and the Central Committee General Office (see Chapter 2). This obviously militated against the principle of "inner party democracy". Of particular significance was the president's decision to expand the functions of the many leading groups within the Central Committee. This ran counter to the principle of the separation of party and government and the streamlining of the bureaucracy.[6]

These top-level groupings included the Leading Group on Finance and Economics (LGFE), the Leading Group on Foreign Affairs, the Leading Group on Ideology and Propaganda, and the Leading Group on Taiwan Affairs. Those formed in the mid-1990s included the Leading Group on Rural Work and Leading Group on Science and Technology. It was signifi-cant that while the leading groups had existed since the early 1980s, they were far more active under Jiang than during the Hu Yaobang and Zhao Ziyang eras. In the 1980s, most of the units, which only had a threadbare structure, functioned as top-level vehicles for brainstorming and did not have executive functions. Because of their secretive nature, the leading groups were not accountable to senior cadres, not to mention the National People's Congress or the public. However, Jiang gave them a key role, probably with a view to promoting his protégés.[7]

A case in point is the LGFE. It became practically dormant in the first two years after the June 4 massacre. Until 1993, it was a shadowy advisory organ that played no role in day-to-day policy-making. However, it soon went through major expansion to become a policy-setting, and in many instances, policy-implementing and supervisory organ. New units added in the mid-1990s included the departments for macro-economics, industry and agriculture. Shanghai Faction affiliates in the group included Zeng Peiyan and Hua Jianmin.[8]

The Revival of the Rule of Personality and the Personality Cult

One of Deng's contributions to political reform in the early 1980s was to do away with the rule of personality. Rules were passed to abolish Maoist trappings such as hanging the portraits or calligraphy of senior cadres in public places.[9] After June 4, 1989, the pendulum swung back to the quasi-Confucian — and feudalist — ideal of finding reliable or "saintly" personalities to run the state.

After Tiananmen Square, the so-called Gang of Elders was anxious to counter the peaceful evolution conspiracy: "hostile foreign forces" sowing the seeds of liberalisation in the fourth- or fifth-generation cadres. Hence the elders' stress on finding the proper philosopher-kings or trustworthy Marxists as leaders. "Whether we can have a long reign and perennial stability depends on the quality of the cadres," Deng reportedy said not long after the June 1989 crisis.[10]

Deng's ideal was repeated verbatim by Hu Jintao at a meeting on organisation work a few years later. "The key [to successful rule] lies in the quality of the party and the people," he said.[11] By the people, Deng and Hu did not mean the "Old Hundred Surnames" but senior cadres. Following Jiang, Hu pointed out that ideological and political work was the priority task of party construction. This meant helping cadres "establish firmly a Marxist worldview and philosophy of life". Hu believed that through a new quasi-brainwash campaign, the party could be made "impregnable in ideology, politics and organisation" — and its mandate of heaven could be extended indefinitely.[12]

In spite of Deng's well-known reservations about the ability and reformist inclinations of Jiang, the latter continued to receive "imperial" blessings for succession. And Deng's commitment to collective leadership notwithstanding, he helped Jiang consolidate his hold, particularly on the PLA. The patriarch made Jiang CMC Chairman a few months after the latter's accession to the post of general secretary. By contrast, Zhao Ziyang was only made CMC first vice-chairman a year or so before his fall. Deng also lent his formidable prestige to shoring up Jiang's PLA credentials. It was the patriarch who advised him to devote the bulk of his time to "seizing army work".[13]

In turn, the Jiang Zemin Office began to engineer a personality cult that was almost as elaborate as that of Mao or Lin Biao (see Chapter 2). This went against party regulations endorsed in the early 1980s. For example, the Central Committee passed a circular in July 1980 entitled "Instructions on Making Less Propaganda on Individuals". This set of regulations said that the media should desist from publicising "activities and talks of leaders that lack major significance". It deplored the fact that there had been too many Mao pictures and quotations in public places. "This is a sign of lack of propriety in politics," the instructions said.[14]

Offspring of Senior Cadres and the "Secretaries' Faction"

Given the renewed emphasis on Marxist trustworthiness, it is not surprising that the sons and daughters of senior cadres — or princelings — again had a new lease of life. This is despite the avowed aims of Deng and Jiang not to give special treatment to the "high-born proletariats" (see Chapter 6). The following case of princelings in action in Shenzhen is instructive.

The power of pedigree: The case of Shenzhen

The democratic ideal of dissident astrophysicist Fang Lizhi — that "nobody need be afraid of anybody" — was achieved, albeit in topsy-turvy fashion, by the sector of the population with the requisite pedigree. While Fang was talking about "equality before the law", what transpired was that *gaoganzidi* ("princelings") and other members of the post-1949 elite could defy the law and even the president thanks to their revolutionary bloodline.

The kidnap of princeling businessman Chen Xianxuan by the cronies of fellow princeling millionaire Wang Bing in the special economic zone (SEZ) in mid-1995 had a huge impact. Chen, reputedly married to the granddaughter of the late vice-president Ulanfu, was the president of Shenzhen Dong Hui Industrial Share Company. Wang, the eldest son of another late vice-president, Wang Zhen, headed the China Ocean Helicopter Corporation (COHC), also based in the SEZ.[15]

While an employee of Wang's in the late 1980s, Chen reportedly committed 10 million yuan of COHC funds to a risky investment. The matter had not been settled when he left China Helicopter to set up Dong Hui. According to Shenzhen sources and Hong Kong media reports, the abduction took place on June 24, 1995, after Chen had finished teeing off at the exclusive Shenzhen Xiangmihu Golf Club.

Chen was taken away by force by several Wang associates, including plainclothes officers from the People's Armed Police (PAP). He was later whisked by helicopter to a remote town in Guangdong. The Shenzhen party committee was holding a regular weekend session when it was alerted minutes afterwards. The first reaction of then party boss Li Youwei and police chief He Jinghuan was not to go after the suspects but to impose a news blackout. Orders were also given to "isolate the case", meaning asking relatives and staff of both parties to hush things up.

Mindful of the *gaoganzidi* status of the antagonists, the Shenzhen committee immediately called the General Office of the Central Committee for "guidance from on high". However, a day later, the shocking event was revealed to the Hong Kong press after friends and employees of Chen staged a demonstration at the golf course. Shenzhen residents also learnt about the scandal through the Hong Kong media. However, even under pressure, all that the Shenzhen authorities thought fit to do was to quietly persuade Wang to let Chen go. The 33-year-old princeling was handed over to Shenzhen police in late June. He was put under police guard at a luxurious villa in the outskirts of the zone.[16]

Under prodding by the Hong Kong press, the Shenzhen authorities claimed they had decided on a "two-pronged strategy": to investigate the "abduction" as well as Chen's alleged misuse of COHC funds. That the law-and-order mechanism was not exactly working to international norms was evident from the apparent kid-gloves treatment of Wang. Shenzhen and Beijing sources said he never came under police detention — but was allowed to take his time to work out a "compromise" with the authorities after the glare of publicity had subsided.

Wang apparently decided to relent only after the personal interference of Jiang Zemin, a family friend who was disturbed by the scandal's effect on foreign businessmen. A week after the incident, Jiang called Wang to offer what he called "an uncle's advice". Wang was urged to "practise self-restraint" and to "minimise the social fallout" of the affair. The *gaoganzidi* was given an opportunity to go to Beijing to explain himself. The matter was not settled until early 1996. As a punishment, Wang was asked to transfer his business out of Shenzhen. A handful of his underlings — including the PAP personnel involved in the kidnap — were given internal disciplinary punishments. The case never went to the law courts. Neither was it explained to people in Shenzhen and other parts of China.[17]

For Shenzhen cadres and police officers, princelings, particularly those with PLA credentials such as Wang, were simply untouchable. The *gaoganzidi* often cruised around town — well above the speed limit — in limousines with PLA or PAP licence plates. They entertained in exclusive clubs, guarded by their own security staff. An informed source said the municipal party committee had a list of the *gaoganzidi* with businesses based in the zone. "Security, commercial, even tax departments are urged to exercise caution when dealing with these high-powered executives," the source said. He added that the Shenzhen leadership had known about the "irregularities" between Dong Hui and COHC, which also had PLA connections, for a long time.[18]

However, the hands of the municipal authorities were tied because of their illustrious backgrounds. Allied to Wang were the children of Gu Mu, a former vice-premier known as "the father of SEZs". At least two sons of Gu, who are surnamed Li, ran army- and PAP-affiliated corporations in Shenzhen. Dong Hui was reportedly linked to the Ye clan, a reference to the late Marshal Ye Jianying and his son, former Guangdong governor Ye Xuanping. The wife of the ex-governor, Wu Xiaolan, a former vice-mayor of Shenzhen, was an honorary director of the company.

Other *gaoganzidi* strutting their stuff in the SEZ included the kin of patriarch Deng Xiaoping, former vice-president Rong Yiren, the late party elder Chen Yun, and former mayor Li Hao. Political observers feared that after the July 1, 1997 handover of Hong Kong, the special administrative region could like Shenzhen become the battleground where the *gaoganzidi* vied for supremacy.[19]

The role of secretaries and aides

Next to their sons and daughters, the CCP grandees could trust their *mishu* (secretaries and personal aides) best. Hence the rise of the so-called *mishubang* or secretaries' faction: the large number of secretaries who took "helicopter rides" to the top. The use of *mishu* cut across the political spectrum. Prominent members of the liberal camp, Tian Jiyun and Bao Tong, were former aides to Zhao Ziyang.[20]

The Chen Xitong affair (see following story and Chapter 2) exposed to the full the possible abuses of the *mishu* clique — and gave new impetus to reform in this arena. Wang Baosen, the Beijing vice-mayor whose suicide opened up the scandal, had been a personal secretary of Chen's. Other personal secretaries of Chen and Wang were major culprits in the entire Beijing network of corruption. To top it all, Chen himself first cut his teeth in Beijing politics as a secretary of a former party boss of Beijing, Liu Ren.[21]

There were calls for institutionalising practices already in existence since the late 1980s against the *mishubang* phenomenon. For example, under normal circumstances, a senior cadre could not take along his secretaries when transferred to another post or location. Thus, the only aide that Jiang brought with him to Beijing in June 1989 was Zeng Qinghong. Moreover, the feudalistic, master and apprentice-like relationship between a top official and his secretary would be phased out.[22]

Shaanxi Governor Cheng Andong created a stir in early 1995 when he departed from tradition by hiring members of his personal secretariat through open competition. Of the four, only the top secretary was a permanent appointment. The other three were on two-year contracts. All four *mishu* were professionals who made their careers in business and academe rather than in the party or government hierarchy. One of the four aides, Zhao Jun, a former judge and law professor, was asked by the local media whether he had some special connection to Governor Cheng. Zhao replied: "I knew the governor only from the media; the governor didn't know me at all."[23]

However, by 1997, the influence of *mishu* had hardly abated. Many secretaries and personal aides of the Shanghai-affiliated leaders — Jiang Zemin and Zhu Rongji — were calling the shots in central and regional positions. That even such a modernisation-minded "Mr Clean" as Zhu had to fill top positions with his former personal aides testified to the difficulty of political reform. One of the "dark horse" members of Zhu's cabinet in 1998 was the

Minister of State Security Xu Yongyue. Xu made his mark as a secretary of the late conservative patriarch Chen Yun.[24]

The Rise of Cliques

Yet another fallout of the rule of personality and the premium put on "trustworthiness" was the resurgence of "small circles" or factions. This was despite the emphasis put by elders such as Deng Xiaoping and General Liu Huaqing on the principle of the "five lakes and four seas". Moreover, in a meeting on personnel issues in 1996, Jiang warned against "making selections time and again only amongst small circles close to leading cadres".[25]

Apart from Deng's patronage, the rise of the Shanghai Faction reflected the relatively narrow power base of Jiang, who lacked the national exposure of a Hu Yaobang or Zhao Ziyang. Working closely with Jiang's Shanghai Faction was the nascent Zhu Rongji Faction, comprising ideologically conservative technocrats (see Chapters 2 and 7).

Apart from Jiang's mainstream clique, other cabals also hit the big time. Consider, for example, the Shandong Faction, which worked hand in glove with the Shanghai Faction. The party's Organisation Department had since the early 1980s been a bastion of Shandong politicians, which might account for the fact that a relatively large number of faction affiliates won senior slots in the regions. The clique's influence was particularly strong in the PLA.

It is perhaps more than a historical coincidence that during the last part of the Cultural Revolution, there was a power pact between ambitious politicians from Shanghai and Shandong. All four members of the Gang of Four either were born in Shandong or spent their early careers there. However, there was inevitable friction between the two cliques. Shandong Faction alumni often complained about being upstaged. While Shanghai politicians were ensconced in cushy posts in Beijing, Shandong cadres were made to defend the frontiers in hardship jobs. For example, the party secretaries of Xinjiang and Inner Mongolia, Wang Lequan and Liu Mingzu, who were appointed in early 1995, came from Shandong.[26]

As in the case of the Shanghai Faction, the rise of the Shandong Faction had aroused jealousy. Then vice-premier Jiang Chunyun, the "patriarch of Shandong", received an unusually large number of negative ballots from NPC members when they voted to confirm his position in 1995 (see following story). There were complaints from cadres from other regions, in particular, the rich coastal zones, that Shandong's so-called economic miracle was based on favouritism — and vastly inflated figures. Shandong cadres were also characterised as boot-lickers eager to please the family members of elders such as Deng or Chen Yun. The officials were said to have their political future in mind when they readily complied with Beijing's requests for special contributions.[27]

Apart from factions defined geographically, there were groupings associated with a university or work unit. Since the late 1980s, the Qinghua Faction, or engineering graduates from Qinghua University, had monopolised a large number of technocratic posts. Twenty-nine full or alternate members of the 1992 Central Committee were Qinghua alumni.[28] Qinghua graduates who hit the big time included Zhu Rongji, Shanghai party secretary Huang Ju, Jiangxi and later Shandong party boss Wu Guanzheng, former Guangdong governor Zhu Senlin, former Sichuan governor Xiao Yang, and former Guizhou governor Chen Shineng.[29]

Then there were cabals based on affiliation with a certain ministry or trade. The Petroleum Faction wielded a big clout in the late 1970s and early 1980s. It had an unexpected revival in the Zhu Rongji cabinet formed in March 1998. Two new ministers, Sheng Huaren and Zhou Yongkang, who headed respectively the State Economic and Trade Commission and the Ministry of Land and Natural Resources, had worked long years as top executives of petroleum companies. Other big shots with connections to the oil industry included foreign-trade tsar Wu Yi and Zeng Qinghong.[30]

Of equal importance were the alumni of the ministries of electronics and machine-building, led by none other than Jiang Zemin. Among distinguished clique members were Vice-Premier Li Lanqing, the party secretary of Beijing, Jia Qinglin, and the party boss of Chongqing, Zhang Delin. Officials who had worked in the car industry also had a leg over the competition. Affiliates who made it to the top included Vice-Premier Li Lanqing, the former head of the Taiwan Affairs Office Wang Zhaoguo, and the former party boss of Shenzhen, Li Youwei.[31]

THE CADRE SYSTEM

On the issue of "party construction", the leadership seemed by early 1998 to have been consumed with narcissism. Instead of casting its glance outwards for new ideas and political groups to rejuvenate the party, the CCP looked inwards in a perhaps quixotic search for Marxist-Leninist saints to give it a new lease of life. A key task of the 15th Party Congress was to identify fourth- and fifth-generation cadres. The emphasis was put squarely on loyalty and "trustworthiness".

Identity and Traits of Post-Deng Leaders

The search for a corps of "cross-century cadres" had reached new urgency by the mid-1990s. In 1995, each ministry and province was told to identify at least 100 cross-century standard bearers, or promising neophytes in their late 30s and 40s who could assume senior positions around the turn of the century.[32]

A premium was put on equipping particularly the younger generation with the trappings of modern management. With the computerisation of offices in larger cities such as Shanghai and Shenzhen, information technology classes were *de rigueur* for the upwardly mobile. Everybody was taking English lessons. Even in relatively backward Liaoning Province, cadres were required by the year 2000 to know a foreign language. Facility with an alien tongue was defined as "mastery of at least 2,000 foreign words and basic grammar". In late 1996, the Organisation Department dispatched circulars to party and government units nationwide asking cadres to take legal courses.[33]

Modernisation also received a boost from foreigners. With the help of Hong Kong and overseas donors such as property magnate Lina Wong, senior cadres were able to study management in top schools overseas. Beginning in 1996, China sent cadres, SOE managers and PLA officers for training sessions of three to nine months at Harvard University's business school and the Kennedy School of Government. In 1996, the Canadian government provided US$7 million to help the State Statistical Bureau improve data collection and analysis.[34]

Yet there was little doubt the party's Organisation Department was looking for both redness and expertise, the proverbial mixture of *de* ("Marxist morality") and *cai* ("talents"). And while Deng in the late 1980s had put *cai* before *de*, he complied with conservative elders' predilection for redness after the June 4 disaster. Jiang Zemin, in particular, sought officials who could measure up to his criterion of "talking more about politics".[35]

For organisation supremo Hu Jintao, senior cadres must first of all be "knowledgeable and expert in their own fields". Even more important, Hu pointed out they must be "loyal Marxists who uphold socialism with Chinese characteristics" and "political experts who know how to run the party and the country". At his major speech on the CCP's 75th birthday in 1996, Jiang Zemin listed five major criteria for being "red and expert". They were: "having lofty and magnificent Communist ideals"; "ability to serve the people and close linkage with the people"; "liberated thoughts and the ability to seek truth from facts"; ability to pursue clean government and a lifestyle of "plain living and hard struggle"; and good professional knowledge and skills.[36]

Jiang's obsession was similar to that of the elders: to beat back infiltration from the West. He pointed out that cadres must "self-consciously resist the decadence [of Western thoughts] and counter peaceful evolution". He called on them to resist the "influence of the corrupt thoughts and culture of capitalism" as well as the "residual influence of capitalism". This message was repeated in his political report to the 15th Party Congress, which was generally touted as Jiang's most liberal pronouncement.[37]

The Goal of Rejuvenation

By the mid-1990s, the CCP indicated it was proud of its achievement in rejuvenation. Three-quarters of officials with the rank of cadres were under 45. In late 1995, the number of under-45 cadres who had the rank of vice-minister or vice-governor doubled that of 1991.[38] In spite of the low salary levels, party and government departments were able to attract hundreds of scholars with advanced degrees from well-known universities in the US, Europe and Japan.

Beijing stipulated that by the late 1990s, each county must have at least several cadres around 35 years of age occupying positions of deputy heads of department or above. In mid-1996, the Organisation Department kicked off the so-called "6, 8, 10 game plan". This meant locating suitable candidates who were born in the 1960s and educated in the 1980s, and who had around 10 years of sterling track record. The top criterion, however, was still "a self-conscious ability to resist Western-style democracy".[39]

Cadres in their 40s to early 50s who already occupied important positions in the mid-1990s included Vice-Governor of the People's Bank of China, Chen Yuan; Vice-Head of the State Assets Bureau, Pan Yue; Director of the State Administration of Exchange Control, Zhou Xiaochuan; and the Executive Vice-Chairman of the China Securities Regulatory Commission,

Li Jian'ge. Examples at the regional level included the then Party Secretary of Jilin Zhang Dejiang; the Vice-Party Secretaries of Guangdong, Hainan, Tibet and Fujian, respectively Huang Huahua, Du Qinglin, Danzeng and Xi Jinping; Vice-Governor of Jiangsu, Zhang Lianzhen; and the Vice-Mayor of Beijing, Duan Jiang.[40]

A closer analysis of the background of these rising stars, however, would suggest that many were chosen at least partially on the age-old ground of *guanxi*. Cadres who came from the right clique or who had a revolutionary bloodline seemed to enjoy an unfair advantage (see foregoing section). Among the high-born titans were Chen Yuan (son of Chen Yun); the Executive Vice-Governor of Guangdong and former People's Bank of China vice-governor, Wang Qishan (son-in-law of the late vice-premier Yao Yilin); Pan Yue (son-in-law of General Liu Huaqing); Xi Jinping (son of Xi Zhongxun); and a political commissar of the PAP, Liu Yuan (son of the late president Liu Shaoqi).[41]

Cross-century cadres without *guanxi* tended to be technocrats or career apparatchiks more noted for their readiness to toe the central line than originality of thinking. This was evident from the corps of local leaders selected in late 1994 and early 1995, when more than half of the provinces and major cities underwent reshuffles. Unlike *gaoganzidi* destined for greatness, who had benefited from unexpected transfers and "helicopter rides" to the top, the plebeian rising stars had humdrum, predictable career paths. They spent long years as mid-echelon engineers, administrators or party functionaries in the localities, sometimes in relatively parochial factory or farm settings.[42]

This is true of the new governors of Shandong, Hebei, Henan, Liaoning, Shaanxi, Gansu, Anhui and Hunan, respectively Li Chunting, Ye Liansong, Ma Zhongchen, Wen Shizhen, Cheng Andong, Zhang Wule, Hui Liangyu and Yang Zhengwu. They seemed to lack the fire and independence of earlier-generation mavericks such as former governor of Guangdong, Ye Xuanping; former governor of Sichuan, Xiao Yang; and the former vice-governor of Guangxi, Lei Yu.[43]

How Good Are the Cadres?

Apart from the ability to withstand the sugar-coated bullets of capitalism, one of Jiang's key standards for promotion was loyalty to himself. Beginning in mid-1995, the Organisation Department sent dozens of teams to 30 provinces and major cities to check the suitability of cadres being groomed for elevation at the 15th Party Congress. For example, in July 1996, a team of 50 personnel experts studied the credentials of cadres in the party, government, people's congress, consultative conference, and disciplinary inspection commission of the Beijing city apparatus. A key criterion was the cadres' ability to "toe the line of the leadership with Jiang Zemin as its core".[44]

While the calibre of the younger generation discovered by Jiang's talent scouts could only be ascertained several years down the line, doubts were cast on the ability or integrity of cadres appointed in the 1990s. For reasons including factional balance, Jiang and his top colleagues such as Li Peng had a track record of giving important jobs to officials who had already proved to be loafers and time-servers.

Take, for example, Li Guixian, named in 1994 as the first president of the Academy of Administration under the State Council. The institute was China's highest unit for research into government efficiency and administrative modernisation. It had the same status as the Central Party School. Open to mid- to senior officials, the academy's goal was to bring about a "Western-style" civil service.[45]

But was Li the man for the job? In July 1993, he was sacked from his post of PBoC governor by Zhu Rongji for mismanagement. The state councillor was blamed for failing to stop his subordinates from using bank deposits to speculate in the property and stock markets. During earlier confirmation hearings at the NPC for the posts of PBoC governor or state councillor, Li was repeatedly snubbed by deputies for sloppy performance and general lack of qualifications. His star continued to rise, however, thanks to his being a member of Li Peng's "Soviet Faction". After losing his PBoC job, he was given responsibilities in areas including auditing and fighting graft.

The same duplicity surrounded the appointment in 1993 of former Guizhou party boss Liu Zhengwei to the post of vice-head of the Work Committee for Central Party and Government Organs. In the last year of his tenure in Guizhou, a scandal involving the corruption of his wife had already erupted. The suitability of Liu was further questioned as a vital role of the work committee was to check on the ethical standards of senior cadres. In 1995, Liu's wife was formally arrested, and later executed. However, it was not until late that year that Liu was forced to resign after what was reported to have been a failed suicide attempt.[46]

Emergence of a Civil Service?
"Scientific" recruitment and dismissal

In his speech on the party's 75th birthday in 1996, Jiang pledged himself to modernising the cadre system. He raised the banner of "democratic partici-pation by the broad masses" in the selection and assessment of cadres. "Only when we pursue the mass line and seek a synthesis between leaders and the masses can we do a good job of selecting good cadres and using them well," Jiang said. "We must implement various forms of democratic recommendation, democratic tests and assessments."[47]

Some progress was made in building up a rudimentary civil service. First of all, there was public recruitment of government, and in some in-stances, party cadres. In mid-1996, 61 departments in the party and govern-ment recruited 737 positions "from society at large". These included "sen-sitive" units such as the Organisation Department, the Central Commission for Disciplinary Inspection, and the General Office of the State Council. This followed the opening up of 495 positions in 1995, which was contested by nearly 10,000 people in examinations. For the first time in 1996, govern-ment positions were open to peasants, employees in the private sector, and non-Beijing residents. The same year, open contests were conducted by 12 provinces and directly administered cities including Yunnan, Henan, Anhui, Fujian, Liaoning, Jilin, Shandong, Sichuan, Guizhou and Shanghai.[48]

For understandable reasons, the ranks of *zhongyang* positions made available for public recruitment were only those up to *keyuan*, or junior-level executives. Comparable positions in the regions were more senior. For example, posts to be contested in Sichuan, Shandong and the Beijing municipality were up to the rank of vice-chiefs of departments. In mid-1996, 627 people in Sichuan applied for 10 positions at the level of vice-director. They included the vice-head of the provincial court, vice-chief of the foreign affairs office, and vice-heads of the departments of justice, statistics, electronics and environmental protection. In the capital, 244 competed for five positions at the vice-director level. Of the winners, two had PhDs and four were under 40.[49]

At the same time, a "scientific" dismissal system was licked into shape, in effect quashing the proverbial iron rice bowl. The practice began in 1989 in the national Police and Customs departments. By the mid-1990s, it had spread to other units and a dozen-odd cities. From 1992 to 1995, 2,700-odd officials were dismissed. Reasons given included breaking laws, infringement of discipline or just poor performance. Then state councillor Li Guixian said the firing system would be extended nationwide, with the view to building a "clean, streamlined, and highly efficient national civil service". In Shenzhen, 33 civil servants were axed in 1995 for going against regulations or dereliction of duty.[50]

Another pivot of the modernisation programme was the rotation of cadres. The Ministry of Personnel indicated in mid-1996 that all cadres and civil servants would be moved to other posts after serving in one position for five years or less. "The new system is particularly intended for leading officials from divisional chief up to ministers and provincial governors," *China Daily* quoted ministry officials as saying. "It is designed to increase efficiency and to help build an honest and clean government." After three to five years, officials would be transferred to posts in another system or geographical location — or at least other slots within the same ministry. Beijing, Sichuan, Jiangxi, Heilongjiang, Jilin and Guizhou took the lead by rotating around 45 per cent of their civil servants that year.[51]

In the year ending March 1998, at least half of State Council cadres were transferred to the provinces, and vice versa. An unprecedented number of officials were also "exchanged" between the coast and hinterland areas. The rotation was so extensive that aggressive lobbying was undertaken by *zhongyang* cadres — as well as those from the poorer provinces — to have themselves moved to the rich coastal belt. In some instances, these officials indicated they would not mind a slight downgrading of their ranks provided they could end up where the money was.[52] In spite of possible abuses, the authorities insisted that the rotation system had yielded the desired effects of rooting out "the phenomenon of mountain strongholds" and of promoting efficiency.

The limits of administrative reform

In late 1996, an official newspaper boasted that after 18 years of experimentation, administrative reform had scored basic results. It cited achievements such as cutting down on bureaucratic fat, in particular the separation of government and business. For example, several "professional economic ministries" had been turned into economic entities with no governmental functions. In the mid-1990s, bureau-level units in Shanghai were reduced by one third from 84 to 53.[53]

However, the same paper pointed out that the point of departure of administrative tinkering was "China's actual conditions", and that only gradual steps would be taken. Many of these "actual conditions" seemed to have to do with the neo-conservative agenda of recentralisation — as well as the peculiar requirements of the Jiang leadership.

Take, for example, efforts begun in the mid-1980s to cut down on CCP administrative organs — or at least those party units that overlapped with government counterparts. Some of these efforts were supposed to continue even after the June 4, 1989 crackdown. For example, when the Pudong Zone was set up in 1994, local officials boasted to the foreign community that there would be a minimal number of party organs in the zone. Yet by 1996, Pudong had become no different from Shanghai — or any other Chinese city — in having parallel party and government offices for practically all areas of governance.[54]

Moreover, modernisation efforts such as rejuvenation stopped at the top levels of the party. Rules such as retirement at 65 or rotation after five years did not apply to members of the Politburo or its Standing Committee. Moreover, actions such as the trimming of bureaucratic fat were often politicised. For instance, the Jiang leadership tried hard to cut down the staff of the NPC and CPPCC not so much out of a zeal for streamlining as because the two organs had become bastions of opposition. Throughout the 1990s, "proletarian-dictatorship" organs such as the police, the Ministry of State Security and the PAP kept expanding thanks to the political decision to maintain stability "above all else".[55]

Is the Leadership Up to Scratch?

Efficient dictatorships last longer than inefficient ones. This apparent truism acounts for the fact that while Beijing was adamant about the "dictatorship of the proletariat", the improvement, if not democratisation, of decision-making was touted as a major thrust for political reform in the post-Deng era. However, by the mid-1990s, the kind of leadership paralysis that made possible the June 4, 1989 conflagration had resurfaced: an inward-looking top echelon concerned with little more than preserving its own privileges; worsening cliquishness; and failure to broaden the CCP's power base.

The trappings of modern statecraft notwithstanding, decision-making had become top-heavy, lacking in initiative, and prone to procrastination. That CCP-style administration which was neither scientific nor democratic also manifested itself in the fact that the cadre-managers were given to unsystematic, ad hoc troubleshooting: fighting fires wherever they arose, and often arriving at the scene only in time to do a rough body count.

The Imperative of Recentralisation

With specific reference to centre-regional relations, the obsession with strengthening the *zhongyang* led to a Song dynasty-style syndrome called "a strong tree trunk coupled with weak branches": to implement its decisions, Beijing revived Draconian measures such as fiats characteristic of the "command economy" of the pre-reform years. The recentralisation drive was a product of two things: lack of a management system and fear of losing control.[56]

What some liberal scholars claimed to be a "return to the old road" manifested itself in almost all areas of decision-making, particularly those concerning the economy. Economic tsar Zhu Rongji's mid-1993 16-point programme to restore fiscal discipline to the overheated economy was a reassertion of Beijing's heavy-handed authority over areas including currency, finance, investment and foreign trade. This was followed by the re-imposition of control over the prices of more than two dozen commodities and services in early 1994. The *zhongyang* also resumed its monopoly over the distribution of farm produce and producer goods. Macro-economic adjustments and controls would not be lifted during the Ninth Five-Year Plan period (1996–2000).[57]

The most common method used to preserve central control was also the most primitive: the imposition of fiats and quotas. Since 1993, they were slapped on provinces and cities in areas including the conservation of arable land, promoting grain yields, stabilisation of prices, clamping down on real-estate and stock market speculation, helping poor regions develop, maintaining law and order, and tax collection.

By 1996, such fiats and levies had bordered on the politically risky. Under the principle of "each region ensuring its social order", almost all provinces and cities were handed targets concerning the number of big-time triad, drug-trafficking and "subversive" gangs they must smash. Cadres in Guangdong and a number of rich provinces and cities were scandalised in late 1996 upon receiving similar quotas for nabbing "big tigers" in corruption and smuggling. With the advent of the "perpetual" Strike Hard campaign in May 1996, the law-and-order portfolio of regional cadres became crushingly difficult. Different provinces soon resounded with the gunshot executions of hard-core criminals — many little more than suspects if strict Western standards of jurisprudence were applied. Yet the political cost that these officials had to pay could be astounding.[58]

To ensure that the targets were met, the Jiang administration revised a quasi-Maoist responsibility system for governors, party secretaries, and mayors. In 1993, the central authorities began to institute a so-called "local leader responsibility system": the party secretary and governor of a province were given a task to perform or a quota to fill. Regional officials were assessed on the basis of how well they had acquitted themselves; seriously deficient performances could lead to dismissals.[59]

The most well-known was the so-called rice-bag and the vegetable-basket responsibility system, meaning that provincial governors would be held responsible for high grain yields and mayors for ample supply of vegetables. The high-grain-yield campaign was best implemented in provinces including Hunan, Henan, Jilin, Zhejiang, Jiangsu and Guangdong. For example, Zhejiang pledged in 1995 that counties with strong economies must also be prodigious grain producers. Guangdong vowed to be at least 70 per cent self-sufficient by the end of the century. Jiangsu cadres went one better by going after total self-sufficiency in rice and wheat. Its goal was a per capita production of 450 kilos of grain by 2000 (see also Chapter 5). Grain-production targets were handed down from provincial capitals to cities, counties and villages.[60]

The "Cadre Responsibility System"

The "cadre responsibility system" was yet another testimony to Beijing's superstitious belief in the rule of personality. In the absence of a rational system, appeals were made to the Lei Feng or Jiao Yulu genes of individual cadres so they could live up to the expectations of the leadership.[61] Faith was pinned on the zeal of fire-fighters when it was evident the city's fire-prevention system and fire engines had gone into disrepair.

Given the lure of honour and promotion, there was no lack of gung-ho cadres willing to shoulder responsibility for missions impossible. For example, in a meeting of officials responsible for rural affairs in Shanxi province, some 50 cadres signed "responsibility certificates" for eradicating poverty in the countryside. They included the vice-party secretary and vice-governor in charge of agriculture, Zheng Shegui and Wang Wenxue, as well as the party secretaries of 46 poor counties. The latter-day Jiao Yulus vowed never to leave their jobs until areas under their charge were out of poverty.[62]

The same went for the fight against crime. Dozens of provincial and municipal leaders vowed to personally take on the criminals. For example, in Guangdong in May 1996, the party secretaries or mayors of cities including Guangzhou, Zhanjiang and Mouming took personal command of the anti-crime fight. These officials adopted a hands-on approach in devising anti-crime strategies.[63] The problem was: could a party secretary or governor be expected to personally handle dozens of different portfolios in addition to their daily jobs of running their provinces and cities?

Given the prevalence of the "every man for himself" psychology of the primitive stage of capitalism, it was not easy for cadres to live up to their "responsibility certificate". For example, to have a fully stocked vegetable basket, mayors had to come up with multitudinous tricks. These included setting aside a "risk fund" to stabilise prices; ensuring arable land for vegetable production; and helping with the deployment of trucks and other distribution methods.[64]

In Guangzhou, the ability of a cadre to lock away felons and miscreants was a key factor for career advancement. The Guangzhou Committee for the Comprehensive Management of Social Order ruled that poor performance on the law-and-order front would mean demotion or dismissal. A notable victim of this responsibility system was Heilongjiang party boss Sun Weiben, who was summarily fired when Zhu Rongji toured the region in April 1994. Sun's "crimes" were failure to maintain fiscal order, rein in speculation and turn government firms around.[65]

Government by Work Teams

Nothing illustrated the ad hoc nature of the Jiang administration better than the frequency with which troubleshooters and plenipotentiaries were sent to the regions to solve problems or twist the arms of a warlord. Since early 1995, Beijing had commissioned hundreds of squads to bust graft cases; to crack down on price fixers; to sniff out "piggy banks" maintained by regional administrations; and to prevent localities from raising loans overseas or over-spending on investment projects. Bureaucratic fire-fighters were also sent to seize smugglers, fight smut dealers and to ensure the fire-safety standards of entertainment centres.[66]

For example, in mid-1995, eight work groups went to the provinces and cities of Beijing, Shanghai, Guangdong, Jiangsu, Hebei, Henan, Zhejiang and Guangxi to find out whether they had overspent on capital construction. In the wake of the Chen Xitong affair, investigation teams led by State Council Secretary-General Luo Gan flocked to Guangdong to follow up on clues to corruption scandals. Several big-name Shenzhen cadres were reportedly nabbed.[67]

Sometimes, these so-called "imperial emissaries" could be concerned with apparently trivial matters such as stopping localities from setting up roadblocks to collect illegal fees. For example, in the summer of 1995, the State Council dispatched three inspection teams to check out the highways in 12 provinces. The object of an "imperial" crackdown could also be surprisingly detailed. For example, in early 1996, eight central-government squads were sent to specifically check on the prices of agrarian chemicals and fertilisers in 14 provinces.[68]

In its public relations campaigns, the Jiang administration made much of the fact that its cadres had set the post-1949 record for periodic tours of the provinces. This was particularly true of trouble spots such as Liaoning Province, which had been racked by periodic labour problems. In 1996, more than half of the Beijing-based Politburo members made inspection trips to Shenyang and neighbouring cities.[69] From one perpective, the frequent provincial tours by either top leaders or "ambassadors" was a sign of "staying close to the people". However, this "governance by work teams" approach begged this question: if the normal system of administration was working well, why the urgency to send inspectors to hotspots?

The "Inter-departmental Approach"

The opposite to the "personalised" approach to governance was the inter-departmental approach. Given the lack of systematic solutions, the leadership thought it wise to tackle new or difficult issues by setting up teams of experts from different party and government departments. After all, should things go wrong, responsibility could be spread among the participating units.

The "collective-responsibility" approach often took the form of a *lianxi huiyi*: convening a joint committee from as many as a dozen departments to tackle a problem. While governments of all countries sometimes convene inter-departmental conferences to handle "inter-disciplinary" matters, the frequency of this approach was astounding in China. It showed up the rudimentary nature of institutions: demarcations of jurisdictions and responsibility were murky. Moreover, this "let's do it together" work-style reeked of Maoist anarchism. Mao's mass movements including the Cultural Revolution were perhaps the messiest manifestations of the mentality of throwing everything — government and PLA units and a stirred-up populace — at a difficult issue.[70]

The party authorities periodically organised *lianxi huiyi* to tackle crime. Typically, units including the ministries of public security and state security, the courts and procuratorate, the People's Armed Police, the propaganda departments and the party's Political and Legal Affairs Commission took part. Sometimes, an apparently straightforward subject warranted this multi-pronged treatment. In mid-1996, a special task force was set up to counter fake yuan bills. The anti-counterfeiting unit's cadres came from public security units, the banks and other departments.[71]

In the autumn of 1995, the State Council called a *lianxi huiyi* to ensure that "experimental work" on enterprise reform would be carried out properly. The inter-departmental conference drew cadres from 15 commissions and ministries including the party's Organisation Department, the State Planning Commission, the State Commission for the Reform of the Economic Structure, the State Securities Regulatory Commission, the People's Bank of China, the ministries of finance, personnel, labour, foreign trade, the All-China Federation of Trade Unions, the auditing and tax administrations, and other financial and banking units. The high-level *huiyi*'s principal job was to prevent unauthorised privatisation: SOEs must not indiscriminately issue stocks, form subsidiary companies or fire workers.[72]

By 1997, countless inter-departmental task forces were put together to tackle matters large and small: ensuring wheat and cotton production; fighting smuggling; hitting out at intellectual property rights (IPR) violations; and plugging leaks of state secrets. Even such a relatively straightforward matter as fire prevention merited the inter-departmental strategy. In late 1997, units including the police, Labour Ministry, Agriculture Ministry, the official trade union and the Industrial and Commercial Management Bureau issued a joint notice concerning fire safety for factories that doubled as warehouses and dormitories.[73]

The frequency with which the *lianxi huiyi* approach was taken cast doubt on the competence of individual party and government departments. This anti-institutional method of governance reached its height in the run-up to Jiang's historic summit with Bill Clinton in October 1997. Top cadres from dozens of departments and think tanks in the party, government and army were pulled away from their daily duties since the spring of that year. In the two months preceding the trip, much of the party and government ground to a halt because the best brains in Beijing and Shanghai were devoting so much of their time to drawing up Jiang's position papers.[74]

The Atrophy of Ministries and Departments

The dysfunction, and in some instances even atrophy, of the ministries and commissions was becoming obvious in the mid-1990s. We can take a look at three typical units: the State Commission for the Reform of the Economic Structure (SCRES), the Ministry of Public Security, and the Ministry of Foreign Affairs (MFA).

The SCRES was formed by Zhao Ziyang in the early 1980s to be the "head engine" for economic liberalisation. By the mid-1990s, however, the commission was keeping a low profile and did not seem to be doing much. Part of it had to do with changing times. The neo-conservative leadership was less interested in market reforms. It did not trust the SCRES, several of whose avant-garde economists were implicated in the June 4, 1989 "turmoil". The then SCRES chief, Politburo member Li Tieying, was deemed a "has-been" who did not get on well with the Shanghai Faction. Other reasons had to do with turf wars. Functions of the SCRES were taken over by the State Economic and Trade Commission, the revitalised State Planning Commission, and the party Central Committee's Leading Group on Finance and Economics. It came as no surprise that the SCRES was abolished in March 1998.[75]

The police also felt their power waning. The Ministry of Public Security had to share power with a newly assertive Ministry of State Security (MSS) — and in particular, the vastly expanded People's Armed Police, which was seen as a potent force to impose the dictatorship of the proletariat (see Chapter 4). Some traditional intelligence-and-surveillance functions of the police and the MSS had been usurped by spy operations run by the army and the Central Committee General Office. The latter were under the direct control of President Jiang. This "division of labour" seemed a deliberate attempt by the Jiang team to prevent one law-enforcement unit from becoming too powerful, particularly when security had used to be a principal domain of arch-foe Qiao Shi. The result, however, was bureaucratic infighting which often manifested itself in street battles among different security units.[76]

As the Taiwan Strait crisis of 1995 and 1996 had shown, the foreign affairs bureaucracy had lost much of its lustre and authority to the generals. Even within the central government apparatus, the MFA had to contend with the rising clout of the Foreign Affairs Office (FAO) of the State Council. Under its ambitious director, Liu Huaqiu, the FAO had visions of transforming itself into an American-style National Security Council (NSC). FAO cadres liked to tell foreign visitors that in countries and areas including the US, Russia and Taiwan, NSC-like outfits played principal roles. In 1996 and 1997, the FAO upstaged the MFA in areas including relations with the US.[77]

For similar reasons, party and government units with partial diplomatic functions, the CCP International Liaison Department and the Taiwan Affairs Office of the State Council, also saw their power truncated. In many instances, powerful figures such as Jiang or individual generals reduced ministries — and institutions — to little more than echoing chambers. For example, Jiang formulated most Taiwan-related policies in his capacity as head of the party's Leading Group on Taiwan Affairs.[78]

Test Case: Can Beijing Tame the Regions?

From the perspective of the recentralisation campaign, governance by fiat seemed to have worked temporarily in certain areas. For instance, local governments were forced to curtail investments and to make more contributions to central coffers. Overall, the score card was disappointing. Regional cadres remained pastmasters at the time-tested game of "You [the zhongyang] have your strategy, I have my counter-strategy."

Take, for example, the quotas imposed on the provinces to arrest big-time criminals. In 1996, Guangzhou trumped Beijing by meeting the latter's stricture on netting the requisite number of heavyweight smugglers and graft-takers. The catch was that the culprits were not Guangdong natives but officials and state entrepreneurs from nearby Guangxi and Hainan.[79]

An even more cost-efficient method of cheating Beijing was the falsification of figures (see Chapter 5). As Gong Wenxiang, a statistics expert in Hubei Province indicated: "Some localities and departments do not concentrate their efforts on increasing production and improving economic efficiency but on inflating figures to fish for fame and personal gain." Or as NPC deputy Chen Shunli put it: "Officials concoct figures, and such figures in turn ensure their promotion." Chen warned against the reappearance of Great Leap Forward-style inflation of statistics, when "the production fig-ures in many places are as fantastic as the richness of their leaders' imagi-nation".[80]

In early 1996, the NPC passed a Statistics Law making falsification of figures an offence. "Over-reporting and under-reporting of micro-economic figures happen all the time," said State Statistics Bureau Director Zhang Sai. To be sure, most of the "over-reporting" belonged in the good news department, and under-reporting, the bad news department. A 1994 investigation of official data uncovered more than 60,000 cases of falsified data.[81]

It is perhaps ironic that while discussing the implementation of the Statistics Law in late 1996, then vice-premier Zou Jiahua slapped yet an-other duty on local officials: to aid in the "correct statistics campaign". "Party committees and governments of all levels must support statistics departments to obey the law," Zou said. "They [local leaders] must not shelter illegal operators. They must not directly or indirectly be involved in the falsification of statistics." An underlying reason for the national pastime of cooking the books was Beijing's penchant for laying down hundreds of quotas and fiats on regional cadres.[82]

NPC SUPERVISION: THE ROAD TO CHECKS AND BALANCES?

The Beginnings of NPC Power

Then vice-premier Zhu Rongji caused a stir in Beijing in the summer of 1996, when he shed tears during a performance of the drama on the life history of "legalist" Shang Yang (390–338 BC), the legendary reformer in the Era of the Warring States. A fierce exponent of "stern laws and severe punishments", Shang laid down Draconian but effective statutes and gov-erning systems which made possible the eventual triumph of the Qin King-dom (see also Chapter 2).[83]

Legions of administrators ancient and modern have, like Zhu, ex-pressed admiration for Shang. Apart from Confucianism, the legalist ap-proach has been central to the Chinese philosophy of governance. While this tradition did not necessarily tally with modern Western democratic ideals, its incarnation in Beijing in the mid-1990s — clear-cut laws, stern application, and "everybody being equal before the law" — represented some degree of progress. "Legalism" also meshed in well with the empowerment of the National People's Congress (NPC). After all, investing more power in the NPC meant a truncation of the "party as supreme" principle. In the Chinese context, the NPC seemed the only means through which cadres or citizens outside the party elite could exercise influence.

The rise of Chinese-style parliamentary power in the 1980s and early 1990s was partly due to the perception of Deng-style reformers that economic reform could not succeed without legal reform: business activities, particularly those involving foreigners, had to be based on statutes. The NPC's clout also expanded with the appointment of strong leaders beginning with Peng Zhen and Wan Li in the 1980s and Qiao Shi in the 1990s. A long-time rival of both Mao and Deng, Peng took the first steps towards shaking off the Chinese parliament's rubber stamp image. The tradition started by Peng of establishing the NPC as a possible counter-balance to the party and government was continued by Wan Li. In May 1989, the Standing Committee almost went ahead with a motion to declare void the state of emergency announced by Li Peng.[84]

Legislative power experienced a leap forward after Qiao Shi and Tian Jiyun took the helm in early 1993. During the NPC that year, senior cadres such as Li Peng, Li Tieying and Li Guixian were humiliated — in the form of surprisingly high negative votes and abstentions — when they were confirmed as premier and state councillors. At the regional level, deputies in the people's congresses in Guizhou and Zhejiang provinces threw out nominees for governor put forward by the party's Organisation Department.[85]

The Vision of Qiao Shi

While Jiang Zemin's perspective of governance was party-centric, the point of departure of Qiao Shi, who retired in March 1998, was the legislature. As spelled out in the preamble of the Chinese Constitution, the legitimacy of CCP rule was based on history: that the party had led the nation in throwing away the yoke of colonialism and Kuomintang misrule. For Qiao and modern-day legalists, the basis of legitimacy was the legislature as an "organ of the people".

While recognising the historical — and theoretical — supremacy of the party, Qiao indicated that the CCP should not be involved in the day-to-day affairs of the state — and that the NPC should live up to its status as the "organ of supreme power". In an interview with American media, Qiao quoted from the CCP and state charters that "the party must act within the parameters laid down by the constitution and the law". "No organisation or individual has the special privilege to go above the constitution and the law," he said.[86]

Qiao also revived to some extent the ideal of the separation of party and government that was enshrined by the 13th Party Congress of 1987. In the same interview, he quoted a 1956 Deng speech on the subject: "The party should not directly give instructions to state organs." Qiao stressed that under the Chinese Constitution, the NPC and its Standing Committee "exercise the highest state powers in a united manner".[87]

It is interesting that while even relative liberals such as Li Ruihuan acknowledged that quasi-democratic activities such as "consultation and multi-party cooperation" must be undertaken under CCP leadership, Qiao hardly mentioned the imperative of party suzerainty. Since becoming NPC chairman in early 1993, Qiao seldom mentioned the Four Cardinal Principles of orthodox Marxism and party leadership. In spite of his continued links with the state security apparatus, he never cited the principle of the "dictatorship of the proletariat" in public.

Qiao was the first to advocate the ideal of "using the law to rule the country". "While we had the idea of 'rule of law' very early on in the history of our nation, it was impossible to accomplish this in thousands of years of feudalist society," he said in 1996. "After 1949", he added, "we have for various reasons been unable to systematise and legalise either democracy within the party or democracy in our socio-political life". "To safeguard the people's democracy, we must strengthen the legal system," the then legislative supremo said.[88]

On two occasions in 1996, Qiao pointed out that democracy must be fleshed out with institutions, systems and a legal basis. Quoting Deng Xiaoping, he said in an interview with a German newspaper: "We must boost the legal system to guarantee the people's democracy. We must render democracy systematic and legalistic." The goal, Qiao said, was that these systems, institutions and laws "will not change because of the change of leaders or because the perspective and concentration of a certain leader has changed". All party units and members must "self-consciously obey and safeguard the constitution and the law". All cadres, Qiao added, must "operate within the parameters of the Constitution and the law". "They must seriously do things according to the law," he said.[89]

Putsch for NPC Power

In April 1996, Qiao laid down a cogent vision of NPC power while visiting a couple of former states of the USSR, China's erstwhile Big Brother in economic and political development. At a press conference in Moscow, he cited the expansion of the powers of the legislature — and those of regional governments and enterprises — as the fruits of political reform. "The political system in China is the NPC system," he said, adding that the latter meant "the people being the masters" of the country. "The reform of China's political system began in the late 1970s, and it has never stopped," he said. "We have made major reforms to the electoral system [for the legislature] and expanded the autonomy of the regions and enterprises."[90]

While, perhaps because of the sensitivity involved, Qiao did not elaborate on the significance of regional and entrepreneurial power, he was straightforward about NPC empowerment. He said different branches of the polity including the government must accept the supervision of the legislature. "We must fully develop the enthusiasm and creativity of the masses in constructing socialism," he said. "The State Council, the Supreme People's Court and the Supreme People's Procuratorate were put into place by the NPC. They are responsible to it and must accept its supervision." Both in Moscow and later, Qiao said the NPC had jurisdiction over the armed forces.[91]

Qiao and his deputies such as Tian Jiyun were convinced the NPC systems at the central and regional levels were the most effective organs for "arousing the masses' enthusiasm" for taking part in government. Congresses of all levels were a manifestation of the will and the "enthusiasm" of the people, Qiao said in 1995. "And the congresses safeguard and develop the democracy of the people," he added.[92]

As we shall see later, Qiao was the first senior cadre to elaborate on the theory and practice of NPC supervision of other sectors of the polity. "The neglect of law, and even the suppression of laws with administrative power, are serious in some localities and departments," he said in 1996. In such instances, Qiao wanted to assert the legislature's role as the conduit of "people power". Part of the NPC's brief, he said, was "to safeguard citizens' rights to sue government departments for violating their rights and to get government compensation".[93]

Tian Jiyun argued that it was useless to enact laws if they could not be fully implemented. He was disturbed by the high level of obstruction to law enforcement. "While exercising our supervisory powers according to law, the question of overstepping our frame of reference does not exist," he said in late 1995. "Yet we do not have enough supervisory powers. The situation of [government units] not obeying laws, and not implementing laws correctly is very serious. And people feel very strongly about this."[94]

Apart from drafting laws and supervising the government, top NPC leaders also wanted to play a role in non-traditional areas. These included diplomacy. "Congress diplomacy is an important part of China's foreign policy work and more effort will be made to improve relations with legislatures of other countries," said Tian in late 1996. He added that the legislature had a unique role to play in easing China into the world theatre. "Such work can never be replaced by government-level diplomacy," he added.[95]

An Aggressive Law-drafting Programme

Up to 1993, the principle of "party supremacy" precluded too much initiative being given to the legislature. However, starting from the mid-1990s, the NPC had seized the initiative in areas including the shaping of legislation — and using this power to influence the behaviour of the party and government.

The very process of law-drafting had changed. In the past, bills were put together by law drafters in government departments. As liberal lawmaker Nie Dajiang put it: "So far as legislative work is concerned, it's the commissions and ministries that are guiding the State Council, and the State Council that is leading the NPC." He said the NPC had displayed insufficient control over legislation. Nie also advocated borrowing the legislative experience of foreign countries.[96]

The NPC began putting together a team of legal experts and drafters in 1994. Many a new piece of legislation had implications and nuances that could prove embarrassing to the powers that be. Take, for example, the late 1995 statute on the declaration of Martial Law. On the surface, the statute served the Jiang leadership's need for stability: should chaos break out in the post-Deng era, there would be a legal basis for slapping a State of Emergency on the people. Thus, the law not only empowered the police, who were to "manage any state of martial law", but also stipulated that the PLA might be called in if the other forces were "insufficient".[97]

However, from another perspective, the law amounted to an indirect critique of the way the 1989 "turmoil" was handled by the authorities. This

became evident in the debate in the NPC. The Chinese media quoted unnamed NPC members as saying the country's first legislation on martial law
lay down precisely the terms of reference and powers of martial-law
personnel — and the "rights and duties" of citizens under a State of Emergency. Other deputies said there must be stringent supervision of police
and soldiers enforcing martial law. "We must ensure that martial law officers strictly use powers given them by the law," the *Legal Daily* quoted them
as saying. There were also calls for the proper differentiation between turmoil, riots and disturbances. "Utmost care should be exercised in implementing martial law," an NPC member said. "It should only be declared
when law and order cannot be maintained by normal means."[98]

It was obvious individual deputies had taken advantage of the debate
to criticise Beijing's handling of the 1989 pro-democracy movement. In
May and June 1989, there were no regulations supervising the Martial Law
Command, which reported only to senior PLA officers. NPC law drafters
revealed that a group of legislators had, after June 1989, discussed with
regional cadres and military officers the lessons to be drawn from the imposition of martial law in Beijing that year. The statute carried measures
against possible abuse of power such as the stipulation that "martial law
personnel should as far as possible avoid using weapons".[99]

Other laws and regulations passed in the mid-1990s would also impinge
on the prerogatives of the party and government. Examples included the
Administrative Procedure Law and the State Compensation Law. They permitted citizens to sue different government departments for negligence,
wrong-doing or dereliction of duty (see Chapter 6).

The Criminal Procedure Law of 1996 and 1997 put at least theoretical
restrictions on the powers of the police and judicial organs such as the
procuratorate. Foremost, the statute abolished the provision of "shelter and
examination", which allowed public security personnel to lock up suspects
for three months or more. Other changes included allowing lawyers early
access to suspects and affirming the principle of presumed innocence. The
new law also made for greater supervision over police in areas such as the
prevention of the use of torture and the collection of excessive fines. In a
meeting with police chiefs after passage of the law, then minister of public
security Tao Siju ordered "systematic training" for officers to "improve their
understanding of laws and their ability to enforce them".[100]

Some of the legislature's efforts at "power grabbing" were less successful. Take, for example, the laws on banking and education enacted in 1995.

Individual legislators lobbied for tighter control over fiscal policy, particularly the money supply. They wanted the People's Bank of China to be independent of the government — and answerable to the NPC. Other deputies wanted to set up a new National Monetary Committee that should report to the legislature. However, the final legislation did not give the NPC such powers.[101]

Similarly, NPC members lost a battle with regard to the 1994 Law on Budgets. The earlier drafts contained specifications that congresses of various levels had the right to supervise how their governments implement their budgets: for example, whether the funds were spent wisely or whether excessive deficits were incurred. Deputies would have been given the authority to call ministers or department heads to explain items of expenditure. The final version of the statute only invested local congresses with some powers of supervision. At the central level, only broad principles such as the judicious use of funds were endorsed, and the NPC was given no new powers.[102]

Legislators also waged a fierce battle with the government over education, particularly guarantees that sufficient funds be spent on schools. Famed musicologist Wu Zuqiang wanted a stipulation on minimal spending, for example, four to five per cent of GNP. Expenditure on education was a mere 2.2 per cent of GNP in 1994. NPC member and Qinghai professor Ren Weidong lobbied for more subsidies to poor areas — as well as restrictions on the commercial activities of colleges. The final version merely forced the State Council to make a theoretical commitment to boosting education — but there were no clear-cut requirements on funds.[103]

The Power of Scrutiny and Supervision
A semblance of checks and balances

In 1997 and 1998, legislators were pushing for a Law of Supervision that would give the NPC teeth over party and government units. The bill would give legislators authority to call senior cadres from the State Council and judicial organs to explain their policies — and to impeach them should they fail to either justify questionable policies or make amends. For example, if inflation was two or more percentage points higher than that predicted in the Government Work Report, the minister concerned must appear before the NPC up to two times. If he failed to satisfy the legislators, he might be impeached.[104]

Among the most enthusiastic supporters of the bill were members of Beijing's municipal congress. Hurt badly by the Chen Xitong scandal, such parliamentarians were concerned about the need to supervise government finances and cadres' involvement in business. In March 1996, 34 deputies led by Yang Zhounan tabled a motion to second early passage of the law and to set up a special NPC Supervision Committee. As a group of parliamentarians led by Chen Lunfen put it: "We must institutionalise and legalise powers that the constitution has vested in different levels of the NPC to supervise the government."[105] Party and government cadres, however, were putting up obstacles — and the bill was postponed until late 1998 or 1999.

Through the mid-1990s, much progress was made by the NPC in boosting supervision over government units, the procuratorate and the courts. The legislature increased the number of "supervisory" trips made by deputies to the ministries and provinces to check on administrative probity and the degree to which laws were being implemented. In 1995, five groups of key NPC investigation teams were sent to the provinces, cities and districts to investigate the issues of fake goods and agricultural production.[106]

Since 1991, congresses in 29 provinces and major cities had undertaken periodic assessment of officials, beginning with the police and judicial organs. For example, in 1994, various levels of congresses inspected and gave assessments to 66 courts, 16 procuratorates, 55 PSBs and two judicial bureaus. Deputies made more than 11,000 suggestions. As a result, an undisclosed number of party and government cadres who had broken laws and regulations were subject to investigations and "a group of major cases was handled properly".[107]

Zhejiang, which had a long association with Qiao, was an exemplary province in this respect. In 1995, 80 per cent of its cadres were assessed by parliamentarians. The appraisals were carried out through seminars, visits, reports and group discussions. Then governor Wan Xueyuan said although the assessment had been focused on exposing shortcomings in the administration, it had helped improve performance. He urged cadres to face criticisms and suggestions with a "correct attitude".[108]

In tens of provinces and cities, the institution of officials making periodic reports to the congresses had been established by the mid-1990s. The system began in relatively backward Shaanxi in 1994. Within the first year, 14 heads of departments, including the chief of the provincial court, Jiao Longting, had appeared before the local legislature to take questions from deputies. Jiao reportedly accepted criticism that the local judiciary had not done enough in civil, economic and administrative cases. The Shantou SEZ pioneered the reporting system in Guangdong. Not only the mayor and vice-mayors but a whole range of officials including heads of departments and bureaus gave annual accounts of their work to the local congresses. Deputies had the right to dismiss those guilty of under-performance.[109]

According to Guizhou deputy Meng Liankun, the assessment process confirmed the "master-servant relationship" between citizens and cadres. "It has boosted the consciousness of staff of executive and judicial departments to be servants of the people and to accept supervision," he said. However, by the mid-1990s, only relatively junior cadres had been fired or demoted by fault-finding deputies. Almost all of them served in the police and judicial establishment. For example, in Guangdong, 578 police officers working for the public security and court systems were penalised or dismissed in 1995 and 1996.[110]

Parliamentary cut and thrust

At both the yearly plenary session of the NPC and the bi-monthly Standing Committee sessions, an element of cut and thrust had become evident between deputies and ministers. State Council cadres had a rude shock at the 1996 NPC when deputies blasted the government for "worshipping" the West in buying equipment and other goods for infrastructure projects. "Individual high-level leaders do not have faith in Chinese-made mechanical and electrical products," said some deputies. "They have a superstitious belief in foreign goods." They cited the machinery for the Three Gorges project. Chi Haibin of the Finance and Economics Committee said more than 50 per cent of the electrical equipment needed for the Ninth Five-Year Plan period was imported. "As a result, Chinese factories producing such goods are working under capacity," he said.[111]

A few deputies were bold enough to indirectly assail then premier Li Peng. According to Lu Yansun, vice-head of the Finance and Economics Committee, the Huaneng Corporation carried the stipulation that it would only use foreign-made machinery for electricity generation and some other business. Huaneng was reported to have close connections with the premier and his relatives. "We should not let foreign companies dump their merchandise in China," he said. Lu, a former vice-minister of machinery, said at least 40 per cent of equipment used should be Chinese-made. "The technological level of some Chinese products is not low," he claimed.[112]

The NPC increased the frequency of voting to show its disapproval of policies. At the same March 1996 session, a surprisingly high number of members declined to endorse the reports submitted by the Supreme People's Procuratorate and the Supreme People's Court. The reason was mass dissatisfaction with the work these two law-and-order organs were doing to fight crime and corruption. Thirty per cent of the 2,682 deputies either voted against or reserved judgment on the annual work report of the procuratorate while negative votes and abstentions for the court report accounted for 20 per cent of the total. "The anti-corruption campaign needs to be intensified because the people are very concerned about this problem," said a deputy from Heilongjiang province.[113]

At a remarkable Standing Committee meeting called in the summer of 1996 to examine the economic situation in the first half-year, several firebrands staged a virtual revolt. They expressed dissatisfaction with then state planning minister Chen Jinhua's characterisation of the economy as "good at the macro-level and problematic at the micro-level". A number of parliamentarians including Wang Guangying and Li Yining demanded to see the "real figures", adding that the government only showed the deputies — and the public — the good picture. Wang jokingly said he and his colleagues would not leak the "real figures" if they were later provided by the central authorities.[114]

At another Standing Committee session, Tian Jiyun took issue with the party leadership's decision to wage a long-term Strike Hard Campaign against hard-core criminals. He said Beijing's instructions to police and court authorities to "speed up arrests and incrimination procedures" went against the principle of the rule of law, in particular recently passed legislation on criminal procedures. "This is the 1990s and the country must be run according to the law," he said in mid-1996.[115]

The power of the ballot box

After the debacle of the governorship elections in Guizhou and Zhejiang provinces in the early 1990s, the party's Organisation Department took extra care to ensure that party power would not be truncated. It pulled out the stops to prevent party-nominated candidates from being snubbed by the deputies. However, congresses in many provinces had extended the range of elections from governors to heads of departments. At the municipal level, most heads of bureaus had to be approved by the local congresses.

At the plenary NPC session in 1995, Jiang's choice for vice-premiers — Jiang Chunyun and Wu Bangguo — met with an unexpected setback. Thirty-six per cent of the 2,752 delegates refused to endorse Jiang, and 21 per cent snubbed Wu. The circumstances of the embarrassment merited close study. In the course of the administration's lobbying, the two candidates were given a big build-up. Li Peng said in his motion that Wu was "resolute in politics and liberated in thoughts" and that he had a "high consciousness about reform and innovation". Jiang was said to be "capable of carrying out the party line" and "familiar with agriculture management".[116]

However, the deputies seemed to have had enough of cliches. Speaking in private, several NPC members said Li failed to explain the need for two more vice-premiers. Wu was denigrated as a lacklustre technocrat who had got where he was because of his Shanghai Faction credentials. Jiang was hurt by his age, lack of formal college education, and undistinguished achievements. He was also tainted by allegations that his relatives were involved in questionable business deals. During the provincial poll for the replacement of Jiang as Shandong party secretary a month earlier, Beijing had also encountered opposition. The Organisation Department was barely able to convince Shandong deputies to endorse its nominee, vice-governor Li Chunting. "A number of Shandong deputies favoured more liberal candidates including the party boss of Qingdao, Yu Zhengsheng," a Shandong source said.[117]

During elections for positions ranging from municipal department heads to provincial governors, local-level people's congresses had, since the early 1990s, rejected dozens of party-nominated candidates. "Many party cadres have criticised the NPC for 'usurping power' by throwing out candidates favoured by Beijing," an NPC source said. "However, in more and more provinces and cities, party and government heads are beginning to curry favour with parliamentarians through elaborate lobbying rituals."[118]

In Shenzhen, the positions of all bureau chiefs and heads of administrative districts had to be confirmed by the local congress. These were in addition to the mayor, the five vice-mayors, and the heads of the courts and procuratorates. SEZ deputies were also active in putting forward candidates: the signatures of only 20 parliamentarians were sufficient for nominating purposes. In the mid-1990s, three senior members of the Shenzhen administration were non-Communist Party members. They were Health Department chief, Liu Jiashen; vice-head of the Futian District, Wu Jingtian; and his counterpart in the Lowu District, Pang Yanming.[119]

The Future of the NPC
People power and the NPC

By early 1996, Qiao Shi had mapped out concrete plans for enhanced NPC empowerment. He said in internal meetings that the NPC Standing Committee must be given more powers to scrutinise the administration. These included shaping important policies and a big say on the budget and other money bills. "The NPC should have more supervisory powers," he said in an internal meeting that year. "This can be accomplished through lawmaking, ensuring that laws are observed, and in some instances, impeaching officials."[120]

Qiao also wanted to change the method for selecting NPC members — in particular Standing Committee members — in order to make the body more professional. For example, more legal experts and politically neutral professionals should become full-time legislators. Qiao was trying to do away with the time-honoured practice of assigning retired cadres to the NPC and the CPPCC. He said NPC work was not "second-line operations" worthy only of retired cadres.[121]

The then NPC chief indicated in early 1996 that more attention would be given to lowering the average age of Standing Committee members. Tian Jiyun underscored the need for rejuvenation. "If you look at NPC members from the back of a meeting room, you see a lot of bald heads," he said. "There should be more black ones."[122] Qiao and Tian even suggested that while the NPC could recruit elite cadres from the party and government, legislative cadres could also be posted to party and government units.[123]

To justify what his opponents said was a power grab, Tian invoked a kind of people power with Chinese characteristics. The former vice-premier said the NPC had the people's backing for a much larger supervisory role. He indicated that the people were increasingly dissatisfied with the phenomena of cadres "using their words to replace the law; using their powers to suppress the law; and violating the laws even as they are implementing them". "The people have pinned high hopes on the NPC," he said. "They have raised higher demands on the NPC to exercise its supervisory powers."[124]

Perhaps to better play the people-power card, an *NPC Daily* was planned for 1997. "The idea is that new ideas for legislation should first be floated in a newspaper to get public feedback," a Chinese source said. "More people should get involved in the legislative and supervision process." NPC cadres hoped it would be more lively than papers already run by the CPPCC and various democratic parties.[125] Other symbols of a new-look NPC included a proposed NPC building and a four-star hotel for parliamentarians. As of mid-1998, however, only the hotel had been built.

Constraints on NPC power

The constraints on parliamentary power became apparent by the mid-1990s. Firstly, the degree of popular participation would be restrained. The Revised Election and Organisation Laws, passed in early 1995, made it clear direct elections to people's congresses would not be held beyond the county level. Thus, balloting at the municipal, provincial and national level would still be in the form of indirect elections where party authorities had a high degree of control. Qiao Shi Xiaoyang, vice-head of the NPC's Legislative Affairs Commission, said this state of affairs matched "the present national conditions of China". "Democracy requires a gradual process," he claimed.[126]

The NPC's bid for power inevitably pitted it against holders of vested interests such as party and State Council bureaucrats. They tried to limit the yearly increase of the budget and staff of the NPC — to four per cent in some instances. This led to Qiao Shi protesting in an internal meeting: "We shall determine the staff according to actual needs."[127] The NPC's effort to start a newspaper became bogged down. Cadres who opposed it said ordinary people should not be allowed to meddle in such a solemn affair as law-making.

Leading the campaign to limit NPC power were Jiang Zemin and Li Peng. This was despite the frequency with which they told foreign dignatories the NPC system was one manifestation of the "superiority" of Chinese-style democracy. For Jiang, there would be no watering down of the principle of CCP supremacy. In response to Qiao's oft-repeated assertion that all cadres must obey the constitution and the law, Jiang implied in a leftist speech in December 1995 that the party was above the constitution and the law. "The party leads the people to establish the constitution and the law," he said. "It also leads the people to implement the constitution and the law."[128] Or as the NPC's own Qiao Xiaoyang put it: "Strengthening the function of the NPC did not mean lessening the role of the party." He added that the leadership position of the CCP "is formed by history and is written into the Constitution".[129]

By early 1998, the future role of the NPC remained uncertain with the replacement of Qiao Shi by Li Peng as parliamentary chief (see Chapter 7). Deputies were certain, however, that Li could not turn back the clock. World attention on the Chinese parliament would also be boosted following the election of 36 Hong Kong-based legislators to the NPC. While none of the Hong Kong deputies was expected to "make trouble" for the leadership, they would at least ensure that the tradition of law-making and legislative supervision begun by Wan Li and Qiao would be continued.[130]

DEMOCRATIC EXPERIMENTS

Liberalisation at the Grassroots

Grassroots democracy, particularly in the form of the direct election of village administrators, had made some headway by the mid-1990s. Beijing's goal was to make "village self-rule" universal by the end of the century. This was to be accomplished through the election of village administrative committees by universal suffrage. While at least in theory, village Communist Party cells still retained ultimate authority, such committees had jurisdiction over matters including education, transport, rural enterprises, security and poverty relief. They carried out some national and provincial policies relating to tax and grain collection as well as family planning. Moreover, the committees periodically called villagers' assemblies to discuss major issues of governance.[131]

The experiment of village self-government was handled by the Ministry of Civil Affairs (MCA), which counted a number of liberals among its leadership. Beginning in the late 1980s, they visited countries, including the US, to study grassroots elections. Aid was received from the Ford Foundation and other American charitable organisations. Foreign experts who worked with MCA cadres were impressed by their liberal outlook and diligence. "MCA officials are not unduly troubled by the fact that the help they are getting from the US and other countries might play into the hands of their enemies, in particular leftists," said a foreign specialist on Chinese democracy.[132]

As former vice-minister of civil affairs Yan Mingfu indicated, village self-rule was decided upon by the central authorities in 1981, even though the Law of the Organisation of Village Committees was not enacted until 1987. Yan, who used to be close to Zhao Ziyang, was confident that all villages would have self-elected committees by 2000. The Village Organisation Law provided for the direct election of the committee chairman, vice-chairmen and other executives. China had more than one million village committees and more than 4.5 million rural cadres. Balloting had, by mid-1995, taken place in 600,000 villages in all but four provinces.

As Yan put it, elections had incorporated elements of free competition, including secret ballots and open campaigns by candidates. "Villages in some places call it *haixuan* [ocean-style election]," Yan said. "This means the voters choose the candidates just as fisherfolk go to the sea to get pearls." *Haixuan* essentially meant that candidates were no longer seconded by superior party or government units. They were nominated by villagers.[133]

Surveying new elections conducted in early 1997, senior MCA cadre Wang Zhenyao pointed out the following improvements: the near-universality of *haixuan*; growing popularity of secret ballots; and more lively campaigns such as candidates giving policy speeches. Poll results confirmed the gradually declining influence of party elements in the grassroots. An unofficial estimate pointed out that around 40 per cent of elected village executives were non-party members, even though about half of these were subsequently "invited" to join the CCP. The clout of the so-called three *zongs* — *zongzu*, or clans, *zongjiao*, or religion, and *zongpai*, local factions — was expanding. Moreover, those with economic means, largely private entrepreneurs, were gaining more seats (see Chapter 5).[134]

This limited exercise of popular suffrage even had a spill-over effect on the way village-level party secretaries were being appointed. The universal practice had been that party organisation bureaus at the county level would pick the heads of village-level party cells. However, reports from Henan and other provinces in the mid-1990s indicated that after becoming accustomed to electing the heads of village committees, a sizeable number of rural people wanted a say in choosing the party chiefs.[135]

Wang Zhenyao was upbeat that grassroots-level experiments would spread nationwide. He disclosed that Deng Xiaoping had in April 1987 — the heyday of liberalisation — expressed the conviction the country would be ready to hold its first "national election" within half a century. "The crux of the matter is that if we can conduct direct elections properly at the grassroots level and build an excellent foundation, development at higher levels will progress more quickly," he said. Wang confessed that he had encountered many officials who were shocked by the elections. "They tell me 'peasants can't do democracy. That's impossible,'" Wang said. "But peasants can manage democracy very well."[136]

How Powerful are the Elected Village Committees?

By the mid-1990s, a kind of grassroots-level democracy with Chinese characteristics had attracted worldwide attention. In March 1997, the respected Carter Center in Atlanta, US, sent a delegation to observe the polls in Fujian and Hebei. Wang Zhenyao said he had invited former US president Jimmy Carter and other US experts to have a look and "to advise us on ways the village elections could be improved".[137]

What potentials did village-level elections really have? Could they be Mao's "spark that lit up the entire plain"? It would not be fair to say that the village committees were merely "flower vases", or public-relations gimmicks. They had aroused the democratic enthusiasm of peasants. In rich coastal areas, villagers who had gone to work elsewhere were known to have taken charter flights to go home to vote. In some strictly administrative matters, the effect of democracy was palpable. For example, when cadres in Malianzhuang Village in the Laixi District of Shandong wanted to buy a car, the village committee called a villagers' assembly to discuss the issue. The motion was turned down, and the money was used to buy irrigation machinery.[138]

However, the leadership had no immediate plans to try out elections at higher levels of administration, for example, in counties or towns (see Chapter 7). After all, if the electoral districts became larger, the CCP had to lift the ban on the formation of political parties to enable meaningful politicking such as the canvassing of voters to take place. As some Chinese observers pointed out, the Politburo's "first choice" was still party committees running the show everywhere. It became evident in the early 1990s, however, that grassroots CCP committees were crumbling — and being replaced by "evil forces" such as triads, underground churches, and *zongpai* ["feudal clans"] organisations. The party leadership had neither the moral authority, organisational ability, nor money to revive the party cells. It saw in directly elected village committees a "lesser evil" or a buffer that could keep the anti-party forces at bay.[139]

Moreover, the system of self-rule amounted to a safety valve against the dissatisfaction of the peasants — a channel for the government to explain policy and for farmers to express their views. Take, for example, the counties of Renshou and Pengshan in Sichuan. In 1993, both were hit by excessive government taxes and other levies, including forced contributions of labour to build highways. Renshou erupted into a now-famous series of confrontations between peasants and police. Yet according to Chinese Academy of Social Sciences rural expert Bai Gang, the problem was solved smoothly at Pengshan thanks to the go-between role played by village committees.[140]

In mid-1998, there were reports that several MCA officials who had played a big role in soliciting foreign support for the village polls were demoted for being "too friendly" with overseas, particularly US, institutions. Indeed, the CCP leadership never seemed to have given up the ideal of tight party control even at the lowest levels of government. For Politburo stalwart Hu Jintao, the key to "regime building", as the Chinese put it, was still boosting rural party leadership. "Secretaries of party organisations at the county level should play a key role in building rural grassroots branches," he said at a conference on rural party networks. In a speech on "boosting grassroots-level regimes", Jiang Chunyun made it clear the "encouragement of grassroots enthusiasm" must go hand in hand with party dominance. "We must ensure that the broad masses of peasants become their own masters and we must fully arouse their enthusiasm," the then vice-premier said in late 1995. "While grasping well the task of self-rule by the villagers, we must uphold the leadership of the party and strengthen party leadership."[141]

Watered-down Version of Experts Running the Country

Forward-looking officials such as Yan Mingfu and Wang Zhenyao were at the liberal end of the political spectrum. At the other end was the neo-conservative leadership. For them, "democratic participation" manifested itself in the familiar theory of "experts running the country". The party was willing to go some way to listen to the views outside its fenced walls; yet this would involve a small group of elite, mostly academics and professionals willing to offer "constructive opinions". The latter did not have the power to influence the course of events. The experts' source of authority was their patrons, not the people or a particular sector of society.

On occasions, even conservative leaders revived the old goal of tapping "outside experts" to render decision-making scientific and democratic. Li

Peng expressed such an ideal while talking to 800 experts from the Chinese Academy of Science and the Chinese Academy of Engineering who met in Beijing in mid-1996 to discuss economic, social and technological development. Senior cadres made the pledge that the intellectuals' views would go all the way to the top. "The party and government hope the academics can offer suggestions on scientific and technological policy to benefit economic and social development," said Li. "This will help render macro-level decision-making more scientific and democratic."[142]

Beginning in the mid-1990s, experts were periodically called to speak in seminars in Zhongnanhai for cadres including Politburo members. The most popular topics included high technology, the information revolution, and the law. Most party and government departments expanded their think tanks and policy research units. Several official polling and opinion-survey units were started to gauge public reaction to policies. In many instances, non-party and non-government scholars were tapped. For example, one quasi-private research outfit sponsored by units including the Ministry of State Security and the State Council General Office carried out periodic surveys on issues such as the Chinese attitude towards the US or the level of popular acceptance of reform measures. Organs that were particularly eager to collect public and expert opinion included the Central Committee General Office, the Ministry of Public Security and other intelligence operations.[143]

However, there was no national, coordinated plan to consult expert or outside-the-party views. This was often left to the initiative of local leaders. The way in which advice was offered — and taken — also varied. For example, it could be at a series of ad hoc meetings where experts expressed their views and leaders selectively took down their suggestions. In 1995, Shanghai Mayor Xu Kuangdi started occasional seminars by intellectuals on legal and scientific topics. Shanghai cadres joked that this was a far cry from the "salons" of an earlier era, when physicians talked about common diseases that befell first- or second-generation revolutionaries.[144]

Leaders in the coastal provinces and cities proved most receptive to new ideas. The Guangdong Policy Science Research Association was set up in 1996 to give advice to the local government. It comprised social scientists from party and government research units including the provincial Social and Economic Development Research Centre. The semi-official China News Service said the outfit would provide the leadership with "research and analysis in the drafting of major policies". Vice-party secretary of Guangdong, Huang Huahua, hailed this as a "new era" in policy-making. The same year,

Shenzhen broke new ground by forming a hi-tech think tank that enlisted overseas-Chinese expertise. The Shenzhen Technology Advisory Committee boasted 40 mainland experts and six Hong Kong scientists.[145]

The consultation bug also hit the relatively backward county of Rui'an in Zhejiang Province. In 1996, experts there took part in the formation of an "education development strategy" as well as the Ninth Five-Year Plan. The local administration had relied heavily on an old boys' network: the 1,000-odd specialists and academics who were graduates of the elite Rui'an High School. Spread out in various posts throughout the country, these experts offered their views to their home-county government.[146]

The CPPCC and Multi-party Cooperation

Despite the often energetic leadership of Li Ruihuan, the Chinese People's Political Consultative Conference (CPPCC or *zhengxie*) and the eight *minzhudangpai* (democratic parties) largely failed to live up to their billing as the locomotive for promoting scientific and democratic decision-making. This was despite some notable developments in the mid-1990s. These included suggestions that the CPPCC be rendered into the Upper House of China's unique parliamentary system. Other *zhengxie* liberals suggested that it become a channel and platform for members of the "new class" of private entrepreneurs and professionals to air their views.

In theory, of course, the consultation process with the *zhengxie* and the democratic parties was broadened and deepened. Beginning in the early 1990s, the CCP leadership briefed members of democratic parties before major policies or documents were announced. These included the Ninth Five-Year Plan and special papers relating to minority peoples and foreign policy. In the mid-1990s, senior cadres including vice-premiers often briefed the CPPCC Standing Committee on the latest government policies.[147]

In 1995, the party Central Committee issued a document on "inserting political consultation [with democratic parties] into the decision-making process of the party and government". Party and government cadres had to abide by the theory of the so-called "three ahead-ofs". This meant that democratic party members must be consulted before the party leadership made a particular decision, before the NPC endorsed it, and before the government carried it out.[148]

Progress was also made in promoting non-party politicians to relatively senior positions. In 1996, the Organisation Department and the

United Front Department issued a paper entitled "On further improving the propagation and selection of non-party cadres for leading positions in the government and judicial organs". By the mid-1990s, senior non-CCP politicians included then vice-president Rong Yiren, nine NPC vice-chairmen, and 23 cadres with the rank of vice-minister in the State Council, the Supreme People's Court and the Supreme People's Procuratorate. A major role for the Organisation and United Front Departments in 1997 was grooming non-party politicians for senior positions at the 15th Party Congress.[149]

It was obvious, however, that there was a lack of qualified *minzhu-dangpai* candidates. "Capable people who are in the right age range and who are willing to toe the CCP line are not easy to find," said a political observer. In fact, the eight democratic parties had been daunted by failure to recruit qualified members. The pathetic state of ageism was illustrated when the eight parties went about choosing a new slate of leaders in 1997. Seeing the dearth of new blood, the CCP leadership gave them a special dispensation: the party chairman could be up to 80 years of age, and vice-chairmen, 75.[150]

As CPPCC deputy and Hainan University law professor Wang Junyan put it, it would be a "long way off" before the CPPCC or *minzhudangpai* could exercise a real supervisory role. Wang cited the case of a provincial CPPCC member who was criticised by the authorities for "disrupting the work of the government". All that the enthusiastic fellow had done was put forward some dissenting views at a local *zhengxie* meeting. Another deputy, Zhang Wenshou, said CPPCC work had yet to go beyond the relatively passive phase of "raising views". "We have to explore new means of exercising supervision over the government," he said.[151]

Beijing's lack of tolerance with difference of opinions was evident from the extreme caution with which it viewed the very small minority of fire-brand *zhengxie* and *minzhudangpai* members. In internal meetings, these avant-garde deputies had raised sensitive matters including the revision of the verdict of the June 4 massacre. There was no possibility, however, that these liberals could broadcast their views in the national media, let alone persuade the leadership to consider them.[152]

In 1996, Li Ruihuan again affirmed the overall leadership of the CCP over *zhengxie* work. "CCP leadership is the fundamental guarantee that the CPPCC can play a correct role in Chinese political life," said the Politburo Standing Committee member. "In China, the democratic parties, people's groups and representatives of various sectors who join the CPPCC all accept the leadership of the CCP," he added. "They are neither opposition parties nor opposition factions." The ideal of the *zhengxie* becoming an "Upper House of the Chinese parliament" seemed a long way off.[153]

FAILURE OF THE SYSTEM:
THE ANTI-GRAFT CAMPAIGNS

The anti-graft campaigns, which had been conducted on a perennial basis throughout Jiang Zemin's tenure, were a good gauge of the efficiency of the party and government apparatus. Jiang was no more successful than Deng in eradicating the scourge, which had become endemic to the system. This illustrated above all the leadership's failure to erect *zhidu* ("systems and institutions") to promote administrative probity. As the president liked to say about the perils of corruption: "The easiest way to conquer a castle is from within."[154] Only through mechanisms of checks and balances could the cancerous cells be rooted out. Yet these institutions would militate against one-party dictatorship, which Jiang and company were adamant in preserving.

"Personalised Nature" of the Clean
Government Crusade

The fight against corruption was hampered by the contradiction between two approaches to clean government. One was Jiang Zemin's quasi-Maoist argument that the key was to churn out thousand upon thousand of Lei Fengs. This would be accomplished through using ideological and political indoctrination to "change the worldview of cadres". As he put it in the 15th Party Congress report, cadres must be trained to "self-consciously resist decadent thoughts". The other approach was building *zhidu*, including more effective mechanisms to supervise party and government units. Jiang's basically *weixinzhuyi* ("subjectivist") game plan held sway.

CCP cadres at both the central and local levels persisted with Jiang's ideal of fighting corruption through building up "spiritual civilisation" or the cultivation of virtues. In a throwback to the rule of personality, the public was continuously fed propaganda that the world would be spotless if all cadres were converted into modern-day Bao Qingtians. This was a reference to legendary Judge Bao, the Song Dynasty legend who struck fear into the heart of big and small officials alike.[155]

Hu Fuguo, the Party Secretary of Shanxi Province, was lauded in the media as a Hu Qingtian, or a latter-day Judge Bao. Speaking on the question of clean government, Hu said: "Whether the people have a decent living depends on the quality of the 'standard-bearers'. If the cadres take the lead and set a good example, the masses will follow suit." On fighting corruption, Hu indicated that "the flag of anti-corruption must be raised high and raised often".[156]

Even such a fierce cadre as Zhu Rongji looked at the graft phenomenon from a "personalised" perspective. In a mid-1996 speech on the art of governance, the then vice-premier attributed corruption to "the air of philistinism in cadres and in society". Zhu put his emphasis on rectifying their "corrupted morals and lack of shame". On another occasion, Zhu looked upon fighting corruption as a personal duel or a fight among gladiators. "Take out 100 coffins for corrupt officials," he said. "Prepare one for me too, in case I get gunned down in the battle."[157]

Half-hearted Efforts to Build Up Institutions

However, this was not to say that the "institutionalists" did not put in some efforts. Cadres at the Central Commission for Disciplinary Inspection (CCDI) admitted at a conference in 1996 that the "construction of a good party style and clean government" had to be anchored upon the establishment of institutions and laws. The commission vowed to build up laws and regulations governing the prosecution, investigation, handling of graft cases, as well as the overall management of cadres. CCDI officials said there would be a clean break from the rule of personality.[158]

In mid-1996, the Personnel Ministry passed a set of regulations on *huibi* ("avoidance") in an attempt to minimise bureaucratic conflict of interests. The rules were in theory as vigorous as those in the Western world. Thus, couples and close relatives were discouraged from working in the same department. Cadres related to each other could not be employed in the same unit if one of them was the supervisor of the other — or if they were in departments covering finance, auditing, personnel, or supervision. Moreover, a civil servant must not handle a file or case of his relative if it involved auditing and taxation, personnel assessment or authorisation to travel abroad. "Relatives" included cousins, nephews and nieces as well as in-laws.[159]

Apart from political considerations such as fighting empire building, cadres were subjected to regular rotation beginning in the early 1990s as part of a new series of measures against graft. This practice was carried out even within individual provinces. In Shanxi, for example, the heads of police units, procuratorates, and courts in the province's 100-odd counties would be rotated once every five years.[160]

New graft-fighting units were sprouting like bamboo shoots in the spring. More than 1,700 Anti-corruption Bureaus had, by mid-1996, been set up within 29 provincial, 289 district- and municipal-level, and 1,400 grassroots procuratorates. Mechanisms for citizen participation in the graft-busting campaign were introduced. In 1995, the Supervision Ministry received about 1.5 million complaints about official misdemeanours, including 280,000 cases of corruption. This compared with 168,000 counts of whistle blowing of all categories in 1989. There were 2,929 centres or hotlines where citizens could file reports or complaints. As a result of such zeal, the government was, in the mid-1990s, able to recover at least three billion yuan a year.[161]

Why the Scourge cannot be Cured

In theory, anti-corruption work should have proven successful with the mobilisation of so many resources. As then procurator-general Zhang Siqing boasted in 1996: "With the determination of the *zhongyang* and various levels of CCP leadership — as well as the support of the broad masses — there is no case that cannot be cracked."[162] But the reality was much different.

Many liberal graft-crusaders cited British thinker Lord Acton's adage — "absolute power corrupts absolutely" — when they explained why the scourge had lasted so long. As CPPCC member Zhang Deqin put it, wherever there was power, there must be effective supervision. "Power that is not supervised will necessarily corrupt," he said. "Ineffective supervision is the same as letting power overflow."[163]

The problem lay in the fact that the "*zhongyang* and various levels of CCP leadership" had monopolised the function of graft-busting. Anti-corruption organs such as the Central Commission for Disciplinary Inspection, the Supervision Ministry and the Anti-Corruption Bureaus were under the solid control of top party organs such as the Politburo or the Commission on Political and Legal Affairs (CPLA). In a retrogression from Zhao Ziyang's ideal of the separation of party and government, most of the functions and staff of the CCDI and the Supervision Ministry were combined in the mid-1990s.[164]

It was well known that the Politburo Standing Committee and the CPLA were hardly unbiased when investigating senior cadres; and the handling of such cases was heavily politicised. For example, cadres on the upswing were seldom penalised for their own misdeeds or those of their cronies and children. Graft-takers who ended up in jail were invariably those whose political fortunes had taken a nosedive. As illustrated by the case of Chen Xitong (see following section), corrupt cadres could also save their necks if they could threaten the authorities with implicating those still in power.

So far as popular opinion went, not enough senior cadres or "princelings" were nabbed to show the graft-fighters were working without fear or favour. In the period under survey, only two sons of senior officials were brought to justice. They were Zhou Beifang, an executive with the Capital Iron and Steel Works (Shougang), and Chen Xiaotong, the businessman son of Chen Xitong. The two were heavily involved in the so-called scandal of the Beijing mafia. Zhou was given a suspended death sentence in 1996, and Chen, a 12-year jail term in 1997. During the *yanda* ("Strike Hard") campaign of the mid-1990s, however, thousands of plebeian criminals were summarily shot for relatively minor offences such as manufacturing pornographic videos or even stealing a few dozen head of cattle.[165]

There was widespread suspicion that Zhou and Chen were caught only because their fathers, Zhou Guanwu and Chen Xitong, had become politically exposed. In Zhou's case, there was the added consideration that Zhou senior only got into trouble after it became apparent in early 1995 that his principal patron, Deng Xiaoping, was no longer fit to offer protection to the Zhou family.[166]

The Politicisation of Graft-busting
The case of Chen Xitong

It was politics more than graft that was responsible for the disgrace of Chen Xitong, the first Politburo member to be removed from office for alleged "economic crimes". The fall of Chen and his Beijing colleagues was mainly due to the rivalry between Chen's Beijing Faction and Jiang's Shanghai Faction. Yet it was also related to the declining health of a clutch of elders including Deng Xiaoping, Peng Zhen, and Wan Li. All three had, to different extents, been supporters of the Beijing Faction.[167]

Soon after the enormity of the "black-money scandal" was exposed by the supposed suicide of Chen crony, vice mayor Wang Baosen in April 1995, it was expected that Chen would be given a heavy jail term at least. Given the fact that Wang had allegedly "swallowed" 18.3 billion yuan, the nature and profundity of "godfather Chen's" guilt could be gauged. The size of Chen's money-making machine could also be estimated by the fact that both his son, Chen Xiaotong, and his girlfriends had made — and squandered — huge fortunes.

At the Fifth Plenum of the Central Committee in September 1995, the leadership vowed to leave no stone unturned in tracking down his alleged crimes. Indeed, even among higher levels, calls for Chen's blood — or head — were vehement at that time. About two months before the plenum, Beijing set up a multi-departmental investigation team to crack the Chen case. It consisted of elite agents from the police, the Ministry of State Security, the procuratorate, the Ministry of Supervision, and the Central Commission for Disciplinary Inspection.[168]

However, it soon became apparent that Chen would be spared a harsh fate. The reasons: having spent four decades in the capital, he knew too many secrets. According to an informed source, the Chen investigation was practically suspended by October 1995. The wily ex-Beijing boss laid all the blame on senior officials, including at least one Politburo-level cadre and his relatives. "Every time that it threatens to expose the complicity of a top official, the investigation comes to a halt on orders from on high," the source said. In a talk to members of the eight "democratic parties" in late 1996, President Jiang hinted that the Chen affair would be down-played. He reportedly said that while Chen had siphoned off huge sums, the bulk of the funds were wasted in ill-considered projects rather than used for his personal enjoyment.[169] The soft-pedalling on the Chen case was disturbing in view of the fact that by *yanda* standards, a criminal could be caught, investigated, found guilty and executed in a matter of a week or so.

Western diplomats believed Jiang had decided to "spare" Chen for various reasons. Apart from the residual pressure from Chen patrons among the party elders, the president needed the support of the politicians Chen had threatened to expose for his campaign for a new term as party General Secretary. Moreover, the dozen-odd senior Beijing cadres who were affiliates of the Chen Xitong–Wang Baosen cabal would be allowed to keep their Mandarin caps — or to retire gracefully. In late 1996, Zhang Baifa, the vice-mayor who was considered close to Chen, volunteered to Western reporters in Beijing that Chen would only be responsible for "dereliction of duty" — he would not even be charged with a criminal offence.

It was not until July 1998 — more than three years after his detention — that the case of Chen was closed, in a manner of speaking. Following a brief secret trial, the putative dragonhead of the "Beijing mafia" was sentenced by the Beijing Higher People's Court to 16 years in jail for taking graft and dereliction of duty. However, the denouement posed many intriguing questions. Chen was mainly accused of misappropriating 22 gifts worth 555,000 yuan and maintaining two luxurious villas for his own enjoyment. The prosecution said he led a "corrupt and decadent life" and followed illegal procedures in approving certain property deals. But few details were given.[170]

This murky account contrasted with widely circulated reports that numerous cadres and their offspring, as well as well-connected businessmen in and out of China, were involved. Yet, apart from Wang Baosen, no names were cited by the prosecutors. It was assumed that no further action would be taken against Chen's "accomplices" and that the former Politburo member would be given "medical parole" after a few years. While President Jiang would like to take the credit for nabbing a "big tiger", his handling of the Chen case showed that, to use Mao's words, politics was still largely in command.

The case of regional fat cat Ouyang De

The kid-gloves treatment accorded Ouyang De, one of Guangdong's most corrupt cadres since 1949, also cast doubt on Beijing's commitment to eradicating graft. Misgivings about a cover-up had arisen even before the case went to the Guangdong courts in February 1996.

The former vice-chairman of the Guangdong People's Congress was only charged with corruptly taking 500,000 yuan. This was despite the fact that internal documents and the Guangdong media referred to Ouyang, the long-term honcho of prosperous Dongguan County, as head of an "empire of black money". It was well known that under Ouyang's influence, at least eight of his children and relatives were able to migrate to Hong Kong. And in their capacity as "Hong Kong businessmen", these "emperor's relatives" became multi-millionaires soon after returning home.[171]

After much suspense, the official media reported in July 1996 that

Ouyang had been given a 15-year jail term, a slap on the wrist by *yanda* standards. The special treatment vouchsafed Ouyang also appeared jarring given reports in mid-1995 that the administration of Jiang Zemin would implicate tens of Ouyang's colleagues. These reports had it that the "nab-the-tigers" campaign would be used to teach a lesson to Guangdong, long considered lax in toeing the *zhongyang* line. In late 1995, however, the Hong Kong and Taiwan press said that the Jiang leadership had struck a deal with the nation's richest province: in return for Guangdong's support for some unspecified political goals, only Ouyang would be implicated and his head would not roll.[172]

The Ouyang denouement highlighted suspicions that Beijing had a double standard regarding politically sensitive suspects, particularly those with good connections. The same phenomenon repeated itself in Shenzhen. Soon after the Chen Xitong affair, State Council secretary-general Luo Gan led a delegation to check on graft cases in Shenzhen. Soon afterwards, a number of senior officials, including two former vice-mayors, were put under investigation. A year later, however, the political wind had shifted and no "tiger" was netted in the booming SEZ.[173]

Beijing was in the mid-1990s awash with rumours that a number of corrupt officials in Shandong and Shanghai — the two regions on best terms with the *zhongyang* — had eluded the long arm of the law because of their political clout. In November 1997, a Hong Kong newspaper ran an article implicating the wife of a senior Shandong cadre. Beijing denied the story. Yet the innuendo remained. Few ordinary people trusted the official versions: the impression of the body politic having been poisoned with greed and graft was strong in everybody's mind.[174]

TEST CASE: THE RURAL QUAGMIRE

A New Social Contract?

By the mid-1990s, farmers were looking for a new deal, a virtual new social contract with the state. As was the case with the USSR, the industrialisation of China has since 1949 been made possible by the exploitation of the countryside, the so-called "scissors' differentials" between the world-market value of Chinese farm produce and the actual amount state procurers pay the peasants. Beijing's inability to improve the economic standards and political status of farmers was a potent indictment of the system.

As theoretician-futurologist Wang Shan made clear in his 1995 best-seller *Looking at China with a Third Eye*, Mao got away with the rural problem by virtually confining the peasants to their fields. Under the strict residency-permit system, farmers were destined to spend their entire lives on the farm. However, this had changed radically by the early 1990s. While, owing to reasons including a high illiteracy rate, conditions in many remote villages remained backward, the bulk of peasants had been hooked up, to some extent, to the global village through television and a much faster rate of news dissemination from the coast. More important, the "stay-put" residency requirement had been broken down as a "floating population" of up to 150 million hit the towns in search of work.[175]

The vast inequality under which they were living was becoming obvious to peasants. In the mid-1990s, the average per capita income in the countryside was 1,550 yuan, against 3,855 yuan in the cities. Moreover, city dwellers were entitled to a world of amenities and hidden subsidies in the areas of housing and education. While the purchase price of produce had been raised almost annually, peasants were suffering from what they perceived as more injustices. For example, large numbers of farmers were asked to forsake lucrative commercial pursuits for grain and wheat. And there were those never-ending taxes and forced contributions of money and labour.[176]

A 1995 survey of 10 villages outside the city of Yancheng in well-off Jiangsu found 8.5 per cent of the 4,200 households lived below the poverty line. Some 249 families had become destitute in the past two years. The survey identified several causes of poverty at a time of relative prosperity. One main reason was the disappearance of government subsidies. It now cost more than 10,000 yuan to send a village kid to college. Hospital costs were exorbitant. Fees for "not observing" the one-child-per-family stricture had gone up to 15,000 per child.[177]

In an interview, Wang suggested that the state took the initiative in renegotiating a social contract with the farmers. "All sectors — the party and government elite, businessmen and city-folk — must come together to negotiate a new deal with the peasants," he said. "The new deal should cover the purchase price of grain as well as the rural sector's rightful share of the state budget and other resources."[178]

A New Deal for the Peasantry?

There was no sign the CCP leadership would be proactive on the rural front. There were only pledges galore of a new dispensation. "All leaders must make increasing agricultural production a priority and they must devote their energy to agriculture work," said a *People's Daily* editorial in January 1996. "We have to give rural workers more initiative and lessen their financial burden."[179]

Politburo member Wen Jiabao, a relative liberal among the younger generation of leaders, called on all cadres to give peasants a fair shake. "We must fully safeguard the economic interests of farmers and fully guarantee their democratic rights," he said in a lecture at the Central Party School. "We must manage well the relationship between 'give' and 'take'," he added. "We must give more and take less." Wen suggested increasing government investment and decreasing tax and other levies. Moreover, farmers must have a right to choose their own production line and ways of production.[180]

The central government decreed in late 1996 that taxes and other burdens on farmers must not exceed five per cent of the latter's net income the previous year.[181] In potential hot spots, local cadres were given explicit orders to pacify peasants in terms of cancelling or lowering tariffs — or giving out emergency relief funds. The experience of the 1993 peasant riots in Renshou, Sichuan, over excessive taxation (see earlier section) was made into a "negative teaching material" for rural cadres nationwide.

After the People's Armed Police had reimposed order, the Renshou government tried to win back the goodwill of the people. There was a thorough reshuffle of the county administration. More than 100 cadres, including the party secretary and head of the county, were dismissed. The new party boss, Zhuo Mingan, tried to endear himself to the locals by visiting "troublemakers" including Zhang De'an, who had played a role in organising the 1993 protests. There was a clampdown on corruption. Official media claimed the clean government campaign was so successful that the 60 upmarket restaurants in the county seat, where banquets used to be held on a nightly basis, suffered a drastic decrease in business. After 1993, no cadre was allowed to postpone settlement of restaurant bills.[182]

The new Renshou party committee examined 66 official documents which had been the basis for the imposition of around 115 levies. Most of the taxes were either abolished or reduced. The new administration reached an agreement with farmers: tax collected each year must not exceed five per cent of the per capita income of farmers earned the year before. In 1994, the average tax burden was 21.59 yuan, just 4.42 per cent of the per capita income of 1993.[183] However, this local-level dispensation did not add up to a national policy for improving the economic prospects of farmers — or to place them in a more exalted station in the polity. As in other arenas, the Jiang administration relied on piecemeal solutions to pacify the disgruntled.

The *Shangfang* as Safety Valve

It is ironic that at a time when Internet cafes were sprouting in the cities, the leadership had to rely on the archaic institution of *shangfang*, a shorthand for peasants going to Beijing or the provincial capital to lodge a petition or to air grievances with the authorities. Like the Judge Bao syndrome, *shangfang* was one aspect of the "personalisation of justice". It was essentially unchanged from dynastic times, when peasants who were victims of injustice trekked hundreds, sometimes, thousands of kilometres to hand a petition to the governor or the emperor. In Beijing, it was not unusual to see crowds swarming outside the *shangfang* or *xinfang* ("hand-in-a-letter") departments of the party Central Committee, the State Council and the NPC. Some were destitute, illiterate peasants from thousands of kilometres away who slept in the subways or parks.

In the mid-1990s, the number of *shangfang* cases kept going up. An internal survey of 12 such cases of villagers in a Hebei county revealed that eight of them were in protest against the "state of financial chaos" of local cadres. The document decried cadres who used their authority to start private enterprises. There were also instances of officials levying excessive taxes to finance prestige projects.[184]

More disturbing were cases of lower-level officials punishing peasants who dared take their case to the *zhongyang*. In March 1995, four cadres in Xulou Village near the city of Dengzhou, Henan, were executed for torturing to death peasant petitioner Chen Zhongshun. From 1992 to 1994, Chen had sent repeated petitions against the village administration for illegal land use, excessive levies, and indiscriminate attacks on farmers. He was murdered in July 1994. According to the China News Service, "after the incident, the central leadership gave instructions to relevant departments to handle the case in good time".[185]

In a national meeting on *shangfang* in late 1995, Zhu Rongji said it was a "major component" of party and government work. "Showing concern for, and laying emphasis on *xinfang* work, is a superior tradition and style of the party," he said. "The older generation of proletariat revolutionaries established a model on this aspect." Zhu also said that *xinfang* was a "channel, bridge and beltway" for senior cadres to maintain contact with the masses. It was beneficial for "raising the masses' consciousness in taking part in, and discussing, politics; promoting clean government; and pushing forward the construction of socialist democracy and the legal system".[186]

Attempted Resuscitation of Grassroots Cells

Typical of the "two-fisted" approach of the Jiang administration, Beijing tried to promote ideological control over the countryside even as it pledged to raise the economic well-being of peasants. Beijing believed that if all the rural party cells were in a "combat-ready" condition, the challenge of dissatisfied peasants could be defused.

In 1996, 470,000 full-time functionaries were sent by the organisation departments of different levels to the countryside to resuscitate party cells and conduct ideological training. A year earlier, 450,000 cadres were assigned the same chores. Some 99.7 per cent of all counties had set up "responsibility systems" to ensure that party units were not overrun by the forces of corruption and bourgeois liberalisation.[187]

Internal party documents admitted that at least one-third of the nation's 3.4 million grassroots cells had ceased to be "fortresses of Marxism-Leninism". A major reason was that instead of being good shepherds, party functionaries spent most of their time in either feudalistic or business pursuits. The New China News Agency said in a 1996 report that at an initial phase — presumably the 1994–1995 period — the party had concentrated on rectifying "weak and lax" party cells in 50,000 villages. Eighty per cent of these units had since been given a clean bill of health. In 1996, the rectification campaign targeted 90,000 villages. In the half year ending in the spring that year, 210,000 village and township cadres and 660,000 rural party secretaries and village committee chiefs received special training in party ideology and administration.[188]

There were many reasons for party cells losing their Marxist purity. An early 1990s study commissioned by the late vice-president Wang Zhen decried the rise of the influence of religion, clans, triads as well as private businesses.[189] By the mid-1990s, the commercialisation of party cells had become more serious, with the result that private businessmen in many villages had usurped the leadership role of the apparatchiks (see Chapter 6).

An equally important challenge to party authority was posed by the mushrooming underground church. For example, an internal paper showed the attractiveness of the illegal faith in remote, landlocked Guizhou Province. There was an upsurge of Christian zeal in the backwater district of Bizhe. In 1991, 151 cadres joined the church. The number rose to more than 2,000 by early 1995. Some of the churches were run by self-proclaimed Christian denominations and offshoots such as the Life Society, which was broken up by police. According to the internal report, even party members who joined the CCP in the 1950s had turned to the church. One destitute veteran said he was attracted to Christianity because church workers took good care of him whereas party functionaries were only concerned with making money. The situation in Bizhe drew the attention not just of security units but the Organisation Department.[190]

Farmers as an Interest Group

As of mid-1998, the fear of party elders such as Wan Li of the appearance of latter-day Qin Dynasty peasant rebels Chen Sheng and Wu Guang had not been realised. Thanks partly to the pacification campaigns as well as strengthening of the ranks of the PAP, the countryside seemed quiet. However, the roots of discontent were growing just under the surface.

More significantly, there were signs of farmers emerging as an interest group if not a "new class". This manifested itself not just in fighting for higher produce prices and lower taxation but also adequate income from real estate and the overall commercialisation of rural resources. Along the coast, there were hundreds of instances of confrontation between farmers on the one hand, and cadres and developers on the other. The former complained that corrupt officials had acted in collusion with Chinese, Hong Kong or foreign property companies to cheat them of their land — and that they had been given compensation that was a mere fraction of the market price.

In September 1995, 200 peasants in the township of Chashan in Dongguan, Guangdong, surrounded the local government offices to demand compensation. Earlier in the year, Chashan cadres sold a 70,000 square metre plot to a Hong Kong company at the bargain price of 1.1 million yuan. The per square metre price was several times below what locals had to pay when they bought land to build their own houses. Peasants suspected the cadres had received a huge kickback. The protesters were dispersed by police. By early 1998, such cases were reported even in inland provinces. For example, 3,000 farmers clashed with PAP officers over the same issue of land rights in the village of Xinzhuang near Zhengzhou, Henan Province.[191]

A related cause of discontent was the phenomenon of *zaigeng* — or the recommitment of "commercialised" rural plots to farming. At the height of the property boom in 1992–1994, thousand upon thousand of hectares of prime agricultural land along the coast were re-zoned for industrial or residential purposes. The land had been flattened and covered with gravel. In the wake of the austerity programme, the relevant areas were supposed to revert to agricultural use. However, farmers who had originally worked there had already taken up other economic activities. Conflicts arose when local governments obliged them to return to their old profession. The farmers refused to cooperate unless they were given hefty compensation or grants. In protest, they planted trees on the land instead of growing rice and vegetables. However, this was seen by the cadres as a waste of land. In the mid-1990s, confrontation with the authorities led to frequent demonstrations in the boom towns of the Pearl River Estuary.[192]

Thanks to the residual strength of its control apparatus, the CCP had yet to face a large-scale challenge in the countryside. After all, the peasants were not organised. Yet instances of disorder and rioting were multiplying. Farmers seemed more ready to stand up to the authorities, as graphically shown by the early 1998 case of villagers near the new airport of Nanjing staging protests at the runway to demonstrate against noise pollution. Moreover, rural folk who had sold their plots or lost their livelihoods kept spilling into the cities. In troublespots such as Xinjiang and Tibet, ethnic tensions were exacerbated by peasants' rebellion against corrupt rural cadres. By 1998, the prospect of the Jiang administration forging a new social contract with 700 million farmers remained slim.

TEST CASE: WORKERS AS A "NEW CLASS"
Rising Labour Unrest

The tragedy — and changing "class nature" of the proletariat — was apparent from the plight of thousands of laid-off workers in Wuhan in October 1997. These destitute labourers and their families paid out more than one million yuan to the Hubei Changrui Technology Company for a shot at a supposedly hi-tech agri-business: rearing ants for medical purposes. Each would-be entrepreneur was asked to put down a deposit of 550 yuan for 100-odd super-ants, which they could rear at home. The promise was that the ants would enable each household to earn at least 1,000 yuan a month. The company soon closed and the culprits escaped with the deposits. Protests by workers were fruitless. The years 1997 and 1998 also saw a spate of desperate and quasi-terrorist actions by workers, which ranged from self-immolation to bombing buses.[193]

It was also clear that workers had lost their status as the "vanguard of the proletariat" and "masters of the nation" (see Chapter 7). Official statistics from 1995 to 1997 put the urban unemployment rate at around three per cent. However, this was based on the five to six million jobless registered with local administrations. The unofficial rate was estimated to be at least three times higher. Moreover, most estimates did not include the "hidden unemployed" — the estimated 28 million "superfluous workers" in SOEs. While still on the payroll, these excess hands had little to do in factories and merely received a cost-of-living subsidy of around 200 yuan a month. An internal State Planning Commission study said if SOEs were allowed to raise the rate of "unburdening their excess labourers on society" by one percentage point, the ranks of the jobless would swell by one million.[194]

While top cadres repeatedly issued statements backing the workers, it was clear that the leadership considered the unemployed a burden — and that "class antagonism" was developing between labourers and the party elite. After all, senior officials and media commentators kept blaming workers for their nostalgic attachment to the iron rice bowl. An editorial published in the *Workers' Daily* after a spate of labour riots in mid-1997 was typical. "Some laid-off workers are sitting idle, waiting for the government to give them jobs," said the paper. "They do not think of going into the market to find jobs for themselves."[195]

That the labour problem could be a time bomb was evident from the bout of seemingly endless troubles from the estimated 500,000 unemployed in Sichuan in the second half of 1997. In July, nearly 10,000 workers marched through the streets of the medium-sized city of Mianyang after they lost their jobs with the closure of several textile factories. Police detained nine ringleaders. They also slapped an arrest warrant on dissident intellectual Li Bifeng, who fed the news to a Hong Kong human rights organisation. A month later, 500 retired workers staged a rally outside the government offices of Dujiangyan in southwest Sichuan to protest dwindling pension cheques. That week, more than 1,000 idle pedicab drivers clashed with police in the same city. Then came the face-off between 300 workers from the No. 2 Radio Factory and riot police in the city of Zigong in early October. The firm had not paid salaries for nearly a year.[196] Similar incidents occurred throughout 1998.

The "Class Interests" of Workers

Despite condemnations by institutions including the International Labour Organisation and Hong Kong trade unions, Beijing maintained its ban on unofficial labour units. The goal was obvious: preventing workers from crystallising and venting their new "class sentiments". However, a record number of wild-cat unions — or at least ad hoc worker committees — had sprung up in factories that were laying off or mistreating workers. It would be wrong to exaggerate their importance. Most of these outfits were dissolved as soon as workers achieved their basic goals. And no national network of underground unions was formed. However, never since 1949 had workers been so aware about the loss of their vested interests — and about the need to press their demands more effectively.

China did not publish statistics of strikes. However, official figures for workplace-related arbitration cases were illustrative. In 1995, labour departments handled 33,000 arbitration cases, up 73 per cent from the year before. The figure for cases that went through the courts was 28,000 in the same year. The New China News Agency said that "workers' consciousness about — and ability towards — protecting their rights through the law has been raised tremendously".[197]

Most of the arbitration and industrial action was about money. However, there were indications of a new-found awareness about the dignity of workers. Take the numerous instances of employees protesting over the inhumane treatment they had received from SOE managers and the bosses of joint ventures. For obvious reasons, official media only exposed cases involving "ugly" Taiwan bosses or Hong Kong factory owners. Such was the case of a Taiwan executive in a hat-making factory in Zhongshan, Guangdong. In late 1995, three workers were caught for allegedly stealing raw hide from the factory to make shoes for themselves. As punishment, the Taiwan manager forced them to kneel for two hours in the presence of everybody. They were also slapped with shoes. The same day, about 600 workers went on strike and 200 of them later resigned.[198]

There was anecdotal evidence of disgruntled workers going after political aims. Most disturbing to the authorities was the fact that some labour activists did not just want money. They also broached taboo subjects such as reform. Take the case of protests by about 300 workers in Shenyang in mid-1995. The demonstrators came mainly from a bicycle and a machine-tool factory, both of which were working below half capacity. According to local sources quoted by a Western news agency, slogans chanted by workers included: "We want rice"; "We want freedom; we don't have freedom of speech"; "We want democracy; we have no autonomy". They were dispersed by police.[199]

Piecemeal Solutions Versus Institutional Improvement

Unsurprisingly, the Jiang administration failed to come up with thorough-going solutions to crack the labour problem (see previous section). Apart from exhortations from President Jiang and his colleagues that "the long-term future of labourers is good", the leadership came up with a barrage of upbeat statistics and forecasts to reassure the dispossessed. Beijing authorities announced that the official unemployment rate would not be allowed to go beyond 3.2 per cent in 1996. They added that by 2000, the ranks of the jobless should not exceed 8.5 million, meaning the unemployment rate would remain within four per cent.[200]

As in the case of farmers, the top leadership slapped a "responsibility system" on regional administrations to ensure that workers were pacified. Each city was told to start a re-employment programme — and the assessment of local cadres was partly based on how many jobless workers could be placed. Employment agencies were set up in all municipalities. In 1996, Guangzhou established a re-employment foundation with a fund base of 25 million yuan. For the Ninth Five-Year Plan period, Shanghai expressed confidence it could keep the jobless rate below three per cent if economic growth could be maintained at 11 per cent a year. In the first half of the 1990s, 660,000 laid-off workers in Shanghai found new jobs thanks to re-employment schemes. Indeed, when nominating Shanghai cadres such as Huang Ju and Xu Kuangdi for promotion, the Jiang Office cited the lack of labour troubles in the metropolis.[201]

In relatively poor Anhui, the "responsibility system" swung into high gear after the 15th Party Congress. In November 1997, 20 top provincial officials led by Governor Hui Liangyu convened a meeting to ensure that 380,000 laid-off workers would not make trouble in the run-up to the Spring Festival. Cadres at every level were asked to secure more funds for "re-employment engineering", social welfare and emergency payouts. By late 1997, more than 232 million yuan had been raised for these purposes.[202]

Optimistic figures on the job front suffused the newspapers in the mid-1990s, even though some statistics were dubious. On October 29, 1996, the New China News Agency reported that "some 171,000" laid-off workers in Hebei had been re-employed by enterprises "thanks to the efforts of the local government". They included 70,000 who found newly created jobs in the services sector. The figure for re-employment, however, was lowered to 40,000 in an NCNA dispatch on the same province two days later.[203]

By late 1997, the administration had mustered two "institutional means" to attack the problem. One was the grandiose-sounding scheme to "change workers into bosses". In the wake of the green light for *gufenhua* ("shareholding") companies given at the 15th Party Congress, labourers in loss-making factories were asked to dole out 5,000 yuan or so to "buy back" the concerns and to become the owners. However, economists and cadres alike decried major problems of unfairness and inefficiency. Many workers were forced to borrow money to refloat factories that had poor track records. According to economist Wu Jinglian, managers in some SOEs refused to let workers return to work unless they had paid their "shares". But after theoretically becoming the "new bosses", decision-making still stayed with the original cadre-managers.[204]

More solid results seemed to have been attained in putting together a rudimentary social insurance system. In Beijing, 17,064 work units had, by late 1996, set up unemployment insurance. In the 10 years up to 1996, social welfare units in the capital allocated more than 20 million yuan in relief funding for jobless workers in addition to the regular dole payments. The same year, Shanghai forked out more than 100 million yuan in unemployment benefits to 95 per cent of the jobless in the metropolis.[205] Even with aid from the United Nations and other international agencies, however, it would take many years to build up a social security net for the millions of workers.

CONCLUSION: PITFALLS OF AN OUTDATED POLITICAL SYSTEM

Time to Act? Or to Procrastinate?

A book published in mid-1997 by former Zhao Ziyang aide Wu Guoguang on political reform in the late 1980s has thrown new light on the genesis of liberalisation begun by the ousted party chief. In their discussions in 1986 and 1987, members of Zhao's short-lived Central Committee Research Office on Political Reform underscored the urgency of action: they must seize the day when conditions were favourable. Then Politburo Standing Committee member Hu Qili urged speed. "Now that we have such a liberal leader as [Deng] Xiaoping, we should tackle the problems immediately," he told a meeting of the group in October 1986. "We should pursue it in a big way. If not now, when?"[206]

Hu was displaying uncanny prescience. The situation would change radically with the removal of Hu Yaobang in January 1987, the June 4 massacre — and the hardline turn in Deng's thoughts. However, Hu was also right in terms of the broader socio-political perspective of the country.

As noted by political observers such as Wang Shan, the late 1980s were a time when radical reform could still be accomplished from the top and with minimal social cost. At that time, China had still not been divided into distinct social sectors or strata, each vying to maximise its political and economic benefits. The cadres at both the central and regional level — as well as the intelligentsia and populace — were more prepared to take orders from the *zhongyang*. Officials also had a relatively free hand to pursue reform because they were less tied to interest groupings such as quasi-state business corporations. With the rapid stratification of Chinese society in the 1990s, reform became a much more cumbersome proposition (see following section).

In the mid-1990s, the Jiang administration was vacillating between two mind-sets: on the one hand, a desperate need to bring about change; on the other, finding excuses to stay put for fear of taking risks. The crisis mentality was described with urgency by Jiang aide and the Vice-Chief of Propaganda, Xu Guangchun. In an internal briefing on the challenges besetting the administration, he said: "The coming one to two years will be an extraordinarily severe, critical stage. It will be the most difficult period in the party's history."[207] Li Ruihuan, deemed a liberal in the Politburo, also felt the urgency to make a move. "We must face the problems squarely and not try to evade them," he said in a discussion on "mass politics". "We must overcome shortcomings instead of trying to cover them up. We must dispel the resentment among the people, rather than neglecting it."[208]

However, even Li offered an apology for not revving up the engine. He claimed that for historical reasons, China could only move forward slowly on democratisation. "The Chinese economy is not very well developed, and science and culture are relatively backward," he said in June 1996. "China experienced more than 2,000 years of feudalistic society and still lacks a democratic tradition." Li said the construction of democracy would be a "relatively long process" because it required the solutions of "questions that demand deep research and careful treatment".[209]

During his visit to the US in late 1997, Jiang reiterated Deng's pledge that "without democracy, there will be no modernisation". Yet, as he pointed out during the joint presidential press conference with Bill Clinton in Washington, stability was still the over-riding concern. "Without social and political stability, such a populous country as China cannot enjoy the prospect of reform and the open-door policy," Jiang said. The president used the familiar pretext of China having its distinct culture and history to justify foot-dragging on democratisation.[210]

The Importance of Institutions
Personalities versus institutions

Since radically overhauling the CCP would seem impractical, most moderate and liberal cadres were aiming to make changes within the system through building up *zhidu* ("systems and institutions"). As Hu Qili said in late 1986: "It is very rare to have such a brilliant leader as Xiaoping; yet we must have well-established *zhidu*. Otherwise, it won't do." By *zhidu* Hu meant ways and means to rein in abuses and other excessive acts of the party leadership.[211]

Other members of Zhao Ziyang's political reform unit pointed out it could be futile to rely on the "saintliness" and "high cognitive level" of leaders. As then vice-premier Tian Jiyun put it: "The issue is how to check and balance the powers of the *zhongyang*. Chairman Mao was the greatest genius and yet he made such a terrible mistake." Zhao Ziyang agreed. "It will not do to count on the knowledge [of leaders]," he said. "Chairman Mao was not reliable in his old age. Who can put a restraint on himself?"[212]

Calls for institutional building resumed in the mid-1990s after a break of a few years. Writing in a mid-1995 issue of the *China Market Economy Paper*, professor at the Central Party School, Wang Jue, said the phenomenon of corruption and maladministration exposed by the "Beijing mafia" required a detailed study of institutions. "We must put forward concrete requirements and strategies with regard to institutions, mechanism [of governance] and systems," he wrote. Wang, a noted liberal, quoted Deng Xiaoping on the imperative of good *zhidu*: "If the system is good, bad people can't have their way. However, good people can't do good deeds in a bad system; they may even go bad."[213]

Hu Qili suggested two plans of action at pivotal meetings called by Zhao Ziyang's political reform research office. One was the separation of party and government. "We must settle the question of whether the party runs everything," he said. "According to the existing system, the party is in charge of all things. Only God can do all things well."[214] The goal of the separation of party and government was played up at the 13th Party Congress, but as we saw earlier, under Jiang, the momentum swung back to depositing all powers in the *zhongyang*.

Hu also mentioned NPC empowerment. He strongly hinted his support, even though he also deplored the fact that NPC members were not up to scratch. "As to the existing deputies, they won't do in terms of quality, aptitude and structure," he said. "There are more than 3,000 people. They can be engaged in a mass meeting but it is difficult for them to make decisions."[215]

The labour crisis and institution-building

On a micro level, the urgency of *zhidu*-building also became apparent in view of the growing ineffectiveness of ministries and departments. A case in point was the labour crisis. By the mid-1990s, three bodies had a role in handling disgruntled workers: the Labour Ministry, the All-China Federation of Trade Unions (ACFTU), and the Ministry of Civil Affairs, which was mainly involved in giving aid.

The ineptness of these departments was demonstrated by the number of fire-fighting units that central organs had to send to the provinces. In mid-1996, the NPC Standing Committee dispatched special inspection teams to seven provinces to check on labour abuses. The areas ranged from rich Guangdong and Jiangsu to poor Gansu and Inner Mongolia. "The main problems we want to investigate include child-labour abuses, delayed wage payments and deducted wage payments," one official said.[216] Both central government units and provincial authorities also engaged in ad hoc operations to pacify destitute or laid-off workers.

The ACFTU, which had more than 600,000 branches and 110 million members nationwide, was a Stalinist institution which had less and less legitimacy as the embodiment of the voice of workers. The 1992 Trade Union Law rendered "private" labour organisations illegal. A sizeable number of dissidents detained in the early to mid-1990s were trade unionists. They included such well-known names as the Beijing-based Yuan Hongbin, Zhou Guoqiang and Liu Nianchun. Liu Jingsheng, who tried to organise the Free Labour Union of China in 1992, was sentenced to 15 years in jail in 1994.[217]

There were problems galore with the *zhidu* of the ACFTU. Its president, Wei Jianxing, was also head of the party's Central Commission for Disciplinary Inspection — and party chief of the Beijing municipality from 1995 to 1997. In many factories, the party secretary or director doubled as the leader of the local ACFTU unit. To lessen industrial disputes, local ACFTU units were discouraged from playing an active role. By late 1997, many were reduced to the role of giving alms to workers. This was despite the fact that the union representatives were theoretically authorised to take part in management.[218]

Maoist Movements and the Myth of Sisyphus

By the mid-1990s, there were signs the Jiang leadership was embracing Maoist-style statecraft, in particular the *qunzhong yundong* ("mass movement"). From one perspective, a *qunzhong yundong* is an effort to "lay siege to" or "overwhelm" problems through mass mobilisation instead of tackling them through working out fundamental, systemic solutions. The classic example was the Cultural Revolution, when Mao egged the Red Guards on to attack feudalism and bureaucratism.

The Jiang administration was also taking the cue from the Great Helmsman. Take for instance, the issue of clean government. In early 1997, party disciplinary authorities in Linzhang County, Hebei Province, called on the masses to report instances of cadres pigging out at huge banquets. Citizens were encouraged to gate-crash lavish parties or to report them to anti-corruption authorities. The reward was 1,000 yuan. The goal was to save 10 million yuan that year.[219] Ordinary urban residents were encouraged to blow the whistle on corrupt officials through hotlines and other facilities (see previous section).

The authorities even called on the people to expose the extra-budgetary expenditure of local governments. In 1995, regional authorities spent more than 300 billion yuan on projects that were not provided for by the official budget (see also Chapter 5). A mid-1996 meeting organised by units including the Finance Ministry and the People's Bank of China concluded that "the broad masses must be fully mobilised to report on irregularities regarding the management and use of extra-budgetary funds".[220]

Another fallout of the decay or lack of *zhidu* were Sisyphean frustrations. With inadequate institutions and little political will, the CCP administration found itself treading over the same ground year after year. Frequently cited examples were campaigns to fight graft and to trim the bureaucracy: they had been staged almost every year since the mid-1980s. The same was true for cracking down on crime — and even tackling the floods. The Strike Hard Movement against felony had by the early 1990s become an annual event. Surveying the return of catastrophic flooding almost every summer, *Outlook Weekly* called on the administration to think of long-term solutions as well as ways to render decision-making scientific.[221]

The New Classes and the Question of Legitimacy

Part of the problem with the Jiang administration was that there were too many engineers and self-styled technocrats — and too few social scientists — running the country. A sociologist would have recognised that whether the party liked it or not, a new class structure had emerged. The façade of classlessness had been shattered by the emergence of socio-economic sectors including cadres, state entrepreneurs, private entrepreneurs, workers, farmers, the army, "intellectuals", and the nascent middle class.[222]

As in the case of countries East or West, each group wanted to maximise its economic — and to a large extent — political advantages. It was for this reason that leftists issued repeated war-cries over the fact that the inchoate "new class" would do battle with Communist orthodoxy by challenging the "dictatorship of the proletariat". As one leftist "10,000-character petition" put it: "Once we have decided to revive elements of the private economy, it is unavoidable and natural for the capitalist and petite-bourgeois classes to reappear." The tract added that the private bosses "had already raised their independent political demands".[223] Or as a Chinese Academy of Social Sciences sociologist put it, the party must renegotiate with the emerging classes new formulae for the division of the economic and political pie. A new social contract needed to be drawn up.

Put in the East-Asiatic context, the concept of the social contract is similar to the theory of the mandate of heaven, or legitimacy of govern-ance. Rebel literary theorists Liu Zaifu and Li Zhehou were criticised for declaring their "farewell to the revolution". Yet even neo-conservatives had to accept the fact that nearly 50 years after the Red Army swarmed into the cities, the party's so-called "revolutionary legitimacy" was in tatters. After the dissolution of the Soviet bloc, Deng recognised that only through raising the standard of living of the people could the CCP justify its ruling status. It was perhaps for this reason that practically every time they met foreign delegations, leaders such as Jiang Zemin and Li Peng harped on the apparent success of the leadership in "feeding and clothing 1.2 billion people".[224]

Yet as Hong Kong's maverick publisher Jimmy Lai put it in his "open letter to Li Peng" of 1994, the then premier would be terribly deluded if he were to congratulate himself on being the head of a farm of 1.2 billion pigs. By 1998, six years after Deng's tour of southern China, Chinese society had become heterogeneous, class-fractured, and intolerant of a party whose second nature seemed to be complacency.

There might be a considerable time lapse between the appearance of the "new classes" and the development of democracy. As American Sinologist David Zweig put it in mid-1997, the middle class, including pri-vate entrepreneurs, remained very small. So long as the government could ensure that SOEs remained the backbone of the economy, it would be quite a while before owners of private capital became a major force in the economy and in politics.[225] And as much as the nation's disparate classes were dissatisfied with their share of economic resources, they were not galvanised into active opposition against the CCP. In the long term, how-ever, the party would find that it had to share power to survive, or else the other social sectors would succeed in forcing it to give up its monopoly on power. Real democracy would start at that point.

4 More Power to the People's Liberation Army

INTRODUCTION: THE PLA'S GROWING CLOUT

The three million-strong People's Liberation Army (PLA) wielded a clout far larger than their numbers would suggest. At a time of declining central authority and increasing centrifugalism, the armed forces — including the People's Armed Police (PAP) — were in many instances the only institution that the party leadership could call upon to impose national unity and cohesiveness. A heavy army presence was essential to suppressing "splittist" forces in Tibet and Xinjiang. More and more frequently, PAP units were summoned to quell social unrest sparked by labour troubles.

For President Jiang Zemin and his faction, the importance of the defence forces grew larger in the run-up to and after Deng Xiaoping's death. After all, one key factor that enabled Jiang to elbow aside potential challengers such as former National People's Congress (NPC) chief Qiao Shi was his solid control over the top brass.

In return for the support of the generals, Jiang, the civilian chairman of the Central Military Commission (CMC), had to keep giving them goodies: not just a bigger budget but a larger say in foreign and domestic policy. The Taiwan crisis of 1995 and 1996 — which is examined in some detail in this chapter — illustrated the extent to which the top brass had augmented their authority. Military officers also threw their weight around in economic policy, including the distribution of resources.

At least in Western eyes, the growing muscle of the PLA became doubly dangerous because of the lack of progress in real defence modernisation. Given Jiang's stress on the troops' "absolute loyalty" to the party, the goal of depoliticising the army and converting it into a government department subject to checks and balances was put on the back-burner. Efforts to promote military transparency and accountability proceeded at a snail's pace.

The PLA, therefore, remained in many ways a quasi-Maoist institution on the eve of the 21st century. Which might be just as well for Jiang, who wanted the men in uniform to spearhead the crusade to promote "spiritual civilisation" and nationalism. The armed forces would also be at the forefront of the campaign to urge all Chinese to profess loyalty to the "party centre with Comrade Zemin as its core". As its weapons — and political clout — became more formidable, however, the PLA remained a source of concern both in and out of China. Liberal intellectuals and cadres regarded the troops as a millstone round the neck of reform. And China's Asia-Pacific neighbours conjured up the spectre of a new "China Threat".[1]

This chapter will examine major developments in the PLA and PAP from 1994 to 1998. There are sections on Jiang's relationship with the generals; the roots of factional intrigue; the scourge of corruption and other disciplinary problems; the campaign to build an "elite force"; and near-futile efforts by liberal cadres to make the armed forces accountable to the legislature. The careers of fast-rising officers such as General Zhang Wannian will also be examined. The concluding section will explore the prospects for reforming military institutions in the next decade.

DOCTRINAL REGRESSION

Deng's Short-lived Liberalisation of Army Doctrine

At least in his "liberal phase", Deng Xiaoping made major contributions to the liberalisation of army theory and practice. Firstly, Deng put a curb to the PLA's status as a "state within a state". Tentative but important steps were taken to give the defence forces a rightful place in the polity. Deng also made attempts to depoliticise the army. Secondly, the late patriarch ensured that the PLA would become a force for peace. Given the improvement in the international environment, military needs would be subsumed under civilian ones — and the PLA would serve the overall goal of economic construction.

Deng realised that to reduce the special privileges of the army, efforts must be made to wean it away from the party. Initial steps were taken towards the separation of party and army — as well as the army's gradual *guojiahua* ("civilianisation" or coming under state control) — in the early 1980s. For example, the State Central Military Commission was created. There were suggestions that the Ministry of Defence (MOD) be given more powers. Sponsors of the *guojiahua* of the army reportedly included former state president Yang Shangkun and ousted party chief Zhao Ziyang, who was briefly First Vice-Chairman of the party CMC.[2]

The patriarch realised that an unnecessarily strong army could be an impediment to economic construction, which Deng deemed to be the "core" work of the country. Steps taken by the master reformer included a truncation of the PLA budget, which fell steadily throughout the 1980s. More importantly, Deng put forward the theory of "army construction in peace times". In his words, "the army must subserve the overall [national] situation of economic construction". Or as Jiang Zemin put it: "The modernisation construction of the PLA must be based on the economic construction of the country. The army must obey and provide service to the overall situation of economic development."[3]

Deng could pull off the trick partly because of his prestige in the PLA. Tiananmen Square, however, intervened. After June 1989, Deng himself reversed many of his earlier doctrines. He boosted the party's "absolute leadership over the gun" by almost immediately appointing Jiang Zemin as CMC chief. His previous teachings on army modernisation were superseded by one central concern: to ensure that the PLA become a "steel Great Wall" that would protect the party against the onslaughts of hostile foreign forces.

Reversal of Deng's Ideals after Tiananmen Square

The reversal of Deng's ideals was reinforced by Jiang Zemin and his military aides. For example, rising star General Zhang Wannian indicated in 1996 that it was a "plot" of the West to try to drive a wedge between party and army by promoting the latter's *guojiahua*. "Western countries think the PLA is their stumbling block to overthrowing the CCP and socialism," Zhang wrote in the theoretical journal *Qiushi* ("Seeking Truth") in mid-1996. "That's why they go out of their way to advocate the depoliticisation of the PLA and severing its links with the party. They want to sow the seed to poison the relations between party and army."[4]

To a degree that Deng himself would not approve, the PLA would be intimately involved in civilian affairs. The Maoist principle of "unity of peace-time and war-time needs" was again raised. As CMC vice-chairman Chi Haotian put it while revising Mao's adage: "If the army and the people are united, they can beat everybody under the sun." The army was needed to ensure the success of reform and development. Thus Long March veteran General Liu Huaqing urged the PLA to further increase its capabilities to safeguard the achievement of China's trans-century development goals. "The PLA will pledge its firm support to reforms," he said. "It will play an active part in the country's economic construction."[5]

Most importantly, the PLA shifted its orientation from "peaceful construction" to preparation for "localised", or regional war. This was despite claims by the 1995 White Paper on Defence that "the precept guiding China's army-building has been strategically shifted from always being prepared against a massive war of invasion to peace-time construction". General Zhang Wannian reiterated in the mid-1990s that the PLA's new goal was "localised warfare under conditions of high technology".[6]

In his first public appearance after clinching the CMC vice-chairmanship in late 1995, General Zhang pointed out that the PLA must "adapt itself to the requirements for preparing for military struggle in the new era". He said he was pleased to see a "revolutionary high tide" sweeping the officers and rank and file. This consisted in confidence in "winning a localised warfare under [conditions of] modern technology, in particular, high technology".[7]

The top brass saw in the slogan "a hi-tech people's war" as having expressed to the full the synthesis of modern warfare and Mao-era concern for indoctrination. Chief of Staff General Fu Quanyou, normally regarded as a wizard in defence modernisation, called this "the strategic thinking of fighting a people's warfare with modern equipment". "The basic law that the decisive factor in warfare is the human and not the material factor has not changed," he said. "The major role that militiamen, the reserves corps and the broad masses play in warfare has not changed." General Zhang Wannian concurred. After masterminding the war games off the Taiwan coast in October 1995, he called it "a manifestation of the characteristics of people's warfare under modern conditions".[8]

THE POLITICISATION OF THE ARMY
Enhanced Indoctrination

The renewed emphasis on politics in the mid-1990s was as important a development as the aggrandisement of weaponry. Early in 1995, Jiang laid down five conditions to evaluate the army: "We must pass muster politically; be strong in combat; have a superior work style; have strong discipline; and have guaranteed effectiveness." This so-called "five-point edict" was later enshrined as a mantra-like doctrine. Of the five, at least three had to do with political rectitude. As the president put it on another occasion: "We must put ideological and political construction in the foremost position; we must encourage a correct political direction for the army."[9]

It was a mark of changing times that Jiang had gone against the injunctions of Deng — and the pitfalls in contemporary history. One of the crimes cited against former chief political commissar General Yang Baibing, who fell from grace in late 1992, was his excessive politicisation of the PLA. Yang's most famous caper was his having boasted about the army providing "an imperial escort" for the patriarch's reforms announced during his tour of southern China in early 1992.[10]

Under Jiang's aegis, an ideological campaign that went one better than Yang Baibing's was waged. Its intensity recalled a quintessentially leftist, Maoist *qunzhong yundong*, or mass movement. According to General Chi Haotian, "ideological and political work should be put at the top of the army's agenda". In a 1996 speech, he urged the army to follow the party leadership with Jiang as its core, and to "ensure smooth implementation of both political and military orders". It was left to Zhang Wannian, however, to flesh out the details. While touring the northeast, where PLA personnel had a tradition of independence, General Zhang urged that "recurrent, continual" work be done to promote loyalty. "Cadres must pay more attention to grasping well recurrent and continual ideological work as well as management," he said in 1996.[11]

Officers of military regions and districts were asked to adopt a hands-on approach to ideological and political work (IPW). In an early 1996 commentary, the *Liberation Army Daily* urged PLA cadres to be personally involved in indoctrination work. "Some units merely pay lip service to ideological and political education, and such work has not been done well," the paper said. It called upon commissars and other IPW specialists to conduct surveys on the ideological levels of officers; they should also organise classes and make investigations and assessments.[12]

To do a better job at promoting loyalty, Jiang in 1995 authorised what was known as "sealed-off management" for PLA personnel. During intensive IPW sessions, soldiers were not allowed to leave the barracks except for brief vacations, when special rules applied. They had to stay away from the business activities of relatives and friends. Bars, karaoke lounges, massage parlours and certain kinds of barber shops were off limits. Access to barracks by civilians was restricted.[13] On the one hand, this strict regime would seem to violate the party's edicts about "mixing with the masses". On the other, it meshed with Jiang's objective that the PLA be converted into a "special spiritual force".

Maoist-style indoctrination campaigns were re-launched with gusto. The Learn From Lei Feng movement went through different guises from 1995 onwards. One was the Emulate Kong Fansen variation — after the cadre who died in Tibet in the wake of decades of selfless service in a poor hamlet. Different PLA units came up with latter-day Lei Fengs or Kong Fansens. One Kong Fansen-style cadre was Lin Zhengshu, a former commissar in the city of Zhenjiang in the Shenyang Military Region. According to the official biography, he died of liver cancer in December 1994 after having served in the northeast frontier for 22 years. "He went for the most difficult jobs in the most dangerous terrain," the *People's Daily* reported. "While harbouring no thoughts for himself and his family, he was willing to remain a nameless hero."[14]

But what specifically was IPW about? Troops were told to be aware of political trends in China and abroad — and to toe the Beijing line. Yang Baibing's successor as chief political commissar, General Yu Yongbo, quoted Jiang on the importance of studying "[Marxist] theory, history, economics, technology, management, law ... all that needs to be learned". For Zhang Wannian, it was an arduous task of "ideological and moral construction". "We must assiduously develop socialist spiritual civilisation, and resolutely counter Mammonism, hedonism, and extreme individualism," he told the officers in 1996. It was clear, however, that the focus of the IPW campaigns would be loyalty to the *zhongyang* ("central authorities") and to President Jiang in particular.[15]

"Talk More About Politics"

The "talk more about politics" campaign was the military version of the one waged by Jiang in 1995 in the civilian sector to promote loyalty to the centre (see Chapter 2). As the CMC chairman pointed out: "The army must at any one time pay attention to politics. This is the most important demand made of the military forces." The president specifically stipulated that senior officers "personally grasp" IPW work. "Officers with the rank of division chief should be even more concerned with and resolute in talking about politics," he said. "They should grasp well the task of the ideological and political construction of the army."[16]

Enemies of Jiang including then CMC vice-chairman Liu Huaqing went along with the crypto-Maoist slogan. For General Liu, the "talk more about politics" movement was essential to "maintaining the nature and goals of the people's army". Officers and soldiers were asked to "comprehensively and dialectically" analyse the domestic and international situation. "Troops must unify their thoughts under the objectives and principles affirmed by the party centre," he said.[17]

Much was made of the Red Army tradition of the "gun obeying the party leadership". Jiang Zemin put it most succinctly: "The troops must forever listen to the orders of the party," he said in a 1995 speech to National Defence University students. "The party's absolute leadership over the army must be guaranteed. The gun must be held by people who are totally loyal to the party." Or as General Zhou Ziyu put it: "Inferior ranks must obey superior ranks; and the entire party obeys the *zhongyang*." "This has traditionally been the political principle and political superiority of the party," the deputy chief political commissar said.[18]

Quite inevitably, the focus of the loyalty to be proffered was narrowed down to Jiang, the "leadership core". Chief of Staff General Fu Quanyou repeatedly asked the army's leading bodies to "firmly safeguard the authority of the party Central Committee and the CMC with comrade Jiang Zemin as the core".[19] In fact, said army analysts, the PLA would provide an "imperial escort" for Jiang's passage to the position of helmsman.

It was again General Zhang Wannian, a latter-day Yang Baibing, who put things in the most grandiloquent terms. The general regarded "talking more about politics" as the "soul of army construction". "Under any circumstances, we must, in thoughts, politics and action, remain in the highest unison with the *zhongyang* with Jiang Zemin as its core," Zhang said. "There should absolutely be no ambiguity about this."[20] In speeches to civilians in the run-up to the 15th Party Congress in 1997, Jiang largely abandoned the "talk politics" slogan because of criticisms about its Maoist overtones. The shibboleth, however, continued to be used in army IPW work.

Soldiers as Model Socialists in Combating "Infiltration"

The PLA would be a handy weapon against the infiltration of Western values and other decadent rubbish. In the words of General Chi Haotian, the army would become "an ideological Great Wall against corruption and [bourgeois-liberal] changes". The senior general claimed that "some people in the party had been corrupted and had gone astray" because they had succumbed to capitalist thinking as well as the "remnant decadent thoughts of the exploiting classes".[21] The PLA would apparently show them the light.

By late 1995 and early 1996, the PLA propaganda machinery had joined in the polemic against Western values. The quality of the anti-Western fusillades was crude — about on a par with those issued the first year after the Tiananmen Square massacre. Take, for example, the series of commentaries in the *Liberation Army Daily* of April 1996 that savaged Western democracy. "Although the two-chamber parliamentary system and the separation of powers may seem very democratic, this [system] only represents the interest and will of the bourgeoisie," the *Daily* said. "The nature of democracy is determined by which class controls the power of the state and which class exerts a dictatorship over the others."[22]

Yet another *Daily* commentary railed against "all-out Westernisation" as well as the "blind worship" of foreign things. "We must counter the infiltration of the decadent thoughts and culture of capitalism," it said. "We must raise our guard against the private ownership system of capitalism as well as its political system, which are fundamentally against socialism and alien to our national conditions."[23]

The PLA would set an example to the nation in ideological rectitude. At an enlarged CMC conference in late 1996, Jiang Zemin called upon the army to be "ahead of the nation" in the propagation of spiritual civilisation.[24] The idea that soldiers would set the pace for some otherworldly values was not new. It harked back to the Maoist campaign of "the whole nation learning from the PLA" during the Cultural Revolution.

Jiang, however, gave it a new, *fin de siècle* urgency. One paragon unit touted by the national media was the Wonderful 6th Company of the Spiritually Civilised Shenzhen Special Economic Zone. Members of this superb unit were models of the new socialist man. They boasted the "four attributes" and "four loyalties": this meant they had "ideals, morality, culture and discipline" and they were "perpetually loyal" to the party, the motherland, the people, and socialism. As General Chi Haotian put it during an inspection tour to this *ne plus ultra* unit: "You have hoisted a big and bright banner against Mammonism, hedonism and extreme individualism."[25] In the PLA hall of fame, the 6th Company of Shenzhen was on a par with other lionised units such as the Wonderful 8th Company of Nanjing Road, Shanghai, and the Hard-as-Steel 8th Company of the Hainan Beachhead.

What distinguished the Shenzhen corps was its ability to withstand the sugar-coated bullets of capitalism, particularly temptations emanating from Hong Kong. After all, there were 150-odd karaoke bars, massage parlours, sauna baths and assorted clubs within a 500-metre radius of platoon headquarters. Members of this saintly company did not smoke, drink, swear, or gawk at women. They also spurned the favourite national pastime: dabbling in the stock market. Shenzhen papers said there were two heavily patronised stockbrokers less than 300 metres from the platoon office. None of the exemplary troops so much as snapped up a share.[26]

How real was the 6th Company? It was well known that practically all PLA units along the coast were, to use an army euphemism, enthusiastic participants in the commodity economy. Former Shenzhen-based commissar Lei Mingqiu, an early candidate for the post of commander of the Hong Kong Garrison, was in 1995 praised by the official media as a successful army entrepreneur. Instead of promoting socialist values, fantastic propaganda about the otherworldly exploits of PLA units could feed the feelings of cynicism that the populace had towards the PLA.

The Patriotism Card and Foreign Policy
"China will no longer be bullied"

Part of the indoctrination that the army — and civilians — was subject to was that a strong PLA was essential to prevent China from once again becoming the victim of colonialism. Jiang Zemin called on the people not to "forget the lesson of history, that a weak country would be susceptible to bullying and drubbing". The president's recommendation: "We must prepare well for a military struggle" against the neo-imperialists. A beefed-up

PLA was the only guarantee the country could thwart the plots of "neo-imperialists".[27]

Throughout 1995, the generals made use of a series of anniversary events — including the end of World War II — to hit home the point of patriotism. The top brass called for a new drive to promote "national consciousness in defence" and "national defence education". The unspoken corollary was that the PLA should be given a larger share of the economic pie. General Chi Haotian made much of the fact that before 1949, when there was no national defence to speak of, "the Chinese people were subject to bullying and humiliation". The veteran lamented that the development of national defence education was "not balanced nationwide". "Effective measures must be adopted to boost the concept of national defence among the populace and to infuse it with patriotic spirit," he added.[28]

By the mid-1990s, Jiang and the generals were playing up plots by unnamed hostile foreign powers to split up China. "Some foreign powers have made use of 'human rights' and issues of minority nationalities and religion to put pressure on our nation and perpetrate infiltration and subversion," Jiang told a gathering of retired PLA veterans. "While living in peace, we must think about dangers and raise our guard."[29]

Some members of the top brass sketched a Manichean struggle between the forces of good and evil: the former was China's effort towards peace and prosperity; the latter, schemes by hostile foreign forces — usually a reference to the Washington-led "anti-China alliance" — to prevent China from claiming its status as a world power. "In the course of China's construction and development, hostile foreign forces in the West will not change its plot to 'westernise' and 'split up' China," said General Fu Quanyou in another pep-talk to the rank and file in 1996.[30]

After Lee Teng-hui's visit to the US, the Taiwanese independence movement was seen as the latest — and most evil — manifestation of the Western plot to keep China divided. The generals pointed out that even when faced with this threat, the PLA had confidence to pursue a course of self-reliance and justice. As General Zhang Wannian put it while meeting a foreign delegation in early 1995: "The Chinese army will never become hegemonist; it will not invade other countries; it will not form an alliance with another army; it will not set up a military base anywhere in the world."[31] But the leadership would develop an army commensurate with its conception of China's greatness.

New definition of Chinese sovereignty and rights

General Liu Huaqing struck a popular chord when he reiterated in the 1990s that "Chinese, having stood up, will definitely not allow any invaders to tread on China's sovereignty and interests".[32] The reason why the US and some Asia-Pacific countries discerned a "China Threat" could be the perception that the CCP and army leadership had moved the goalposts as the country became stronger. That is, the new "sovereign rights and interests" that the PLA was called upon to protect might disturb some countries as hegemonist. The senior cadres and generals, however, saw this as natural. The country had new requirements and aspirations after it had become rich economically.

Up to the early 1990s, the PLA's goals were defined in a loose manner as protection of territorial integrity. By the mid-1990s, however, the army's multiple tasks consisted of "consolidating national defence; resisting foreign aggression; defending the nation's sovereignty over its land, sea and air space as well as its maritime rights and interests; and safeguarding national unity and national security".[33] "Power projection", though not necessarily involving territorial ambition, was pretty much recognised as a legitimate component of Chinese sovereign power. With the improvement of China's relations with Russia and India, the focus of Chinese concern shifted from the northeast and northwest to the southeast, primarily the Taiwan Strait, the South China Sea and the Pacific Ocean. And Chinese power projection in these areas had raised eyebrows throughout the Asia-Pacific region.

In 1996, the leadership, scientific and academic communities held a series of meetings on China's oceanic rights. The consensus was that they were vital to China's security and economic development — and that the PLA and ordinary citizens should strengthen their "consciousness about the oceans". The semi-official Hong Kong China News Agency quoted relevant experts as saying: "The ocean is a blue-coloured national territory and it should be protected the same way as territory on land."[34] The agency added that the development of oceanic resources was indispensable to the "third-stage strategic goal of China's economic development in the 21st century".

In late 1996, China passed relevant rules and regulations asserting rights over the three million square kilometres of "economic zone" which fell within 200 nautical miles of China's lengthy coastline. The rights included exploring, exploiting and managing mineral and fishing resources. As then premier Li Peng put it, the law would "guarantee the exercise of

China's sovereignty and jurisdiction over its exclusive economic zones and continental shelf, and safeguard its maritime rights and interests".[35]

Many diplomats indicated they were disturbed by China's apparent revival of the concept of *lebensraum*: to survive, the large and populous nation needs more "breathing space" in its vicinity. This was despite the fact that in the mid-1990s, the civilian and military leadership by and large showed restraint concerning disputes over the Spratlys and the Diaoyu (Senkaku) islands. Analysts pointed out, however, that Beijing might have adopted a relatively low profile to soften the image of bellicosity conjured up by the Taiwan-related war games. On the Diaoyu islands, Chinese authorities exercised the utmost restraint for fear that the spread of anti-Japanese sentiments — which were widespread in Hong Kong and Taiwan in the summer of 1996 and 1997 — might affect domestic stability (see Chapter 6).[36]

Given the PLA's new powers and mandate, however, it was possible that Beijing might become more assertive in the first decade of the new century. Apart from oceanic rights, the leadership also became much more conscious about safeguarding a reliable supply of petroleum and other raw materials to ensure fast-paced economic development.[37]

THE ARMY'S ROLE IN DOMESTIC POLITICS AND FOREIGN POLICY

It is a truism in Chinese politics that while the three million-strong PLA accounted for only 0.25 per cent of the population, it packed a lot of punch. Since the June 4 crackdown, the CCP was reliant upon if not beholden to the army to maintain its "ruling party" status. In return, the PLA augmented its power through formal, and more importantly, informal channels of influence.

Starting in the mid-1990s, top generals began taking part in — or at least sitting in on — important civilian meetings, particularly those in the economic and fiscal areas. One eye-catching example was the national meeting on economic work held every December to finalise plans for the year ahead. Starting with the 1992 session, not just CMC vice-chairmen but the heads of the three headquarters departments and the PAP commander attended as observers. The top brass's brief was hardly secret: they wanted more say in the distribution of resources (see following section).[38]

By the mid-1990s, PLA representatives were routinely working with their civilian counterparts in meetings and functions in areas ranging from culture to law and order. In a throwback to Cultural Revolution days, army officers or retired PLA personnel were seconded to party and government units. In 1995 and 1996, *People's Daily* director Shao Huaze, a former army officer, appointed several ex-PLA cadres to high positions in the party mouthpiece. In late 1996, head of the Culture Department of the General Political Department, Major-General Liu Xiaojiang, became a Vice-Chairman of the All-China Federation of Literary Circles.[39]

PLA preponderance was reflected in the expanded structure of the Central Military Commission. In late 1995, the number of CMC vice-chairmen was increased from two to four. One reason was to make way for the retirement of Generals Liu Huaqing and Zhang Zhen. However, another reason was that the CMC had taken on more responsibilities, including reunification and foreign affairs. In 1996 and 1997, the top brass was contemplating yet one more expansion of the CMC. Under this schema, a CMC Standing Committee would be created. Apart from the vice-chairmen and the chiefs of the three headquarters departments, the heads of the main divisions and the regional commands would be inducted into the high council.[40]

PLA Influence in Economic Policy
Which comes first: The economy or defence?

The top brass still paid lip service to the Deng goal of the PLA subserving the economy. As General Zhang Wannian indicated in mid-1995, "national defence construction and army construction must be based on economic construction". "The army must obey the overall situation of economic construction," he said. Or as Admiral Wang Xugong, the commander of the Naval Air Force, put it: "Only when the country has been strengthened and the economy developed can the troops have their own development." Added General Chi Haotian: "Only when the water has risen will the boat be at a higher level." "As in the past, the PLA will actively support national economic construction and make its contribution to achieving the country's trans-century development goals," he vowed.[41]

However, it soon became apparent that the message was on the flip side of the coin: that the country should first and foremost build a strong defence to ensure there was a peaceful environment for development. As the Chinese proverb put it, the host and the guest had changed places. At the very least, economic and military pursuits had become equally important. As General Chi Haotian said in a 1995 speech: "To raise the comprehensive strength of the nation, we must have a strong economy and a strong defence." "The two contribute to each other and one can't do without the other," he added. Jiang protégé and former PAP commander General Ba Zhongtan said it most explicitly: the PLA needed a bigger share of national resources. "At the moment, economic construction has not given enough consideration to the needs of national defence," he indicated at the 1996 NPC.[42]

The logic was as eloquently laid out by General Zhang Wannian, considered a hawk. "Without national defence, the Chinese people cannot maintain long-term stability, let alone development," he said in 1995. Noting that a peaceful environment could easily lead people to belittle the significance of a strong military, he warned that misguidedly pacifist notions could spawn "an ideology of off-guardedness".[43]

The PLA's high assessment of its importance was undiminished by the decision in late 1997 to demobilise 500,000 men, which was opposed to by older generals such as Liu Huaqing. Jiang was able to have his way by absorbing many of the laid-off PLA personnel into the beefed-up PAP. Moreover, the president told the top brass that money saved by cutting personnel would be used to boost facilities and develop weapons.[44]

The concept of "interchangeability"

Apart from his "power grows out of the barrel of a gun" axiom, one of Mao's secret weapons for defeating the Kuomintang (KMT) was the "interchangeability" of the military and civilian sectors. As General Ba Zhongtan put it in 1996: "I suggest we give more thoughts to the development strategy of the fusion of peace-time and war-time [needs] and the fusion of [the goals of] the military and civilian sectors."[45]

The fusion of peace and war manifested itself in many arenas. In addition to combat duties, soldiers built hospitals, grew rice, fought natural disasters and smashed "counter-revolutionary" rings. In return, government and industrial units as well as civilians provided unconditional contribution to the army effort. In their spare time, teachers and factory hands trained as reservists. Factories combined ordinary industrial goals with those of PLA-related research and development.

Jiang lent his authority to the Maoist theory of the so-called "double support": "The army supporting the government and loving the people; the people supporting the army and giving preferential treatment to their kin." A New China News Agency report in mid-1995 said regional party and government units as well as the masses regarded the support of army construction as an "unshirkable responsibility". In aid to the PLA exercises off Taiwan in 1995, residents in the city of Luoyang in Henan Province provided the troops with 2,800 houses, 40,000 pairs of shoes and other amenities.[46]

By late 1995, 150 cities had established regulations on "double support". Duties for civilians included finding jobs for demobilised soldiers; providing education and welfare benefits to army relatives; and ensuring that PLA units have sufficient and subsidised supplies of food, electricity and fuel. Contests were held among hundreds of cities for the title of "paragon unit" for the double-support drive.[47]

At the macro level, an important manifestation of the "fusion" and "interchangeability" principles was a bigger budget (see following section). Equally significant, however, was the fact that military men were having a bigger say in the use of economic resources, even in industrial policy.

Under the pretext of the "fusion of peace and war", General Chi Haotian asked that the army play a bigger role in civilian transport and telecommunications. "Even in ordinary times, national and regional development in the area of transport and telecommunications must take into account the needs of defence," he said in a conference on communications in 1995. Thus the planning of civilian railways, highways, airports and other communications facilities must have military needs in mind. "This means one set of investments can serve two purposes," he claimed.[48]

Much more than previous PLA representatives on the Politburo, General Liu Huaqing spent time inspecting economic facilities and making comments on economic and industrial policy. For example, in mid-1995, he toured electronics facilities in Nanjing in the company of then minister of electronics Hu Qili. While talking to personnel in one factory, General Liu said: "Army production should take precedence over the civilian sector." The official NCNA wire quoted the general as making comments on "the fusion of the army and the people; the synthesis of war and peace". He also asked managers and workers to give more support to the army. The senior general said he hoped efficiency in the electronics sector would improve so that it could "make more contribution to national defence and to the livelihood of the people".[49] It was significant that in his remarks, General Liu put the army before civilian purposes.

General Liu seemed particularly interested in forming some sort of an alliance between the PLA and the southeast coast, the country's economic powerhouse. In return for supporting the continuation of the open-door policy, the PLA apparently wanted more contributions from the coast. While meeting NPC delegates from Shandong in March 1996, the then CMC vice-chairman praised Jinan's policy of "developing the economy both on land and at sea". The general praised the rich province for not neglecting agriculture and for maintaining social stability.[50]

As for Guangdong, the Long March veteran reassured the go-go province that Deng's policy of favouring the southeast coast had not changed. "Leading cadres of various levels in Guangdong have been effective in carrying out the policy of the *zhongyang*," he said during a provincial tour in 1996. "The people of Guangdong have made a great contribution to reform and the open-door policy." He urged cadres and citizens in the "advanced province" not to forget spiritual civilisation. Guangdong, and in particular Shenzhen, had, of course, always done well in rendering special aid to the PLA. In 1995, the special economic zone contributed more than one million yuan for a local PLA unit to build a hall. Electricity and water bills for Shenzhen-based troops were calculated at cost. And in 1996, Shenzhen mayor Li Zibin listed "double support" as a key goal of the city's spiritual civilisation campaign.[51]

The other municipal leader who bent over backwards to accommodate PLA requirements was Shanghai party boss and Politburo member Huang Ju. In an interview with the *Liberation Army Daily* in late 1996, Huang said development in the civilian sector should take place "in lockstep" with that in the army. The Shanghai leader listed five areas for "commensurate and simultaneous developments" in the Ninth Five-Year Plan and beyond: planning, provision of facilities, institutional mechanisms, education and "way of life". Huang said PLA affairs should be given "special consideration" in the city. For example, enterprises would have to make provisions for its staffers joining the militia or reserves.[52]

Apart from economic concerns, the "interchangeability" ideal had an impact on social policies. The most obvious instance was education. In 1995 and 1996, tens of cities adopted municipal laws on propagating "national defence education". For example, in Shanghai, education in patriotism and national defence would be integrated. "We must from an early age inculcate in youths concepts and consciousness about national defence," Huang Ju vowed in 1996.[53]

The PLA Budget and the "China Threat"

Beginning in the 1990s, a major theme of the speeches made by military and civilian cadres to foreign audiences was the groundlessness of the "China Threat" theory. As General Chi Haotian told a delegation of American defence officials in 1996: "China will not become hegemonist now and it will never do so in the future. Stories about the China threat are the biggest joke on earth."[54] Among international observers, the most worrisome prospect was that the larger say given the PLA would result in a bigger budget, more deadly weapons, and a more aggressive military-foreign policy. In the mid-1990s, the Chinese propaganda machinery pulled out all the stops to try to defuse the "Yellow Peril" theory. For example, judging by official figures, the rate of increase in military spending dropped in 1996. In that year, the NPC allotted 70.23 billion yuan to the army, a boost of 11.3 per cent over 1995. However, this figure was lower than the year-on-year increase rates for 1990 to 1995: respectively 15.2 per cent; 12 per cent; 12 per cent; 13.5 per cent; 20 per cent and 21.25 per cent.[55]

In late 1995, China used its first White Paper on National Defence and Disarmament to underscore its pacifist intentions. "The Chinese people love peace, and the theory of 'China threat' spread by some people overseas is false," the paper said. The document further pointed out that "as long as there is no serious threat to the nation's sovereignty or security, China will not increase its defence spending substantially".[56]

The paper then cited a spew of figures to show that China's military outlay was low by international standards. For example, the 1994 budget of US$6.39 billion was but 2.3 per cent that of the US and 13.9 per cent that of Japan. As a proportion of GDP, Chinese defence spending dropped from 5.6 per cent in 1979 to 1.3 per cent in 1994. Moreover, the White Paper claimed that 34 per cent of the PLA's military spending was used on salaries and food. The same percentage was earmarked for the research, development, procurement and maintenance of weapons.[57]

In 1997 and 1998, the army budget resumed the pattern of leaps forward when the NPC awarded 80.57 billion yuan and 90.99 billion yuan respectively for defence purposes. They represented year-on-year increases of 14.7 per cent and 12.8 per cent respectively. However, the senior generals lost no time in downplaying the figures. The then head of the Commission of Science, Technology and Industry for National Defence (COSTIND), General Cao Gangchuan said in 1997 that the limited budget meant the PLA had no choice but to postpone many research and development projects. "We have to feed and clothe three million-odd soldiers," he said. "What's left after that?"[58]

Retired deputy chief of staff General Xu Xin also groused that the PLA's outlay was lower than that of Taiwan. "Our budget is lowest in the world," he said at the 1997 NPC. "Living expenses for each soldier are less than US$1 a day." When reporters asked Xu whether the manoeuvres off the Taiwan coast in 1996 had cost too much money, General Xu blew up: "Why don't you criticise the Americans, who are conducting war games all the time?"[59]

The problem, of course, was the perceived lack of transparency of PLA operations, including its budget. Most independent analysts said actual spending was up to three, four times more than official statistics. For example, a report published by the London-based International Institute of Strategic Studies claimed that in 1994, real PLA expenditure was US$28 billion, or four times the official figure. The institute cited "the falsification in military accounting whereby military-related expenditure is listed under non-defence headings in the central government budget".[60] Moreover, in the wake of the theory of the "fusion of war and peace", much of military expenditure could be absorbed by civilian units.

That the PLA had gained a larger say over how the pie was sliced would reinforce suggestion that covert military outlay had increased. The series of war games off the Taiwan coast also buttressed the impression that for domestic and foreign reasons, much spending went unreported (see following section). Moreover, in the atmosphere of accentuated arms race in the region, the requirements of research and development specialists kept rising by the day. After all, in the second half of the 1990s, the PLA was gunning to upgrade its equipment to prepare for a "hi-tech, multi-dimensional and electronic warfare".[61]

Resources were particularly concentrated on the navy and air force, which had been neglected up to the late 1980s. Moreover, these two units, in addition to the Second Artillery or missile brigade, were most useful in force projection. President Jiang underscored the priority accorded the navy at its eighth party congress in late 1996. PLA watchers said it was unusual for a party general secretary and CMC chief to attend the party congresses of individual PLA units. "The navy must resolutely carry out ... the principles of military strategy in the new period, and enhance its overall combat capability," Jiang told the proud admirals.[62]

Military analysts said priorities in the mid- to late-1990s included the

following: the building or acquisition of an aircraft carrier; a new generation of submarines; development or co-production of fighter aircraft as
sophisticated as the Russian SU-27s or the American F-16s; and development of a new generation of missiles such as the new DF-31, a solid-fuel
projectile fired from a mobile launcher.[63]

Diplomacy: The Hawks' Last Laugh

It is true for almost all countries that the military leadership takes a more
hardline attitude on foreign policy than its civilian counterpart. The PLA
was no exception. What was disturbing was that the Chinese military was
not subject to enough checks and balances. And despite its opaqueness and
lack of accountability, its say in diplomacy increased dramatically through
the 1990s.

Compared with civilian units such as the Ministry of Foreign Affairs
(MFA), the top brass took a consistently tougher line on a range of foreign
affairs. They ranged from the South China Sea to nuclear testing. For example, on the Spratlys, the diplomats leaned towards joint development
with the other six claimants. Individual hawks in the PLA favoured the use
— or threat — of force. By the late 1990s, these hardliners were targeting
Vietnam, the claimant that had the most formidable military machine.[64]

The top brass showed signs of relative belligerence towards the US,
which, after all, posed the biggest obstacle to PLA aggrandisement.
Anti-American sentiments reached their height during the Taiwan Strait
crisis. In late 1995, Deputy Chief of Staff Xiong Guangkai left his mark on
history by threatening to nuke the West Coast. This implicit threat was
made when General Xiong told a former senior US defence official that
Americans "cared more about Los Angeles than Taiwan".[65] Military think
tanks sponsored elaborate computerised war games with the latest PLA toys
pitted against elements of the Yankee war machine.

By 1996, the generals also boosted their "military diplomacy" — making trips abroad to push their foreign policy line. Issues covered by the PLA
diplomats went beyond defence matters such as exchanges with the armies
of host countries. According to NCNA, delegations were sent to more than
50 countries in 1996. The CMC and Defence Ministry also received visits
from military groups from more than 60 countries.

"Sino-foreign military exchanges are an important component of China's diplomacy as a whole," NCNA quoted an officer from the Defence

Ministry's Foreign Affairs Bureau as saying. "In implementing the country's independent foreign policy of peace, the PLA's military diplomacy has also helped promote the all-round development of China's relations with other countries." The officer was careful to point out that the generals-turned-diplomats had "abided by the basic principles of the country's foreign policy".[66] However, it seemed evident the PLA officers could also be pursuing distinct goals of their own.

TEST CASE: TAIWAN, THE ACME OF PLA INFLUENCE

The Taiwan crisis of May 1995 to March 1996 perhaps marked the height of PLA influence in the 1990s. Taiwan became the focus of the contradictions between Jiang Zemin on the one hand, and elements of the civilian leadership and the top brass on the other. The generals were to some extent successful in holding Jiang hostage and in boosting their own powers.

Is Jiang Zemin — or the Politburo — in Control?
Jiang's reunification dream shattered

Jiang Zemin wanted Taiwan policy to be his contribution to history, in particular, the one area where he had "advanced beyond" Deng Xiaoping. His would-be masterpiece was the eight-point initiative on national unification unveiled on January 30, 1995. While Jiang was ideologically conservative, his proposals were largely conciliatory and positive. The olive-branch statement included points such as "Chinese will not fight Chinese" and a call for leaders on both sides to exchange visits. It also envisaged the development of a common, "greater" Chinese civilisation through effects across the Strait.[67]

Yet the president immediately ran into difficulties with the generals, who gave him no face at all. None of the members of the top brass so much as uttered a word in support of the initiative. This was despite the fact that in the national press, the eight-point proposal was lauded as a "far-sighted programmatic document". First of all, the PLA saw Taiwan policy as one of its many preserves. The eight-point game plan was very much the brainchild of top Jiang adviser Wang Daohan, the head of the Association for Relations across the Taiwan Strait (ARATS). The details were hammered out together with cadres of the Taiwan Affairs Office (TAO) headed by

Wang Zhaoguo, a former governor of Fujian Province and head of the General Office of the party Central Committee. It had minimal PLA input.[68]

More importantly, the top brass considered Jiang's olive branch to be dovish to the point of capitulation. Two months before the eight-point initiative, Jiang and the generals had, in November 1994, crossed swords over the infamous Xiamen shelling incident. A Taiwan navy vessel off Xiamen apparently overshot its target during routine drills — and the shells landed on a village on the Chinese side, killing several peasants. Instead of issuing a strong protest, Jiang and such of his aides as TAO vice-chief Tang Shubei suggested to the Taiwanese that Beijing would not allow this to harm relations. In an unusual move, the Taiwanese were also told that Beijing would not be seeking damages. This was despite tear-jerking reports of the villagers' suffering in the Chinese media. The top brass was livid. On a trip to Fujian soon afterwards, then CMC vice-chairman General Zhang Zhen blasted unnamed civilian officials for "cowardly behaviour".[69]

There were more setbacks for Jiang. In April 1995, Taiwan President Lee Teng-hui politely snubbed the eight-point proposal. He issued his own six-point plan which gave nothing away. Then came the bombshell in late May. The Jiang foreign policy and Taiwan affairs teams were shocked by the apparent about-face of President Bill Clinton in granting Lee a US visa. For some strange reason, however, Jiang failed to see that his Taiwan policy was in shambles — and that if he did not act swiftly, the initiative would go to the PLA hawks.[70] For almost three weeks after Washington announced its opening of the door to Lee on May 22, hardly a strong word came out of Beijing. Desperate to continue his Taiwan overture, Jiang allowed Tang to go to Taipei on May 26 to make preparations for the next round of meetings between the heads of the two semi-official units, ARATS's Wang and Chairman of Taipei's Straits Exchange Foundation (SEF), Koo Chen-fu.

After President Lee laid bare what Beijing considered his "pro-independence gambit" in his speech to Cornell University in early June, however, the generals struck back — hard. To military minds, Jiang's "soft" policy had failed dismally; and the civilians had stupidly let themselves be fooled by Washington's promises "never" to let Lee visit the US. Mad that Jiang and his aides had not so much as uttered a harsh reprimand, generals led by Zhang Zhen and Liu Huaqing prevailed upon the leadership to publish a series of anti-Lee fusillades. The first one was run by Xinhua and other media on June 7, way too late for the hawks.[71] Then came the full attack on Jiang. At an enlarged Politburo meeting in mid-June, Jiang, Foreign Minister Qian Qichen and Wang Zhaoguo made self-criticisms, with varying degrees of severity. Beijing unilaterally halted all political contacts between ARATS and SEF. And cross-strait relations went into a tailspin.

PLA-dominated institutions

The generals moved fast to fine-tune the rules of the game concerning Taiwan-related decision-making. First came modifications of institutions and personnel. Subtle but important changes took place at the Central Committee's Leading Group on Taiwan Affairs (LGTA), which had ultimate authority over policy towards the "breakaway island".

The LGTA had traditionally been headed by military or quasi-military personnel such as Deng Xiaoping and Yang Shangkun. Upon taking over the chairmanship in June 1993, Jiang privately indicated that he hoped reunification policy would henceforth stay in the hands of civilians. Group members included Qian Qichen, who was its vice-chief, as well as Wang Zhaoguo, security chief Jia Chunwang, General Xiong Guangkai and Wang Daohan. Wang Zhaoguo doubled as secretary-general. The only PLA representative was Xiong, then an intelligence expert at the PLA General Staff Department.[72]

The Lee Teng-hui incident, however, provided a good excuse for the top brass to assert their power. Heavyweights including Generals Zhang Zhen, Liu Huaqing and Zhang Wannian sat in on LGTA meetings on a regular basis. General Xiong, also the PLA's leading expert on the US, adopted a higher profile. He ousted Wang Zhaoguo as the secretary-general of the group. The English-speaking general also took the initiative of drafting position papers and NCNA commentaries that would represent national policy.[73]

And without full consultation with — let alone supervision by the Politburo or other elements of the civilian leadership — the top brass got ready for quasi-military action. The decision was made to "teach Taiwan a lesson". The CMC and the General Staff Department (GSD) set up a Joint Command Centre on Taiwan in Fuzhou to direct "war preparations" against the "breakaway province". It was headed by General Zhang Wannian and staffed by officers from the GSD and the Nanjing Military Region. The centre upstaged the leading group as the foremost decision-making organ on unification affairs. Together with other military think tanks, it put together a new series of invasion scenarios on how Taiwan would be taken over by force. The game plans ranged from "surgical" attacks on Taiwan military installations to the occupation of KMT-held outlying islands such as Quemoy and Matsu.[74]

The army lost no time in building up the infrastructure for the "war effort". First the Nanjing and later the Guangzhou military regions were turned into "war zones". By March 1996, the Nanjing and Guangzhou war zones were amalgamated into an East-South War Zone. It pretty much incorporated the operational wing of the PLA Joint Command Centre on Taiwan. Military and civilian units in areas covered by the war zone — Shanghai, Jiangsu, Zhejiang, Anhui, Jiangxi, Guangdong, Guangxi, Hainan, Hunan and Hubei — were asked to give maximum contributions to the "patriotic mobilisation". A circular from the command centre said: "In order to facilitate the expanded deployment and supply of troops and material during war time, national and local units must ensure that the PLA has priority over the allocation of resources and transportation."[75] There was minimal party or governmental supervision of the build-up of this infrastructure.

The "War Games Diplomacy"

The several rounds of PLA manoeuvres off the Taiwan coast that followed laid bare the naked ambition of the hawks — and the potential for disaster fuelled by raised emotions. For a time after Jiang's self-criticism, the top brass not only took over much of day-to-day Taiwan policy but laid down the philosophy and guidelines for cross-strait relations.

Under PLA influence, the goalposts for the so-called military option were shifted. All along, the leadership, including the Foreign Ministry, had cited two criteria for using arms: outright, *de jure*, declaration of independence by Taipei; and involvement by "hostile foreign powers" such as the US and Japan. However, in private discussions, top generals and other hawks in the civilian sector had added other touchstones. They included a so-called *yinxing* ("hidden") independence movement which manifested itself in a policy of deliberate prolongation of separation by perennial refusal to talk to the mainland. Other criteria included: readiness by Taiwan authorities to hold a referendum on whether to declare independence; the outbreak of massive disorder in Taiwan; or evidence that Taiwan was developing a nuclear capability.[76]

Moreover, the PLA's concept of the use of force was markedly different from that of the civilian leadership. For Jiang and the Foreign Ministry, the military option was mostly rhetorical: it would be used as a means of intimidation. For the top brass, however, war and "quasi-warfare" including war games, were a vehicle of policy that could be adjusted for particular targets. This could be deduced from the main PLA slogan of late 1995: "A small-scale military action against a small-scale independence movement; a large-scale military action against a full-fledged independence movement." For example, provocative manoeuvres such as missile drills or flying reconnaissance flights close to the island served the purpose of psychological warfare.[77]

Throughout the course of the war games from July 1995 through March 1996, outright invasion was never intended. However, again without supervision by Jiang and the Politburo, the PLA toyed with different options aimed at upping the ante and putting more pressure on the Lee regime. These included hostile action against Taiwan inhabitants on the outlying islands; PLA aircraft or naval vessels making an apparently mistaken incursion into Taiwan-held territory; deliberately timed run-ins between aircraft or naval vessels from both sides; missiles overshooting their intended "splash zones" and landing closer to Taiwan than earlier anticipated; and using "special" fishing boats to harass Taiwan vessels and inhabitants. By late 1996, an "invasion plan" was also finalised and leaked to selected overseas media. The three-step game plan consisted of: firstly, the occupation of an outlying Taiwan island such as Quemoy; secondly, naval blockade of the Taiwan Strait; and last, the start of "reunification negotiations" on Beijing's terms.[78]

The series of manoeuvres along the Fujian Coast which started in July were carried out with minimal Politburo oversight. Theoretically, each war game was approved by the Politburo Standing Committee and the timing and intensity of the firepower would be communicated to all Politburo members and government ministers. However, a few Politburo members got to know about the August drills on TV. Informed sources said during the two test-firings of missiles in July and August 1995, a couple of projectiles "deliberately" hit areas to the south of the splash zones — or closer to Taiwan than had originally been planned.[79]

Throughout this tense period, news about Taiwan policy or the conduct of the war games was mainly communicated to the outside world through the generals. PLA officers were particularly explicit with US government officials. The most graphic example was what the generals told Chas Freeman, the China expert who visited Beijing in December 1995. Freeman had left his position as assistant secretary of defence several months earlier and the Chinese were sure he would communicate the matter to the US administration. One message was that the PLA had prepared plans for an Armageddon against Taiwan consisting of one conventional missile strike a day for 30 days. Other threatening noises were also made.[80]

Civilian ministers or diplomats adopted the lowest of profiles. Maybe the latter had taken the lesson that Jiang learned in October 1995 when he gave concurrent interviews to *Newsweek* and *US News and World Report*. The interviews, released on October 15, included a statement by Jiang that Lee was still welcome to visit Beijing — and that he himself was also prepared to tour Taiwan. This protestation of friendliness again led to a volley of criticism from General Zhang Zhen and company. "Taiwan has a Lee Teng-hui who shoots from the hip," an officer reportedly said. "In the mainland, Jiang Zemin likes to do the same." Jiang was forced to say that he had been misquoted by the two magazines. Soon afterwards, NCNA came out with the "official" version of the interviews, which contained no reference to the proposed exchange of visits.[81]

Jiang ran into further trouble with the generals in his talk to members of the Chinese diplomatic corps in New York in late October 1995. Jiang was on a "working visit" to the US. In his discussion with the Chinese diplomats, the president concentrated on the importance of maintaining good ties with America. He again cited his four-sentence dictum of "lessening trouble and avoiding confrontation" with the US. Jiang reiterated his desire for high-level exchanges between mainland and Taiwan leaders. This conciliatory mood was also reflected in Jiang's talk to American officials. The top brass was understandably angry. In a rare step, they took their case directly to the US media. In an interview with an American newspaper, General Xiong Guangkai played hardball. He stressed that Taiwan was the key issue in Sino-US relations and that if mishandled, "it could be explosive". The general also scolded the US for its alleged about-face concerning the Lee Teng-hui visit.[82]

Gripe from Central Departments and Regions

There was opposition among different sectors of the polity against efforts by the PLA to use "patriotism" and "national unification" to grab power.

Among the central departments, PLA critics included the "losers" in the power game: the Ministry of Foreign Affairs, the International Liaison Department of the party Central Committee, and the TAO of the State Council. Also dissatisfied with the hawkish policy was the foreign trade establishment because of the adverse impact on foreign investment and trade along the coast.

Surprisingly, the CMC also fought a bitter duel with the party's Propaganda Department over the dissemination of news relating to the war games. Only the army media and other units under the General Political Department were allowed to cover the missile tests of July and August 1995. Footage and stories from the PLA propaganda units were then given to the civilian media. This led to protests by propaganda chief Ding Guan'gen and other ideologues. Ding told the top brass that propaganda aimed at Taiwan would be much more effective with the participation of civilian professionals.[83]

CCTV was allowed to cover the Yellow Sea exercise in mid-October. However, after the TV news was aired on October 18, General Zhang Zhen called up Ding to complain that the focus of the footage was establishing the authority of "core" Jiang Zemin, not a blitz against Lee Teng-hui. Despite Ding's protests, the November exercises were again closed to the civilian press.[84] News about the manoeuvres was disseminated by the army media on November 25, a Saturday. Ding immediately called up General Zhang to complain that PLA propagandists lacked "common sense about news operations". The Taiwan stock exchange was closed on Saturdays and the impact on the local economy was thus diminished.

Opposition to the sabre-rattling also came from the regions. This was despite claims by the national media that even frontline provinces such as Fujian were supportive of the quasi-war effort. Apparently under instructions from Beijing, a pro-Chinese paper in Hong Kong pointed out that "for the sake of the unification of the motherland, the people of Fujian are willing to put up with the sacrifice". Then Fujian party boss Jia Qinglin was quoted as saying that his province would give its all to the mobilisation effort. "Various levels of administration [in the province] will devote the most in the way of financial and material resources to support national defence construction, and assiduously do concrete things [to help the PLA]," he said.[85]

The party boss also indicated that civilian and military forces would "work hand in hand to maintain the safety and stability of the Taiwan Strait area". That Jia did not mention aggressive tactics such as war games, however, could be interpreted as a vote against military adventurism. In fact, the sabre-rattling inflicted sizeable economic losses on Fujian and Guangdong due to its disastrous impact on Taiwan and other foreign investment and business activities.[86]

In August, Jia went to see Jiang Zemin and presented the viewpoints of the coast. While expressing his support for national reunification, Jia urged caution. "We must guard against impetuousness in policy towards Taiwan," Jia reportedly said. "We must take a comprehensive, all-embracing approach. It is relatively easy to take over Taiwan. But how to pick up the threads? Is it good for China's economic construction and international image?" Jia's words carried weight because of his long association with the president. However, there was little that Jiang could do at this point.[87]

At the 1996 NPC, which saw the height of the anti-Taiwan fusillades, General Chi Haotian expressed thanks to Fujian. "Fujian is facing a very tough situation," he said. "It has borne the brunt of the conspiracy by the Lee Teng-hui clique to foster two Chinas." The CMC vice-chairman went on to praise Fujian for being "in the front rank of the nation in patriotism and in showing support for the army".[88] It was hardly surprising, however, that the tough PLA veteran did not say sorry for the economic havoc his men had wreaked on the province.

The Height of PLA Power

In spite of the controversy over their missile diplomacy, the generals had become so full of themselves they seemed to be wallowing in hubris. Members of the top brass were particularly agitated over the decision by President Clinton in early March 1996 to send two aircraft carrier battle groups to the Taiwan Strait. General Zhang Wannian was quoted as telling army officers in Guangdong and Fujian that if American or Taiwan naval vessels were to infringe upon Chinese territory, "they will surely not be able to go back home". Referring to the American armada approaching Taiwan, Chengdu Military Region's General Bi Hao said: "It's no big deal. China and the US have fought once or twice before. It's the US that has always ended up the loser."[89]

The war games turned out to be largely unsuccessful. Owing to the onset of the foggy spring season, the last manoeuvres scheduled for March 1996 could only be partially implemented. Worse, while the Taiwan public was genuinely scared, the exercises helped Lee Teng-hui score a landslide victory at presidential polls later that month. Moreover, China's reputation in the Asia-Pacific region was dented as alarm bells were sounded from Tokyo to Jakarta about the perceived bellicosity of a rising power. However, the top brass decided to follow the Mao maxim of "making a good thing out of a bad thing". They blamed everything on Clinton's "neo-imperialist" gambit of sending two aircraft carriers to the area.[90]

The American armada also provided an excuse to the PLA to clamour for a bigger budget. Hawkish military elements wanted to speed up the armaments programme to thwart "future American intervention" in the Taiwan Strait. The top brass pointed out that the reunification issue could be solved much faster if the PLA had the wherewithal to repel "American interference".[91] In the evaluation sessions over the manoeuvres, PLA officers expressed overall satisfaction with China's missile and naval capabilities. But the generals showed disappointment over the performance of the air force as well as its lack of sophisticated weapons. From that spring onwards, training of air force units was stepped up. Some of the extra drills were carried out with the help of a newly acquired, state-of-the-art electronic simulator. "The generals want to get more funding to beef up the modernisation of the air force and other units," an army source said. "The PLA is convinced that it can 'catch up' with the Americans early next century."[92]

In April 1996, the *Liberation Army Daily* ran an especially bold call for more money to develop air force facilities. It pointed out that neighbouring areas had "ceaselessly" expanded their capacities in this area, thus "rendering our country's tactical situation more complicated". "We face a serious challenge," it concluded. "China must strengthen control over aerial space and land and sea territories."[93] Analysts said the "neighbouring areas" referred to Japan; and that the PLA wanted money to develop or procure advanced warning systems and mid-air refuelling equipment. They said it was the first time the PLA had so crudely called for an expansion of hardware in a public forum.

JIANG ZEMIN AND THE ARMY, 1994–1997

A major reason why the PLA remained a wild card and a potentially destabilising force in Chinese politics was its intimate involvement in factional intrigues. This was evident in its relationship with president Jiang Zemin, the Central Military Commission (CMC) supremo with no military credentials.

From 1989 to 1997, Jiang seemed on the one hand to have succeeded in riding the PLA tiger. His hold over the army had increased and this had ensured his frontrunner status in becoming China's next helmsman. On the other hand, Jiang became a quasi-hostage to the generals. In return for their support, the putative commander-in-chief had to acquiesce in the PLA's growing clout. The possibility could not be ruled out that the generals would exploit their strategic high ground and force the CMC chairman, the party and country into adventures they did not want.

Jiang's Relationship with the Top Brass
Jiang-style *quanshu*

Jiang's military prowess was based almost entirely on *quanshu*, or Chinese-style Machiavellianism. It was predicated on the CMC chairman's famed ability to win friends and sideline enemies through means such as regularly rotating generals and granting them promotions and larger budgets. However, backroom manoeuvres could never invest Jiang with the aura of authority commanded by Mao or Deng. Officers did not have the kind of emotional attachment or loyalty that they felt towards the early CMC chairmen.

Upon being made head of the political section of the Central Committee's Policy Research Office, Wang Huning, a top Shanghai academic, was asked by Jiang for ideas on how to control the top brass. Wang, a former Fudan University political science and law professor, offered his mentor the following six-point advice: ensure the party's leadership over the gun; fill top PLA posts with officers with no obvious factional affiliations; boost the powers of the People's Armed Police (PAP) as an "alternative army" and enhance control over it; offer promotions and other perks to generals who will be useful politically; propagate the "fourth generation of leaders" among different PLA strata; and boost the authority of the position of CMC chairman.[94]

Professor Wang's advice was similar to the instructions Jiang was given by Deng Xiaoping on eradicating the phenomenon of the "mountain strongholds" in the PLA. In a letter to the Politburo that effectively removed the military powers of Yang Shangkun and Yang Baibing in late 1992, Deng breathed new life to the theory of the "five lakes and four seas", meaning that top positions must be given to officers with different backgrounds and affiliations.[95] The departure of generals with a large factional base would make it easier for Jiang to impose his own stamp on the top brass.

Beginning in late 1996, Jiang started propagating the ideal of "using the law to run the army". It was to be an integral part of the president's "military thoughts" (see section below). However, as with most of Jiang's initiatives, military laws and regulations also served the Machiavellian motive of power grabbing. One of the rules that Jiang pushed in 1995 and 1996 was a strict retirement system: meaning that all generals, including chiefs of headquarters departments and regional commanders, had to step down at 65 (it was 63 for their deputies). For example, in late 1996, the heads of the Commission of Science, Technology and Industry for National Defence (COSTIND), the air force and the navy, Generals Ding Henggao, Yu Zhenwu and Zhang Lianzhong respectively, had to call it quits.[96]

The strict retirement regulations enabled Jiang to flush out people he did not like — and to appoint younger officers, most of whom were less tainted with factionalism — to the top. For example, General Ding went out under a cloud because of alleged mismanagement and questionable business practices. Being the son-in-law of Marshal Nie Rongzhen, Ding turned COSTIND, where his wife also occupied a high position, into a virtual fiefdom. Jiang, however, had a way of keeping loyalists working well beyond 65. One was General Yang Dezhong, the former head of the Bodyguards Bureau of the party Central Committee and the CMC. Yang, 74, had officially retired from that position in 1995. However, he managed that portfolio by "remote control" from his other position as Vice-Director of the party Central Committee General Office. The party had no retirement stipulations.[97]

Another favourite means for Jiang to score points was promoting senior officers to full generals. These included quite a number of not-so-friendly veterans who would, however, be grateful to Jiang for the perks that would come with the new titles. In three rounds up to early 1997, Jiang presided over the elevation of 29 full generals. The president also introduced measures making it easier for officers to buy their own flats. According to rules introduced in mid-1995, soldiers could enjoy a discount of at least 8 per cent in purchasing state accommodation. This was beyond ordinary privileges already enjoyed by most cadres. Moreover, retired officers who had taken part in pre-1949 Red Army warfare could enjoy further discounts of up to 12 per cent.[98]

Jiang was the commander-in-chief who paid the most trips to PLA units, particularly those in the regions. And he often promised concrete benefits to the soldiers — such as more supplies of food and other benefits. For example, the president ensured that even in installations as far away as Tibet, soldiers would at least have one egg per day. It was also Jiang who suggested that, to enrich the "spiritual life" of the rank and file, each barrack should be equipped with karaoke facilities. Every year since 1990, there was a rise in food allowance for the troops. And even though the increase was meagre — the raise for each soldier in early 1997 was a nominal 0.4 yuan per day — this helped to some extent in boosting Jiang's popularity.[99]

Opposition to the "Jiang Dynasty"

In spite of his success in ingratiating himself with the top brass, Jiang was never sure how secure his position was. This difficulty was evidenced by his problematic relationship with the two senior generals, former CMC vice-chairmen Generals Liu Huaqing and Zhang Zhen. In theory, the two were recalled from semi-retirement by Deng Xiaoping at the 14th Party Congress in 1992 to help Jiang maintain his hold over the army. Yet until their retirement in late 1997, the two octogenarians posed repeated challenges to the president's authority.

There seemed to be never-ending run-ins between Jiang, on the one hand, and Generals Liu and Zhang on the other. Apart from the Taiwan issue (see previous section), the altercations in 1995 and 1996 centred on power relations. The two Long Marchers refused to take Jiang's hint that they step down. Citing the fact that it was Deng who authorised their comeback, the generals would only retire upon an express order from the patriarch.[100]

Generals Liu and Zhang, but particularly the former, opened fire on Jiang's alleged attempt to build up a Shanghai faction in army and civilian circles. On this point, Liu joined forces with Jiang's foes in the party such as then NPC chief Qiao Shi. Both Liu and Qiao liked to harp on the fact that Jiang had violated Deng's principle of the "five lakes and four seas" when making appointments. "We must not restrict ourselves to a certain sector or region in selecting future leaders," General Liu said in an internal meeting in mid-1995. "We must open new vistas in organisation and personnel work."[101] He was uncompromising in attacking Jiang's "self-serving" promotion of Generals Zhang Wannian and Chi Haotian (see following section).

A late 1995 *Liberation Army Daily* commentary betrayed Jiang's suspicion of factional activities against himself. The article castigated unnamed officers for "not concentrating on studies or work". "They are very enthusiastic about calling on each other, seeking out hearsay, taking in and spreading rumours," the paper warned.[102] Yet with Generals Liu and Zhang, even such a skilled manipulator as the president had to wait until the law of biology took its toll.

Line-up at the Fifth Plenum of September 1995

PLA personnel changes at the fifth plenum of the party Central Committee in October 1995 carried Deng's imprimatur: it was arguably the very last time that the patriarch participated in a major policy of state. The personnel moves also enabled Jiang to consolidate his hold over the army. The most notable development of the enlarged CMC meeting that followed the plenum was the elevation of Generals Zhang Wannian and Chi Haotian to the CMC vice-chairmanship. General Zhang was groomed by Jiang to be a successor to General Liu. Jiang figured that since General Zhang did not have a broad power base in the PLA, he would reciprocate his patronage by staying loyal to him.

General Chi was perhaps the one member of the top brass who became closest to Jiang soon after the latter's transfer to Beijing in 1989. Chi's loyalty also involved a repayment of favours. According to a Chinese military source, the general had a dubious record during the Cultural Revolution, including alleged "cooperation" with the Gang of Four. "There was an internal order saying General Chi could not be promoted to top PLA posts such as CMC vice-chairman," he said. "When General Liu [Huaqing] objected to General Chi's promotion on that ground, Jiang ignored it."[103]

Jiang had defended Chi in the early 1990s. At that time, the Yang brothers were reportedly forcing General Chi to retire from his position of chief of staff — and manoeuvring to have his deputy, General Xu Xin, take over. Jiang's message to General Chi: "Don't lose heart. Hang in there — stay strong." General Liu's opposition to Chi's advancement, however, had its effects. The CMC chairman was forced to make a compromise by letting General Zhang take precedence over General Chi in terms of protocol. This was despite the fact that General Chi outranked General Zhang in seniority.[104]

Among officers freshly inducted to the CMC, Wang Ke, the newly appointed logistics chief, could also be counted a Jiang protégé. A fellow native of Jiangsu, General Wang began to catch the president's eye from the early 1990s. It was partly due to Jiang's endorsement that General Wang was promoted from vice-commander to commander of the Shenyang Military Region in 1992. General Wang accompanied Jiang when the latter toured the northeast provinces in 1993 and 1994. The CMC chief was on hand when General Wang masterminded a major exercise in the Liaodong Peninsula in August 1994.[105]

The Shanghai and Jiangsu Connection

To a large extent, Jiang was successful in elevating officers from his home province of Jiangsu and his Shanghai power base. In late 1992, the president surprised many observers by reviving the position of assistant chief of staff after a hiatus of eight years. Among those who filled that position were two generals from Jiangsu: Wu Quanxu and Qian Shugen. Both were promoted vice-chiefs of staff in 1995. Jiangsu Faction heavyweights also included the then commissar at the General Logistics Department, General Zhou Kunren; the then vice-commander of the air force General Wu Guangyu; and the fast-rising commissar of the Nanjing Military Region General Fang Zuqi.[106]

An even more pronounced example of Jiang's factionalism was the rise and fall of General Ba Zhongtan. Ba, a police chief in Shanghai, was called to Beijing to head the PAP in late 1992. He became a full general in 1995. By late that year, Jiang was hatching plans to induct Ba into the CMC. Never before had a PAP chief been considered for such an elevated position.

The "helicopter ride" of General Ba, however, had engendered jealousy — and widespread opposition. Born in 1930, he should have retired in 1995. His enemies finally ganged up on Ba in February 1996 upon the murder of NPC vice-chairman Li Peiyao by one of his PAP bodyguards. Originally, Jiang tried to wriggle out of the situation by making a lower-level officer the scapegoat. On February 13, the official media announced that the commander and political commissar of Beijing's No. 1 PAP Brigade had been cashiered because of the Li affair.[107]

Jiang could not hold the tide. Two days later, the decision to sack General Ba and PAP commissar General Zhang Shutian was announced at the headquarters of the military police. General Ba had to take "moral responsibility" for the scandal. The replacement of Ba was General Yang Guoping, a former vice-commissar at the National Defence University (NDU). Reportedly the son of famed general Yang Chengwu, General Yang was believed to be close to General Zhang Zhen, a former NDU president.[108]

Another Shanghai-affiliated stalwart, You Xigui, seemed to have fared better. Jiang's security chief when he was party secretary of Shanghai, General You became in 1995 the Director of the Central Bodyguards Unit of both the General Office of the party Central Committee and the CMC General Office. Shanghai sources claimed You was a very mediocre police officer whose only strong suit was his ability to please his boss. It was indicative of Jiang's lack of confidence that security at Zhongnanhai had to be run by his boys.[109]

The PLA as Jiang's Closest Ally

Part of the secret of Jiang's staying power was his ability to manoeuvre the army to his own benefit. His troubles with the generals over Taiwan and other foreign-policy issues notwithstanding, the president was often able to emulate Mao and Deng, who were past masters in using the PLA as an extra-constitutional means to get things done. For example, the Great Helmsman called in the troops to restore order during the Cultural Revolution. Army support was essential to the success of Deng's *nanxun* or tour of southern China in 1992.

The PLA media often heralded ideas that Jiang would later disseminate across the system. Take, for example, the campaign to study the so-called "Seven Differentials", or how to distinguish between orthodox Marxist views and bourgeois-liberal thoughts (see Chapter 2). This ideological movement was first launched by eight articles in the *Liberation Army Daily* in April and May, 1996. What was interesting was that Jiang had first laid down his ideas on the subject in a meeting with the party's propaganda officials in January that year. However, Jiang chose the army media to launch the controversial campaign because of the PLA's conservatism and political clout.[110]

In early 1997, the PLA began a movement to study Jiang Zemin Theory. This was seen as a move by the president to lay claim to being the country's philosopher-king (see Chapters 2 and 7). As the pro-Chinese Hong Kong monthly *Wide Angle* saw it, "Jiang Theory will first be established in the PLA before it is popularised in the party and the country".[111] Owing to widespread criticism that Jiang was establishing a personality cult, he decided in mid-1997 to put off a national propaganda campaign to study Jiang Theory. The quasi-hagiographic movement, however, went on in many PLA units.

In any case, the PLA was at the forefront in trying to establish Jiang's helmsmanlike stature. Sometimes the adulation displayed in the army media seemed over the top. In major ceremonies such as Army Day, propaganda units invariably played up the portraits and calligraphy of Mao, Deng and Jiang. In the Cultural Revolution, Mao's sayings were said to pack the punch of an atomic bomb. The same was happening with Jiang or Jiang Thought. According to the *Liberation Army Daily*, "Chairman Jiang's five-point instruction [on army building] is not only pasted on the walls of grassroots brigades, it has penetrated the hearts of every soldier".[112]

Chief Political Commissar Yu Yongbo seemed a latter-day Lin Biao when it came to glorifying the CMC chairman. "At a time when [international] competition is hotting up in the run-up to the new century, Chairman Jiang has a lofty and comprehensive vision," General Yu told troops in the Beijing region in mid-1996. "He has asked us to study, re-study and study once more the Marxist canon. It has a big significance."[113] This canon, of course, included Jiang's teachings.

FACTIONAL DYNAMICS AND THE SEEDS OF INSTABILITY

While the PLA top brass and propagandists liked to say that the army was "as united as one piece of well-wrought iron", the reality was different. In the run-up to the June 4 crackdown, CMC leaders including Deng Xiaoping and Yang Shangkun had difficulty securing the support of the military regions. And by 1997, generals who originally opposed the massacre, including Zhang Aiping and Xiao Ke, continued to make trouble for Deng's successor, Jiang Zemin, by voicing opposition to a wide range of policies.[114]

Other factors that undermined unity included foreign policy. It was well known that "hawks" within the army were opposed to efforts by Jiang and a minority of "dovish" officers to promote ties with the US and Russia in 1996 and 1997.[115] Yet the most common reason behind factionalism was power: overt and behind-the-scenes machinations by ambitious cliques and individuals to augment their bases. After the demise of the clan of the Yang brothers, the most obvious factional activity was Jiang building up his cadre of loyalists.

The CMC chairman tried his level best to prevent other real or potential cliques from coalescing. Soon after mid-1989, PLA authorities slapped a ban not only on non-official organisations but also quasi-private gatherings such as "salons", or discussion groups. Before June 4, 1989, these salons were hotbeds for new ideas such as the separation of party and army. However, the commissars were not entirely successful in stopping the activities of PLA veterans. Reports of their activities cropped up now and then in the official media. For example, in October 1995, around 300 old-timers held a get-together at the Great Hall of the People "to recall their old days", according to NCNA. They belonged to two secretive organisations, the October 1 Fellow Students Association and the Long March Park of the Red Army.[116]

In a late 1995 commentary, the *Liberation Army Daily* admitted there were individuals who did not heed central control. "In our party, we do not allow the existence of special persons who ride roughshod over party organisation and party discipline, and who do not accept supervision," the paper said.[117] We seem to hear the voice of Jiang inveighing against veterans such as the Yang brothers. The president could also have been casting subtle aspersions on still-active elders such as Generals Zhang Zhen and Liu Huaqing.

The Basis of Factional Intrigue

Assessment of factional dynamics based on the officers' affiliation with the pre-Liberation field army system was becoming less important in the late 1990s. However, this exercise still had substantial reference value. Looking at the background of senior officers elevated at the late 1995 CMC, it was evident that Third Field and Fourth Field alumni had gained the upper hand.

The Second Field, which used to be headed by Deng and Yang Shangkun, was a dying force. It pretty much petered out with the retirement of General Liu Huaqing in 1997. Indeed, after the eclipse of the Yang clan, it was a foregone conclusion that Second Fielders could never revive their historical glory.[118] The same was true of the remnants of the First Field, whose only top-level representative was Chief of Staff General Fu Quanyou. However, it was true that even in its heyday, the First Field was hardly the PLA's mainstream clique.

The Third Field became arguably the dominant faction in the second half of the 1990s. Stalwarts included Generals Zhang Zhen, Chi Haotian and Wang Ke. The influence of the Third Field was particularly strong among retired generals such as the formidable former defence minister Zhang Aiping, one of Jiang Zemin's nemeses. Generals Zhang Aiping and

Zhang Zhen were close allies.[119] General Zhang was reportedly among a group of senior generals who wrote a petition to the authorities in 1997 asking for better treatment for ousted party chief Zhao Ziyang.

Standard-bearers of the Fourth Field Army were Generals Zhang Wannian and Yu Yongbo. General Zhang earned his spurs in the northeast in the mid- to late-1940s (see following section). Since the early 1990s, Fourth Fielders had experienced some form of revival following a couple of decades of eclipse after the fall of Lin Biao, the former defence minister and a founder of the elite group. One factor behind the resuscitation of the Fourth Field was the partial rehabilitation of the reputation of Marshal Lin. Before his death in 1995, conservative patriarch Chen Yun had lent his support to Fourth Field alumni. The most important reason, however, was Jiang's perception that given their weakness, Fourth Field affiliates would present him with the least threat.[120]

Apart from affiliation with the Field Army system, camaraderie borne out of participation in battles such as the Korean War of 1950–1951 and the Vietnam War of 1979 was a basis for mutual support and cliquishness among officers. By early 1998, many top generals were high-fliers who earned their first decorations in the 1979 conflict. They included the commanders of the Beijing, Chengdu and Lanzhou military regions, respectively Generals Li Xinliang, Liao Xilong and Guo Boxiong.[121]

Other Foci of Loyalty

The "five lakes and four seas" notwithstanding, geographically-based affiliation was always an important factor behind PLA factionalism. Depending on the era, generals from a particular province tended to dominate the scene. Under Deng Xiaoping, it was the Sichuan boys who towered over heaven and earth. Veterans from the most populous province in China included the patriarch and members of the Yang clan. The other important home province of generals was Hubei, one of whose most well-known representatives was the late president Li Xiannian.

Under Jiang, the Shandong generals had pretty much the run of the place. And the preponderance of this group went further than that of the Sichuan clique. Among CMC members, Generals Zhang Wannian, Chi Haotian and Wang Ruilin were from the east coast redoubt. Other senior representatives included former PAP chief Ba Zhongtan; Beijing commander General Li Xinliang; Shenyang commissar General Jiang Futang;

former naval commissar Admiral Yang Huaiqing; former COSTIND commissar, General Li Jinai; the President of the National Defence University,
General Xing Shizhong; and the President of the Academy of Military Science, General Xu Huizi.[122]

Factionalism could also be based on professional affiliation. Until the
retirement of General Liu Huaqing in 1997, officers who had served in the
navy had a head start over the competition. The Second Artillery Unit, or
missiles squad, was catapulted into the limelight by the Taiwan Strait crisis
of 1995–1996. Following the first missile test off the Taiwan coast in July
1995, eight Second Artillery officers were given instant promotions.
Vice-commander Major-General Zhao Xijun was made a lieutenant-
general. And seven senior colonels were elevated to major-generals.[123]

Even more than the civilian sector, the PLA was the bastion of
gaoganzidi or offspring of party elders. Princelings who packed a punch
included the former head of the Equipment Department and prominent
PLA entrepreneur, He Ping (son-in-law of Deng Xiaoping); the former
chief of COSTIND, General Ding Henggao (son-in-law of Marshal Nie
Rongzhen); Navy Vice-Commander Admiral He Pengfei (son of Marshal
He Long); Head of the General Political Department's Liaison Office, General Ye Xuanning (son of Marshal Ye Jianying); and a PAP divisional commissar, Liu Yuan (son of former president Liu Shaoqi). In addition, the sons
of the following first-generation leaders occupied senior posts: generals
Chen Yi, Yang Yong, Peng Dehuai, Liu Bocheng and Su Yu.[124]

However, at the 15th Party Congress in late 1997, President Jiang's
intention to curtail the influence of the *gaoganzidi* became clear. On both
the civilian and military sides, princelings suffered a reverse so far as promotion to the Central Committee was concerned. It was anticipated that
more PLA *gaoganzidi* would seek lucrative careers in army-affiliated businesses.[125]

Zhang Wannian: Commander of the 21st Century?

Zhang Wannian, 70, surprised many observers in September 1995 by being
ranked ahead of Chi Haotian when the two were named CMC vice-
chairmen. General Chi was not only one year younger than General Zhang
but also the latter's predecessor as chief of staff. Moreover, Chi, a Korean
War hero, became a full general in 1988, six years earlier than General
Zhang. The latter might also have suffered political damage during the

June 4, 1989 crisis. Then commander of Guangzhou military region, General Zhang was one of the last regional leaders to profess support for Deng Xiaoping's suppression of the Tiananmen Square rebels.

A major reason behind General Zhang's rise was his perceived innocuousness in the eyes of his boss, President Jiang. The Shandong native did not have an independent power base or circle of close followers. It was, however, also true that he had impressive professional credentials. The CMC vice-chairman distinguished himself in the 1979 Vietnam War as well as the crisis with Taiwan in the late 1950s. As chief of staff, he oversaw the PLA's aggressive drive to modernise weaponry and upgrade training. General Zhang was credited with boosting the number and quality of specialised units such as the rapid-response and amphibious divisions, as well as the army's ability to deploy different units and weapon systems simultaneously.[126]

By late 1995, however, the fast-rising general had displayed disturbing dimensions of ambition and ruthlessness. He seemed to have exploited the series of war games off Taiwan to promote his image and power. As discussed earlier, the CMC vice-chairman, whose portfolio included Taiwan, was most vociferous in urging "resolute action" against the KMT stronghold. In national coverage of the military manoeuvres, General Zhang got top billing as a master strategist. In some official news releases about the exercises, he was the only PLA officer mentioned.[127]

By 1997, General Zhang was firming up his power base. As CMC vice-chairman, he had a big say on personnel issues, and this role increased following the retirement of Generals Liu Huaqing and Zhang Zhen. Protégés General Zhang had promoted included Beijing commander General Li Xinliang and the commissar of the Shenyang military region Jiang Futang. General Jiang worked with General Zhang in the Jinan region in the early 1990s. General Li, who also distinguished himself in the Vietnam War, worked under General Zhang in the Guangzhou region in the late 1980s. That the former was transferred to Beijing, the most important region, after just two years of stewardship of the Shenyang region showed he was a man to watch.[128]

General Zhang also wasted little time in broadening his portfolio to include ideology and political indoctrination, even though these were more the province of General Chi and General Yu Yongbo. Dubbed a second Yang Baibing, General Zhang engineered a quasi-cult of personality around President Jiang. According to military sources, General Zhang would often surprise his fellow officers when, in the midst of meetings devoted to operational matters, he stood up and invited his colleagues to proffer their allegiance to the CMC chairman. After Deng Xiaoping's death, General Zhang was the first senior officer to swear loyalty publicly to Jiang.[129]

In terms of ideology, General Zhang was a dyed-in-the-wool hawk. He was tough on reunification issues including Taiwan and Tibet as well as foreign policy. Western diplomats said that on policy with the US, General Zhang had largely given up Deng's "pro-American" stance. General Chi Haotian, by contrast, still subscribed to the late patriarch's theory that good relations with America were essential to the fast-paced development of the country.[130]

General Zhang, however, might have gone overboard, in the process alienating large numbers of his colleagues. By late 1996, General Liu Huaqing had in private meetings begun attacking him for empire building. Sources said General Liu again cited the "five lakes and four seas" dictum in putting down the upstart. In the run-up to the 15th Party Congress, General Liu was successful in his effort to prevent General Zhang from getting into the Politburo Standing Committee.[131] There were also unconfirmed reports of his having given patronage to officers with dubious characters.

THE PROBLEM OF DISCIPLINE

The Odour of Corruption

"From ancient to modern times, corrupt armies will not have real combat power," General Zhang Zhen said at a meeting on army disciplinary work in early 1996. "In this new historical period, there should be higher standards and conscientious action against corruption in the army." Stricter rules were set for areas including standards of accommodation, and the use of official residences, cars, and personal secretaries.[132]

At the most obvious level, most infractions of discipline had to do with problems of what army ideological and political work (IPW) specialists called "money, power and pretty women". Beginning in the early 1990s, there was a series of high-profile cases such as car-smuggling in Shandong and Liaoning provinces. Other common crimes included offering "protection" to gangs and illegal businesses (see following story).

Officers snared by sex traps were a comparatively new phenomenon of the 1990s. In a 1995 raid on a Fuzhou entertainment parlour with show girls and masseuses, police nabbed two colonels, one from the navy and the other from the air force. While TV was initially installed in barracks to enhance the "cultural life" of troops, the *Liberation Army Daily* decried the fact that "pornography is secretly penetrating the camps". "People's thoughts turn rotten" from pornography, the paper said. It recommended that "all sorts of measures be taken to prevent 'yellow poison' from infiltrating barracks even deeper".[133]

Disciplinary problems included ill-treatment of recruits, which was common in Western armies but relatively rare in the PLA until the mid-1990s. In late 1995, Wang Kaifeng, a Xining-based platoon leader from the Lanzhou military region, was sentenced to three-and-a-half years for beating up a conscript. The victim had reportedly cheated during an army examination. Ill-treatment was supposed to be the cause of the notorious incident in Beijing in September 1994, when a People's Armed Police officer ran amok and killed more than ten of his colleagues and Beijing residents.[134]

A measure of PLA humanitarianism was prescribed. Authorities at the Chengdu military region said they had abandoned the method of forcing greenhorns to go through an unreasonable degree of hardship. "Training must progress from easy to difficult and take a gradual approach," a division chief in the region said. Officers in a division of the Second Artillery Corps said they believed recruits should be treated with "the heart of parents and the feelings of brothers".[135]

The PLA as an Agent of Instability

More serious a concern for the Jiang leadership than disciplinary problems, however, was the fact that the PLA had become a source of political instability in different areas. Instead of a Great Wall of Steel buttressing the authority of the party and the Jiang faction, PLA units in many provinces and cities became a law unto itself. They fought for turf with other law-and-order units — and posed grave security risks.

Consider the following scandal, which shook the CMC. In October 1995, a private entrepreneur with good PLA connections, Yun Dabin, got into an altercation with Guangzhou police while taking a joy ride with his girlfriend. Yun called his PLA cronies, who came out in force. A dozen-odd policemen from the Shahe branch of the Guangzhou Public Security Bureau were badly beaten up. It turned out that Yun had "rented" a military licence plate at a few thousand yuan a year. Soon after the incident, which was widely reported in the Hong Kong and Taiwan press, there were rumours that Jiang would intervene to punish the culprits. Yet only a platoon leader was cashiered. The affair did not even go to military courts, not to mention the civilian judicial process.[136]

In rich Guangdong, there were cases galore of soldiers not paying after going to karaoke bars, snatching pricey consumer items, or extorting money from Hong Kong lorry drivers. Military supremoes, however, were often able to stop local media from running critical exposés. This took place when a Shenzhen newspaper wanted to print a story on military vehicles breaking traffic regulations. Shenzhen garrison commander Li Youlie protested, and succeeded in suppressing the article. Other Guangdong residents complained that it was often difficult to distinguish between real and fake PLA units. In a swoop in mid-1996, 28 fake PLA groups were cracked and more than 700 bogus soldiers arrested. The official media claimed that the culprits were crooks with no PLA connections. In reality, quite a few of the bogus army concerns were backed by real army units or demobilised troops.[137]

Even more alarming for the CMC leadership was the phenomenon of army officers "colluding" with regional cadres. Consider the 1996 scandal involving the head of a unit in the General Staff Department (GSD), a major-general surnamed Liu. In charge of PLA facilities such as hotels and other establishments, General Liu had excellent ties with local civilian leaders. He reportedly used these *guanxi* ("connections") to find a plum job for a crony who had been in jail for 13 years. After certifying that the crook had been "in PLA service" for 13 years, the general got him the position of vice-mayor in a medium-sized city in Guangxi Province.

The impostor's true identity was exposed while he was seeking a promotion in early 1997. However, the GSD immediately dispatched a few officers to Guangxi to bail him out. These officers claimed that President Jiang had approved of the crook's promotion and that he was on a "special mission" in the province. After the scam came to light, the CMC chairman set up a high-level work team headed by Politburo member Hu Jintao to look into the matter. Liu and several officers in his division, including another major-general and a few senior colonels, were suspended or detained for further investigation. For Jiang, what was most disturbing was the infringement of the rule, set by Chairman Mao, that army personnel should not be allowed to develop political ties with local cadres.[138]

Escalation of Ideological and Political Work

Perhaps reflecting his belief in the rule of personality, Jiang Zemin set a lot of store by boosting the *xiuyang* ("virtue and self-cultivation") of officers and soldiers (see Chapter 2). In a talk to the students of the National Defence University in 1995, the president said that given the "fast-shifting circumstances", soldiers must "ceaselessly" study the thoughts of Marx, Mao, and Deng. "If they [officers and soldiers] don't understand history, if their knowledge of science and culture is low, and if their ideological level, spiritual state and leadership quality are not high, it will be difficult for them to do their work well," Jiang said.[139]

In early 1996, the CMC promulgated a series of "regulations on strengthening the management and education of medium-ranking and senior officers in the army". "The long-term construction of the army and the stability of the country," the commissars said, "hinged on the success of this programme." What the ideological gurus recommended, however, seemed hardly new: "to uphold the party's basic principles and fundamental lines; to establish a correct world view, philosophy of life and values; and to maintain a vibrant revolutionary spirit".[140]

In 1997, the theme of ideological and political work (IPW) went back to basics. In the words of General Fu Quanyou, soldiers had to observe the Maoist ideal of "plain living and hard struggle". The army papers urged troops to "self-consciously combat Mammonism, hedonism and individualism". "Army officers must accustom themselves to tightening their belts," said the commentator of *Liberation Army Daily*. "They must boost their self-consciousness in avoiding extravagance."[141]

Yet even as IPW was being escalated, the ranks of the suspects of corruption kept rising. By late 1995, CMC disciplinary organs were investigating officers including the commissar and head of the political department of a group army as well as the head of the logistics department of a provincial military district. One million yuan was found in the home of the group army commissar. Then came reports in 1997 of a large-scale car-smuggling scandal in Liaoning. The culprits, who were illegally bringing in Japanese sedans worth more than 100 million yuan, were PLA and PAP officers. The case came to light when the army and para-military units opened fire on each other because of arguments over the division of the spoils.[142]

The Army Business Empire Runs Amok

As political scientist Wang Shaoguang indicated, the PLA was the only force in the world that maintained a substantial business empire. Dr Wang pointed out that *bingshang* ("army business") could encourage corruption and hurt morale.[143] By late 1997, however, this phenomenon was only discussed among a small elite of liberal intellectuals. As with most aspects of army life, *bingshang* was shrouded in secrecy.

Throughout the 1990s, Jiang and the CMC leadership made many attempts to curtail the PLA's commercial activities. The number of *bingshang* companies shrank from about 20,000 in the early 1990s to roughly 10,000 by 1997. An effort was made in 1995 to unify all PLA business units under the General Logistics Department. This followed steps taken in 1993 and 1994 to close down outfits beneath the level of the regional commands. Senior Politburo members such as Zhu Rongji were personally involved in negotiations with the generals in closing down *bingshang* units.[144]

By early 1998, apparently more thorough efforts to restrict *bingshang* were reported by the Hong Kong media. For example, the range of non-military activities that soldiers could engage in was restricted: some PLA units could only grow vegetables for their own use. Army departments that maintained substantial or controlling interests in shareholding corporations were asked to decrease their holdings and gradually transfer ownership rights to local administrations. Jiang was reported as having given instructions that the separation of army and business should be accomplished in three years.[145]

Some analysts argued that unless the army was given adequate compensation and its budget was raised, PLA businesses would continue to flourish. Huge sums were at stake. Exports from all *bingshang* units reportedly reached US$7 billion in 1997. The bulk of the profits went into improving the standard of living of soldiers. The commercial activities also provided an outlet for demobilised troops who could not be absorbed by civilian units.

That PLA Inc had become an important component of the economy could be seen by the fact that by 1996, army businesses had put in applications for nearly 3,000 patents, and more than 1,600 had been granted. Fully half of the 2.1 million-strong ground forces were believed to be working in industrial or commercial entities. Like ordinary companies, *bingshang* units were in 1997 becoming conglomerates and shareholding corporations. Offshoots of giants such as the Poly Group of the General Staff Department were listed on the Shanghai and Hong Kong stock markets. However, as the number of *bingshang* multinationals grew, so did cases of alleged impropriety and even scandals in both the economic and political arenas. The most famous of this was contribution allegedly given to the Clinton presidential campaign by a company run by the daughter of General Liu Huaqing. Ms Liu Chaoying denied the story, which made it to the front pages of American papers on the eve of Clinton's visit to China in June 1998.[146]

It was not until July 1998 that Jiang grasped the nettle by declaring a ban on *bingshang*. "All military and armed police forces must not engage in business activities," the CMC chief said. This surprising development was followed by a ritualistic show of support by members of the top brass. Yet army sources said that the generals would be given generous compensation for closing down enterprises or turning them over to civilian authorities. On top of an anticipated boost in the PLA budget, they would be getting compensation of at least 30 billion yuan a year from Beijing until the early 2000s. And provincial and municipal administrations would be footing bills totalling more than 100 billion yuan when they take over PLA businesses and assume more responsibility for providing social welfare and employment for soldiers.[147]

Moreover, the proscription on *bingshang* could not be accomplished in a year or two. It would take a long time for huge companies such as the Poly Group to be restructured or "civilianised". Nor would the ban be comprehensive. Army units would be allowed to keep their most lucrative line: the sale and procurement of armaments. Chinese sources said in 1998 that many generals were actually happy about the prospect of getting rid of loss-making factories — and securing hefty compensation for them. Premier Zhu, who had to find the funds to pacify the generals, was said to be unhappy about Jiang's sudden decision. This was despite the president's argument that the payout for the PLA would be more than covered by money saved through eradicating corruption and smuggling by *bingshang* units.

THE PROBLEMATIC NATURE OF THE PEOPLE'S ARMED POLICE

The Dubious Goals of the PAP

By late 1997, the People's Armed Police, or *wujing* in Chinese, was poised to become one of the most important units of China's defence forces. Yet the 15-year-old division, which had come under the total control of the CMC by the mid-1990s, illustrated the whole range of ills plaguing the PLA: factionalism, lack of public scrutiny, and worsening discipline. After all, no other country had a comparable institution — and its rapid expansion under Jiang raised queries about the possibility of maladministration and abuses.

In theory, the PAP worked alongside the PLA to ensure national security. They helped guard the borders and maintained law and order in areas ranging from forests to railway lines. Yet under Jiang Zemin, the *wujing* became mainly a tool of the dictatorship of the proletariat, that is, a juggernaut against challenges to the regime posed by elements including gangs, religious sects, underground political organisations, and workers on industrial action. The dramatic increase in the PAP establishment coincided with the party leadership's need to crush growing internal disorder. And unlike the police and state security departments, the PAP was immune from administrative downsizing ordered by Zhu Rongji in March 1998.

PAP officers were particularly on the lookout for *tufa* ("suddenly developed") manifestations of anti-government sentiment. The classic example was the incident in Renshou county, Sichuan, in mid-1993, when up to 30,000 peasants held rallies to demand a cut in taxes and government levies. They were dispersed by the PAP.

Former commander General Ba Zhongtan highlighted the importance of the PAP as the defender of the administration in what he called the "new historical period". "The PAP must pay close attention to developments in the international and domestic situation," he said in late 1995. "It must boost its sense of danger, keep up its guard and assiduously elevate its level of combat-readiness." The Jiang confidant was referring to efforts by domestic and foreign enemies to unseat the party dictatorship.[148]

The PAP as Jiang's Personal Army

Soon after his rise to power in 1989, Jiang devoted much energy to turning the *wujing* into his preserve. The president figured that given his lack of military credentials, it would be difficult for him to exert full control over the PLA. And the police — the third "tool of proletarian dictatorship" — was still under the influence of heavyweight politicians such as Qiao Shi and Li Peng.[149]

Given its short history, the PAP was much less riven by factionalism than the PLA. Jiang took advantage of the purge of the *wujing* soon after the June 4 massacre to install his protégés in the top echelons. The president did not encounter much resistance when he recalled former Shanghai police chief Ba Zhongtan from retirement and appointed him PAP commander (see previous section).

By mid-1995, Jiang had hatched a plan for the dramatic expansion of the PAP to more than 1.5 million men by the end of the century. Heavy-duty armaments that would normally go to the PLA were ordered for the *wujing*. These included tanks, armoured personnel carriers, heavy artillery, helicopter gunships, and reconnaissance equipment. During a PAP ceremony in late 1996, Jiang commended the force for acquiring state-of-the-art hardware in the areas of riot control, nocturnal operations, anti-chemical warfare, and reconnaisance.[150]

The PAP was growing at the expense of the army as Jiang went ahead with plans to lop off at least 500,000 soldiers from the PLA establishment. At least 150,000 of the demobilised soldiers — including more than 15 mechanised units — were absorbed by the *wujing* in early 1997. This strategy served many purposes. The much-hyped PLA demobilisation enabled Jiang to boost his international prestige. And the PAP's expansion served to strengthen his power base.

By 1996, even experienced army officers were absorbed into the *wujing*. This could be seen from the appointment of four vice-commanders in the middle of the year. Three of them were from PLA units. The newly promoted PAP officers were the vice-commander of the Chengdu military region, Zhu Chengyou; head of the security department of the General Political Department, Zhu Shuguang; vice-commander of the Nanjing Army Academy, Zhang Jinbao; and PAP chief of staff, Wu Shuangzhan. Of the four, only Major-General Wu was a PAP veteran. Moreover, the ranks of the appointees were surprisingly high, which suggested that the *wujing* had been upgraded to the same level as the army, navy and air force. For example, a PAP vice commander would not until now have been as senior an officer as Zhu Chengyou, a lieutenant-general.[151] And to cap it all, commander Yang Guoping made history for the PAP when he was made a full general in 1998.

Lack of Public Scrutiny

While the PAP was in theory under the dual leadership of the PLA and the

State Council, it was subject to even less public scrutiny than even the army. Even its size was a matter of controversy. The official media put it at 650,000 or so in the mid-1990s. Yet most Western and independent Chinese analysts said its strength had reached at least 850,000 by the end of 1995. By early 1997, the PAP had exceeded one million. While the NPC endorsed the official PLA budget each March, outlays for the PAP were shrouded in secrecy. There was no publicity surrounding the CMC's formal assumption of control over the PAP in mid-1997.[152]

Since the early 1990s, the PAP had suffered from the problem of being given too much power when not enough qualified officers could be found. Across the cities — but particularly in the southeast coast where there was money to be made — turf wars between the PAP and the police took place almost on a weekly basis. This internecine struggle often erupted over "protection fees" to be solicited from entertainment and even vice establishments, many of which had connections with police or quasi-military units. An internal report said that in 1995, there were 211 incidents of conflict between the PAP and local government units, enterprises or members of the public. In Shenzhen, the PAP and related businesses were so powerful they were often outside the purview of local government authorities. In early 1996, the wife of mayor Li Zibin was reportedly beaten up by PAP officers after an altercation between her driver and a few *wujing* roughs.[153]

The murder of NPC vice-chairman Li Peiyao by a PAP guard — and the fall of General Ba — provided *wujing* critics from around the country with an excuse to hit out at the unpopular force. At the NPC session in March 1996, many regional deputies groused about the dictatorial behaviour of para-military brigades in their home cities. These complaints resulted in a temporary delay in the PAP's expansion plans.

Quite a number of senior *wujing* cadres were frank about disciplinary problems in the force. As the head of the Shandong PAP brigade Yang Jiajie put it: "Nowadays, temptations in society are too numerous, and there is interference from various thought currents." He said given the poor salaries of PAP officers, leaders had to boost ideological education to ensure that they stay straight. Si Qiuyi, the commander of the Yunnan PAP brigade, agreed. "The troops are hardly segregated from the world," he said. "Social trends will infiltrate the barracks." General Si recommended more political classes to make sure that the rank and file would be imbued with the "correct philosophy of life and the correct values".[154]

It could also be argued that by coming under the control of the military commission, the PAP would be affected by the same problems that plagued the PLA. In an internal speech in 1996, Commander Yang Guoping listed six "weak links" in the PAP hierarchy. They included "not paying enough attention to ideological work"; lax party organisation; problems in the "self-construction and work habits" of top officers; near-chaotic internal administration; lax organisational discipline; and poor relations with the local administration and the public.[155]

In a speech to a *wujing* detachment in late 1996, Jiang called on PAP officers to do more to "combat the infiltration of corrupt thoughts and culture". "You must be able to withstand corrosion and never get corrupted," he said. Yet there was no magic formula to ensure that the PAP would have a better track record than the PLA. This perhaps explained the note of urgency — if not desperation — in General Zhang Wannian's plea that the PAP must observe the party's "absolute leadership". General Zhang told a gathering of *wujing* representatives in early 1997: "You must at any time and under any circumstances safeguard resolutely the authority of the party leadership collective with comrade Jiang Zemin as its core." "You must resolutely abide by the instructions given by the party central authorities and the CMC with comrade Jiang Zemin as its core," he added.[156] Such Maoist — or Lin Biao-like — rhetoric, however, only called into doubt the ability of the party to turn the *wujing* into a modern and civilised force.

THE PLA IN THE 21ST CENTURY
A Real "Elite Force"?

Jiang Zemin went some distance in reviving Mao's ideal of an elite troop: a superior cadre of soldier-citizens who would set the pace for the nation. The enlarged Central Military Commission (CMC) meeting of late 1997 enshrined Jiang's idea that the PLA and PAP should be "one step ahead" of the nation in putting into practice the spirit of the 15th Party Congress. This new-era vanguard of the proletariat would serve many purposes for Jiang and the party: promote loyalty to the CCP "with comrade Zemin as its core"; suppress domestic unrest; play up nationalism; and in general prolong the party's mandate of heaven.

Much of the CMC's effort in the second half of the 1990s was to build up an "elite corps". While talking about the military version of the Ninth Five-Year Plan (1996–2000) and the 15-year Long-term Development Blueprint (1996–2010), Jiang said in late 1995: "We must concentrate on quality construction and insist upon the road of building up an elite corps." As General Chi Haotian put it in 1997, the army leadership was gunning for a "twofold transformation": "Soldiers must convert their ability to win a regional warfare under ordinary conditions to one that is under hi-tech conditions; they must seek qualitative excellence instead of quantitative superiority."[157]

In deference to the "small is big" principle, the CMC decided in late 1996 to demobilise a further half a million soldiers by the end of the century. Out of the remaining 2.5 million troops, one-fifth or half a million men would be converted into the cream of the cream. This select group would have access to new equipment and be trained in special skills including rapid-response tactics. Quality control would especially be boosted in crack units in the air force, navy, and missile forces. General Zhang Wannian, who played a key role in upgrading personnel, said: "We must build up a fighting corps with an adequate numerical strength; a scientific organisation and division of labour; high quality; advanced equipment; and advanced theory."[158]

By early 1998, officers and the rank and file were following Jiang's instructions on the priority given to training: "We should nurture talents first and let equipment catch up later. It won't do to lavish resources on equipment first and then wait for qualified personnel." By late 1997, 56 per cent of all officers had some form of college qualification. Special efforts were made to recruit "intellectuals". Among the 5,300 university graduates who signed up in 1997, nine per cent had master's or doctoral degrees. For example, 140 college graduates had attended classes at the famous Shijiazhuang Army Academy, the largest in Asia.[159]

The Class Nature of the PLA

Jiang and CCP leaders realised, of course, that even the most elite army could be a double-edged sword. Apart from problems of discipline and corruption (see previous section), military forces could make mischief in the political arena. Hence the promulgation in late 1995 of a code on the punishment of a host of crimes and cases of dereliction of duty among soldiers.

Fifty-nine kinds of felonies and disciplinary infractions were cited in the legislation. They included rebellion, harming national security, obstructing wartime orders, undermining combat power, and harming troop management. The death penalty and life imprisonment would be meted out to the "masterminds and perpetrators of armed rebellion". Culprits for leaking PLA secrets could be liable to imprisonment ranging from seven years in jail to life incarceration. This Draconian law was seen as an effort by Jiang to ensure that the PLA — or certain army factions — would not become an agent of instability.[160]

What Jiang and company might be reluctant to recognise was the fact that China had become a class society (see Chapter 3) and that, like workers, farmers and intellectuals, the PLA had become a "class" with its own distinct interests and demands. In a late 1997 commentary, the *Liberation Army Daily* asked the PLA to subsume its economic demands under national requirements. "Some people will get more out of reform and some less," the mouthpiece said. "A minority of units and people may have to make temporary sacrifices." The *Daily* referred to the PLA as an "armed group with the spirit of self-sacrifice".[161] The fact of the matter, however, was that time could not stand still. The economy and society were moving on — and officers and foot soldiers alike had to claim their share of the pie.

Conflict of interest between the Jiang leadership and the PLA came to a head with the demobilisation of half a million men, which was not officially announced until September 1997. Although the personnel decision had been made earlier, senior officers including General Liu Huaqing opposed the move all the way. This was despite his public protestation of support for Deng's idea about "improving the quality of the army through taking the road of fewer but better troops". The officers stressed that money saved through reducing personnel must be spent on boosting the weapons programme.[162]

Finding jobs for demobilised soldiers also presented one headache after another to party and government authorities. In the end, Beijing had to resort to a familiar tool: imposing a "quota" on provinces, cities and counties to take up a fixed number of former PLA officers and soldiers. A joint circular by the CMC and the State Council warned that local leaders "failing to meet resettlement targets or refusing to hire demobilised soldiers" would be punished.[163] By mid-1998, the PLA had functioned fully as an interest group by lobbying vigorously for economic benefits and diplomatic clout (see foregoing sections).

Lack of Legislative Accountability
The PLA and the NPC

In an early 1996 speech on army discipline, General Zhang Zhen advocated "strengthening and perfecting inner-party supervision". He decried "special people who are above party organisation and party supervision".[164] It was significant that the Long March veteran did not mention supervision by the National People's Congress (NPC). This was despite the fact that the Chinese constitution stated clearly that the state CMC was in charge of the armed forces and that it was accountable to the NPC and its Standing Committee.

It was no coincidence that then NPC chief Qiao Shi raised the issue of the accountability of the armed forces during a trip to the Ukraine in early 1996. While briefing the Ukrainian press, Qiao pointed out that the NPC "exercised state power in a united manner". The power of the Chinese parliament, said the liberal cadre, included "the leadership of the armed forces".[165] However, President Jiang did not agree. It was true that throughout the mid-1990s, Jiang made much of the slogan of "running the army according to law". What the CMC chairman meant, however, was only that officers and soldiers must follow instructions and codes laid down by the party CMC — and in some instances rubberstamped by the NPC. Examples included the retirement-at-65 rule for senior officers such as heads of regional commands.

In spite of aggressive lobbying by Qiao and company, the question of the legislature exercising substantial power over the PLA did not arise. The NPC, of course, fulfilled theoretical functions such as approving the annual defence outlay. In practice, parliamentarians had no say over the decisions of the CMC or the behaviour of officers. For example, the legislature had no power to combat army-related graft. Practically all major corruption cases involving military personnel were handled by PLA courts and "disciplinary inspection" organs.[166]

Among the raft of PLA-related laws passed in the 1990s, a couple or so seemed to enshrine the principle of the NPC supervising the defence forces. For example, the 1996 draft law on the declaration of hostilities upheld the constitutional point that the NPC had ultimate control over the armed forces. It stated that only the NPC Standing Committee had the right to determine whether the country had entered into a state of war or a state of emergency — and whether the PLA should "retaliate against foreign invasion". The formal declaration of hostilities against a foreign country had to be made by the state president and carried out by the CMC.[167] Analysts agreed, however, that whatever rights the NPC had gained through this legislation were largely theoretical.

Most statutes enacted in this period, however, invested the PLA with real gains in power. A common principle enshrined in these codes was the "marriage" between peace-time and war-time needs — hence the PLA's "legitimacy" in grasping a bigger slice of resources. For example, the Law on the People's Air Defence saluted the "fusion" principle. It said that funds for air defence should be shared between the state and the PLA. Moreover, the requirements of air defence should be meshed with those of city planning and economic development.[168]

The National Defence Law of 1997

The National Defence Law of 1997 turned back the clock of defence modernisation by enshrining the PLA's status as a "state within a state". It seemed a trade-off between Jiang and the top brass. The law protected the PLA's special privileges even as it codified the army's need to be loyal to the party leadership. Firstly, the principle of the CCP's "absolute leadership" over the PLA was highlighted. "The armed forces of the People's Republic of China accepts the leadership of the CCP," the law said.[169] Since Jiang was both the "leadership core" of the party and the CMC, the law fuelled criticism that the PLA was becoming a Jiang Army.

The PLA got much in return. The law saluted the Maoist principle of the "interchangeability" between the military and civilian sectors. It upheld the principle of "the fusion of the [needs of the] army and the people and those of peace and war". In industry, the statute said, "army production would have priority" in the allocation of resources. The code also stipulated that the army budget would increase at a rate "commensurate with the needs of national defence and the development level of the national economy".[170]

Even more important than a bigger share of the economic pie, however, was the elevation of the PLA's status. And this went beyond stipulations that soldiers were entitled to society's "respect and priority treatment". In his preamble to the code, Defence Minister General Chi Haotian played up the fact that "national defence is a security guarantee for the nation's survival and development". General Chi vastly expanded the frame of reference for army work. Apart from repelling foreign aggression, the PLA would play a key role in combating internal rebellion, "armed turmoil" and "splittist" activities perpetrated by pro-independence elements in Taiwan, Tibet and Xinjiang.[171]

The code also said the PLA had legal competence over "activities in the political, economic, diplomatic, technology and education areas that are related to military affairs". It could thus serve to legitimise the PLA's attempt to extend its tentacles to civilian life. Needless to say, this development ran counter to Deng's insistence that the army adopt a low political profile and that it must be subordinate to the requirements of economic development.

It was not surprising that liberal academics and legislators had questioned the constitutional basis of the new law, including its clause about absolute "party leadership" over the PLA. Nowhere does the Chinese Constitution state that the PLA is the party's preserve. The charter points out that the armed forces "belong" to the people. It says that the defence forces are led by the state CMC, which reports to the NPC (see previous section).

An NPC insider pointed out it was precisely those concerns of unconstitutionality that had bogged down the drafting of the defence law, which began five years ago. He added that military authorities had made tell-tale adjustments to earlier versions of the draft. For example, the mid-1996 version said the PLA "obeys" the CCP leadership. The word "accepts", used in the final version, seemed somewhat more neutral — and less of a blatant violation of the spirit of the constitution. The drafters also used a sleight of hand in an apparent effort to befuddle the distinction between the party and the state CMC. The final draft stated that the "Central Military Commission leads the country's armed forces", without pinpointing whether it was the party or the state commission.[172]

In any case, the codification of the "party commands the gun" doctrine might have torpedoed efforts by reformers to wean the army away from the party. After all, Deng's decision in the early 1980s to establish the state CMC was precisely an attempt to shift some of the responsibilities of looking after the army from the party to state organs.

Test case: The NPC and the Taiwan issue

The NPC's near-impotence in military matters was illustrated by the March 1996 legislative session, which coincided with the height of the tension over the Taiwan Strait. This was despite the fact that the PLA leadership had cunningly used the occasion to let on that its aggressive posture towards the "breakaway province" had the support of legislators from all over the country.

First of all, the PLA set the tone for the legislature by announcing a new series of missiles tests off the Taiwan coast at 6 am, March 5, 1996, just a few hours before the plenary session was to open. The leitmotif having been laid down, doubts raised by individual legislators about the propriety of the war games — or the rhetoric of the generals — could be construed as expressions of lack of patriotism.[173]

Because of the news blackout, many deputies were unaware of what kinds of bombs and other weapons had been used. For example, most NPC members did not know that the missiles that were splashing down near Taipei cost US$2 million apiece. At a time when numerous deputies from the central and western provinces were beating their chests over the failure to get development funds from Beijing, the extravagance of the PLA must have struck a jarring note. Moreover, the entire bill for the half year of manoeuvres ran into billions of yuan. Since ordinary NPC delegates lacked even basic information about the war games, they were not in a position to criticise the PLA.

The generals were given ample media exposure to whip up a nationwide enthusiasm for patriotism — and for arms procurement — by decrying Washington's decision to send two aircraft carriers to the Strait. "We're not afraid of aircraft carriers," said General Ding Henggao. "If there is a need, we have an ability to build our own."[174] General Ding and his colleagues seemed to have forgotten that the decision to spend even one yuan on military supplies should be made by the people and the NPC — and not army officers apparently bent on expansionism.

With the exception of Hong Kong's irrepressible deputy, the late Liu Yiu-chu, who was an incorrigible dove, not a single parliamentarian so much as expressed a view on whether the PLA should continue with the quasi-war preparations. There were moments when even top civilian leaders seemed mere puppets of the military machine. President Jiang and Vice-Premier Qian Qichen read from prepared scripts when they briefed deputies and foreign journalists on the Taiwan question. On the same occasions, however, the two did not use prepared notes while discussing other subjects such as the economy. The standard line on Taiwan had been laid down by a "collective leadership" with a heavy military component.[175]

Residual Doubts About PLA "Adventurism"

In the wake of the two Sino-US presidential summits in October 1997 and June 1998, bilateral military relations were pretty much restored to levels before 1989. In 1997, PLA officers toured a record 70 countries and regions.[176] While the global prestige of Chinese military forces had improved, this did not mean that it was looked upon as a modern, responsible institution worthy of the trust of the international community. Familiar problems cited by foreign observers included the lack of transparency and public scrutiny in and out of China.

So long as the PLA remained the army of the party — or its dominant faction — it was not subject to the checks and balances considered the norm in the developed world. What China's neighbours worried most was that under this quasi-feudalistic setting, possibilities of generals seeking foreign adventures to boost their clout could not be ruled out. The issue of Taiwan — which remained a flashpoint in the Asia-Pacific region in 1998 — again yielded good examples of the overweening ambition of PLA generals. The party leadership had, in the summer of 1996, ruled out strong-armed tactics at least for the time being. In the interest of a smooth Hong Kong handover and a trouble-free 15th Party Congress, hardball measures such as military manoeuvres were mothballed. Moreover, while the Jiang leadership continued with its time-honoured carrot-and-stick approach, the president seemed predisposed to another charm offensive in early 1998.[177]

The top brass, however, never stopped their sabre-rattling. At a CMC meeting in late 1996, the generals switched into a belligerent mode at least at the rhetorical level. They again underscored the imperative of a "military solution". At the conclave, General Chi Haotian used an old Red Army slogan against the Kuomintang to hit home his point against the "Lee Teng-hui clique": "If we don't smash their pots and jars, they won't know we mean business."[178]

While the civilian leadership had shelved "war preparations", task forces under the CMC and the still-active Taiwan Command Centre continued in 1997 and 1998 to come up with ultra-modern, missiles-aided strategies against the island. By 1997, the favoured scenario of exerting direct military pressure on Taiwan was to temporarily take over outlying islands such as Quemoy and Matsu. This might be followed by "surgical strikes" against military installations on the island. While no attempts would be made to engage the Taiwan air and naval forces in full-scale combat, PLA strategists were confident that such limited action could bring Taipei authorities to their knees.[179]

General Zhang Wannian, too, had resumed his hawkish taunts of the KMT regime. The CMC vice-chairman reportedly indicated in an internal meeting in mid-1997 that should tension escalate, the PLA would "chop off Taipei's arms" — a reference to Quemoy and Matsu. The *de facto* military chief also supported hardliners who believed a "liberation timetable" should be established for recovering Taiwan. General Zhang reportedly cited the year 2020 as a "deadline" for reunifying the island.[180]

In 1997 and 1998, the top brass largely went along with Jiang's foreign policy, most notably on the US and Russian fronts. For example, the generals supported the rapprochement with Washington. In late 1997, the official *China National Defence News* seconded Jiang's US policy of "seeking development and lessening confrontation". "Strengthening military cooperation is not only in the interests of one side, but this can benefit both," the mouthpiece said.[181]

However, there was little doubt that this support was given in return for an unprecedented level of say by the generals. PLA officers were closely involved in preparations of Jiang's historic trip to Washington in October 1997. Generals such as intelligence expert Xiong Guangkai were playing a diplomatic role that would be quite unthinkable for a PLA cadre in the days of Mao or Deng. Moreover, voices of dissent were never far beneath the surface. In internal speeches, a number of generals expressed doubts about cozying up to either the US or Russia. One gripe they had was that the supposed detente with Washington had not translated into ability to import American military high technology. And since the purchase of Russian weapons had run into difficulties, military cooperation with Moscow slowed down dramatically in 1997 and 1998.[182]

Jiang Zemin and the PLA's Future
Jiang's military prowess at the 15th Party Congress

At least superficially, the 15th Party Congress marked the zenith of Jiang's military clout. Octogenarian Generals Liu Huaqing and Zhang Zhen left the scene. The new CMC was dominated by the president's two main protégés: Vice-Chairmen Generals Zhang Wannian and Chi Haotian. There was no visible opposition to the CMC chairman. And as younger, less faction-conscious officers took over, the underlings of such Jiang foes in the PLA as Yang Shangkun or Zhang Aiping were becoming marginalised.

At the 15th congress, even Liu Huaqing, who had seldom acknowledged Jiang's "core" status, was obliged to give the president a big salute. "The party Central Committee with Jiang Zemin as its core is a staunch and mature leadership collective," the retiring general said at the congress. And General Zhang Wannian pretty much went over the top with his praise of the boss. "Mao Zedong enabled Chinese to stand tall," the CMC vice-chairman said at the watershed conclave. "Deng Xiaoping let the people get rich. The third-generation leadership with Jiang Zemin as its core will enable China to become a strong country." General Zhang also urged the rank and file to "rally more closely around the Central Committee with Jiang Zemin as its core".[183] Jiang's power was not affected by General Zhang's bout with cancer in early 1998. Should his conditions deteriorate, Chief of Staff Fu Quanyou, who had good relations with Jiang, was expected to be appointed CMC vice-chairman.

Yet a kind of give-and-take was involved. Jiang and fellow neo-conservative leaders had apparently signed a life-and-death pact with the top brass. The generals' support was predicated upon this increasingly assertive and greedy power bloc getting more goodies by the day. And the president had to do his share of back-slapping. As the CMC chief said in late 1995: "Without a people's army, the people will be left with nothing. While doing a good job building up the economy, we must strengthen national defence construction."[184]

A quasi-institutional provision for the PLA's lofty status was given by Li Peng in his NPC address of 1997. The then premier called the army a special "guarantor" of economic development; other government units were asked to furnish the PLA with unquestioned assistance. "Strengthening defence construction is an important guarantee of economic construction and the long-term stability of the country," Li said. "All levels of government must support the PLA." Li lent his support to the theory of the "fusion of peace and war". He went so far as to ask other government units to help PLA factories sell their products and "help money-losing army enterprises get out of their difficulties". On a social level, Li said that "national defence consciousness" and education should be boosted to ensure "the legal rights of soldiers".[185]

Military reform plans in 1998

Even though he was riding high, Jiang realised that he had to implement some form of institutional modernisation of the PLA before leaving the scene at the 16th Party Congress in 2002. A team of his advisers under former law professor Wang Huning was busy drafting reform plans for the army in 1997 and 1998. At the operational level, this involved a high level of restructuring in tandem with the demobilisation drive. Obsolete divisions such as those in infantry, as well as non-combat departments such as academies and propaganda outfits would be slashed. Units would be merged or reorganised with a view to boosting the use of technology and the level of coordination among different forces. The entire PLA staff establishment was expected to be down to 1.75 million by 2010. Western, principally American, systems of command and control were examined. There was even talk of fine-tuning the system of regional commands so that the number of military regions would be curtailed.[186]

Many of the more far-reaching reforms — particularly those involving institutional change — had been raised by former party chief Zhao Ziyang in the mid-1980s. By the late 1990s, time was running out for the PLA's integration with international norms, a move that would both ensure stable political development in China and promote China's acceptance by the world community.

A major theme of the institutional reforms was that the PLA should undergo some form of "civilianisation" (see also Chapter 7). For example, the Ministry of Defence would be given real powers and more ministry officials should be civilian cadres instead of military officers. It might be put in charge of drawing up the PLA budget, supervising the expenditure, managing PLA-related construction and properties, and laying down principles of organisational reform. In internal discussions in mid-1998, Wang tabled the proposal that the new generation of officers must have "more scientific and specialised knowledge as well as a higher level of overall intellectual capacity". PLA sources said because not that many professional soldiers could meet this criteria, Wang was suggesting in a roundabout manner that civilians be given some senior army posts. The generals' reaction was understandably lukewarm. As a counter-proposal, members of the top brass such as General Chi Haotian said even if "positions for civilians" would be made available, they should be filled by demobilised officers or those who had worked in civilian departments.[187]

The PLA sources added that Jiang's ambition was that by the time he retired from the position of party general secretary — and probably CMC chairman as well — in 2002, the possibility of military interference in civilian life would be minimised. Moreover, Vice-President Hu Jintao would likely succeed Jiang as CMC chairman. And given Hu's lack of a national stature, it would be much more difficult for him to control the generals if some institutional changes were not implemented from 1998 to 2002.[188]

However, as Western military analysts saw it, the only long-term solution for PLA modernisation was the separation of party and army — and subjecting the army to the scrutiny of institutions such as the NPC. By mid-1998, there was no sign that Jiang was ready for such a radical move. Most of the reforms suggested by Professor Wang remained on the drawing boards and were not even divulged to the public. Despite his growing clout, the CMC chieftain was still too dependent on the support of the top brass to risk an open confrontation with the generals.

The Scourge of Regionalism

5

Introduction: The Dynamics of Power-sharing

In a 1996 book, controversial economist Hu Angang urged the "new-era" chieftains of post-Deng Xiaoping China to blaze new trails. "China's new generation of leaders must be the founding fathers, like Madison and Jefferson in America," he said. "We must set up new, durable institutions in order to maintain China's economic and political stability." Otherwise, he said, the country risked going through the fate of the former Yugoslavia after Marshal Tito. "We need a new banking system, a new tax system, new rules of the game between the centre and local governments," he added. "We need a new modern state system."[1]

Hu was addressing a focal point of political debate in the second half of the 1990s: the need to strike a new balance between the *zhongyang* ("central authorities") and the regions. On the one hand, the powers of Beijing needed to be strengthened to solve the increasingly complex issues of the country. On the other, regional initiative must not be blighted — and the gap between coast and hinterland must be narrowed.

Internal politics in the nine years after the Tiananmen Square massacre were characterised by a blitz against centrifugalism. Neo-conservative leaders such as Jiang Zemin and Zhu Rongji undertook herculean efforts to rein in the independence and assertiveness of regional cadres. After all, notable elders including Deng Xiaoping and Chen

Yun had highlighted the crisis of regionalism. "If the *zhongyang* cannot exercise full authority, the party and nation could disintegrate and nothing can be accomplished," Deng repeatedly warned.[2]

Not enough, however, was done to nurture a healthy degree of autonomy in the regions. Nor was Beijing successful in building institutions to ensure the equitable sharing of resources and clout among the provinces and major cities. And while individual think tanks had done research on federalism, the Chinese Communist Party (CCP) leadership shied away from thorough-going solutions to a problem that dated back centuries.

This chapter will look at the Jiang team's recentralisation efforts, including Mao-style fiats to force the "warlords" to fulfil Beijing-imposed quotas in the economy and other arenas. Particularly colourful was the protracted bickering between Beijing mandarins on the one hand, and maverick cadres in Guangdong and the coastal special economic zones on the other. Long sections are devoted to the future development of these exciting areas. While the *zhongyang* seemed to have scored superficial victories, their antagonists were becoming increasingly adept at crafting counter-strategies.

Failure to come up with a power-sharing formula could engender a lose-lose situation: political as well as economic resources were wasted in the never-ending tug-of-wars between the *zhongyang* and the regions. By the late 1990s, signs of an equally ferocious struggle among the provinces and cities had emerged over the division of the spoils and other issues of economic and political turf. Regionalism seems destined to remain one of most intractable problems for the Jiang leadership and its successors.

RECENTRALISATION OF POLITICAL POWERS

The Top-down Chain of Command

Beijing was poised to return to the Song Dynasty style of governance: a strong tree trunk and weak branches. While the central bureaucracy seemed to be swelling, it was difficult for orders to be carried out in the regions and the effectiveness of overall administration was dubious. This in part was due to Jiang Zemin's statecraft: putting powers in his personal office and various Central Committee organs as well as transferring members of the so-called Shanghai Faction to high party positions (see Chapters 2 and 3). Another reason was the CCP leadership's fear of losing control. Thus the crusade to centralise powers, talents and resources in the *zhongyang*.[3]

President Jiang and Premier Zhu Rongji practically reversed the trend begun by Deng Xiaoping of devolving power to the localities. The patriarch and such of his disciples as Zhao Ziyang had pursued decentralisation for two reasons: they thought it was better for economic reform; and they needed the warlords' support in the battle against the conservatives led by Chen Yun.

Apart from elevating members of "friendly" factions such as the Shanghai and Shandong cliques, Jiang kept the regional cadres further and further from the power centre. After the retirement of former Sichuan party boss Yang Rudai in 1992, there were no representatives from the western provinces on the Politburo. At the 15th Party Congress in September 1997, five "regional" party secretaries made it to the Politburo: Beijing's Jia Qinglin, Shanghai's Huang Ju, Shandong's Wu Guanzheng, Guangdong's Xie Fei, and Henan's Li Changchun. However, it became obvious by early 1998 that Xie would be transferred to the All-China Federation of Trade Unions and Li would take his place in Guangdong. Jiang failed to live up to the promise he made in early 1997 of awarding Politburo memberships to Chongqing or to a major province in central and western China.[4]

Moreover, power had since the early 1990s been concentrated in the Politburo Standing Committee rather than the Politburo, which met once a month at most. The clout of regional Politburo members was questionable. For example, Huang derived his power more as a protégé of Jiang than as a regional "warlord". Xie was periodically criticised by leaders such as Jiang and Zhu for dereliction of duty. As we shall see in the following section, strong-willed regional cadres such as Guangdong's Ren Zhongyi, Fujian's Xiang Nan, and Guizhou's Zhu Houze — who were in power in the early to mid-1980s — were a thing of the past.[5]

The Personnel Card
Jiang cracked the whip

In a political culture characterised by rule of personality, the top leadership could move heaven and earth by cunningly executed promotions, demotions and transfers. The party could to some extent still maintain an aura of authority so long as the Politburo Standing Committee and the Organisation Department retained the personnel card. In spite of the emerging phenomenon of senior cadres leaving their positions for the commercial world, an appointment to a top position in the provinces and cities was still much sought after.[6]

Throughout the 1990s, Beijing did not encounter serious difficulties in firing and transferring cadres, or forcing recalcitrant ones to retire. Then vice-premier Zhu Rongji set an example of resoluteness in 1994, when he sacked Heilongjiang party boss Sun Weiben on the spot during an inspection tour of the northeast. By 1998, there were signs that Beijing was able to breach the last regional stronghold of Guangdong by transferring non-native sons to senior positions in the southern province. Jiang took full advantage of newly beefed-up retirement rules to ease out maverick regional chieftains. Thus, cadres with the rank of provincial governors or the equivalent must quit at 65, and vice-governors or vice-mayors had to step down by 63. By 1996, regional potentates such as Sichuan governor Xiao Yang and the vice-governor of Guangxi Lei Yu had disappeared into the sunset.[7]

Jiang also gave more teeth to the Maoist practice of the rotation of civilian and military leaders to undermine warlordism. At the summer meeting of leaders at the Beidaihe resort in 1995, the regular rotation of cadres was institutionalised. Officials would be moved around regional postings at intervals of about three years; alternately, local cadres would be posted to the State Council and party headquarters. By the end of 1995, 900-odd central and regional leaders had been reshuffled and rotated both vertically and horizontally. For example, 54 bureau- and department-level cadres were transferred from Beijing to the provinces.[8]

The leadership wanted in particular to rotate cadres between coastal and hinterland areas. In many instances, a protocol for the exchange of cadres was established between pairs of provinces. This began in 1991 between Jiangsu and Shaanxi. Since then links were established between Beijing and Xinjiang; Zhejiang and Ningxia; and Shandong and Shaanxi. More than 10,000 officials of various levels were moved around from 1991 to mid-1994. For example, officials from coastal Shandong and Jiangsu worked in 59 counties and cities in the west. And more than 300 officials from impoverished Gansu were posted to relatively rich provinces and cities such as Zhejiang and Tianjin.[9]

Effects of personnel policy

These rigorous measures had an inevitably negative fallout. One aspect concerned morale. Officials in rich coastal areas were reluctant to relocate to either backwater areas in the west or the quasi-industrial wasteland of the northeast. This was despite the fact that cadres from the "privileged areas" were often given promotions of at least half a rank upon transfer to a disadvantaged province or city. A case in point were cadres from Shenzhen, many of whom were persuaded to go to the west or northeast in the mid-1990s. Li Youwei, who was party secretary until 1998, turned down several offers of vice-governorships in western areas.[10]

An even more serious effect of the new cadre policy was that it could result in mediocrity. Units such as Jiang's personal office and the Organisation Department were basically looking for docile, malleable cadres who would toe the Beijing line — not bush-whacking mavericks with original ideas. Thus cross-century cadres identified by the mid-1990s tended to be technocrats or career apparatchiks who tended to play safe rather than take risks.

This was evident from the corps of local leaders selected in late 1994 and early 1995, when more than half of the provinces and major cities underwent reshuffles. These included the new governors of Shandong, Hebei, Henan, Liaoning, Shaanxi, Gansu, Anhui and Hunan, respectively Li Chunting, Ye Liansong, Ma Zhongchen, Wen Shizhen, Cheng Andong, Zhang Wule, Hui Liangyu and Yang Zhengwu (see also Chapter 3).

The same went for the regional stars being groomed by the Jiang leadership at the time of the 15th Party Congress of 1997: then Henan party secretary Li Changchun, Shandong party boss Wu Guanzheng and Shanxi party secretary Hu Fuguo. All three acquitted themselves of their tasks in economic development but failed to make their mark as visionary modernisers. Media coverage of the three concentrated on their loyalty to Beijing and their service to the masses. Much was made of their image as "latter-day Bao Gongs" or Mr Cleans — and their anti-graft campaigns. Chinese sources said these cadres owed their rise partly to factional reasons: having jumped on the bandwagon of the Shanghai faction and professed allegiance to President Jiang.[11] For example, soon after becoming party boss of Guangdong, Li helped Jiang promote a number of the latter's associates to senior party and government positions in Guangzhou.

Political Edicts and Campaigns against the Regions

Despite his complaints about "mountain strongholds", Mao was largely successful in imposing his will over the regions. Apart from his charisma, there was the factor of the heavenly mandate: even fierce warlords felt duty-bound to profess allegiance to the equivalent of a dynastic monarch. Deng could still command some of the authority due a latter-day Son of Heaven.

However, President Jiang had to rely mostly on regulations and campaigns to rein in recalcitrant regional cadres. This would have been a good thing if the party leadership had been really committed to the rule of law. However, the edicts and crusades aimed at countering regionalism smacked of Maoist-era fiats that were problematic on two scores: they were much less effective in the 1990s; and they could blight local initiative as well as engender anti-Beijing feelings.

In early 1996, the Central Commission for Disciplinary Inspection (CCDI) put forward four criteria for upholding the *zhongyang*'s authority. First, local cadres must "remain in unision with the central authorities with Jiang Zemin as their core"; they were urged to combat "regionalism and departmentalism" so as to ensure that Beijing's orders would be enforced. Cadres were told "to stop making things up, to avoid filing false statistics and to refrain from exaggerating their achievements". "Local leaders must resolutely counter and suppress opinions that are opposed to the party's basic lines," the CCDI said. "They must put an end to anti-*zhongyang* rumours — nor must they believe in those rumours."[12]

Jiang revived Maoist rituals to ensure the loyalty of the regional chieftains. One such mechanism was periodic exercises to ask them to *biaotai*, or profess allegiance to the party core. This was first tried out in late 1994, when Deng began fading from the scene (see Chapter 2). On a more practical level, Beijing slapped quotas on local cadres to meet goals in areas including grain production and helping the poor.

Yet it was Beijing's use of the anti-corruption campaign against selected targets that brought cold sweat to the backs of many local officials. Much has been written about how the Jiang Zemin administration used the monkey businesses of Chen Xitong to bring down the Beijing Faction. In the latter half of 1995, a veritable earthquake swept Guangdong as "work teams" were sent there to sniff out the "Chen Xitongs of southern China" (see Chapter 3).

Beijing even slapped quotas on the number of corrupt officials each province and city must arrest. The instructions were handed out in 1996 at a closed-door session by Ren Jianxin, then secretary of the policy-setting Commission for Political and Legal Affairs. Ren said the provinces should go after the "big tigers" among bribe-takers and other economic offenders. In return, local party committees and governments were promised a higher degree of autonomy in operational matters. In the past, provincial and municipal party committees had to secure central-level approval before they began investigating cadres with the rank of bureau or department chief. Now, only the authorisation of the province's party boss was needed.[13]

Ren stopped short of spelling out how many "big-time culprits" each province or major city should nab at a given period. However, local cadres were given to understand in no uncertain terms that assessment of their performance would be based on how well they acquitted themselves in this task. But some provinces came up with counter-strategies in an effort to protect local interests. For example, the Guangzhou administration sought to fill its quota by cracking down on corruption, smuggling and other economic crimes committed in Guangdong by Guangxi, Hainan and other out-of-province cadres.[14]

THE CENTRALISATION OF ECONOMIC POWERS: REINING IN REGIONAL INITIATIVES

The Central Economic Work Meeting of December 1995 marked the peak of Beijing's reassertion of economic powers. The conclave's communique said: "The thoughts and actions of different departments and localities should be subsumed under the ideas, objectives and policies of economic work on which the *zhongyang* has decided."[15] The conference confirmed Zhu Rongji as the Great Rectifier. While the then vice-premier underwent somewhat of an eclipse because of the flak he received for the initial phase of the austerity programme, he also scored points in restoring order to an economy ravaged by the unruly and hyper-inflationary activities of parties including the warlords.

The years 1995 to 1998 saw aggressive efforts made by the *zhongyang* to claw back powers, revenue and other resources. Marathon edicts were issued to rein in regional initiatives in the name of curbing inflationary, speculative or corrupt activities.

Control over Taxation and Finance

A central theme of the warlord period from the 1910s to the 1940s was fighting over the control of taxation. It was no surprise that the first move by the neo-conservative leadership was to grab hold of the purse-strings. As the late Chen Yun reportedly told Jiang Zemin: "The political authority of the *zhongyang* must be based on economic authority." The conservative patriarch added: "The *zhongyang* should centralise whatever power, in particular financial power — that needs to be centralised."[16]

Then vice-premier Zhu Rongji claimed at a closed-door meeting in mid-1994 that he should be given the Nobel Prize for Economics for "inventing" the dual-tax system, whereby tax bases for Beijing and for the regions were clearly demarcated. The benefits for central coffers were obvious, according to statistics Zhu provided in early 1996. From 1993 to 1995, national revenue rose on a year-on-year basis by 99 billion yuan, 95 billion yuan and 86 billion yuan respectively. This compared with a yearly increase of only 20-odd billion yuan in the 10 years ending 1992. "In the past, taxes were all collected by the local governments and it was difficult [for the *zhongyang*] to take the tax dollars," the economic tsar said. "Now, the taxes are first collected by the *zhongyang* and returned to the localities. Not a single yuan has been withheld by Beijing."[17]

In reality, Zhu was claiming too much. It was true that because the entire tax pie was expanding, Beijing's share was increasing. Yet the benefits were considerably bigger for the localities. For example, central revenues grew by 9.1 per cent in 1996, against 27.5 per cent for the regions.[18] In rich areas such as Guangdong, tax revenues rose by around 30 per cent in the mid-1990s. Most importantly, the size of state revenue as a proportion of GDP continued to slide. According to the official *Outlook Weekly*, it dropped from slightly more than 30 per cent in 1980 to just 10.9 per cent in 1996.[19]

One reason was that in spite of Zhu's assertions, a substantial portion of the taxes owed to central authorities were by 1997 still collected by local administrations first. For example, by late 1996, Beijing was fuming over the fact that the provinces and cities had only surrendered 60 per cent of the levies they had gathered on behalf of the *zhongyang*, down from a comparable figure of 70 per cent in 1995. And regional cadres often gave incentives, such as remissions and even "discounts", to persuade enterprises and other economic entities to pay local taxes first and national taxes later.[20]

At least according to Beijing's mandarins, local chieftains often set up private "treasures troves" or "piggy banks" to hide income and other funds from central tax collectors or auditors. In 1995, investigators found what they called "private golden vaults" in Guangdong totalling 201 million yuan. In mid-1996, central authorities launched a campaign to crack down on "extra-budgetary funds" kept by the warlords. Some sleuths from Beijing believed as much as 300 billion yuan could be stowed away in hidden accounts both in China and overseas.[21]

Apart from frequent checks and investigations, Beijing promulgated rules and regulations to rein in regional over-spending. A State Council circular of early 1995 forbade regions from having a "deficit budget". This stricture included bans on raising loans abroad or establishing a credit rating with international financial institutions. Local administrations had to secure the approval of central banking and planning agencies before they could sell bonds overseas. The move was in response to ambitious plans by scores of provincial governments and state corporations in 1995 to sell bonds and other securities in financial centres such as Tokyo, New York and Hong Kong.[22]

Shortly before he became premier in March 1998, Zhu struck hard at regional autonomy by taking away powers of local administrations to make loans. As part of a major plan to restructure the banking system, 15 or so new regional branches of the People's Bank of China (PBoC) would be established in 1998 and 1999. Henceforward, only the PBoC headquarters and the regional offices would have authority to grant credit (see also Chapter 8). "In the past, provincial governors and mayors had authority over local banks and this became a big problem," Zhu said in an internal meeting in late 1997. "From now on, heads of bank no longer need to heed orders from regional officials." One of the first regional PBoC offices was based in Guangzhou, which would cover Guangdong, Guangxi, Jiangxi and Hainan. Of the four, Guangdong and Hainan had received the most flak for disorderly financing procedures.[23]

Constraints over Economic Projects

While Beijing had made headway in adopting selected "Western" administrative and business practices, Stalinist control mechanisms were retained to impose control over the regions. Maoist-era institutions such as the State Planning Commission kept track of a wide range of economic activities by local administrations and corporations. A key crusade by economic tsar Zhu Rongji was to prevent duplication in infrastructure and industrial projects.

A *cause célèbre* in the mid-1990s was the no-holds-barred construction of ports, container terminals, highways and airports along the southeast coast. In a briefing for journalists in 1996, Zhu said that only in the area of railways, which were kept under solid control by the Ministry of Railways, was redundancy kept to a minimum. He decried "mindless duplication" in most infrastructure items. Mushrooming ports and airports in Fujian and Guangdong were singled out for special criticism. "In these provinces, one airport comes after the next in close proximity," he said. "In future, pilots may have a hard time telling which airport they should land at."[24]

The then vice-premier was especially bitter about schemes that involved central participation. For projects approved by the *zhongyang*, Beijing as a rule footed 60 per cent of the bill, and the provinces and cities the rest. During the 1996 NPC, Zhu complained about the large number of cases when an infrastructure item had been started with central money, but the local administrations refused to pay. For fear of more wastage, Beijing was often obliged to pump in more than its agreed share.[25]

Unbridled property development proved to be the Waterloo of many a boom town. By early 1998, mistakes made by local leaders at the initial phase of the *nanxun*-related euphoria had hardly been remedied. Disaster zones such as Hainan, Huizhou and Beigang were still burdened with half-built houses and unoccupied skyscrapers. The malaise also hit Shanghai and Pudong, which went through a rash of construction in 1995 and 1996.[26]

Again, Beijing resorted to fiats to limit local autonomy. The powers of individual provinces and cities to grant land-use rights were curtailed by a spate of local rules and legislation in the mid-1990s. One regulation said SOEs could only be allocated extra land if their economic performance was satisfactory. Administrations along the coast were urged to exercise utmost caution when allocating land for office or residential blocks. The central and western provinces, however, were exempted from this restriction. Beginning in 1995, land in Guangdong which had been approved for real estate purposes had to be re-zoned as farmland if it was obvious the development was going nowhere. All vacant sites in the suburbs had to be reassigned for agriculture and other uses.[27]

On a more micro-level, the fight against the duplication of production lines was waged with ferocity well into 1998. Take automobiles, which were listed by 22 provinces as their "pillar" or "priority" industry. But in 1996, the entire output of the country's 124 manufacturing and assembly plants was a mere 1.47 million vehicles. There was tremendous wastage and minimal economy of scale. In contrast, the giant automakers in Detroit alone produced around 10 million cars a year.[28]

In an internal speech in late 1997, Zhu vowed to clamp down on the "mad rush" for manufacturing trendy electronic goods. "Once a product is seen as making money, the whole country bends over backwards to produce the same item," he said. "Look at VCD machines. Already, more than 20 so-called brand products are being promoted in nationwide advertising campaigns. Once all these products have hit the street, prices will collapse. I'm getting ready to attend the VCD's funeral."[29]

The Battle over the Growth Rate

At least superficially, a major victory over the warlords was scored in the mid-1990s on the issue of growth rate: Beijing breathing down the necks of local cadres to put an end to inflationary growth. After the central government promulgated the Ninth Five-Year Plan (1996–2000) and the 15-year blueprints in 1995, all provinces and major cities put out their own road maps to match national norms. Local officials demonstrated a willingness to scale down development to accommodate the overall goal of a GDP growth rate of eight to 10 per cent in the coming decade.

In 1996, prosperous Guangdong announced that it was seeking a yearly GDP increase of only 11 per cent, while the boom cities of Guangzhou and Shenzhen indicated they could live with a mere 13 per cent. Pointing to the fact that the yearly expansion of the provincial economy had dropped from 21 per cent in 1993 to 15 per cent in 1995, a Guangdong cadre said: "We have shifted gears from super high-speed growth to steady advancement."[30]

Comparative growth figures for ambitious areas such as Shanghai, Shandong, and Guangxi were set in 1996 at 14 per cent, 10 per cent, and "at least 10 per cent" respectively. Would-be over-achievers included the quasi-capitalist haven of Wenzhou on the Zhejiang coast, and the "ahead-of-the-times" Pudong zone of Shanghai, which were gunning for 16 per cent and 20 per cent respectively. The two exceptions, however, illustrated the rule of toeing Beijing's line about eschewing the Great Leap Forward-style game plan of the Deng Xiaoping era. Even the "cowboy province" of Hainan was playing by the rules. For 1996, it first publicised a growth target of 15 per cent, and then scaled it down to 10 per cent, and later, 7.2 per cent.[31]

The same willingness to heed Beijing's call was evident in the relatively depressed *zhongxibu* (central and western areas) as well as the northeast. The development targets for Heilongjiang and Liaoning were respectively 9.5 to 11.5 per cent and nine to 10 per cent for 1996. The targets for Sichuan, Shaanxi, Ningxia, Yunnan and Qinghai were respectively 9 to 10 per cent, 10.5 per cent, 10.5 per cent, 10 per cent and 9 to 10 per cent.[32]

By the mid-1990s, Beijing had intensified efforts to use work teams to rein in overspending. In 1995, the State Council dispatched eight work groups to Beijing, Shanghai, Guangdong, Guangxi, Hebei, Henan, Jiangsu and Zhejiang to try to turn off the development-fund tap. Enforcers included senior cadres from the State Planning Commission, the State Economic and Trade Commission, the Ministry of Finance, the People's Bank of China and the Auditing Administration. Underlying the urgency of the move was the fact that in the first half of 1995, fixed-assets investments were 376.4 billion yuan, or 22.2 per cent more than the comparative period in 1994.[33]

The national mood — and the preoccupation of the recentralising cadres — shifted abruptly in 1997 and 1998, when the order of the day was expanding, not limiting, growth. The Chinese economy was hit by sluggish demand, as well as the spill-over effects of the Asian financial crisis (see Chapter 8). In 1998, a top priority of the government was to ensure that the eight per cent growth target be reached. Strict orders were slapped on every province and city to reflate the economy through boosting expenditure on infrastructure and other projects.[34] These fiats illustrated the fact that despite the trappings of a market economy, the Jiang administration still had to rely on age-old production quotas to maintain economic — and political — stability.

The Imperative of Agriculture

Neo-conservative titans such as Jiang and Zhu seemed to have made progress in forcing regional chieftains, even those along the industrialised coast, to accord agriculture top priority. There would be no slippage in implementing the so-called rice-bag and vegetable-basket programmes. To satisfy the *zhongyang*, local officials were jostling for superlatives to describe their achievements in grain self-sufficiency, in arresting the decline of arable land, and in producing fantastic yields.

For example, the two agricultural provinces in the northeast,

Heilongjiang and Jilin, pledged in 1996 to raise grain production by respectively 7.5 billion kilos and five billion kilos by 2000. Guangdong and Guangxi cadres vowed to at least equal their 1995 feat of boosting grain output by 1.29 billion kilos and 320 million kilos respectively. Fujian declared in 1997 that it had attained self-sufficiency despite the fact that per capita distribution of arable land in the hilly province was 0.56 *mu* (15 *mu* = one hectare), one of the lowest in the country. Increase in grain yield in the previous five years had been 129,000 tonnes.[35]

Throughout the mid-1990s, the media kept a close tally of the grain output in each province — so that leaders in poor-performing ones were put to shame. Grain production was an important criterion for the promotion of regional cadres. Among the star performers was Anhui, which reaped 28.5 million tonnes of grain in 1997 — up 5.6 per cent from 1996 — despite poor weather. From 1993 to 1997, Anhui invested 7.7 billion yuan in farming, representing an annual increase in rural capital outlay of an astounding 23 per cent.[36]

Yet it was perhaps the sea-change in Guangdong that did the re-centralisers most proud. According to the provincial Ninth Five-Year Plan, the total value of production of the farming and fishing sector should reach 96.9 billion yuan by the year 2000, representing a laudable annual growth rate of five per cent. The figure for the heavily industrialised Pearl River Estuary area was fixed at six per cent. Fifty new commodity grain bases would be established in this period.[37] The rich province used to import grain from neighbouring provinces and countries including Australia. In the mid-1990s, Guangzhou promised Beijing it would attain at least 70 per cent self-sufficiency in grain. The erosion of arable land was stopped. In 1995, 520,000 *mu* of land which had been diverted to industrial or commercial activities were recommitted to agriculture. Thirty million *mu* of land was classified as "farming conservation zones".[38]

The *Fupin* Campaign

The *fupin* ("save the poor provinces") campaign became a handy excuse for central authorities to interfere with the way in which local governments spent their money. In deference to the *zhongyang*'s new imperative about egalitarianism, prosperous coastal areas bent over backwards to bail out the disadvantaged in their own backyards — as well as in the impoverished western provinces (see also following section). By 1998, Beijing took much credit for the fact that the population of the extreme poor — defined as a per capita income of 300 yuan a year — was being reduced at the rate of three milliion a year. The goal for most provinces was that poverty eradication should be achieved by 2000. Central authorities, however, were oblivious to the argument that *fupin* and reducing regional disparity should have been the primary responsibility of the *zhongyang*.

Guangdong, long criticised by Beijing for its people's extravagant lifestyles, was eager to pacify the *zhongyang* by devoting more resources to *fupin* campaigns. In 1995, then party boss Xie Fei vowed to wipe out poverty in his province — a reference to the 800,000 inhabitants of the hilly counties in the north — by 2000. In early 1998, provincial authorities said they had already achieved this goal.[39]

But it was at a hefty cost. Eight developed cities in Guangdong were made "responsible" for the fast-track development of 16 poor counties. The amounts involved could be gauged from the fact that from 1991 to 1995, Shenzhen and Zhuhai had already spent 400 million yuan and 120 million yuan respectively on development aid to remote counties. Individual officials were made to shoulder the burden. The Guangdong media disclosed that cadres in the province had in 1997 made donations worth 20 million yuan to the *fupin* cause. Some 103,000 officials had volunteered or were assigned to be "sponsors" of 120,700 destitute households with the goal of promoting "common prosperity".[40]

The province had to fork out even larger sums to help "sister" provinces and cities such as Guizhou and Qinghai. Within Guangdong, Shenzhen acquitted itself best. Mayor Li Zibin pointed out in 1997 that since the early 1990s, the special economic zone had invested 15 billion yuan in industries in backward provinces. While touring Shenzhen in 1996, then premier Li Peng praised its devotion to egalitarianism. "Shenzhen often donates funds and material to the hinterland, and builds schools there," Li said. "This is very good. It helps Shenzhen establish a good image."[41] And in 1998, cities in Guangdong such as Shenzhen, Guangzhou, and Dongguan were given the additional task of "taking over" loss-making enterprises in the northeast as well as absorbing laid-off workers there (see Chapter 8).

Are the Centralisation Measures Working?

The age-old strategy of the warlords — "you [the *zhongyang*] have your strategy, we have our counter-strategy" — was as vibrant as ever. Chinese economists decried the reappearance of the *fukuafeng* ("the wind of exaggeration") of the Great Leap Forward era: local officials making up figures to hoodwink the "imperial inspectors". This was despite repeated injunctions of central officials against the four nos: "Not to say empty words; not to go in for superficial effects; not to put up a show; and not to indulge in formalism."[42]

In 1996, the official media admitted that Shandong, the reputed model province, had succumbed to *fukuafeng* to the extent it had hired specialists to confect rosy statistics. One example was the supposed "miracle development" of the county of Taichang, which chalked up a yearly growth rate of 141 per cent. Revulsion against Shandong-style showiness was one reason why 36 per cent of NCP deputies refused in 1995 to endorse the promotion of then Shandong party boss Jiang Chunyun as vice-premier. The situation in other provinces was not much better. Moreover, even senior regional cadres were playing the numbers game. Heads of provinces and cities often fixed "desired production targets" for lower-level units including counties and villages. These figures were later sent to Beijing regardless of actual performance.[43]

State Statistics Bureau officials conceded that they had doubts about the numbers they were working with. For example, in calculating the 1994 figure for the value of industrial output, they made provisions for the fact that the regions had exaggerated their tallies by as much as 730 billion yuan. The bureau also found that the 1995 figure for the sale of consumer goods had been artificially swollen by 30 billion yuan because many department stores had cooked the books in their attempts to be named national pacesetters.[44]

However, the phenomenon of bogus figures was much less important than possible damage to the economy and the reform enterprise by excessive interference in regional autonomy. After all, it was impossible to run such a complex country as China by *diktat*. Part of the semi-economic miracle achieved in the Deng era was due to the patriarch's famous principle of devolution: *yindizhiyi* or "to each region according to its characteristics".

Given their disparate natural endowments and human resources, different provinces and cities should, according to the law of comparative advantage, be encouraged to do their own thing. Many of Beijing's strictures were grounded in political, not economic, considerations. For example, the stress on grain self-sufficiency was in part due to the party leadership's fear of becoming dependent on countries including the US for wheat and other staples. The near-uniform ban on Deng-style, fast-track development was regarded by the "warlords" as insincere because the *zhongyang* was making exceptions for the apples in its eye. The neo-conservative leadership had yet to fully explain why the Shanghai-Pudong region should be exempt from the tight-money policy.[45]

Unsurprisingly, naked coercion bred a mixture of cynicism and hyprocrisy — in addition to a kind of newsspeak with Chinese characteristics. While unveiling his province's master plan for the next five years, then Anhui party boss Lu Rongjing hinted in early 1996 at his disagreement with Beijing's fiats. "Economic work has its own laws," he said, adding that Anhui's development should be "fast-paced, long-lasting and planned". Lu did not elaborate on whether there might be contradictions between the goal of high-speed growth and planning.[46]

Consider also the intriguing remarks of then Hainan party secretary Ruan Chongwu. Mindful of Beijing's criticisms that the nation's largest economic zone had devoted too many resources to sectors including hotels, real estate and entertainment, he cited the following slogan for the provincial five-year plan: "Take agriculture as the basis, industry as the guiding light, and tourism as the dragon head." This please-all-parties, fail-safe formula said much about how the local chieftains were setting a circuitous course to save their necks while beating the system.[47]

NARROWING THE REGIONAL GAP

It would not be as spectacular as the recovery of Hong Kong — or reunification with Taiwan. Yet if Jiang Zemin were to succeed in solving the "east versus west problem" — or the polarisation between coast and hinterland — the president would have achieved something that eluded even Deng Xiaoping.

At least at the rhetorical level, Jiang and company did much to mollify the *zhongxibu* or central and western areas. Money, resources and special policies were pledged through the 1990s. Lessening the discrepancy between eastern and western China was a leitmotif of the Ninth Five-Year Plan of 1996–2000. In the first half of the 1990s, the GNP of eastern China grew by 16 per cent annually, against nine per cent for the heartland. In the same period, the coast, which occupies only 15 per cent of mainland territory, attracted 67.4 per cent of fixed-assets investment. The possibility of redressing this balance remained slim by 1998.[48]

A New Deal for the *Zhongxibu*?

Zhongxibu chieftains were getting more vocal by the day. They began listing their demands in public. For example, officials in the backwater province of Guizhou said in 1996 they needed a fresh injection of 500 million yuan for industry and electricity generation. Poverty-relief funds must be expanded from 360 million yuan to five billion yuan. And budgets for township enterprises should rise from 150 million to five billion yuan to solve local unemployment.[49]

Other warlords were demanding policies. For example, Shaanxi's party secretary Cheng Andong wanted more central projects to be located in his domain. The central-northern province had missed out on the refocusing of central investments from the southeast coast to the Yangtze River. Then party secretary of Qinghai Wen Kesheng said in 1996: "Now we won't lobby the *zhongyang* for money because we can't get it even if we make the demands. The crucial things are favourable policies [for development]."[50]

Both the Ninth Five-Year Plan and the Blueprint for Long-term Development (1996–2010) pledged to address these demands. There would be goodies galore for the *zhongxibu*. Central and western areas would enjoy a "sliding policy in state investments" for infrastructure development and resources-related industries. Labour-intensive industries such as textiles would be moved to the heartland to boost employment levels there. Beijing would increase the *zhongxibu*'s "ability for self-development" through increasing the prices of their product, including agricultural and mineral resources.[51]

At the same time, Beijing was rejigging the system of transfer payments so that financial support for "Third World China" would be boosted. More policy-oriented loans, including those from the newly set up State Policy Bank, would be diverted westwards. At least 60 per cent of soft loans from foreign governments and aid packages from international financial organisations would be destined to the poor regions.[52]

The Help-your-poor-cousin Crusade

To jumpstart the *zhongxibu* economy, Beijing started in 1995 to assign a "poor cousin" to a rich province or city along the prosperous coast. The idea was that by the year 2005 or 2010, the latter would help its impoverished partner to become self-sufficient and to be no longer dependent on central-government largesse.

In some instances, the *zhongyang* laid down the percentage of income that a well-off province or city should devote to the *fupin* crusade. Take, Shenzhen, for example. Since the early 1990s, the SEZ had been obliged to earmark at least two per cent of its earnings as donations and other charity work. In 1995, Shenzhen, in addition to the boom cities of Qingdao and Ningbo, was made "responsible" for the economic takeoff of Guizhou Province. Li Youwei, then party secretary of Shenzhen, pledged that the SEZ would shift some of its manufacturing capacities inland. Earlier, Li had tried to persuade Beijing that Shenzhen should only vouch for the speedy development of poor districts in northern Guangdong. Guangdong, in turn, was asked by Beijing to "take care" of Qinghai, which was deemed a basket case.[53]

Shanghai, which had been paired with Xinjiang, started moving its labour-intensive industries — as well as those dependent on resources — westwards in the early 1990s. Mayor Xu Kuangdi said in 1996 that cooperation between Shanghai and western China was a case of the exchange of capital, technology, information and talent for resources. As Xu put it: "Supporting the *zhongxibu*'s development is on one level our contribution to the national economy; on another level, this also helps Shanghai's own development." Gone, however, was the 1950s-vintage self-sacrifice when part of the cream of Shanghai's college graduates "volunteered" to work in the deserts of Xinjiang. A number of *zhongxibu* leaders blamed Shanghai for giving them low-tech and even obsolete assembly lines.[54]

It was clear that the "forced marriage" of rich and poor areas could only be a stopgap solution. This was seen by both well-off and under-developed regions as a cynical means for Beijing to lighten its baggage. The *zhongyang* could also be accused of trying to drive a wedge between the regions — so that they would not gang up on Beijing. After all, even the best-placed boom towns were reluctant to play Santa Claus to the *zhongxibu*. And recipients of east-coast handouts complained about "exploitation". One common gripe from the heartland was that "First World" cities along the coast were trying to milk them of mineral and human resources under the pretext of cooperation.

More Gripes from the Heartland

By early 1998, there were no signs that the *zhongxibu* was placated. The unsurprising reason: they kept asking for more — and there were lines beyond which Beijing would not go. Cadres in the *zhongxibu* argued that Beijing would reap tremendous benefits from putting its emphasis on the western sector, which would provide a vast domestic market for national products. "China must rely on domestic resources to develop," argued then Qinghai governor Tian Chengping. "We must open up the west in the same way that the US developed the American West and Japan developed Hokkaido."[55]

However, China was different from Japan and the US. Beijing's mandarins feared the whole nation would be bogged down if more money was poured into "black holes" such as Qinghai and Tibet. After all, one factor behind the centre's largesse was the political need to prevent instability in volatile regions such as Xinjiang and Tibet (see following section). Moreover, even more than officials in rich areas, *zhongxibu* cadres had a record of reckless speculation in the real estate and stock markets.

While Beijing might be prepared to channel more funds to the west, it did not trust the cadres there enough to let them raise their own funds. The State Council flatly turned down repeated demands that foreign banks be allowed to set up shop in the *zhongxibu*. As then Gansu governor Zhang Wule said in 1996: "Beijing only allows Gansu to issue bonds worth 50 million yuan a year, whereas an enterprise on the east coast could issue bonds worth a few hundred million yuan." The only concession the State Council made was that local cadres could approve joint ventures worth up to US$30 million.[56]

Central authorities were not sympathetic towards a request from provinces including Sichuan, Shaanxi, Guizhou, Gansu and Xinjiang to start their own special economic zones or bonded areas. According to Liu Xiaohua, a division chief of the State Council SEZ Office, the *zhongxibu* lacked the prerequisites for setting up special zones. He claimed that for reasons including lack of transport networks, "they could not develop export-oriented industries as in the SEZs of the southeast". Liu said the *zhongxibu* should concentrate on mining, energy and resources. Other central cadres said profit margins in the west were not high enough to attract foreign or domestic investors. Then SEZ Office chief Hu Ping simply said: "Times have changed; it is impossible to transplant the special policies to central and western areas."[57]

In internal meetings in late 1996 and early 1997, leaders from several western and northwestern provinces pressed Beijing for "Hong Kong-style autonomy". After all, Deng Xiaoping had stressed the necessity to "create a string of Hong Kongs" in the heartland. According to a party source, these intrepid lobbyists told the *zhongyang*: "If Beijing is willing to give Hong

Kong a high degree of autonomy under 'one country, two systems', we should have comparable powers." The source said the western regions' power bid began in late 1995, when the party secretaries of seven provinces wrote a petition to the Politburo asking for a radical devolution of authority. Beijing, however, stood its ground. The ideological and propaganda departments organised numerous classes to try to convince *zhongxibu* cadres that the Hong Kong experience could not be duplicated.[58]

The main pretext of the *zhongxibu* for "super-special treatment" was that to make up for lost opportunities since the late 1970s, they had to be given policies that would in effect be discriminatory against the rich southeast coast. However, the Fifth Central Committee Plenum of late September 1995 stressed Deng's policy of "letting some areas and some parts of the population get rich first". The only policy adjustment Beijing had made was to enable the Shanghai-Pudong area and selected cities along the Yangtze River to catch up faster with Guangdong. There was no question of a thorough re-stacking of the cards. Said then premier Li Peng: "If areas with the necessary qualifications go faster, this will be beneficial towards strengthening the national economy and supporting the development of backward areas."[59]

The *People's Daily* supported Li's — and Deng Xiaoping's — "trickle-down theory". It indicated soon after the Fifth Plenum that there must be a pecking order for development: "We must let the coastal areas develop first and continue to demonstrate their superiority." "We definitely cannot pay the price of depressing the development speed of the coast" to artificially nudge up the growth rate of the hinterland, the paper said. It added that the *zhongxibu*'s takeoff could only be based on "the augmentation of overall national strength based on the development of the coast". Beijing University professor Wu Shuqing concurred. He said there was no question of a Robin Hood-style robbing the rich to benefit the poor. "The Ninth Five-Year Plan does not recommend sacrificing the development of the east so as to narrow the east-west discrepancy," he pointed out.[60]

The Challenge of Xinjiang, Tibet and Other Areas with Ethnic Minorities

The exacerbation of ethnic troubles in Xinjiang, which culminated in a series of bombings in Beijing in March 1997, heightened the leadership's failure to seek a long-term solution to areas with high ethnic concentrations. Analysts in the capital said the questions of Xinjiang and Tibet were much more than dollars and cents: a new generation of ethnic cadres and residents was demanding political autonomy.

On the economic side, Beijing claimed progress had been made in redistributing wealth in favour of the *shaoshuminzu* ("ethnic minorities"). A new dispensation was announced in mid-1996. For example, infrastructure projects and those geared towards opening up resources would have priority access to state funds. Transfer payments and government loans to *shaoshuminzu* areas would be increased. Most importantly, the prices of raw materials would be "gradually raised so as to enable *shaoshuminzu* areas to accumulate [funds for development]". The leadership said minority areas were given more aid dollars than other *zhongxibu* provinces. For example, Tibet was on a per capita level the largest beneficiary of such largesse.[61]

Beijing also lived up to its promise of liberalising border trade between *shaoshuminzu* areas and neighbouring countries including Russia, Vietnam and North Korea. Until ethnic problems boiled over in early 1996, Xinjiang had enjoyed much latitude in trading and other links with Middle Eastern countries as well as former members of the Soviet Union.[62]

Yet what Xinjiang and Tibet — and to a lesser extent, Inner Mongolia — were demanding was more political and economic autonomy. In internal sessions with central leaders in the mid-1990s, representatives from ethnic-minority areas had made proposals that could be characterised as "you give us autonomy and we guarantee you stability". One demand was that *shaoshuminzu* cadres be made heads of Communist Party committees. In the Chinese hierarchy, the party boss of a province or city outranks the governor or mayor. In areas such as Xinjiang, Tibet and Inner Mongolia, the position of party secretary had except for a few instances never gone to a native Uighur, Kazakh, Tibetan or Mongolian. This was despite the fact that more ethnic officials had been appointed to mid-echelon posts.

Particularly in the tinderbox regions of Xinjiang and Tibet, a key task of the Han Chinese party secretary — together with the Han Chinese heads of the local army and People's Armed Police regiments — was to fight "splittist" activities. Much of the classified information and intelligence about Beijing's strategy against pro-independence groupings was privy only to the party bosses — who were also responsible for liaison with the Politburo and other top cadres in the capital. However, this archaic system had resulted in sloppy decision-making and communication delays. Advocates for vesting more power in ethnic-minority officials alleged that this would not only raise morale but promote efficiency in administration, including the "struggle against splittism".[63]

Beijing, however, was hard put to cede the warlords more leeway. A Chinese source said in 1997 that the Politburo Standing Committee was considering giving the party secretaries of Xinjiang and Tibet more author-ity to handle the anti-splittist campaigns on the spot. However, he said this had made it even more difficult for the leadership to consider breaking with tradition and appointing a Uighur or Tibetan to be party boss.[64]

By early 1998, it was obvious the Jiang administration's strategy towards Xinjiang and Tibet was to continue playing hard ball. The president was not swayed by arguments that the upsurge of violence in Xinjiang in 1997 had been triggered by a Beijing order in the spring of 1996 to "kill off the splittist terrorists". That get-tough instruction had reportedly exacerbated Han-Uighur tension because of the large numbers of separatists who had been arrested — and in many cases executed — in the interim. To prevent "Uighur terrorists" from making trouble during the Hong Kong transition, a large number of known separatists were subjected to "preventive detention".[65] On the Tibet front, prospects of any form of talks with the Dalai Lama re-mained dim. Among all the agents of instability, security departments in mid-1998 still classified separatists in Xinjiang and Tibet — well ahead of dissidents or laid-off workers — as posing the most threat to the regime.

Why a Fair Deal Remains Illusory

As things stood in mid-1998, the Jiang administration was nowhere near defusing east-west tensions. Shortly before he became premier, Zhu Rongji indicated he was dissatisfied with the "trickle down" approach of Deng. In internal discussions, he raised the possibility of a "new plan" to develop western China much the same way that the US government developed California in the late 19th and early 20th centuries. Zhu's initiatve, however, had virtually petered out by mid-1998. The general line of thinking was still President Jiang's admission that "common prosperity" could only be a theo-retical goal. "At any one epoch, even in the distant future, there will still be differences [in income levels] owing to different reasons," Jiang said while touring the south in late 1995. "If there are no differences and no contra-dictions, there won't be progress."[66]

Zhongxibu cadres, however, were unwilling to accept this fatalistic at-titude. The views of the Vice-Governor of Qinghai, Wang Hanmin, were typical. Qinghai, with a mere 4.8 million population, had survived on state handouts. However, this should not have been the case for such a mineral-rich province. Wang called it "begging for alms while holding a gold rice bowl". He complained that each year, Qinghai cadres had to "kow-tow" before central-government departments as well as the coastal provinces for emergency aid. Wang said Beijing dragged its feet on many projects, some of which died natural deaths as a result of procrastination.[67]

However, the fact was that times had changed since the Mao — or Deng — era. Chinese society was becoming stratified along the lines of classes and interest blocs (see Chapter 3). The ideal of "common prosperity" was becoming less practical by the day. From one perspective, the "rulers" in Beijing were representatives of power groupings such as the Shanghai Faction, the coast or the large corporations. None of these — except for the relatively few businesses based in the *zhongxibu* — had much incentive in redressing the regional imbalance. On the contrary, the east China-based blocs might want to perpetuate the disparity to take advantage of cheap labour and resources in the hinterland.

For example, Xinjiang cadres openly complained to foreign visitors that in the course of exploiting local minerals such as oil, major state corporations and their overseas partners received the lion's share of profits, leaving the native Uighurs with the crumbs.[68] By 1998, liberal scholars in official think tanks were arguing that Beijing must bite the bullet by putting together formal laws and institutions on power sharing between the *zhongyang* and the regions.

THE FATE OF THE SPECIAL ECONOMIC ZONES

The special economic zones (SEZs) in Guangdong, Fujian and Hainan are a good barometer of not only the country's open-door policy but the dynamics between the *zhongyang* and the regions. This was particularly the case given the fact that by 1998, Shanghai, and in particular Pudong, had in many areas displaced the zones as the national pacesetter for reform. Market-oriented practices first tried out in Pudong included allowing foreign banks to start renminbi business; the formation of joint ventures in the area of foreign trade; and allowing foreign trade companies from other provinces to set up subsidiaries there. Pudong also set new standards for the ideal of "small government, big society", meaning a relatively lean party-and-government apparatus.[69]

Moreover, the centre of gravity of reform and the open door was beginning to shift northwards to the Yangtze River Estuary area. Other coastal hubs such as Tianjin and Dalian were making substantial headway. How the "original big five" — Shenzhen, Zhuhai, Shantou, Xiamen and Hainan — tried to keep their competitiveness said much about the relationship between Beijing and southern China.

Endgame for the Special Economic Zones?

The zones' first enemies were leftists and diehard conservatives such as the late Chen Yun. As soon as the SEZs were set up in the late 1970s, they were seen as the "tail" of capitalism. In the mid-1990s, however, the threat was coming from a different direction: China's impending accession to the World Trade Organisation (WTO). Joining the WTO required not only lowering tariffs but also abolishing "anti-market" practices such as maintaining special manufacturing or trading enclaves within China.[70] The popularisation of "national treatment" for foreign firms all over the country could make the SEZs obsolete before 2000.

The big five remained dazzling gems in the mid-1990s. In 1996, their combined GDP amounted to 215.5 billion yuan, or 14.3 per cent above that of 1995. Yet SEZ cadres were apprehensive that the good times might be gone for good. After all, in the early 1990s, they were enjoying growth rates of more than 20 per cent. From 1992 to 1995, the SEZs had lost a number of "special treatments". These included keeping the bulk of their incomes in addition to foreign exchange earnings, and tax remissions for importing producer goods.[71]

Then head of the State Council SEZ Office Ge Hongsheng indicated that it was unlikely the zones could keep up their heady pace in the late 1990s. "It is unrealistic to suppose they can maintain the same high growth rate as that during the past 15 years — nor can they go on attracting the same high level of foreign capital," he said in 1996.[72] However, Ge at least did not challenge the *raison d'être* of one of Deng Xiaoping's key "inventions".

The most frontal attack against the zones came in 1994, just two years after the patriarch's *nanxun*, or "imperial" tour of southern China. Neo-conservative economist Hu Angang, a researcher at the Chinese Academy of Science, practically called for the abolition of the SEZs in speeches to the Central Party School and other important units.

"The central government plays the role of determining and overseeing the rule of the game for the marketplace," Hu wrote in a 1995 book. "It should not take the lead in breaking that rule by granting special policies or monopoly conditions to certain areas." Privately, the scholar ridiculed Shenzhen and other SEZs for currying favour with party elders such as Deng to jostle for advantage or to generate publicity. He quoted *zhongxibu* cadres on how they had been ripped off by the zones. For example, the coastal areas bought cheap raw material from the western provinces and made vast profits exporting them. And since the zones could import machinery and other commodities at low rates, they were accused of profiteering when such materials were subsequently sold inland.[73]

However, as with so many other issues in China, the crux of the matter was more politics than economics. SEZ critics such as Hu were lobbyists for not only the *zhongxibu* but also remnant Maoists such as former Politburo Standing Committee member Song Ping, a Chen Yun disciple. Apart from proving their worth through economic performance, zone leaders had to find new patrons in Zhongnanhai.

A Reprieve for the Zones

From late 1995 to early 1996 the Politburo Standing Committee began a concerted effort to reassure the zones. During this period, five Standing Committee stalwarts toured one or more of the enclaves. President Jiang made two trips each to Shenzhen and Shantou, where he upheld the policy of the "three no changes" towards the SEZs. "Beijing's determination to develop the zones remains unchanged," Jiang said. "The basic preferential policies remain intact, and the historical status as well as the functions of the zones in the economic reform programme will continue."[74]

Firstly, the SEZs retained what Liu Xiaohua of the State Council SEZ Office called "the special right to make experiments". During his Shenzhen tour of December 1995, Jiang called on local leaders to continue to "develop the spirit of bold explorations and seeking truth from facts". The enclaves would be allowed to remain pioneers for experimenting with the structural reform of the economy. On other occasions, the president asked Shenzhen and other zones to create "new superiorities and to cross a new threshold". He gave a list of the updated requirements: raising "the level of the open-door policy" by perfecting the investment environment; restructuring the economy and going hi-tech.[75]

Chinese sources said the zones would be allowed to keep their privileges at least until 2000. These included a 15 per cent corporate tax rate compared with 30 per cent elsewhere. Value added taxes would be exempt for products manufactured and sold in the SEZs. The zones could aim for a growth rate that was higher than the national mean. They would have considerable leeway in carrying out experiments such as offshore financing.[76]

The top leaders' reassertions about the principle of "common prosperity" had not hurt the zones. After all, Jiang pointed out in Shenzhen, this edict must not be equated with "egalitarianism". This prompted then Shenzhen party chief Li Youwei to rehoist the banner of Deng Xiaoping's teachings about "one part of the country getting rich first — and helping others get rich [later]". "If we again implement egalitarianism and eat from the common wok, the result can only be common poverty," he said.[77]

Internal Politics and the Zones' Survival

A principal reason behind Beijing's apparent bailing out of the zones was regional politics. While the SEZs were hardly the apple in the eye of the neo-conservative leadership of Jiang Zemin, the president felt he had to sustain the zones so as to protect Shanghai and Pudong. After all, the bitterness of the *zhongxibu* leaders was directed at Shanghai as much as the zones.

Jiang and other Shanghai Faction stalwarts were alarmed by the fact that Hu Angang and other anti-SEZ warriors could be targeting Shanghai and Pudong as much as Shenzhen or Zhuhai. For example, Hu's statements such as "we must stop giving more preferential policies to areas which have already become rich" seemed to have implications for wealthy Shanghai. In a revealing speech to his associates, then Shenzhen party secretary Li said in 1995 he was tired of acting as a shield for Shanghai. "Shenzhen has taken all of 300 million yuan of investment from the *zhongyang*, whereas Shanghai and Pudong have gulped down more than 40 billion in a much shorter period," he claimed.[78]

Zone leaders also sought support from liberal leaders such as Tian Jiyun, a frequent visitor to Shenzhen and Zhuhai. Pro-SEZ statements by moderate leaders were invoked with gusto. For example, the former party boss of Guangdong Lin Ruo cited the late party chief Hu Yaobang's edicts on the zones. "Hu pointed out that 'special areas can go about their business in a special way' and that 'SEZs can have special administrative powers'," Lin said. "What's wrong with this?"[79]

What also gave the zones a new lease of life was an opportune juncture in history. Given the difficult task of ensuring the prosperity and stability of Hong Kong and Macau — as well as the even more daunting challenge of speeding up Taiwan's reunification — Beijing saw a sizeable "united front" role for the SEZs.

A major decision of an early 1996 national meeting on the SEZs was to carve out "radiation spheres" for the five zones plus Pudong, referring to particular markets and partners that the six should woo. Thus, Shenzhen should augment its "radiation effect" over Hong Kong. It was Macau for Zhuhai; Hong Kong and overseas-Chinese markets for Shantou; Taiwan for Xiamen; Southeast Asia for Hainan; and East Asia, particularly Japan and South Korea, for Pudong. Speaking at the meeting, then premier Li Peng expressed high hopes that Shenzhen would "dovetail with the Hong Kong track" and help ensure the well-being of the Hong Kong Special Administrative Region.[80]

Shenzhen Squeaks Through — For Now

Beijing and Shenzhen sang different tunes while marking the *nanxun's* fifth anniversary in 1997. Central leaders played up Deng teachings such as "preserving stability is the over-riding task" and "beware of the Great Leap Forward mentality". However, officials quoted by Shenzhen newspapers cited the patriarch's aphorisms such as "we must be bold enough to smash taboos"; and "we must speed up development by grasping opportunities because opportunities can be gone in split seconds".[81]

Rhetoric aside, what was at stake was whether Shenzhen could maintain its momentum. What had become of the famed "Shenzhen speed" and "Shenzhen efficiency"? It was true that in 1996 and 1997, every Shenzhen cadre was talking about "a second round" of empire building. In the Ninth Five-Year Plan, however, the annual growth rate was projected at a relatively modest 13 per cent and annual increase in the value of industrial production 14 per cent. The plan enshrined many elements of central planning. Take, for example, the principle of the so-called three coordinations. This meant there should be a balanced development of the primary, secondary, and tertiary industries; coordination between economic activities within and without the zones; and synthesis between the material and spiritual civilisations.[82]

Daunting limitations notwithstanding, Shenzhen still led the nation in many important reforms. The SEZ was among the first areas to achieve a high degree of separation of government and business. Enterprises in the zone had arguably the least number of "mother-in-law" units. Shenzhen was the first city to implement the national treatment for foreign corporations. In the first quarter of 1996, foreigners began paying the same price as locals in areas including raw materials and transportation.[83]

Genuflexion towards "spiritual civilisation"

Shenzhen cadres were pastmasters at pre-empting criticism of their being "capitalist roaders". Hence the big budget and the large number of cadres devoted to waging quasi-Maoist campaigns. While such movements were unpopular among Shenzhen people, they helped officials stay out of trouble. In the mid-1990s, the star zone bent over backwards to ensure it passed muster in "building up spiritual civilisation" and in "talking more about politics".

The SEZ was a much-touted model for cementing a "fish-and-water" relationship between civilians and the People's Liberation Army. In 1996, the city was designated a "paragon unit" in the national campaign to "support the soldiers and honour their relatives". While the Shenzhen Garrison was Beijing-financed, the SEZ forked out millions every year on the food, welfare and entertainment of the troops; building and refurbishing army facilities; and job training and placement for the demobilised. Shenzhen also shouldered part of the expenses incurred by the garrison stationed in Hong Kong.[84]

As a local source put it: "Shenzhen leaders know the PLA is the most potent power bloc in the nation. Should a power struggle erupt in the capital, the zone knows it will not be without friends in the forces." Mayor Li Zibin largely agreed, even though he phrased it differently. "Shenzhen's one superiority is support from the troops," he said in a ceremony honouring the soldiers in early 1997. "With a stable political and social environment, the people here can singlemindedly devote themselves to economic construction."[85]

Shenzhen acquitted itself particularly well in taking care of the have-nots. It was among the first cities to introduce a minimum wage system, medical and social insurance, and an emergency fund for workers in moribund enterprises. Welfare and labour units kept detailed dossiers on laid-off workers, destitute families and other disgruntled elements. During the 1997 Lunar New Year, the Labour Bureau gave a special 300 yuan subsidy to 1,800 jobless labourers. And the local branch of the official trade union paid 1,000 yuan each to 390 destitute families. Under the "common prosperity scheme", the government spent 489 million yuan on 137 infrastructure and other projects in poorer parts of town.[86]

Shenzhen also tried to impress Beijing through periodic campaigns against corruption, prostitution and illegal immigrants. "We must not secure temporary 'prosperity' through sacrificing spiritual civilisation," said vice-party secretary Li Ronggen. Li Youwei, an unrivalled reader of Zhongnanhai's moods, organised regular seminars on "political construction" for cadres. Li's goal was to show Beijing he was toeing the party line. In a speech to an "ideological and political work meeting" in 1997, Li urged cadres to "rectify and overcome the wrong tendencies and behaviours stemming out of regionalism and protectionism, liberalisation, individualism and centrifugalism".[87]

Long live the Hong Kong connection!

In the five years since the *nanxun*, the GDP of Shenzhen grew threefold to 95 billion yuan. Yet the metropolis's prosperity in the mid-1990s and beyond had less to do with its SEZ status than the fact that it had virtually become Hong Kong's twin city. Shenzhen was desperately playing up its Hong Kong connection to retain its "special status". In his report to the local people's congress in 1996, Mayor Li Zibin said Shenzhen should "boost ties with the Hong Kong Special Administrative Region and fully take advantage of the latter's superior conditions as a financial, commercial, shipping and information centre".[88]

Then party boss Li Youwei waxed lyrical on a lucrative, symbiotic relationship with his glamorous neighbour. Li claimed in a speech in early 1997 that after the handover, Shenzhen would provide the Hong Kong economy with "many types of contribution and vigorous support", thus ensuring the success of the "one country, two systems" formula. However, Li conceded that Hong Kong would play the role of "big brother" in helping the zone prosper. "Shenzhen should make use of Hong Kong to develop itself and learn from Hong Kong in doing things according to international norms," he said.[89]

Li went on to say: "The better and more intimate Shenzhen-Hong Kong ties become, the broader will be the prospects of cooperation between the mainland and Hong Kong." Beijing, however, did not seem to equate

Shenzhen-Hong Kong synergy with that between the mainland and Hong Kong. Obviously, the *zhongyang* did not want Guangdong or Shenzhen to monopolise the SAR. There was an ingrained fear that Hong Kong and Guangdong cities would "gang up" against Beijing.[90]

Before the July 1, 1997 transition, the Shenzhen municipality had drawn up grandiose plans for economic — and even some degree of political — integration between the two cities. These included the abolition of customs restrictions and control over the flow of people. The relaxation of border control would enable SAR residents to live in Shenzhen — and commute to Hong Kong to work. Moreover, selected sectors of the Shenzhen population, mostly "professionals", would be allowed to seek employment in the SAR under a work permit system. These measures would contribute greatly to the Shenzhen economy and property values would soar. Another radical proposal raised in internal municipal discussions even envisaged Shenzhen being "absorbed" into Hong Kong, that is, the SEZ becoming part of the SAR early in the 21st century. Many Shenzhen cadres reportedly did not mind "working under" the SAR administration. After all, civil service salaries in Hong Kong were many times those of the SEZ.[91]

However, by mid-1998, Beijing was sticking to the point made by President Jiang in mid-1994: that Shenzhen must not become an "expanded Hong Kong". At that time, Li Youwei quoted Jiang as saying: "Shenzhen is a socialist SEZ and it cannot at any time become an expanded part or a continuation of Hong Kong." At most, Jiang instructed, Shenzhen could only seek Hong Kong's help in "going international". In the mid-1990s, Beijing had also held up a number of infrastructural projects that Shenzhen and Zhuhai had proposed, including highways, bridges, and other links with Hong Kong.[92]

The Future: A Rough Ride for the Zones

SEZ officials were largely resigned to the fact that the 1998 NPC confirmed the formal abolition of the State Council SEZ Office. The cadres were given reassurance by Beijing bureaucrats that in the foreseeable future, the zones would still serve as China's "windows" for absorbing foreign investment and technology.[93] What was certain was the pacesetting enclaves were in for a rough ride. In the first decade of the 21st century, the weaker SEZs, including Shantou, Zhuhai and Hainan could lose their lustre as more cities along the coast and in inland areas acquired SEZ-like qualities. Shenzhen and

Xiamen would continue to flourish thanks to their unique links with Hong Kong and Taiwan respectively.

The imperative of regional politics meant Beijing would no longer be as predisposed to meet the zones' demands. For example, Shenzhen and Hainan were in the mid-1990s lobbying for the status of free ports. Cadres there argued that at the very least, the two SEZs should be converted into "bonded zones". It was unlikely that Beijing would grant them this dispensation.[94]

SEZ cadres were also complaining about excessive political and ideological control by Beijing. This manifested itself through repeated admonishments to the zones to bolster spiritual civilisation and to "strengthen party leadership". The second message was struck home by Hu Jintao while on a tour of Hainan in the spring of 1996. The Politburo Standing Committee member played up the orthodox norm of "maintaining the correct orientation" of cadres. "We must self-consciously arm our brains and unify our thoughts," Hu said. "We must prevent and flush out all sorts of mistaken ideas and wrong tendencies." And during his tour of Guangdong in 1996, Li Peng pointed out that Shenzhen must remain a "socialist zone" that excelled in spiritual civilisation.[95]

Direct control was assured through stationing "northern cadres" in the SEZs. In late 1996, Beijing transferred about 50 officials to Shenzhen in an apparent bid to halt centrifugalism. These were young turks many of whom were named deputy heads of party and government units. The rising stars included a former head of department in the Ministry of Posts and Telecommunications, Zheng Tongyang, who became a vice-mayor. The personal secretary of Politburo member and propaganda chief Ding Guan'gen, Zhang Chunlei, became deputy head of the SEZ's propaganda bureau.[96]

Then came the surprising appointment of Guangdong executive vice-governor, Zhang Gaoli, as Shenzhen party secretary, replacing veteran Li Youwei. This was despite repeated resistance by Li to be transferred out of the SEZ. For the first time, a Guangdong provincial heavyweight was made the head of Shenzhen. Shenzhen sources said this signified the loss of the SEZ's relatively independent status. As a local pundit put it: "1997 marked the return of Hong Kong to the motherland — and that of Shenzhen to Guangdong." The apparent emasculation of the zones had the support of Premier Zhu. Another Shenzhen official said privately: "Zhu wants to make sure that just as Beijing is running Guangzhou, Guangzhou should have full authority over important cities such as Shenzhen."[97]

While talking to the press about Li's transfer, Mayor Li Zibin, who had wanted the job of party secretary, indirectly expressed his disapproval. He hinted that Beijing's pretext of removing the party boss — his having reached the retirement age of 60 — was less than convincing given the latter's "excellent health". The imposition of Guangzhou authority ended the hope of some SEZ supporters that Shenzhen would be made into a directly administered city.[98]

GUANGDONG PROVINCE ON THE BRINK

Guangdong as No. 2?

By the mid-1990s, Guangdong, the "ahead-of-the-times" province, was on the point of losing its No. 1 status so eloquently celebrated by the likes of Harvard University guru Ezra Vogel. The growth rate for Guangdong in the Ninth Five-Year Plan period would only be 11 per cent, down from the 13.5 per cent in the 1991–1995 period — and significantly lower than the 21 per cent scored in 1993. The rate of increase in capital construction, mostly infrastructure and plants, was fixed at 30 per cent, or five percentage points lower than the national mean. For the late 1990s and beyond, the emphasis would be on stable, sustained, and non-inflationary development, not a spectacular new takeoff.[99]

The amount of foreign capital and loans to be absorbed in 1996 was set at US$11.5 billion, or five per cent less than that of 1995. Of these, foreign direct investment was projected at US$9.55 billion, or 6.2 per cent short of the previous year's. This was the first time since the start of the open-door policy that overseas fund injections in the province had been reduced. A near-moratorium was put on activities that had contributed most to the wealth of the province's tens of thousands of nouveau riche "red capitalists": property and stock market speculation, as well as questionable deals this side of smuggling via naval vessels.[100]

Beijing's insistence that Guangdong boost agriculture cast a pall on its real estate business. By the mid-1990s, the province had passed strict laws against the building of golf courses or "luxurious villas". In the first half of 1996, land devoted to real estate totalled slightly more than 10,000 *mu* (15 *mu* = one hectare), or 55 per cent lower than that of the same period in 1995. Guangzhou announced later that year that a moratorium would be placed on the release of land for property development. It also stipulated that plots earmarked for non-farming purposes should not exceed 18 per cent of the province's entire land stock.[101]

In the meantime, land and labour costs in a dozen-odd Guangdong boom towns had become prohibitive. These "First-World" prices were expected to hamper Guangzhou's ambitious plans to go hi-tech. In his Ninth Five-Year Plan, former governor Zhu Senlin outlined bold plans for automobiles, electronics and petrochemicals. Then party boss Xie Fei admitted in a 1996 seminar that productivity was going down and the economic structure was "less than rational". Losses from state-owned enterprises (SOEs) in 1995 totalled 2.05 billion yuan, or 50 per cent more than the year before.[102]

Above all, Guangdong had to reconcile itself with the fact that it was being trumped by the Shanghai-Pudong behemoth. There were signs that preferential policies particularly for cutting-edge sectors such as finance and technology were being "reserved" for Pudong, which was anticipating an annual growth rate of 20 per cent for the next decade.[103]

The Imperative of "Spiritual Civilisation"

Yet another sword of Damocles hanging over Guangzhou was the "spiritual civilisation" campaign, often used by Beijing as a pretext for putting Guangdong down. While spiritual civilisation usually referred to matters of ethics and morality, it included the key concept of toeing the party line. Put another way, Guangdong cadres were faulted for failing to "talk more about politics". After all, they were credited with the slogan: "Full steam ahead when you see the green light; accelerate no matter what when you see the yellow light; and try to circumvent the red light."

At the Beidaihe Conference in 1995, then Guangdong party secretary Xie Fei admitted that his province had failed to march in lockstep with Beijing. "My understanding of central instructions may not be deep enough," he reportedly said. "That's why I have modified them to suit the conditions of Guangdong." He claimed that whatever departures there might have been from the *zhongyang*'s line, it was due to misunderstanding only.[104]

There were rumours as early as 1995 that Xie might have to call it quits (see later section). Speculation was also rife that the Jiang Zemin Office would tame Guangdong by "ferreting out tens of southern Chen Xitongs", that is, use graft busting as a pretext to emasculate the province. However, it became apparent by early 1997 that a compromise had been struck.

Guangdong would toe the Jiang line — and be more punctual in surrendering taxes and other contributions. It would devote more resources to propagating spiritual civilisation. In return, there would be no thoroughgoing purge.

Guangzhou, of course, claimed it had done more than its fair share in promoting clean government. In 1995, local procuratorate authorities conducted investigations into 1,860 cases of corruption and related economic crimes involving more than 10,000 yuan each. The number of cases was 28.8 per cent more than the year before. Guangzhou announced in late 1996 tough anti-graft codes that contained "73 no-nos". For instance, cadres were forbidden to take kickbacks and to buy stocks in foreign companies. There were also restrictions on taking free trips abroad or acquiring foreign passports and residency rights in Hong Kong. Analysts said this series of regulations was more detailed than those promulgated in most provinces.[105]

Provincial cadres also did their part in combating polarisation of income, another top priority of the neo-conservative Beijing leadership. Full welfare benefits were paid to the unemployed. Moreover, only firms with the following conditions could lay off workers: three years of continuous losses; loans exceeding assets; plants standing idle for more than half a year; and inability to pay workers their minimum wage for more than three months. Guangzhou also vowed to contain the unemployment rate within three per cent.[106]

Zhu Rongji's Blitz against Guangdong

Shortly before becoming premier in March 1998, economic tsar Zhu Rongji made it clear his top priority would be to combat regionalism — and that he would begin the campaign with Guangdong. In a swing through the province in December 1997, he harped on its failure to abide by central edicts. Guangdong's cardinal sin was what Zhu called a "disorderly and lax" banking and financial system. He scolded local cadres for the fact that many loans in the province had been authorised "not according to market needs but based on the political connections of clients". Touring Shenzhen for the first time since the 1980s, Zhu criticised the local stock market's unsatisfactory performance, saying it had not done enough to provide Beijing with "the adequate experience" for expanding experiments with shareholding companies.[107]

Other complaints of the then premier-designate included Guangdong's failure to collect enough taxes for central coffers. Zhu said it lagged behind comparable areas along the coast such as Shanghai and Shandong. He also expressed concern about a rising crime rate. The Great Rectifier criticised a top Guangdong official for failing to "put his own house in order". Law and order in the cadre's home county had deteriorated to the extent that the People's Armed Police had to be called in.[108]

Shortly before the Guangdong People's Congress in March 1998, Zhu pulled off a coup by appointing key protégé, former banker Wang Qishan, as First Vice-Governor. Moreover, with the support of President Jiang, Zhu finally succeeded in moving Xie Fei out of Guangdong. Former Henan party secretary Li Changchun was installed as party boss in late Feburary. Li, who was inducted into the Politburo in September 1997, was seen as a protégé of Jiang (see Chapter 7). Xie would have to be contented with the "second-line" position of NPC vice-chairman.[109]

Zhu and Jiang seemed to have quashed Guangdong cadres' time-honoured opposition to Beijing posting "northerners" to senior slots in the province. In private, Guangdong officials liked to cite the "unwritten agreement" between Deng Xiaoping and Guangdong native Marshal Ye Jianying that only Guangdong-born cadres be appointed to top positions there. Sensing widespread resentment against himself, Li kept a low profile in the first few months of his tenure, telling local cadres that he would "learn the ropes first and make statements later". Wang Qishan, however, began his crusade to shape up Guangdong sooner. One of Wang's roles was to crack down on financial irregularities and graft cases. Here, Premier Zhu went further than Jiang Zemin in 1995. The president called a moratorium on the anti-corruption campaign after what local analysts called a "junior fat cat", Ouyang De, was nabbed (see also Chapter 3). Now Zhu and Wang seemed to be going after the "real tigers".[110]

Governor Lu Ruihua's state-of-the-province report to the people's congress in 1998 was suffused with reassurance to Beijing that most of its concerns were being addressed. The super-aggressive province would follow the national norm of steady, non-inflationary development by "seeking progress in the midst of stability and ensuring that growth is based on productivity". The GDP was forecast to grow by a relatively paltry 10 per cent, or 5.4 per cent below the average rate for the past five years. Lu vowed to end speculative activities in real estate and stock markets. Other aberrations the governor pledged to rectify included too much funding being tied up by inefficient enterprises; interfering with the loan-making policies of banks; inability to eradicate illegal banks; and failure to stamp out economic crimes.[111]

However, the big question was while Zhu and Jiang seemed to have won temporary battles against Guangdong-style warlordism, they risked losing the war of reform. The reimposition of the *zhongyang*'s straitjacket could stifle initiative on the part of local officials and private entrepreneurs. In 1998, Guangdong was already suffering from factors including high land and labour costs; dwindling investments for Hong Kong and overseas; as well as competition from countries with devalued currencies. Liberal scholars argued that unless Guangdong secured a new dispensation from Beijing to lure investments, restructure enterprises and experiment with new products, the province's energy and drive could fizzle out.[112]

Strategy for the Future

Guangdong, of course, could yet bounce back. In the mid-1990s, the wealthy province scored quite a few victories — political and economic — over the *zhongyang*. For example, Zhu Senlin's replacement as governor in 1996 was Lu Ruihua. While not a distinctive reformer, Lu was a native son who had strong support in the Pearl River Estuary. In his departing state-of-the-province address, Zhu indirectly thumbed his nose at the Jiang administration by mentioning "core Jiang" only once in his 48-page, two-and-a-half-hour address.[113]

Somewhat in defiance of central edicts, the Guangdong media had in the mid-1990s played up statements by Deng and other reformist elders on the bright prospects of the province. A notable example was the memoir published in late 1996 by former governor Liang Lingguang. Liang, who worked closely with liberal Guangdong party boss Ren Zhongyi in the early 1980s, recalled the many blessings the top cadres had bestowed on Guangdong. One example was the extension of the boundaries of the SEZs beyond Shenzhen or Zhuhai. "The [concept of the] special economic zones should cover the two provinces of Guangdong and Fujian," Liang quoted Deng as saying. "It will not do to merely make a go of a few small places. What the *zhongyang* has in mind are the two provinces."[114]

Former vice-premier and NPC chairman Wan Li was quoted by Liang as telling local officials that Guangdong could afford to make mistakes in the course of reform. "It does not matter if you commit mistakes, the State Council will be fully responsible," Wan reportedly said. "You go one step ahead of us. Your mistakes will have significance for the entire nation because proper lessons can be drawn."[115] Significantly, Liang's book was not reported in the national media and it had a relatively small circulation.

At the provincial people's congress of 1996, Governor Lu Ruihua denied that the golden age of Guangdong was coming to an end. "I don't think our golden time has passed," he said. "Perhaps the period of the Ninth, Tenth and Eleventh Five-Year Plans will also be our golden age."[116] Yet it was obvious that shorn of its patrons in Beijing, Guangdong had to handle itself cautiously. Some cadres used the analogy of the duck moving across the pond: on the surface, the fowl does not seem to be moving even though beneath water, its feet are paddling frantically. Splashy gestures, on the other hand, would invite criticism and crackdowns by a *zhongyang* committed to "macro-level controls and adjustments".

Guangdong's Trump Cards

Despite the slings and arrows discussed above, Guangdong seemed to have retained its ability to cross new thresholds. A 1998 survey on the competitiveness and productivity of major cities and provinces ranked Guangdong just below champion Shanghai but above Beijing, Tianjin, Jiangsu and Zhejiang. Since Guangdong is a huge province with numerous poor areas, it could be argued that the large Guangdong cities were on average more "advanced" than Shanghai in terms of efficiency and attractiveness to foreign capital. The ingenuity of Guangdong entrepreneurs and engineers was attested to by the fact that the province held 88,000 patents, one-tenth that of the entire country. Guangdong also led the nation in terms of taxes collected from individuals as well as private companies.[117]

Part of Guangdong's strong suit was adaptability, including the ability to manoeuvre itself out of thickets of official documents — and dogma. According to Executive Vice-Mayor of Guangzhou Chen Kaizhi, Guangdong was nonplussed when Beijing laid down the austerity measures in mid-1993. "There was no question of going against the *zhongyang*," he said in 1996. "What we have done is to adopt a positive attitude to make the best opportunities under the tight money policy." Guangzhou worked out the 3:3:4 formula with Beijing, meaning that for big projects, the central government, local government and foreign corporations would respectively split up the costs in accordance with this ratio.[118]

Indeed, the province still held trump cards galore to go the extra mile.

It had the highest concentration of private and foreign-trade businesses in the country. It boasted a 40 per cent share of both national exports and use of foreign capital. And its people had plenty of cash in the banks. The well-established entrepreneurial spirit had yet to be cowed by the cold wind from up north.

While speaking to Guangdong deputies in February 1996, outgoing governor Zhu Senlin emphasised enhanced cooperation with foreign capital. Zhu hinted that the province could go faster over privatisation. This would be accomplished through the sale of shares in state corporations to foreign and privately owned firms. The New China News Agency quoted Zhu as saying Guangdong would transfer shares in state companies to overseas investors. "Existing enterprises can be merged with overseas-funded enterprises apart from fields forbidden by the state," he said. The former governor said the province would support conglomerates made up of overseas-funded and domestic enterprises so as to expand production and improve quality. While these innovative steps had in theory been approved by Beijing, they had not been tried out on a large scale in any other province or city.[119]

In 1996, Guangdong cities pioneered the "national treatment" for foreign businesses. A year later, the province became the first to allow overseas companies and private capital to invest in its foreign trade corporations. Reformers were also pushing the experience of Shunde, Jiangmen and Shenzhen as national models for "setting free" medium- and small-scale SOEs (see Chapter 6). While the Asian financial crisis of late 1997 and 1998 exposed to the full the deficiencies of government-backed enterprises, Guangdong's successful experiments in the non-state sector became all the more important.[120]

Then there were the golden opportunities afforded by "integration" with the Hong Kong economy. In his 1997 state-of-the-province report, Governor Lu emphasised strengthening cooperation with the SAR on high technology, so that "industries and products in both places can go upmarket together". Prospects on this front seemed to have improved with the central government's decision to move some of the hi-tech research and production bases from Beijing and Shanghai to Guangdong cities including Shenzhen. For example, at least four new hi-tech industrial parks were planned for the SEZ just north of Hong Kong. In a speech in early 1998, Xie Fei urged Guangdong, Hong Kong and Macau to coordinate the development of infrastructure and high technology.[121]

In the final analysis, the extent to which Guangdong could make a go of the market economy depended on the size of the proverbial bird cage. By 1998, central-regional dynamics had become even more of a two-way street. Efforts by Guangdong's cadres and businessmen to battle the constraints, together with changes in the "larger climate" such as the reabsorption of Hong Kong, were having an increasing impact on expanding that cage.

REGIONS AGAINST EACH OTHER

The relationship between the *zhongyang* and regions was complicated by a relatively new phenomenon: localities fighting each other for economic and other resources. The ability of Beijing to play referee was damaged by its perceived policy of favouritism towards areas such as Shanghai and Shandong. While the central leadership could take advantage of the inter-regional conflict to boost its clout, it was clear that the exacerbation of the problem would hamper political reform and affect economic development.

Take the open-door policy. It had become apparent by the mid-1990s that conditions were ripe for Beijing to open up all the major cities for market reforms and integration with the world economy. Yet for political more than economic reasons, some areas continued to enjoy special advantages. Consider the 10 areas identified in 1997 as candidates for expedited development. They were: the Shanghai and Yangtze Delta Region; the Pearl River Delta Region in Guangdong; the Bohai region (including Tianjin, Beijing, and Shenyang); the Harbin-Changchun region in the northeast; the Changjiao region (mainly Nanchang and Jiaojiang in Jiangxi Province); the Beihai Region in Guangxi Province; the Huangshi Region centred at Wuhan in Hubei Province; the Chengyu Region (mainly Chengdu and Chongqing in Sichuan Province); the Guangzhong Region focused at Xian in Shaanxi Province; and the Upper Yellow River Region centred at Lanzhou in Gansu Province.[122]

Obviously, it would take the inland districts such as the Guangzhong and Upper Yellow River regions much longer to catch up with the coast. And provinces and cities not selected would continue to grouse about "discrimination". Beijing had yet to lick into shape mechanisms and laws governing the distribution of resources and "favourable policies" among the regions.

Shanghai against Everybody Else

Beijing decided in the early 1990s that Shanghai and Pudong would constitute the "dragon head" for a new wave of reform in the 21st century. From
1995 onwards, many favourable policies and market-oriented experiments
would be tried out in the Shanghai-Pudong area ahead of the rest of the
nation (see previous section).

However, the aggressive way in which Shanghai authorities went about
augmenting their turf was a case of adding insult to injury as far as the
feelings of other "warlords" were concerned. In September 1995, Shanghai
Mayor Xu Kuangdi and then Pudong chief Zhao Qizheng unveiled the 18
"super-special" policies that they had wangled out of Beijing. The dream
dispensation included annual government loans of 700 million yuan; permission to float Pudong-based bonds worth 500 million yuan a year; permission for foreign banks to engage in renminbi business; and upgrading
Pudong projects into "priority national projects".[123]

For many regional cadres, the announcement, just one month before
the party Central Committee was scheduled to hold its fifth plenum,
smacked of the Shanghai Faction presenting a *fait accompli* to the rest of the
country. Xu and Zhao's pre-plenum pronouncements had the effect of
pre-empting discussion of Shanghai's share in alleviating the problem of
polarisation of income. After all, a key topic of the plenum was how the
Ninth Five-Year Plan would narrow the east-west gap. Moreover, other
warlords were asking why Shanghai was spared the austerity or tight-money
programme that was still gripping the country.

By 1997, the complaints against Shanghai-Pudong seemed to have hit
the target. It was clear that Pudong had fallen foul of the tight-money
policy and had overspent on real estate. This was evident from the below
50 per cent occupancy rate of the 250 skyscrapers there. Shanghai economist Yang Lujun pointed out that Pudong authorities had from 1992 to
1995 made available 1,800 prime plots for development, which resulted in
the glut. Shanghai and Pudong cadres, however, not only escaped censure
from Beijing but were asking for more central aid. Pudong officials indicated in 1996 that while the city had already absorbed about 50 billion yuan
of government injections, they were seeking at least double this amount for
the rest of the decade.[124]

Meanwhile, top Shanghai cadres were making new enemies by trying to
undercut the competition. During his 1995 US tour, Shanghai Mayor Xu
attempted to puncture the Guangdong "myth". In a speech to business lead-

ers in San Francisco, Xu made an unexpectedly hard-hitting criticism of Guangdong. He claimed that while the success rate for foreigners doing business in Shanghai was 95 per cent — 21 percentage points above the national average — that of Guangdong was only 65 per cent. Xu said it took longer for foreign executives to conclude deals with Shanghai cadres or entrepreneurs. However, those agreements were honoured later. "In Guangdong, you can sign a contract in three hours," he said. "Yet after that, all the troubles begin to surface."[125]

Shanghai even had run-ins with nearby Jiangsu, considered a "sphere of influence" of the Shanghai Faction. Take, for example, the name for the highway linking Nanjing and Shanghai, which opened in 1996. Because 90 per cent of the road lay within Jiangsu — and the bulk of the investment came from the province — Jiangsu natives wanted to call it the Ninghu Highway ("Ning" is a short form for Nanjing and "Hu" for Shanghai). However, Shanghai cadres insisted on the name Huning Highway. The latter reportedly brandished calligraphy by Jiang Zemin of the characters Huning Highway. Yet Nanjing cadres refused to yield. They asked for arbitration from Li Peng when the then premier toured the region in December 1996. The matter remained unsettled.[126]

Shanghai tried to justify its pre-eminence by invoking Deng Xiaoping's name. The message to cadres jealous of Shanghai's special treatment was that it was the patriarch — not members of the Shanghai Faction such as Jiang Zemin — who had decided to heap privileges on the metropolis. In a mid-1996 issue, the official *Outlook* magazine said it was Deng who had decided in 1990 to develop Shanghai and Pudong in a big way. "When I developed the SEZs, I did not do anything with Shanghai; this was a big mistake," Deng was quoted as saying. He said Pudong should become the "dragon head" for the entire Yangtze River delta zone. Deng reportedly told Politburo members in the early 1990s: "Shanghai is our strong suit. Developing Shanghai is a short cut [for national development]."[127]

Shanghai cadres such as party boss Huang Ju tried to mend fences with other regional chieftains by saying the city would always play the *zhonghua* or China card — meaning Shanghai would serve the entire country, not just its own interests.[128] Shanghai liked to boast of the economic aid it had given to the hinterland. Particularly strong was the relationship with Xinjiang, which had benefited from a wave of "forced immigration" of Shanghai intellectuals there in the 1950s (see previous section). *Zhongxibu* cadres complained, however, that in the 1990s, Shanghai only moved westwards low-tech, labour-intensive industries that it did not particularly want.

Regional leaders found in his patronage of the Shanghai Faction a handy weapon to attack Jiang. At the Fourth Plenum of the Central Committee in 1994, a number of provincial representatives expressed reservations about the promotions of Shanghai Faction stalwarts Wu Bangguo and Huang Ju to member of the party Secretariat and Politburo member respectively.[129] *Shanghaibang* affiliates also fared badly at the 15th Party Congress of 1997. Jiang's ability to tame the warlords was considerably weakened.

The Seeds of Inter-regional Conflict
Demarcation over borders

Regional infighting climaxed in the mid-1990s for various reasons. Firstly, central authority had waned. For most cadres, developing the local economy, which brought tangible benefits such as wealth to relatives and business associates, was more important than heeding Beijing's call for national cohesiveness. The profit motive and fight for resources were the main reasons for the escalation of inter-regional disharmony. And central leaders lacked the moral authority to arbitrate because of their long record of favouring one region over the other.

More significantly, the scarcity of resources — land, minerals and other resources — was becoming more acute as even backward provinces joined the craze for development. Raw material prices were soaring in the world market. Provinces that produced coal and oil such as Shanxi and Xinjiang, were no longer willing to part with their products at "brotherly" or "comradely" prices. And areas and districts near major mines and natural resources often slugged it out among themselves over the division of the spoils.

Such jockeying for position was evident in internal border conflicts. From 1980 to 1996, more than 10 bloody clashes took place between cadres and residents in picturesque Guilin, Guangxi Province and the city of Yongzhou in Hunan. Some 1,500 people were killed or seriously injured. The quarrels arose over land and water rights along 380 square kilometres of disputed territory. Equally venomous battles were fought between villagers living on the Qinghai-Gansu border over gold mine rights. Two special work teams sent by the CCP and the State Council to the area failed to solve the problem.[130]

Official reports showed that "thousands" had perished in more than 1,000 disputes over "imprecise demarcation of frontiers" since 1949. Work on a more scientific demarcation of borders did not begin until the early 1990s. Beijing announced in 1995 that after six years of hard work, six segments of disputed boundaries between three provinces and regions had been fixed. Work on 59 other contested areas would continue. "The move is to solve border disputes among provinces and regions, which have reappeared in recent years as local areas tend to claim more territory in the drive towards the market economy," said Vice-Minister of Civil Affairs Li Baoku. Territories that required central government arbitration amounted to 140,000 square kilometres of internal borders, some 1.5 per cent of the total national area.[131]

The fight over water and other resources

Irrespective of whether border problems were involved, a growing number of inter-regional conflicts arose over water resources. The bulk of the controversies over water, whose value as a strategic resource rose dramatically in the early 1990s, concerned rights regarding large rivers. Bitter struggles erupted in the mid-1990s between Shanxi and Inner Mongolia over the middle and lower reaches of the Yellow River. For example, Shanxi wanted to build an artificial duct to channel water from the river, thus severely cutting its flow into arid Inner Mongolia.[132]

The mighty Yangtze was even more of a bone of contention. The decision to build the Three Gorges Dam only exacerbated the enmity between Sichuan and Hubei. Sichuan was opposed to the project because it had to bear costs including sheltering the one million-odd refugees who would be displaced by higher water levels. Hubei was regarded as the major beneficiary because of improved irrigation and electricity supply.[133] Quarrels also broke out over the tributaries of the Yangtze such as the Zhang River, over which Hubei and Hunan had repeated run-ins.

Strong feelings over the Three Gorges spilled over into the controversy over upgrading Chongqing into a directly administered city. When the NPC cast its votes in March 1997, more than 11 per cent of the 2,720 deputies opposed the motion or abstained. A number of the naysayers were Sichuan deputies who resented the fact that the province would become less important after "losing" Chongqing. However, opposition also came from officials from Hubei and other provinces along the Yangtze who did not want

Chongqing to monopolise the vast resources that would accrue to the Three Gorges Dam.[134]

Other areas of discord between less well-off provinces included fighting for central government investments — and for the right to develop "pillar industries" such as automobiles. Practically all of the 31 provinces and directly administered cities squared off against each other over the increasingly common practice of erecting inter-provincial trade barriers. Examples included one district closing its market to the goods of a rival region, or a province that would only patronise local factories. Commodities and products involved in inter-regional "trade wars" ranged from cotton and silk to television sets and washing machines. This protectionist phenomenon was exacerbated by the precipitous drop in consumer demand in 1997 and 1998.[135]

Beijing was embroiled in a fierce competition with neighbouring Hebei province over water, electricity and other supplies. While Hebei cadres reluctantly bowed to central authorities by ensuring that the capital would have priority access to these resources, the rancour never subsided. Given Beijing's failure to play impartial referee, provinces and cities with common interests were forming regional blocs to bludgeon rivals and jockey for advantage.[136]

CONCLUSION: BUILDING INSTITUTIONS
FOR POWER SHARING

By the mid-1990s, central leaders had stopped harbouring illusions about their ability to tightly control the vast expanse that is China. At repeated internal meetings in early 1995, Jiang complained that many local leaders were "running their own show". Provinces that he criticised by name included Guangdong, Sichuan, Guangxi, Hunan, Henan, Hubei, Shaanxi and Guizhou. Provinces and cities that were praised for acting in unison with the *zhongyang* included Shandong, Shanghai, Anhui, Jiangsu, Shanxi and Inner Mongolia.[137]

In 1998, Zhu Rongji tried his level best to impose control over the regions, beginning with a blitz against Guangdong early in the year (see previous section). However, analysts said while the new premier might have won temporary battles against the warlords, he risked losing the war of reform. New strictures on the regions might dampen initiative at a time when the country needed to boost competitiveness to meet the challenge of the new century.

The Decline of Central Power

While leaders such as Jiang and Zhu liked to cite the pre-Cultural Revolution norm of "the entire country acting as a [well coordinated] game of chess", it seemed that the decline of the *zhongyang*'s prowess might be a long-term, irreversible process. Sometimes, the Beijing leadership gave local leaders the impression it lacked self-confidence — and that it was not speaking with one voice.

During a talk with a group of Guangdong-based NPC deputies in early 1995, Jiang played up the fact that Beijing's "favourable policy" towards Guangdong and the zones would not change. He cited Deng Xiaoping's dictum that Beijing's reform policy would remain "unchanged in 100 years". Intriguingly, Jiang asked Guangdong cadres not to take seriously remarks on regional development that other leaders might have made. "Only the views of myself, Li Peng and other members of the Politburo Standing Committee represent official policy," Jiang said. "Other people's views do not represent the official stance."[138]

Despite Premier Zhu's claims about the success of the dual-tax system — particularly towards boosting income for the *zhongyang* — Beijing found it necessary in 1998 to promulgate more rules to rein in the warlords. Since the dual-tax regime was introduced in 1994, various localities had come up with their own interpretations of which types of tax should go to central coffers, and which should benefit local finances. A March 1998 State Council regulation stressed that only central authorities could determine how the tax dollars should be divided. Local governments were strictly forbidden to collect taxes that should go to Beijing — or to remit the tax burden of "favoured" units. Another regulation of the same period indicated that taxes that were to be "shared" between the *zhongyang* and the regions should nonetheless be collected by Beijing first before being redistributed to local governments.[139]

Other legislative moves contemplated by Beijing in 1998 included a possible statute to take away the land-use authority of local administrations at the county and district levels. This would mean that only the central and provincial governments could determine, for example, whether an agricultural plot could be rezoned for property development.[140] While these regulations and fiats illustrated the recentralising zeal of the Jiang administration, they also showed the ability of regional chieftains to repeatedly produce "counter-strategies" to frustrate the *zhongyang*'s plans.

According to political scientists Wu Guoguang and Zheng Yongnian, centrifugalism was caused not so much by the regions getting stronger as the *zhongyang* getting weaker. The crux of the matter, Wu and Zheng said, was less the aggrandisement of localities through a decade-odd period of administrative decentralisation than "the exhaustion of resources on the part of the *zhongyang*" even as it went about recentralising its powers. If Beijing were to mechanically take back administrative autonomy granted to localities, it would throttle economic and other reforms.

The two experts thought the central leadership could only try to claw back lost territory through boosting its political resources and moral authority. As discussed in Chapter 3, however, the *zhongyang* was losing influence for reasons that had little to do with "warlordism". Factors included endemic corruption; a rigid, quasi-Leninist system; and the phenomenon of cadres and military officers focusing on doing business.[141] The best way out for Beijing seemed to be to work out an equitable distribution of powers through institutional reform.

The Regions Fight Back

Casting anti-*zhongyang* aspersions

By the mid-1990s, the warlords were hardly shy about protesting what they called the *zhongyang*'s tyranny. Coastal cadres used to say that the Jiang leadership was "going back to the old road [of Mao]". One common criticism: "The third-generation leadership is embracing the ways and means of the first-generation leadership."[142] During the austerity programme of 1993–1996, relatively outspoken cadres such as Guangdong's Xie Fei and Sichuan's Xiao Yang were bold enough to ask Beijing to consider not applying the tight-money policy to their regions.

Then there was the case of Henan cadres selectively implementing *zhongyang* fiats. In late 1995, Beijing sent to Henan 10 documents on the reform of state enterprises. However, only nine were carried out. Officials in the provincial capital of Zhengzhou refused to heed Beijing's order forbidding state firms from running educational institutions. "We did not disseminate the document [on schools] because there was no way we could implement it," said Vice-Governor Zhang Shiying. He explained that for lack of educational funds, the province had to let enterprises "help out" by running schools. Otherwise large numbers of children would be deprived.[143]

It was, of course, true that local chieftains lived in fear of being demoted by Beijing — or transferred to backwater areas. But in internal discussions, they often thumbed their noses at the party Central Committee's Organisation Department. For example, coastal cadres frequently groused about the regular rotation of officials. "It may not be fair for cadres from rich areas to be posted to poor areas," one provincial party boss said privately. "In backward regions, they will have a hard time demonstrating their talent and ability."[144]

Then there was the near-universal practice of cadres sabotaging Beijing's instructions by going through the motions — and cooking up statistics (see foregoing section). Head of the State Statistical Bureau, Zhang Sai, conceded there was considerable fabrication in economic statistics. In an interview with a semi-official news agency, Zhang was asked to comment on the saying "small villages cheat large villages; large villages cheat counties; counties cheat townships; the cheating goes on all the way to the State Council". He admitted that a fair amount of chicanery went on at local levels, but claimed "it is not at all easy to cheat the State Council".[145]

Under Jiang Zemin, regional tours by Politburo members increased by at least 50 per cent over those in the 1980s. Part of the reason behind the frequent inspection trips was to check whether local officials were telling Beijing the truth. Yet even Jiang admitted that he had been taken in by regional cadres during fact-finding tours.[146]

Initiative going to the regions

In the cutting-edge domain of economic reform, the regions often led the *zhongyang* by the nose. A major area was "privatisation", over which Beijing was super-nervous. In the decade ending 1995, more than 500 billion yuan worth of state assets had been lost. However, a sizeable part of this came from local governments and related enterprises selling off state-owned concerns. Some SOEs were "converted" into private or semi-private companies owned by the relatives and cronies of the cadres. Others were sold to foreign corporations, private entrepreneurs or workers. Foremost practitioners included the provinces of Guangdong, Sichuan and Shandong.

Beijing at first viewed this phenomenon with alarm. Even at the provincial and municipal levels, SOEs belonged to the state — and could not be disposed of by local administrations. Clean sales or conversions into private or semi-private entities had to be approved by the State Assets

Administration, the State Planning Commission and other units. By 1996, however, the authorities were forced to recognise the *fait accompli* — and to give "after-the-fact" approval to such experiments provided they were confined to medium- and small-scale enterprises (see also Chapter 6).[147]

Apart from Guangdong, Sichuan excelled in going at least one step ahead of the *zhongyang*. Shortly before his retirement in early 1996, governor Xiao Yang boasted about his province's achievements in reform. He claimed Sichuan had led the nation in the policy of "grasping hold of the big [SOEs] and rendering the small ones free". The maverick said his province had in 1995 turned 22 large- and medium-scale companies into "guinea-pig zones" for building up a modern enterprise system. Such experiments had been extended to 80 firms by early 1996. And a large number of medium and small SOEs had been radically restructured or privatised through methods including mergers and sales.[148]

By the latter half of 1995, there was an element of militancy in the warlords' demand that Beijing end its footdragging in "equalising" standards in eastern and western China. At the annual Beidaihe meeting that summer, *zhongxibu* leaders were crying foul. The cadres threatened Beijing that if aid was not forthcoming, they could not be made responsible for a host of socio-political ills. The angry officials said without central money and special tax and investment policies, their economies would deteriorate further, leading to more widespread outbreaks of crime and anti-government activities.

Beijing sources quoted the regional warlords as saying they were also losing control over economic crimes such as smuggling and corruption. "Quite a few coastal provinces and cities have become rich because cadres there tolerate dubious economic deals and even smuggling," one *zhongxibu* veteran said at Beidaihe. "Unless Beijing gives us more preferential policies, we may have difficulty stopping our cadres from emulating the coastal areas." Such tactics worked well because Beijing was afraid of worsening law and order, in particular, the possibility of an old-style peasant insurrection.[149]

Protection of Local Rights by Legislation

By 1997, the slogan *yifazhiguo* — "running the country according to law" — coined by Jiang Zemin had become popular (see Chapter 3). Many local cadres came up with the commensurate formula *yifazhisheng* or "running the province according to law". On the one hand, this was a sign of respect for the law. On the other, there was a regionalist dimension: the warlords were telling the *zhongyang* to respect the rights and privileges to which the localities were entitled under the law.

In 1996, Guangdong set up a *Yifazhisheng* Leading Group to ensure that laws were carried out in the province. In the five years ending early 1998, the Guangdong People's Congress had enacted an unprecedented 151 pieces of legislation. Ninety-nine of these covered economic activities, technology development and environmental protection. At a meeting in early 1997, then party boss Xie Fei pointed out that citizens and leaders of all levels must boost their awareness of the law — and that the legislature would increase "supervision" of the government. However, Xie was also subtly telling Beijing that it had a body of self-sufficient codes to govern itself. Even such a darling of Beijing as Li Changchun had to endorse the *yifazhisheng* experiment. Among the first pronouncements of the Guangdong party boss was to endorse the status of the provincial party congress. "We must boost the supervisory functions of the [provincial] legislature," Li said in April 1998, adding he would build an "express through-train" between his office and the congress.[150] The *yifazhisheng* ideal enjoyed the support of liberal cadres such as outgoing NPC chairman Qiao Shi and his deputy, Tian Jiyun.

Law-making in the autonomous regions

Since the mid-1990s, liberal elements in the party leadership had proposed drafting legislation to flesh out the special status of "autonomous regions" such as Tibet, Xinjiang and Inner Mongolia. The existing law on regional autonomy, which honoured in general terms the principles of autonomy and the rights of minorities, had fallen into disuse and become irrelevant. In 1997, Buhe, a former party chief of Inner Mongolia and an NPC vice-chairman, said that the 1984 law must be revised to reflect "the new situation of building China's socialist market economy". He also proposed supplementary legislation on ethnic affairs.[151] The drafting of such codes, however, remained haphazard due to lack of central support.

For example, soon after his transfer to Guangxi in 1992, the well-known reformer Lei Yu began drafting a host of "self-rule regulations" for the autonomous region. "Since Guangxi is called an autonomous region, there should be real devolution of power to us," he said in early 1993.

Lei admitted however, that while some government departments were supportive, "more work needs to be done with other departments".[152] There had been no results by 1998.

Scholars familiar with the issue of Chinese-style autonomy pointed out that the new law should give local leaders, especially representatives of ethnic groups, a bigger say over the allocation of resources. This included the price for minerals, a key source of income for Xinjiang and Tibet. Future legislation could also spell out the level of transfer payment and development funds from the capital. There should also be control over the migration of Han Chinese into the areas — as well as concrete measures to protect religious and cultural traditions and practices.

The series of ethnic-inspired disturbances that began to hit Tibet and Xinjiang in the late 1980s had dealt a blow to this liberal school of thinking. The biggest concession that Beijing had made was to appoint more members of minorities to cadre positions. By 1997, 2.4 million such officials worked in the party, government and legislative bodies.[153] However, the conferment of a set of definite rights would hamper Beijing's desire for control. To contain unrest in Tibet, for example, the authorities would find it expedient to continue restricting the activities and even residence rights of monks and nuns. In the harsh climate of the late 1990s, granting more political privileges to Tibet or Xinjiang would be seen as a sign of weakness. The most that Beijing was prepared to do was to give selective, ad hoc concessions.

Law-making in the zones

Experiments with local-level law-making were more successful in the SEZs, first in Shenzhen and later in Zhuhai. Laws enacted by Shenzhen in the three years after securing quasi-independent legislative powers in 1992 were more than double the tally of the previous 11 years. Then Zhuhai party chief Liang Guangda said in 1996 that legislative autonomy would enable the zone to better serve the hinterland and guarantee the rights of foreign businesses.[154] While there was no question that local laws could contravene the provincial or national norm, this was one step forward for regional autonomy.

Shantou gained the same status in 1996 after overcoming fierce resistance. Opposition came from both the centre and warlords in other provinces. Speaking in support of the SEZ, Fang Bao, a vice-chairman of the

Guangdong People's Congress, said the constitution had empowered localities to make laws. "Because development is uneven in China, some national laws may not be able to take into consideration [the requirements of] different areas," he said.[155]

Fang indicated that the Constitution had adopted a "dual-legislation system" to take into account disparity in income levels in different places. He said SEZ-related laws were required because "in the course of experiments, the zones will encounter all sorts of problems". If laws in the zones were working well, they could be extended to the provincial and even national levels. According to former Guangdong congress chief Lin Ruo, legislative powers for the SEZs accorded with the late party chief Hu Yaobang's dictum on the zones: "Special things can be handled in a special manner."[156]

Wu Bo, the Shantou legislative chief, pronounced himself nonplussed by opposition against giving such law-making powers to his zone. "I don't understand what these people think," he said in reference to the dissenters. "I suppose they are psychologically unbalanced because they can't have something other people have." He said that if Shantou did not get its way, it would circumvent the restriction by promulgating "administrative regulations" in order to run its market economy better.[157] Because of Shantou's relative backwardness and its lack of patrons in Beijing, however, it enacted considerably less local laws in 1996 and 1997 than Shenzhen and Zhuhai.

Prospects for a Loose Federalism

For western Sinologists and liberal scholars, federalism seemed the only way to solve the problem of regional and ethnic tension in such a huge country. In the highly charged atmosphere of Chinese politics, however, federalism was always a taboo subject. Yet it is important to note that leaders from Mao to Jiang had conducted studies on federalism away from the public eye. In Mao's most liberal phase — the early 1950s — the Great Helmsman considered applying some elements of federalism to tackling the Tibet and Xinjiang imbroglio. But this was also a period when he said it was permissible for the CCP and the eight democratic parties to "take turns running the government".

Jiang's think tank members began studying the subject when he was party boss of Shanghai. From the 1990s, official brains trusts that had researched and put out internal papers on federalism included the Central Committee General Office, the Central Party School and the Ministry of

State Security.[158] Jiang was mainly interested in widening the concept of "one country, two systems" to incorporate Taiwan. Yet, according to sources close to the Jiang Zemin Office, the president was aware that a kind of federalism with Chinese characteristics could help defuse tension with the regions. That it was unlikely the neo-conservative leader would implement the concept during his tenure did not mean that research carried out by his think tanks would not be translated into policy in the late 2000s or beyond.

According to academics Wu Guoguang and Zheng Yongnian, China had by the mid-1990s attained a kind of quasi-federalism or *de facto* federalism. They said that a type of checks and balances already existed between the *zhongyang* and the regions — and that many policies affecting the regions were arrived at after lengthy negotiation and give-and-take between central and local leaders. "There is already a rough balance of power between the *zhongyang* and the regions," they wrote. "And both sides exercise a degree of restraint in their interactions."[159]

While a formal federalist structure would remain politically incorrect in the foreseeable future, scholars and think tank members proposed institutions and mechanisms for power sharing — at least in the area of the allocation of economic resources. Political scientist Wang Shaoguang said regional cadres should be allowed to join central leaders in making decisions on different aspects of economic policy. "Each province should have an equal vote on how resources should be distributed," Wang said. "There should be mechanisms for checks and balances in this respect."[160]

Economist Hu Angang proposed that either the NPC Standing Committee or the NPC Finance Committee should be restructured to accommodate representatives from the 31 provinces and directly administered cities. Since these bodies had some influence on the budget, central investment, taxes and transfer payments, this "US Senate-style" arrangement should enable local representatives to have a say on both national and regional development.[161] However, by mid-1998, there was no sign that this and other seemingly modest proposals would be adopted any time soon.

6 Ideas and Trends for the New Century

INTRODUCTION: MAJOR IDEOLOGICAL MOVEMENTS OF THE MID- TO LATE-1990S

President Jiang Zemin liked to tell foreign reporters that it was a "colourful and heterogeneous world" in terms of ideology and beliefs.[1] Mao Zedong liked to wax eloquent about "letting a hundred flowers bloom". In *fin de siècle* China, ordinary Chinese, particularly denizens of the fast-expanding civil society, had more and more ideas and fads to choose from. The Chinese Communist Party (CCP) was hard put to pick out of this plethora of possibilities a new creed that could unite the people even as it continued to shore up the party's legitimacy. After all, Marxism was moribund. And yet Jiang and his comrades could self-destruct if they were to incorporate ideals that smacked of "all-out Westernisation".

The difficulty was all the more acute given the fact that Jiang was singularly deficient in what American commentators called the vision thing. As we saw in Chapter 2, his primary interest was in staying in power. While the party chief was given to delivering long speeches — which were invariably described as "programmatic documents" by his handlers — most of his ideas did not go beyond home truths and safe formulas. They often coalesced into some form of pan-nationalism, which offered a set of lowest common denominators for Chinese from different persuasions.

Jiang's notions of patriotism and nationalism were evident from the way he reinterpreted the Long March spirit in a speech in 1996 marking the 30th anniversary of the end of the Red Army epic. The president gave a multiple-point primer on "saving and developing" China. It consisted in putting the fundamental interest of the people and the Chinese race first; upholding the ideals of the revolution; paying whatever price that was necessary to save the nation and the people; upholding the principles of independence, self-reliance and "seeking truth from facts"; putting emphasis on the requirements of the entire nation and on unity; and reliance on the masses.[2] Jiang hoped these high-sounding ideals could mobilise the masses towards a new era of patriotism.

Throughout the late 1990s and early into the next century, the leadership is expected to play up the twin ideals of patriotism and nationalism. This will be the party's new mandate of heaven, a time-tested means to pull the people together. And with the economy and military getting stronger by the day, the CCP can point to concrete proof that it could lift China's profile and take it beyond the grip of "neo-imperialists". As an internal document put it, while Chairman Mao declared at Tiananmen Square in 1949 that the Chinese had stood up, the third-generation leadership headed by Jiang enabled China not only to enter the nuclear club but to be within striking distance of superpower status. Promoting nationalism also seemed a cost-effective method to divert the people's attention from the sores in the domestic landscape.[3]

Apart from nationalism, this chapter will look at new ways of thinking — or revivals of old ideals and "isms" — in the political and economic arenas up to the pivotal 15th Party Congress of September 1997. Fresh perspectives on reform on different fronts will be analysed in depth. The liberalising impact of the fast-expanding civil society will be assessed. Members of the "new class" of private entrepreneurs and professionals — as well as Internet aficionados — are putting forward their ideals with gusto and clamouring for a share of the action.

After the change of sovereignty, Hong Kong, with its vibrant irreverence and entrepreneurial gizmo, is poised to play a big role as a catalyst for change for the mainland. The significance of the "one country, two systems" formula for all of China will be examined in detail. The final section will cast the spotlight on other trends and ideologies that the nation may embrace in the "Asia-Pacific century". The big question: can CCP orthodoxy survive the onslaught of the new-fangled challenges of the Information Age?

THE TEMPTATION OF NATIONALISM

The Bogey of an "Anti-China Club"

A Xinhua (New China News Agency) commentary in late 1996 summarised the relationship between patriotism, national cohesiveness, and a marauding West. "At present, patriotism is both a great driving force to encourage the Chinese people to revitalise the nation and a banner to unify the whole nation," said the mouthpiece. "In the face of attempts to 'Westernise' and 'split' China by US-led countries, it is highly necessary that the Chinese people become more closely united and move vigorously to promote patriotism."[4] Given the highly dramatised stridency in this "save-the-nation" appeal, however, it was as though the bogey had to be invented even if it did not exist.

The spectre of an evil West out to gobble up China had, of course, been raised by every Communist-Chinese leader since Mao. It climaxed soon after the Washington-led Western alliance slapped an embargo on China after the June 4, 1989 killings. However, there seemed a new urgency in the leadership's call to arms in the mid-1990s.

Immediately after the 1989 "turmoil", Beijing could only point to some vague plots by the CIA and other agents of the "hostile foreign forces" to destabilise the nation. By the mid-1990s, however, it cited palpable dangers to the body politic allegedly posed by "neo-imperialists" aiding the separatists in Taiwan and Tibet. In spite of American President Bill Clinton's decision to de-emphasise human rights and to play up the policy of engagement, the Chinese held the US responsible for the expanded "splittist" crusades of Lee Teng-hui and the Dalai Lama. Then there was the rise of right-wing politics in Japan. The Chinese were convinced the 1996 American-Japanese agreement on boosting security cooperation was aimed at Beijing.[5]

By early 1997, separatist efforts in western China were blamed on what Xinjiang chairman Ablait Abdureschit characterised as the anti-China alliance's efforts to "split up and Westernise" China.[6] Some internal reports specifically cited Western government agencies as backers of the Uigher nationalists. There were also fears that Hong Kong might be turned into a base of subversion against China. Former governor Chris Patten's efforts to promote democracy in Hong Kong were viewed as a plot by the anti-Beijing lobby to bring about "peaceful evolution".[7]

An overarching theme of a fast-emerging xenophobia was the theory that powers led by the US were undermining China's bid to become a strong nation. By the mid-1990s, southeastern parts of China such as Guangdong and Shanghai were within striking distance of joining the ranks of the Four Asian Dragons. In the eyes of CCP strategists, such progress would be blocked by the "China Threat" theory spread principally by the US and Japan. As Foreign Minister Qian Qichen put it in mid-1997: "Some people in the US are spreading the 'China Threat' theory. They believe that as its economy and national strength grow, China is bound to pursue external expansion."[8] Beijing feared that if the China Threat theory gained currency, Washington and Tokyo could persuade more nations to join the "anti-China containment conspiracy".

Warnings against Cultural Invasion
Campaign against "foreign garbage"

As befits a political party that started the Cultural Revolution, the CCP raised the most alarms against "cultural invasion" by a country that produced Coca-Cola, McDonald's and Madonna. One recalls, of course, the Campaign against Spiritual Pollution of 1983 and the Campaign against Bourgeois Liberalisation of 1986–1987. More overt streaks of xenophobia were detected in the mass movement against "foreign garbage" in 1996. This could herald attempts to screen off "harmful" Western culture in the coming decade.[9]

The 1996 Central Committee document on spiritual civilisation decried efforts by the West to infiltrate China, partly through the export of culture. Chinese were told to "obliterate the propagation of cultural rubbish and to withstand the plot of hostile forces to 'Westernise' and 'split up' China".[10] The *Liberation Army Daily* quoted Mao on the fact that one must not "blindly learn from, indiscriminately borrow, and mechanically copy" Western things. It said China must spit out capitalist institutions such as privatisation and Western political systems, which were "fundamentally opposed" to China's interests and conditions.[11]

During intellectual-property rights talks with the Americans, the Chinese made it clear many cultural products were barred from the China market for ideological — not commercial — reasons. Beijing pointed out that American companies would never be allowed to set up wholly-owned or joint-venture factories in China to produce video products. "Cultural products, especially those having to do with ideology, are very sensitive," said Vice-Premier Li Lanqing. "Chinese laws will not allow cultural invasion by America."[12] Beijing also took the strictest measures to bar other American cultural and media products such as newspapers and TV productions from entering the country.

In 1996, the authorities found in "foreign rubbish" an apt metaphor for the Western "plot" to poison China: the tons of American-originated garbage — waste material from households and to a smaller degree, industrial detritus — dumped on China through intermediaries and importers who had been paid by unscrupulous US exporters.[13] As the semi-official China News Service put it, foreign litter was not just a commercial or environment matter. It was a 21st century version of the trafficking of opium. "The essence is the conspiracy of Washington-led Western nations to transfer public poison to China in a planned, organised manner," it said. "This is a grave infringement of the human rights of Chinese."[14]

Campaign against "colonial names"

A resuscitation of Maoist-style xenophobic fervour could be behind the short-lived war against "colonial names" that was waged in mid-1996. In cities ranging from Beijing and Chongqing to Guangzhou and Xiamen, hotels, restaurants, cinemas and enterprises were told to drop names and titles that sounded "Western" or just politically incorrect. Colonial, feudal, offensive or "vulgar" appellations were removed from shops, bill-boards, advertisements and product labels. The names of many streets were changed. At the height of the movement in the spring and early summer of 1996, nearly 4,000 company and product monikers were axed by the authorities.[15]

Names deemed offensive included "imperial", "empire", "queen", "new aristocracy", "mafia", "big landlord", and "pirates". Anything with an excessively foreign, Hong Kong and Taiwan flavour could become taboo. Restaurants, hotels and department stores called Julius Caesar, New York, Arc de Triomphe, Sun Moon Lake (Taiwan), Mainland-Hong Kong and Zhaohe (a Japanese dynastic name) were told to use more proper or elegant substitutes.

A Guangdong nightclub that called itself Herman Goering after the Nazi marshal was given severe warnings. Another restaurant that went by Louis XVIII was penalised because the king was "the head of the reactionary French restoration". The proscription extended to names that were merely in bad taste such as "professional killer", "rich guy" and "rich widow".[16] In several cities, laws were passed to press home the new cultural regime. Guangdong authorities issued regulations forbidding buildings, plazas, and squares from using the names of foreign (including Hong Kong and Taiwan) nationals and places. Corporations were also subject to this Draconian ruling.[17]

Particularly fierce battles were waged to ban names — and cultural paraphernalia — with overtones of imperialist Japan. In the relative backwater of Hunan, 34 enterprise and product names with "Japanese-sounding" flavours were proscribed. More ire was directed at entertainment facilities that sought to make money out of memories of the Sino-Japanese War. Black sheep included photography shops at the holiday resort of Baiyangding, Hebei, which rented out imperial-Japanese costumes to Japanese tourists wanting to take "nostalgia pictures". Four young software technicians at the Tianjin Guangrong Software Company became national heroes for refusing to take part in the production of a computer game, *The Governor's Resolution*, which played up the exploits of Japanese soldiers during the War. After the four were fired, theirs became a *cause célèbre*. The company soon closed down.[18]

In the words of a former adviser to Hu Yaobang, the war against names smacked of the *siqing* ("smash the four evils") movement during the Cultural Revolution.[19] At the height of this frenzy, antiques, ancient texts and foreign books were burnt or smashed to smithereens. Of course, Jiang's fastidiousness with names ran afoul of Deng's teachings against the leftist practice of "surnames" — that a policy can only be carried out if it is "surnamed socialist".

Acme of Anti-American Feelings

While it was uncertain whether the promotion of patriotism would lead to a regeneration of Chinese culture, it served to some extent — and for a limited period — to "unify" the people. Take, for example, the acme of anti-American feelings in 1996, which seemed to have been nurtured by government or quasi-official units including the media and orthodox academics.

Uncle Sam was the bogeyman in ideological sessions in party and government offices, factories, farms and colleges. On a diplomatic and political plain, the US government was held responsible for keeping China disunited or otherwise preventing the nation from gaining its rightful place in the sun. With the common people, however, the administration scored more points with emotional issues not necessarily related to cool-hearted calculus of geopolitics. Somehow, the Olympic Games became a symbol of Yankee high-handedness.[20]

The Chinese government was successful in persuading a sizeable part of the public that it was Washington that frustrated Beijing's application to host the 2000 Summer Games. Upon returning to Beijing in 1992 after the delegation he headed had lost the Olympic bid in Monaco, former Beijing party boss Chen Xitong gave the leadership a briefing on how "hostile Western powers" led by Washington had tried to smear and bad-mouth China. Then came the "discrimination" against the Chinese team at the Atlanta Olympics of 1996. The official media savaged what they called the "shockingly poor standards" of the facilities in Atlanta. Chinese athletes were subjected to accusations of dope-taking by the US media. They were reportedly given poor-quality food in the canteens. The ace swimmers were awakened at night by strange alarm bells. National favourite long-distance runner Wang Junxia complained that during the 5,000-metre race, competitors from different countries were "ganging up on her".[21]

This Olympics complex, together with the Taiwan crisis of 1995 and 1996 (see Chapter 4), precipitated a wave of popular hostility against the US. In a mid-1996 poll of youths conducted by a quasi-official organisation in six cities, 90.3 per cent of respondents thought American actions concerning China smacked of "hegemonism". This feeling towards the US was shared by 95.7 per cent of all college students surveyed.[22]

Anti-American sentiments reached a new high with the publication of *China Can Say No* in the summer of 1996. Hastily put together by five young, market-savvy intellectuals, *Say No* was a caricature-style, fad book which demonised the US. It repeated the familiar charge that Washington had spearheaded a drive to contain China and stunt its development. Yet the tome attracted attention because of its apparently jingoistic overtones and demagogic recommendations. Charging that American movies were a vehicle to pollute Chinese minds, the authors suggested that "Hollywood be burnt down". *Say No* accused the CIA of not only subverting the country politically but fomenting nihilism among youths by spreading the doctrine of promiscuity and "sex education". The book's first edition of 130,000 sold out in a few weeks.[23]

Detrimental Effect on Business

In the economic field, a corollary of nationalism was stress on native indus-try. Soon after the patriotism craze, the media echoed with calls that China should be more discriminating in introducing foreign capital and goods so that enough room be given to domestic manufacturers. There were signs xenophobia was spilling into the business sector. President Jiang himself might have fanned this sentiment. Compared with former leaders such as Deng, Hu Yaobang and Zhao Ziyang, the president paid a lot more atten-tion to the development of the native sector. For example, he outlined this two-pronged approach to development in 1996: "While continuing to in-troduce and to use foreign capital well, we must pay full attention to pro-tecting and developing our own industries."[24] By contrast, Deng and Zhao expressed no reservations in thrashing out their open-door policy.

In mid-1996, nearly 100 National People's Congress members wrote to the leadership to lobby for protectionist measures. The parliamentarians complained that as a result of the "invasion" of foreign products, domestic industries in areas ranging from beer to automobiles ran the risk of either floundering or becoming "vassals" of Western multinationals. The deputies urged Beijing to use more concrete means to nurture local manufacturing capacities. In separate petitions, other NPC delegates blamed foreign compa-nies for exacerbating the economic gap between coastal and western China. "Unscrupulous" Chinese firms were accused of colluding with overseas firms in gouging the mineral resources of central and western provinces.[25]

A late 1996 article in the party mouthpiece *Outlook* linked patriotism to buying Chinese. The "mindless worship of things Western" was bitterly criticised. "If you just stick a foreign label on a product, people will flock to it like ducks," the newsweekly said. "Even if they understand clearly it is a fake foreign brand, consumers still feel good wearing it." *Outlook* said citizens should not be overly credulous when overseas firms claimed they wanted to help the nation's modernisation. The magazine pointed out that buying native products was a concrete action to help the nation — and when China became strong, "nobody in the world will dare bully us".[26] Added the usually moderate *China Business Weekly*: "Traditionally, the majority of Chinese consumers thoughtlessly acquired foreign-made household electrical appliances." The paper said this had led to the atrophy of native manufacturing.[27]

But it soon became clear to the authorities that patriotic sentiments should best be kept out of business. There were two reasons for Beijing's anxiety. First, the rise of protectionism was setting off alarms in foreign capitals at a time when China was eager to join the WTO. The semi-official Hong Kong China News Agency decried a tendency to bad-mouth foreign investments. "Some theorists have published articles saying that as China absorbs more and more foreign direct investment, the status of state-owned enterprises as the mainstay of the economy will be jeopardised," the news agency reported in 1996. Secondly, local governments and numerous SOEs were slyly taking advantage of the rise of nationalistic feelings to ask for more government aid.[28]

Beijing took action in the summer of 1996 to reiterate its commitment to the open-door policy. In an internal meeting, head of propaganda Ding Guan'gen urged the media to downplay calls to "strengthen native industry" or to "protect native manufacturing" for fear foreign investors would get the wrong message. Ding said the media should generate more publicity for China-made brand names, but without giving xenophobic overtones.[29]

In August 1996, the *People's Daily* warned against the indiscriminate rejection of foreign capital. "Opening up the [China] market is the price to pay for absorbing foreign capital," it wrote. "It is also an important measure to use market competition to raise the management level of our national enterprises." The paper noted that while opening up domestic markets would bring about a certain degree of "disruption and shock" to native industry, such detrimental effects would be limited because foreign capital would only be introduced in a planned and gradual manner.[30]

Will Nationalism be the Creed of the 21st Century?

Taiwan President Lee Teng-hui referred many times to the "crypto-fascist" nature of the Jiang Zemin administration's fanning of the flames of nationalism. It was left to Fang Lizhi to provide perhaps the most eloquent critique from the standpoint of "bourgeois-liberal" intellectuals. For the rebel astrophysicist, the rise of "extreme nationalism" in China was proof that it was wrong to assume that after developing its economy, China would automatically embrace democracy. "The economy may have improved; yet if the country still has a dictatorial system, it may gravitate towards a dangerous form of fascism," he said in 1996. Fang added that nationalism was the antithesis of democracy because it went against such principles as diversity and tolerance.[31]

While both Lee and Fang were hardly disinterested observers, their views might not be entirely off the mark. The military — even militarist — overtones of the nationalistic movement was evident in an August 1996 commentary in the *China National Defence Paper*. The official organ claimed the best way to beat "colonial culture" and the encroachment of the West was to raise the level of "national defence consciousness". "Defence consciousness is the core content — and manifestation in a concentrated form — of nationalism," it said.[32] As we saw in Chapter 4, a number of generals were taking advantage of the patriotic movement to clamour for larger budgets and bigger powers.

Indeed, it seemed obvious that over the long haul, the "say no to foreign devils" mentality could hurt as much as help the authorities. Encouraging intellectuals and citizens to vent their frustration via quasi-xenophobic activities might promote national cohesiveness in the short run; it could be self-destructive over a longer perspective. Critics with as different a background as former US ambassador to Beijing James Lilley and Hong Kong-based political scientist Wu Guoguang saw shades of the Boxers in the "say no" mind-set. Moreover, as Wu indicated, only during the closed-door era of Mao could China afford to say no to the US. "If a Boxer-style 'say no' movement were to emerge, the first consequence would be massive domestic disorder," Wu warned.[33]

Moreover, experience in many developing countries has shown that a people given to xenophobia could turn against their own government for failure to "act tough" over real or imagined enemies. As liberal legal scholar Yu Haocheng pointed out, a "say no" movement aimed at the West could ignite a "say no" crusade against the powers-that-be within China. After all, the Jiang administration needed to make concessions to the Americans over trade and other issues.[34]

In the half year prior to Jiang's summit with Bill Clinton in October 1997, the Chinese propaganda machinery began toning down overt anti-Americanism. Books and articles dealing with the US or Sino-US relations had to be subjected to special vetting by the propaganda department and the state publication administration. Scholars and cadres known to be harsh critics of America were asked by their work units to keep a low profile. Organisers of international conferences in Beijing and other cities were told to rein in speakers with reputations of being America bashers. A social scientist and well-known US critic was prevented from addressing the full session of a cultural conference held in Nanjing in late summer.[35]

The episode over the Diaoyu or Senkaku islands in the summer of 1966 proved that Beijing could not "stand up" to the Japanese either. While vocal Chinese in Hong Kong and Taiwan were organising anti-Japanese protests, Beijing appeared to spend most of its effort dousing the outpouring of anti-Japanese feelings. The reason: Beijing felt it could not yet confront Japan; and it feared an outbreak of student action over Japan could lead to a repeat of the 1989 pro-democracy demonstrations.[36]

In late 1996, Beijing showed its displeasure over the sequel to *China Can Say No*, called *China Can Still Say No*. The second book implicitly challenged the conciliatory policy towards Japan first laid down by Deng in the 1970s. It advocated a more hawkish attitude towards Tokyo than Beijing would allow. China, the book said, could be flexible and tolerant towards Asian countries over territorial disputes. With Japan, however, Beijing should be resolute and "fight for even one inch of territory". Referring to Deng's statement in the 1970s that the dispute over the Diaoyu islands be put off, *China Can Still Say No* said: "The great leader hoped that the next generation of Chinese will have the wisdom to solve the Diaoyu islands dispute." However, for this generation of Chinese, the book added, "the goal [of winning back the archipelago] is no longer one that can be postponed".[37]

At about the same time, moderate legislators and CPPCC members wrote the leadership to cool down the growing signs of xenophobia. The petition said while patriotism should be encouraged, it must not degenerate into anti-foreign sentiments. "If signs of xenophobia were to develop, our open-door policy might be threatened," the letter said. The NPC and CPPCC delegates said there was a minority of people, including youths, who thought "things foreign are no good". They said this could affect China's ability to absorb foreign investment and technology. "It's true the influx of foreign capital and goods has brought about certain negative phenomena," the deputies said. "But it is within our means to make necessary corrections. China's door must remain open."[38]

The "say no to the West" and allied schools of thought could not become the state doctrine of the 21st century also because cadres and opinion leaders were hardly practising a vigorous, China-above-all-else lifestyle. Officials who daily mouthed patriotic slogans were scrambling among themselves for perks such as German limousines and Japanese household products. The authors of *China Can Say No* reportedly accepted all-expenses-paid visits to the US and at least one stayed behind for further studies.

In spite of the news blackout, most urban Chinese were aware of the large number of princelings who had gone abroad. Many had obtained US and other foreign citizenships, and those who returned to China became latter-day compradors, that is, salesmen and troubleshooters for foreign corporations. Cadres of ministerial-level seniority or above whose children had either settled overseas or worked for foreign companies included Jiang Zemin, Zhu Rongji, Huang Ju, Lu Ping, and Zhou Nan. At a lower level, a number of top US-based Chinese journalists who had gained fame bashing the US ended up applying for asylum and Green Cards.[39]

The Resuscitation of Marxism

Apart from nationalism and patriotism, Jiang and company also pulled out all the stops to revive traditional Marxist — and Confucianist — values. After all, a call to arms against the containment policy and cultural imperialism would work for the regime for the long run only if it came up with something new and distinctly Chinese. Mired in the poverty of philosophy, however, what many party leaders and ideologues could offer was to recycle old Marxist truths. They insisted on the perennial relevance of Marxism. "Hostile Western forces are spreading anti-Marxist opinions to subvert China's socialist system," said former Beijing University president Wu Shuqing. "We must keep Marxism as the guiding principle."[40] At a time when the entire nation was moving towards a capitalist mode, however, the rehoisting of the Marxist banner would appear superfluous at best.

Neo-conservative leaders such as Jiang kicked off a "spiritual civilisation" campaign to resuscitate interest in Marxism (see Chapter 2). Cadres and ordinary Chinese went through the motions but it was clear the movement would have petered out very soon had it not been for the heavyhanded work of the Propaganda Department. Take, for example, the revival of the movement to emulate Lei Feng, Mao's "undying screw of the revolution". Under instructions from the leadership, each province and city must every two months or so select a Lei Feng-like proletariat paragon. Soon as the Lei Feng of the season was chosen, an elaborate ritual followed as officials tried to outdo each other with outpourings on how important it was to be "totally self-abnegating and to give one's all to the revolution".[41]

While praising the "Guangdong Lei Feng" of March 1996 — an indefatigable labourer called Chen Guanyu from the border area close to Hong Kong — then provincial party boss Xie Fei thundered that the party must never "for a moment sacrifice spiritual civilisation for the sake of economic development". Xie then launched into a bitter condemnation of Mammonism, hedonism and individualism. Yet how could Xie's audience be convinced when the achievements of the go-go southern province hinge upon the unashamed pursuit of private wealth?[42]

Other public relations units tried to appeal to citizens' civic-mindedness and sense of national pride without linking them necessarily to Marxism — or the CCP's greatness. In a late 1996 issue, the journal *Outlook* gave a surprisingly non-ideological interpretation of Marxism and patriotism. "People in various fields should have a high respect for their profession and do their work diligently and solidly, so as to boost the economy and the nation's comprehensive strength," it said. Thus students should master high technology; workers in enterprises should ensure the world competitiveness of their products; and farmers should have good grain yields in addition to providing raw material for industry.[43]

This de-dogmatised version of patriotism sounded more realistic. Indeed, even Jiang sometimes spoke of Marxism as no more than a methodology — a means to "seek truth from facts". The trouble for the party, however, was that if no extraordinary claims were made of the attributes of Marxism or the party's unique role, why should the CCP remain the ruling party? If it was just a matter of finding the best path to productivity and mastering high technology, shouldn't another political force be running the country?

The Propagation of Confucian Culture
The revival of Confucian and Asian values

In yet another subtle admission of the pending irrelevance of Marxism, Jiang jump-started a campaign to revive ancient philosophies and mores. The spiritual civilisation document spoke much about "developing the tradition of the motherland and its cultural quintessence". In a speech marking the 100th birthday of great Beijing opera stars Mei Lanfang and Zhou Xinfang, Jiang pointed out that "the Chinese race is one that has a 5,000-year tradition of splendid history and culture as well as tremendous life force and creativity". He urged Chinese to develop this tradition. If not, he said, China risked becoming a "vassal of foreign, particularly Western culture".[44]

In a frank critique of Dengist materialism, a mid-1995 Xinhua (New

China News Agency) commentary saluted the oriental way of life as a way out for China. "Even though the market economics propounded by Deng Xiaoping has won the support of the Chinese people, complaints about the fall in moral standards have increased by the day," Xinhua said. It characterised the malaise as "the degradation of social norms, the death of morals and the disintegration of traditional values". The agency claimed there was a "near-consensus" among Chinese and Western scholars that traditional Chinese culture as represented by Confucianism was "good medicine" for the country.[45]

Some Chinese scholars expressed the belief that Eastern culture would soon "overtake" the West. They contended that America and Europe, accustomed to their role as "teacher" of the developing world, should perhaps become a student of the Orient. For Guan Shijie, an expert on Western culture at the School of International Studies of Beijing University, Westerners were "blinded by their deep-rooted ethnocentrism"; they had a "bias" against East Asian cultures. "A drastic change will occur in the middle of the next century, when Western countries will re-evaluate these cultures," Guan claimed.[46]

Beijing leaders happily echoed sentiments expressed by Singaporean Senior Minister Lee Kuan Yew and Malaysian Premier Dr Mahathir Mohamad that moral decay in the West would lead to its decline — and that the East would see its place in the sun. They talked vaguely of a counter-offensive to ward off further "cultural imperialism".[47]

What were these "Asian" or Chinese values? Traditional lore — mainly Confucianism, but also a smattering of Taoism, legalism and "Chinese-style common sense" — was vaguely spoken of as the counterweight to Western civilisation. Guan characterised what the East had to offer as "collectivism, family loyalty and frugality" and the Confucian ideal of respect for "universal harmony". Neo-conservative leaders including Jiang cited elements of "time-honoured Chinese goodness" such as respect for elders; good neighbourliness; and helping the community in difficult times. For Guangdong propaganda chief Yu Youjun, traditional values embodied "putting the people first; emphasising the interests of the collective; the synthesis of benevolence and the profit motive; and the philosophy of 'being the first to worry about the country's welfare and the last to enjoy the benefits' ".[48]

Xinhua cited the deciding influence of Confucianism in the economic takeoff of East and Southeast Asia, pointing out that rapid development in these areas was dependent upon "boosting traditional culture".[49] Hu Ping, a member of the Standing Committee of the CPPCC, advocated the Confucian principle of doing business. Hu, a former Minister of Commerce, said the "traditional commercial morality" was based on the Confucian precept of *chengxin* ("sincerity and trust"), and that it was still relevant today. Moreover, *chengxin* was a key to dissolving the contradications that had emerged in the course of reform. Confucian morality, he indicated, was a good way to strike a balance between profits and benevolence, and between making money and altruism.[50]

Many observers found this re-invention of the wheel ironic. After moving heaven and earth in the name of bringing about a Marxist nirvana, the descendants of Mao had to find excuses to rehabilitate the much-maligned *Kungjiadian*, or "the shop of Confucius". The big question was whether the revaluation of Confucianism could be a regenerative force just as it seemed to have been for Singapore in the 1970s.

Not likely. After all, it was no secret that Jiang and his colleagues were reviving a vulgarised — and politicised — form of Confucianism: obedience to elders (particularly party elders); and knowing and sticking to one's station in life (particularly as it was determined by the party). In internal speeches, Jiang pointed out that Confucianism, coupled with Marxist training, would prevent party cells and cadres from succumbing to bourgeois liberalisation.[51] And then, of course, the very *raison d'être* of "Asian values" was called into question by the Asian financial crisis of 1997 and 1998 (see later section and Chapter 8).

The model city of Zhangjiagang

Nothing illustrated better the pitfalls of Jiang's effort to promote Confucianism-cum-Marxism than the national campaign to learn from the model city of Zhangjiagang. The city of 800,000 people in the outskirts of Suzhou, Jiangsu Province, was supposed to be heaven on earth. Or so the propaganda machinery would have us believe.

The pride of Jiangsu boasted an annual growth rate of 60 per cent — and per capita income of more than 15,000 yuan in the mid-1990s, meaning it had already achieved what Deng Xiaoping called "small-scale prosperity". Yet it had not neglected spiritual civilisation. Each year, the municipality forked out more than two billion yuan on education and culture. There were no prostitution, no gambling, no foul language — and almost no crime. Harking back to the Golden Age of legendary emperors Yao and

Shun, residents did not lock up before going to bed. Some 200 million yuan worth of merchandise was left in open stores in the market every night.[52]

Equally important, at a time when at least 38 per cent of the nation's 800,000-odd party cells were considered "weak and lax", Zhangjiagang was a hotbed of communist zeal. According to an official news agency, the city had a "resolute party and government leadership corps" that was immune to the sugar-coated bullets of capitalism. Everyday in 1995 and 1996, more than 2,000 visitors and journalists from all over the country flocked to the mecca to get the gospel.[53]

The campaign to emulate Zhangjiagang reached the fervour of the "Learn from Lei Feng" movement during the Cultural Revolution. As in the case of Mao-related mythology, however, the focus of the propaganda exercise was not so much the model proletariat or pace-setting city as its illustrious patron. After all, Zhangjiagang shot to national fame because Jiang had hailed it as the nonpareil exemplar of Confucian and Marxist rectitude.

According to insiders, the president had originally wanted to play up Shanghai. He settled on Zhangjiagang, which is, after all just several hours' drive from the East China metropolis, to ward off criticism of favouritism. In his paean to Zhangjiagang, former *People's Daily* chief editor Fan Jingyi recalled how, upon stumbling into a large meeting of local cadres, he was impressed by the fact that the participants "observed the strictest discipline and order" instead of reading vulgar magazines or engaging in gossip. It transpired that the conference was devoted to "learning the Shanghai experience".[54]

Zhangjiagang was to Jiang what Shenzhen and Hainan were to Deng. While the two special economic zones grabbed international attention for their vibrant brand of cowboy capitalism, they were also notorious for brothels and drug dens — and the near-irrelevance of party cells. The Jiangsu showcase, on the other hand, was a socialist special economic zone that was as prosperous as it was squeaky clean on the score of both Marxist and Confucian morality. The catch, however, was whether it was also believable.[55]

NEW IDEAS ON POLITICAL REFORM

While touring Singapore in August 1997, then premier Li Peng said it was a "misunderstanding" that China only implemented economic, not political reform. Li claimed that "economic and political reform will be pushed at the same time". "We will further strengthen democracy and the legal system," he said. Significantly, Li dropped the qualifier "socialist" before the two institutions.[56]

It was not the first time that Li and Jiang Zemin had re-pledged themselves to political reform. By 1997, Jiang was citing Deng's dictum that "there is no socialism and socialist modernisation to speak of without democracy". The limits, however, were clear. The late patriarch's proscriptions on reform would also have to be observed to the letter: no Western-style party or parliamentary politics, and no tripartite division of power. It was true that Deng mentioned the possibility of "national elections" by the year 2047. Yet his idea was that even if the polls really came to pass, they would take place under close CCP supervision.[57]

Hope for liberalisation in the late 1990s and early years of the new century comes from mainly two quarters. Moderate and liberal elements in the CCP will be working on "inner-party democracy", that is, building up *zhidu* — systems and institutions — for a more rational and efficient administration, if not democracy in the Western sense of the word. Outside the party, the intellectuals, private-business sector and the civil society will be assuming more power, in the process bringing about political pluralism.

Jiang's New Commitment to Reform

By early 1997, Jiang had made a new commitment to reforming the political structure. In his eulogy at Deng's funeral, the president pointed out that "we must insist on deepening the reform of the political system and other systems". The New China News Agency cited the ability of the "third-generation leadership" to implement political reform that was commensurate with economic reform as proof it had made advancements over the first- and second-generation revolutionaries. Jiang's neo-conservative allies such as Li Peng also told foreign dignitaries after Deng's death that the "next major step" for China would be political reform.[58]

Sources close to the Jiang camp said the president was ready for some changes, but these would hardly amount to a leap forward. Firstly, some progress would be made in the "separation of government and business". This would mean expediting the gingerly process of converting the economic ministries to state corporations, a process which began in the early 1990s. Several ministries including electronics, machine-building, chemical industry and coal industry would be "corporatised". The leadership, however, had to do more in ensuring that the crown corporation-like entities function as real enterprises, not quasi-government offices. Secondly, the party's Organisation Department would gradually stop appointing the managers of large state corporations. Since 1949, the heads of major SOEs had had party and government rankings, often up to the level of ministers.[59]

More significantly, Jiang would promote the ideal of "running the country according to law". For Jiang aide Li Junru, a noted expert on Mao and Deng Thought, Jiang's "legalism" referred to "administration according to law": government departments going about their business based on well-defined statutes. One Jiang adviser gave vent to his boss's thinking on this subject by pronouncing in an internal meeting: "The will of the party manifests itself through laws; and the country should be administered according to these codes."[60]

This party-based "rule by law" concept was miles apart from the "Western" ideal of the rule of law. However, even Jiang critics admitted it was a small step forward. Deng had mentioned in the early 1980s that augmenting and "perfecting" the National People's Congress system would constitute a major part of political reform. The patriarch, however, only laid down vague principles — and it was left to parliamentary chiefs including Peng Zhen, Wan Li and Qiao Shi to substantiate NPC powers (see Chapter 3). Jiang's push for the "rule by law" goal would inevitably add more powers to the parliament. In spite of Jiang's suspicion of Qiao, the president had by early 1997 agreed to allow the congress to have more authority in appointing government officials and vetting budgets. Moreover, the NPC would be allowed to boost law-drafting ability; all along, most laws were fashioned by legal draftmen in the ministries.[61]

Yet another goal touted by the Jiang Office was "running the country using science and technology". Apart from the angle of developing high technology, this meant promoting "scientific" administration under one-party suzerainty through seeking the advice of scholars and experts. The president underscored his respect for academics by scheduling regular Zhongnanhai briefings by scientists and law professors. He also paid a visit to his former Jiaotong University teacher Gu Yuxiu during his American tour of 1997.[62] As discussed in Chapters 2 and 3, some of Jiang's young aides were making much bolder suggestions about economic and political liberalisation. There was no denying, however, the shades of *noblesse oblige* with Chinese characteristics.

Given Jiang's caution and innate conservatism, it could take years for these initiatives to bear fruit. His critics pointed out that Jiang had failed to pick up on the more forward-looking positions of his predecessors. For example, there would be no talk about the separation of party and government, which was favoured by Deng and Zhao Ziyang in the late 1980s.

Jiang's lily-livered commitment to political change was obvious in the political report he delivered to the 14th Party Congress in 1992. Then, the party chief had mentioned traditional ideals such as "perfecting the system of multi-party cooperation under CCP leadership" and "improving the NPC system". Jiang's goal of "scientific and democratic decision-making" was tempered by the need to uphold "democratic centralism". The latter Maoist concept meant while the leadership might listen to different views, final decisions would only be made by cadres at the very top of the apex.[63] The apparent flowering of reform in 1997 could have been an effort by Jiang and company to steal the thunder from the Zhaoists and Qiao's "parliamentary faction" (see Chapter 7). The president had to do much, much more to convince cadres, intellectuals and ordinary people that he really meant business.

Challenge from the Right
Zhao's proposals for reform

The "Zhao Ziyang factor" suddenly regained currency weeks after Deng's demise. This was most evident in the "petition" that Zhao reportedly sent the Politburo on March 5, 1997. The former party chief had been barred from the Deng funeral by Jiang. The four-page "Zhao manifesto" had a wide circulation in Beijing, particularly after they were printed in Hong Kong newspapers in late March. Regardless of whether it was Zhao who penned the piece, it reflected the thinking of the party's liberal wing.

The missive touched on sensitive topics including the Tiananmen Square massacre. For example, it said the suppression of student demonstrations was against "the principle of the revolutionary humanitarianism of Marxism". However, the main thrust of the letter, which according to Chinese sources was written by intellectuals who had worked under Zhao, was boosting inner-party democracy.[64]

The Zhao petition spotlighted Deng's famous 1980 dictum on building *zhidu* or institutions and systems, to combat the rule of personality, so that, in the patriarch's words, "institutions and systems will not change because of the change of individual leaders — or because the focus of individual leaders has shifted". It cited the little-known but authentic "Regulations on Political Life in the Party" of 1980, which were drafted under Deng's directions. The regulations said the party must be run by a collective leadership; they warned against the dangers of "the authoritarianism of one-person [rule]". Two years later, the position of party chairman was abolished as evidence of Deng's opposition to the personality cult.[65]

Zhao pointed out that the dismissal of Hu Yaobang in 1987 and the handling of the "Tiananmen Square turmoil" were instances of failure to implement good decision-making by a collective leadership. Most significantly, the letter said that to avoid further mistakes, the party must abolish the practice of ascribing the "core status" to a single person. It quoted Mao on the fact that only a collective leadership, not an individual politician, could be called a "core". Here, the criticism against "core" Jiang for holding too much power was obvious.

Apart from issues of inner-party *zhidu*, Zhao proposed methods to widen popular participation in politics. They included direct elections of government chiefs below the level of the county. The ousted party chief also suggested "constitutional law courts", where citizens could sue party and government departments and officials for violating the constitution.[66]

Zhao's teachings on reform

Perhaps in reaction to Jiang's efforts to turn back the clock through measures such as reviving the party chairmanship, Zhao's teachings on political reform in the mid-1980s gained new relevance — and popularity — in 1997. In his 1987 speeches to the now-defunct Central Committee Research Office on Political Reform, Zhao laid down important principles for re-engineering the party structure. These internal remarks first saw the light of day in Hong Kong and Taiwan newspapers in 1997 — and they very soon had a big influence in cadre and intellectual circles in the capital.[67]

Zhao largely went along with Deng's instructions about barring Western norms such as the "tripartite division of powers". But in statements in internal meetings in the two years before the June 4 massacre, the ousted party chief put forward bold proposals for inner-party democracy. His point was to dilute the authority of the party leadership. The then CCP general secretary complained that "the party secretary [of party and government units] has absolute authority, like a super-emperor".[68]

First of all, there should be a scientific working relationship between the four major bodies: the Politburo Standing Committee, the Politburo, the Central Committee and the Central Committee Secretariat. Zhao favoured vesting more power in the Central Committee. And since the Central Committee only met once or at most twice a year, he toyed with the idea of a Standing Central Committee, along the lines of the NPC's Standing Committee. In general, Zhao was opposed to vesting too much power in a small council or clique. "We must prevent power in the party from being concentrated in a minority of people, individual cadres, and even one person," he said in 1987.[69]

Even though it was Deng who had first given the green light for the separation of party and government, it was Zhao who fleshed out the initiative. The ousted party chief wanted the party to get out of economic ministries and factories. He also hoped that more non-party-based organisations would assume importance in political and economic life. "If we substitute the government with the party, various kinds of social organisations cannot have their full play," he said. In industry, Zhao said that party cells played a relatively small role in management or production in the 1950s. "Later the party committee [responsibility] system was instituted and political movements were organised in factories," he said. "Factories started to learn from the PLA and political units were strengthened." Zhao hinted they should emulate Hungarian factories, which had but a skeletal party organisation.[70]

The ousted leader pointed out that in Western countries, party organisations shrunk considerably after elections. The party fulfilled its role as "ruling party" through the government and the parliament. Zhao did not say whether he wanted the CCP to emulate "Western" parties. He said in no uncertain terms, however, that it "should no longer give out orders or directly handle administrative matters". "The party should only exercise authority over those members it has called upon to form the government," he argued. The party could, for example, fire those cadres who were assuming senior government posts. However, he said, it "should not interfere with government affairs". At most, he added, the party should make decisions concerning major issues; actual orders concerning implementation, however, had to come from the government. Zhao called this a "responsibility system for heads of government".[71]

The former general secretary kicked around novel ideas about elections with aides such as Hu Qili and Bao Tong. Perhaps with elements of Dr Sun

Yat-sen's theory of *xunzheng* ("supervised democracy") in mind, Zhao indicated he hoped to introduce guided democracy whereby the people would gradually be given more say. And while popular participation would be within the limits — or "cage" — fixed by the party, the cage should be suitably large. For example, in local elections, "the masses can pick 10 out of 15 candidates" nominated by the party. In provincial elections, Zhao said, the governor could nominate two candidates for vice-governor — and the local people's congress could make the choice. "Superior units often do not have a correct assessment [of popular wishes], and it is better for the cage to be bigger," he said.[72]

Zhao proved himself to be a liberal in other matters as well. On the factory floor, for example, the former party chief wanted the trade union to better reflect the opinion of workers. "It should not be said that the trade union [of a factory] should absolutely obey the party committee," he said. "Otherwise, there won't be divergent voices." He proposed that unions should be able to cast "no confidence votes" against factory directors. Zhao also instructed that the examples of Western and East European labour organisations be studied.[73] The liberal leader even asked his underlings to study the possibility of smashing the taboos on freedom of speech, publication, assembly and the formation of non-party organisations. After all, Hu Qili, then a radical, had made this famous remark in 1986: "We must build up a high degree of socialist democracy. We must not let the slogans of liberty, democracy, and human rights be monopolised by capitalists."[74]

The Challenge of Qiao Shi and the NPC Faction
The imperative of *zhidu*

Qiao Shi was a more cautious reformer than Zhao Ziyang. However, while the former NPC chairman never posed a frontal challenge to Jiang, his acts and statements were in support of a statecraft that was to the right of the political spectrum. Together with such other members of the so-called "parliamentary faction" as Tian Jiyun, Qiao was the first to revive the old ideals of Deng when he talked about building up proper *zhidu* ("institutions and systems") for the mid-1990s. As we saw in Chapter 3, Qiao was instrumental in the "empowerment" of the NPC.

In his speeches and interviews, Qiao made little secret of his view that Jiang Zemin's Machiavellian machinations were against the principle of collective leadership and inner-party democracy. In public addresses, the former NPC chief never referred to Jiang as the "core" of the leadership. The only exception was the NPC meeting after Deng's death, when Qiao spoke on behalf of the legislature. In many private conversations with foreign guests, Qiao dwelled on the atrocities of the Gang of Four. There seemed little question that he was referring to imperfections in the party structure and ideology that made possible the kind of factionalism associated with Jiang Qing — or with Jiang, who headed a latter-day Shanghai clique.[75]

Many of Qiao's views were expressed in an interview he gave *Le Figaro* while visiting France in March 1997. He cited Deng's 1980 dictum about the need to build permanent institutions so that they would not change according to the caprice of individuals. The then NPC chief revived the goal of the "separation of party and government". He reminded his audience in France — and China — that it was Deng who first raised this liberal standard. Qiao quoted the patriarch as saying party leadership should manifest itself mainly through the CCP determining "political principles, political orientation, and major policies … and recommending important cadres to state organisations". He sought more clout for the legislature, seen as part of a healthy, enduring *zhidu* of socialist checks and balances. The parliamentary chief said major decisions by the CCP would only become "the will of the nation after going through the legal procedure [of endorsement by] the NPC and its standing committee".[76]

What raised eyebrows, however, was his ideal of the *guojun*, or an army under the control of the state. Qiao told *Le Figaro* that while the CCP had "created" the army, the PLA had become a *guojun* once the troops had entered and settled in the cities in the early 1950s. "The state has set up a central military commission to lead the nation's armed forces," Qiao said. "The commission chairman is elected [into office] by the NPC, and he reports to the NPC and its standing committee." "It is necessary to appropriately define the status of the army within the hierarchy of the state," he added. It was significant that Qiao did not even pay lip service to Jiang's goal of the party's "absolute leadership" over the PLA.[77]

In general, Qiao and colleagues such as Tian Jiyun kept up the atmosphere and spirit of reform. They hoist high Deng's *nanxun* precept that "while the party should guard against rightism, its main task is fighting leftism". Qiao was the first leader to echo Deng's bold slogan in the spring of 1992. And in an interview with the German paper *Handelsblatt* in late 1996, he unexpectedly raised again the anti-leftist banner.[78] This liberal battle-cry had almost dropped out of political debate in 1994 and 1995.

The influence of the NPC faction

Tian Jiyun was a *bona fide* Zhaoist, having been the former party chief's right-hand man. Owing to his long-standing adversarial relationship with Jiang and Li Peng, not much of Tian's activities was reported in the official media. However, it was no secret that the former vice-premier hoped to revive the reform programme of 1986–1988 — and then some.

Tian wanted government officials to be elected into office by legislators — and he was unhappy that very often, people's congress members were offered only one candidate for one position. "Only when the mechanism of competition is added to elections will the able candidates distinguish themselves and the weak ones lose out," he told delegates attending the 1995 NPC. The reformer pointed out that "multiple-candidate elections" should be held not just for vice-governors and vice-mayors but for more senior positions.[79]

Tian campaigned not just for NPC empowerment but the rule of law in general. He was the only top cadre to have expressed reservations about the legality of the Strike Hard campaign. The senior parliamentarian alleged that Beijing's instructions to police and court authorities to "speed up" arrests as well as prosecution and incrimination went against the principle of the rule of law. "This is the 1990s and the country must be run according to the law," he said in mid-1996.[80]

Superficially, Qiao, Tian and the NPC Faction did not seem to have achieved much beyond the Chinese parliament. Yet it is important to remember that in the Chinese context, laying down the theoretical or ideological foundation is the prerequisite for pushing new policies. By the mid-1990s, there were signs the Qiao clique was able to build up a loose coalition of liberals and moderates.

For example, Qiao made some headway in winning the support of key elders, particularly those who had been close to Deng. Qiao's backers included two former NPC chairmen. In 1995, the late Peng Zhen and Wan Li became honorary advisers of a legal think-tank set up under Qiao's auspices. "Even though they have no formal power, Peng and Wan have a big say over the succession issue in accordance with Communist-Chinese tradition," a source said. "In the summer of 1995, Wan incurred the ire of Jiang by publishing a collection of essays that was considered very liberal."[81]

While cadres recognised that Qiao and company were unable to stage a frontal challenge to Jiang, the NPC clique gained widespread sympathy for daring to stand up to the Shanghai Faction. Qiao spoke for many when he started laying into Jiang-style factionalism in 1995. "The president should be the leader of the entire country, not the leader of a certain city or faction," Qiao said in internal meetings that year. He went so far as to draw a parallel between present-day politics and the situation immediately after Mao's death, when the Shanghai Faction was trying to hijack the succession.[82]

It was a broad coalition of moderate cadres and elders which prevented Jiang from reviving the party chairmanship. As a Politburo member put it in the spring of 1997, there was widespread opposition to the restitution of the Maoist institution.[83] The prevailing opinion was that the return of conservative norms ran counter to Deng's legacy. That Qiao was forced to retire at the 15th congress (see Chapter 7) did not mean his viewpoints could be stifled.

The Future of the Party

How long can the CCP last? Soon after the June 4 massacre, the near-universal "predictions" of Western diplomats and democracy activists were that the party would crumble in three to four years. By mid-1998, even CCP bashers were hard put to cite a convincing reason why it could not muddle through for the foreseeable future. While the problems abounded, there was no sign any one of them could mushroom into a major explosion à la 1989 seven or eight years down the road. This was despite the fact that in their private conversations, many cadres expressed doubts about the longevity of the party. It was for this reason that the majority of officials with ministerial ranking or above had sent their children to Western countries to study or to settle.[84]

In the near term, it is unrealistic to expect what the Chinese call "a change of heaven" — a revolutionary development such as the fall of the Eastern bloc in 1990 and 1991. In Eastern Europe and to some extent, the USSR, "alternative power centres" such as the church and unofficial trade unions played a pivotal role in ushering in the new. At the time of Mikhail Gorbachev, the Soviet Communist Party had a relatively weak hold over aspects of the USSR including the government and the army. Moreover, ethnic problems were much more serious in the Soviet Union. In China of the mid-1990s, the CCP's control over the army and the police state apparatus was generally secure, and alternative power centres had yet to emerge.

It is possible that China's mushrooming civil society (see later section) could by early next century grow big enough to upstage if not knock down the CCP edifice. However, it is equally probable that the civil society and other non-CCP forces would join hands with the "healthy forces" within the party to expedite change. If this were to come to pass, there could be a multi-pronged movement towards liberalisation. Initiatives along the following lines would come from the top: diluting the absolute power of the party committees; expanding inner-party democracy; boosting NPC supervision; and so forth. More thorough changes would come from the grassroots. Village-level elections could be expanded beyond small hamlets. Movers and shakers in the civil society, including entrepreneurs who had "purchased" official positions, could be at the forefront of the push for pluralism. Several years down the road, the CCP could evolve into an East European "social-democratic" party.

On the eve of the 15th Party Congress, liberal aides of Jiang had told the president that only if the CCP seized the initiative could it avoid the fate of being swept away by history. A book edited by Jiang adviser Liu Ji contained a chapter on political reform that urged "the gradual expansion of the people's participation and discussion of politics". The article, written by Qinghua University professor Li Li, envisaged "the direct election of the country's top leaders when the time is ripe". The scholar also thought that major decisions should only be made after the people had had their voice heard.[85]

For aides and scholars in the Jiang camp such as Liu Ji, Wang Huning, and Li Li, there was little doubt that a modernised, transformed CCP could win at least the first few popular elections. This, of course, depends on the party's ability to carry out reforms demanded by the people — and the times. However, as will be discussed in Chapter 7, advocates for thoroughgoing change did not have the ears of the neo-conservative leadership. The fact that dissidents and other vocal advocates of change were either behind bars or had *xiahai* ("dived into the sea of business") might have deluded neo-authoritarian cadres such as Jiang Zemin and Zhu Rongji into thinking that they could hold on to near-absolute power forever.

SCENARIOS FOR STEPPED-UP ECONOMIC LIBERALISATION

By late 1997, China — or at least the southeast Gold Coast — was on the point of attaining "newly-developed" status. The economy, tipped to grow at eight per cent for the coming ten years, was expected to be within striking distance of surpassing that of the US in the year 2020.[86] Further integration with international norms was in the works. China was on the threshold of joining the World Trade Organisation. Tariffs had been lowered repeatedly. In individual cities, "national treatment" had been accorded foreign businessmen. Hitherto taboo areas such as insurance, the law, banking in renminbi, trading and other services were opened up to foreigners.

However, stark problems loomed. Domestic and foreign analysts invariably cited state-owned enterprises (SOEs) as the key to the puzzle. Whether the Jiang administration was willing to unreservedly push the unwieldy firms and factories to the marketplace would be the litmus test of its commitment to reform. And SOEs will be examined at length in this section.

Reform of State Firms: Movements after Deng's Death

By 1997, there was a consensus among all factions except diehard Maoists that SOEs needed to be retooled. Some 46 per cent of the roughly 68,500 state companies that were accounted for by the state budget were losing money. The first quarter of 1996 was a milestone in Chinese industry: SOEs registered a net loss — to the tune of 3 billion yuan — for the first time since reform started in 1979. In these three months, losses sustained by state firms increased by 41 per cent while profits chalked up by the more robust ones shrank 58 per cent over the same period in 1995. The situation improved somewhat in late 1996 and 1997, but not by much.[87]

In a mid-1996 internal discussion of the economy, then vice-premier Zhu Rongji cited the following three stumbling blocks to SOE reform. The first was the delay in building up a comprehensive social security system. Secondly, the investment structure was archaic. "You may have lots of money, yet you need the approval of superior [government units] before you can start a business," Zhu said. "In foreign countries, the bosses go ahead whenever there is money to be made." Thirdly, Zhu blamed an outdated financial system which made it difficult for entrepreneurs to raise money.[88]

Understandably, Zhu did not mention Beijing's lack of commitment to reform — or foot-dragging over questions of efficiency and ideology. Nor did he touch on the factional struggle that had wreaked havoc on decision-making. For example, younger members of the Shanghai Faction, including Vice-Premier Wu Bangguo, were gravitating towards faster change, including the overhauling of the ownership structure of state concerns. At least until late 1996, Zhu stood firm on the issue of privatisation. At the same time, the Jiang administration had to protect its flank against criticisms by leftists that it was going down the capitalist road.[89]

After the demise of Deng Xiaoping, Jiang was anxious not only to solve the economic problems that had piled up but to stake a claim as the worthy successor of the patriarch's economic reform. Perhaps the most dramatic development was Jiang's acquiescence in the fact that while *gongyouzhi* or public ownership should remain the dominant sector of the economy, it could manifest itself in many forms (see also Chapter 7). Joint-stock or shareholding companies were recognised as belonging in the domain of public ownership. And *gufenhua* ("the shareholding system") was seen as the new panacea for SOEs.

During a meeting with members of democratic parties and private entrepreneurs in early 1997, Jiang said: "We must be bold in experimenting with the shareholding system." The neo-conservative leader reiterated that China should learn things from the capitalist West. He pointed out that a shareholding company needed not be a capitalist creation because shares could be held by the masses. "The kind of production run by a shareholding company is not capitalist production because it's production for the benefit of an amalgamation of many people," the president said.[90]

Jiang also reaffirmed his administration's commitment to a multi-sector economy. His preconditions included the following: the state sector should retain its overall position of predominance in the economy; and there should be no significant participation by non-state sectors in "strategic" areas. The president reintroduced in early 1997 the principle of *shehuihua shengchan* or "socialised production", meaning economic activities run by entities that were owned by different social sectors. The party chief pointed out that socialised production was a form of public ownership that conformed with socialist principles. After all, private or foreign capital would be a distinct minority within this system of socialised ownership. And *gufenhua* companies qualified as one type of "socialised ownership".[91]

The flexible and open-minded approach was endorsed by Jiang's speech to the Central Party School on May 29, 1997, which was widely seen as an early version of his Political Report to the 15th Party Congress. "We must assiduously find the types of public ownership that will boost production forces the most," Jiang said. "All management styles and organisation formats that reflect the rules of socialised production should be boldly adopted." The president listed the following mechanisms that could forge "new" forms of ownership: restructuring; mergers; leasing; *chengbao* ("contract") management; joint-stock companies and shareholding cooperatives.[92]

Jiang's imprimatur was important given the fact that his neo-conservative leadership had previously been lukewarm towards the concept of stocks. Until late 1996, for example, Zhu Rongji would only endorse mergers and bankruptcies. In internal speeches, the economic tsar was dead-set against the popularisation of shareholding companies. While touring the northeast in July 1997, however, Zhu for the first time endorsed the *gufenhua* experiment. "In the wake of the regularisation of the stock market and its stable development, raising funds on the stock market can be an important means for SOEs to gather capital," he said.[93]

Nobody, of course, expected the *gufenhua* strategy to go fast. Firms in areas deemed strategic or "vital to people's livelihood" — such as banking, aviation, transport and telecommunications — were unlikely to be converted into joint-stock companies. Moreover, the sacrosanct principle that the state should retain control over major enterprises would stay. What was important, however, was the recognition that it was not necessary for the government to hold 51 per cent of the shares to ensure state control. Many ministerial-level cadres argued that as little as 20 to 25 per cent would manifest quasi-state control. Even Li Peng was said to have come round to the idea of a lower threshold of state ownership.[94]

Under this schema, SOEs, particularly those that were losing money, could sell their shares to the following parties: employees; more robust SOEs or collective enterprises such as village and township enterprises (VTEs); private enterprises; and foreign companies. Moreover, debts which loss-making enterprises owed the banks could be converted into "state shares", or shares held by the government. State firms with potential would also be floated in domestic, Hong Kong or foreign stock markets. By the end of 1996, 467 companies were listed on the Shenzhen and Shanghai stock exchanges. Their market capitalisation was more than 980 billion yuan, or 17 per cent of the GDP of 1995.[95]

New Versus Old Ideas

Major differences, however, loomed between the recipes of liberals and those of neo-conservatives. Market-oriented cadres aggressively lobbied for no-holds-barred integration with the world economy. Provided that the social impact of unemployment could be cushioned, they wanted the pace of *gufenhua* and privatisation to quicken. This was largely the thinking of "Westernised" economists including the older generation of social scientists such as Yu Guangyuan, Li Yining and Xiao Zhuoji.

As discussed above, while the neo-conservatives acceded to the *gufenhua* principle, they had reservations galore. There were also doubts as to whether many of the SOEs-turned-*gufenhua* companies were functioning according to market norms. Moreover, in spite of Jiang's reaffirmation of socialised production, "taboo zones" where the shareholding principle could not be applied were still numerous. The guiding edict for SOEs throughout the late 1990s would still be *zhuada fangxiao* ("taking a tight grip on large SOEs and letting the small ones go free"). And building up conglomerates was a major component of the *zhuada* offensive.

Building up conglomerates

Jiang Zemin, Li Peng and Zhu Rongji wanted up to 1,000 key SOEs to be preserved. The reason: Jiang and company would not yield control over strategic areas to the private sector; and they believed that given proper investment and management, such SOEs could not only be turned around but developed into world-class *jituangongsi* or conglomerates. Jiang was confident a corps of Chinese General Motors, Siemens, Toyotas and Samsungs could be nurtured by the first decade of the new century (see also Chapter 2). While as many as half of these conglomerates might eventually take the shareholding format, Beijing would ensure that all such units would be under a high degree of state control.[96]

An internal document of mid-1996 cited a senior cadre as saying that the state now had the wherewithal to concentrate its resources on a relatively small group of "elite SOEs". "We should build some big ships and organise 'joint fleets'," the cadre said. "We should boost the ability of SOEs to withstand the risk of the marketplace." The official quoted Lenin on the fact that provided they were up to scratch, it was better for the state economy to have fewer, top-of-the-line SOEs. "The national economy should put its emphasis on a small number of elite, big and strong companies," he added.[97] No matter that in the eyes of market purists, the slogan "boosting the ability of SOEs to withstand the risk of market forces" was a contradiction in terms: only when the state has ceased interfering can enterprises learn to swim in the marketplace.

Throughout 1995 and 1996, executive fiats were given to state banks and other departments that special loans and preferential treatment be accorded 300 large-scale SOEs, which accounted for about 46 per cent of the total value of industrial production.[98] The SOEs would be given permission to float bonds and to run finance companies on the side. The number of such elite companies grew to nearly 1,000 in 1997 and 1998.

By 1996 and 1997, most large and medium-sized cities with potentials were given directives — and in some instances rough quotas — to form *jituangongsi*. Nationwide, 120 conglomerates were designated "pilot" units. Shanghai indicated it would focus on supporting 54 enterprise groupings, and Guangdong more than 70. In prosperous areas, each town must have at least one such corporation, defined as having assets of over 60 million yuan. In some instances, the performance of regional officials was assessed in proportion to the number of conglomerates they were able to put together.[99]

Guangdong had by 1997 claimed some success for its 70-odd *jituangongsi*, which were based mostly in Guangzhou, Foshan and Shenzhen. The 1996 earnings totalled 190 billion yuan, with 20 of the enterprises raking in more than 3 billion yuan each. Local officials said these "sharks", some of which were subsequently listed on the Shenzhen bourse, were able to energise loss-making factories they had absorbed. Then Guangdong party boss Xie Fei said in early 1997 that enterprises in the Pearl River Delta should band together and exploit the economies of scale. A special task force was put in charge of forming conglomerates in the delta. Officials were hopeful that by 2000, "supersharks" with sales of up to 10 billion yuan each could be nurtured.[100]

Overall, however, it remained doubtful how competitive the conglomerates would be. In theory, those that had been corporatised or undergone the *gufenhua* process should have Western-style trappings such as a board of directors and professional managers. However, mainly because of their national and strategic importance, many were subject to tight political supervision (see concluding section).

Other measures for improving SOEs

That it would be less than full steam ahead for market reform was also evident from the fact that the traditional, "evolutionary" approach had hardly been jettisoned. Even as it was experimenting with more thorough-going solutions, Beijing was throwing its weight behind incremental, "within-the-system" tinkering.

In early 1997, then vice-premier Zhu indicated he favoured mergers and bankruptcies, not thorough ownership changes. At that time, the economic tsar's team set aside 30 billion yuan, mostly for absorbing the bad debts of enterprises that had been declared bankrupt or that were merged. "Factories that should go bankrupt should do so," Zhu said in Chongqing. "Those that can be merged should, to the greatest extent possible, go through this process."[101] However, this restructuring would only take place in 110 "pilot cities", whose leaders must report intended bankruptcies and mergers to Beijing for approval. Enterprises that had gone bankrupt should first of all take care of the livelihood and re-employment of staff. Re-employment centres would also be set up with the help of local governments and special bank loans. Superior units that had merged with inferior ones should undertake to clear up the latter's debt in five years.[102]

More than 5,500 companies declared bankruptcy in 1996, as against 2,200 in 1995, 1,625 in 1994 and 710 in 1993. Even in Liaoning, which was home to 10 per cent of the country's large-scale SOEs, more than 200 enterprises were declared bankrupt in 1995 and 1996. Provincial authorities indicated in late 1996 that even such a mammoth institution as Anshan Iron and Steel Works could be put on the market.[103] While a number of bankrupt companies were privatised, most were merged with the more robust SOEs. Bankruptcies and mergers thus became a way out for SOE dinosaurs without thorough-going structural changes. Zhu made no secret of his preference for mergers over bankruptcies because of the lesser degree of disruption.

Other leaders alleged that SOEs could be turned around mostly through "improving their internal environment". As Wu Bangguo put it while touring Guangdong factories in late 1996, the key was improving management know-how. "We must strengthen management by measures such as cutting costs," he said. "We must boost the construction of the leadership corps and make sure that managers can be demoted as well as promoted. Training of cadres should be ameliorated." In 1996 and 1997, Wu was given the thankless task of making apologies for the unsatisfactory progress in SOE reform. Oftentimes, he resorted to Marxist casuistry. "We must look at the situation of the reform of SOEs from a dialectical-materialist point of view," said Wu. "We must further boost our confidence."[104]

New Deal for Small SOEs

Perhaps a major achievement of the Jiang administration in the mid-1990s was "setting free" and "rendering alive" small, and in many instances, medium-sized enterprises. This dovetailed with the *zhuada fangxiao* slogan of early 1996. It can be argued, however, that the *fangxiao* experiment was achieved in spite of Beijing. It was mostly the initiative of local cadres and entrepreneurs that made it possible for small and medium-scale SOEs to be liberated from the state straitjacket. This was no mean feat because more than 80 per cent of all SOEs were classified small-scale firms — and they employed 60 per cent of the total labour force.

Even before the *fangxiao* dictum was publicised in 1996, regional officials and businessmen had begun their quiet revolution in 1994 and 1995. Small firms were privatised through measures including the formation of shareholding concerns, leasing, contracted operations, bankruptcies — or clean sale of assets to workers and foreign entities.[105] Particularly spectacular results were achieved in Guangdong, Sichuan and Shandong. In 1996, Guangzhou vowed to transform half of its 30,000-odd small-scale enterprises within the year. Chengdu pledged to "liberate" 60 per cent of Sichuan's small firms the same year. The favoured means of *fangxiao* in both provinces was either *gufenhua* or selling assets to workers and foreign firms.

Given Shandong's relatively poor track record for fast-paced reform, the success of its *fangxiao* experiments was astounding. It all developed out of a medium-sized city named Zhucheng, whose party secretary, Chen Guang, was given the sobriquet Chen Maiguang ("all sold out") for the large numbers of firms taken off the state ledgers. Unbeknownst to the rest of the country, more than 90 per cent of the SOEs and collectively-owned enterprises in the city were from 1992 to 1994 "privatised", mostly through conversion into shareholding cooperatives. The shares were sold to workers in the original SOEs, who chipped in 5,000 yuan or more per person.[106]

By mid-1996, even neo-conservative leaders such as Zhu Rongji had toured Zhucheng and affirmed Chen's efforts. Chen himself became a celebrity and was much in demand on the lecture circuit in major cities. While Zhu had second thoughts about officially proclaiming Zhucheng a "national model", the experience of the hitherto obscure city became known nationwide.

By August the same year, the State Economic and Trade Commission issued an "Opinion on Rendering Alive Small-scale SOEs". The document permitted different enterprises to choose the best way for their transformation. "We should not implement just one model or one set of criteria," it said. "After restructuring, such enterprises will have autonomy in management. They must bear their own risks and be financially self-sufficient." The semi-official Hong Kong China News Agency quoted officials as saying the restructuring of the 500,000-odd small-scale state enterprises should be finished in two years.[107]

Challenge from the Right

It was perhaps more than a coincidence that in the summer of 1996, three reform-minded cadres made a tour to the northeast, deemed a disaster zone of SOEs. Then Minister for Economic Restructuring Li Tieying, former state president Yang Shangkun and then NPC chairman Qiao Shi preached the gospel of market reforms in talks to local cadres. Unlike Jiang, these cadres never mentioned the imperative of the "wholly state-owned public sector" remaining the "mainstay" of industry. Nor did they show concern over the fact that privatisation would lead to the death of socialism. A hallmark of the liberals' approach was that they threw dogma to the wind and left it to the masses to decide which production method was best.

Speaking in Heilongjiang, Li, sometimes considered a "foster son" of Deng, repeated the patriarch's famous line: "If we do not reform, there is only the road to the grave." "We must be bold in exploration, because there is no established model from which we can copy," he said. Concerning SOEs, the Politburo member simply said: "We should let the tigers go back to the forests." It was significant that Li's speeches were not reported in major national media such as the *People's Daily*.[108]

While touring the same province, Yang urged local cadres to "dash forward, conduct experiments and reform in a bold manner". It was, however, then NPC supremo Qiao who defended the Deng banner most vigorously. For example, while visiting Liaoning in mid-1996, Qiao called upon state entrepreneurs to be "bold and liberated in thoughts". "Our thoughts must be further liberated and the work of reform grasped tighter," he said.[109]

The NPC Faction's bid for the limelight

As we saw in Chapter 3, Qiao Shi and stalwarts of the "NPC Faction" such as Tian Jiyun cut out new paths in political reform. They were equally valiant in the economic arena. From 1995 to 1997, Qiao and Tian picked up the tattered standard of economic liberalisation. The two were working under heavy constraints: the austerity programme was still in place and control of the economy rested with Li Peng and Zhu Rongji. They lacked heavyweight economists to act as advisers or propagandists. However, the two NPC titans tried to claw back lost territory by hoisting high the ideals of Deng Xiaoping and Zhao Ziyang.

During tours to the provinces in 1995, Qiao raised the Deng slogan that "reform is the second revolution". The then NPC chief pointed out that it was permissible to make mistakes and to take risks. On a visit to Shanghai in late 1996, Qiao reminded the managers there to learn more about the West. "You should boldly imbibe the good things both in and out of China," he said.[110]

Qiao was able to steal the thunder from Jiang and company because the NPC supremo shied away from out-dated shibboleths such as "talking more about politics" and "preserving stability at all costs". Almost every time that they spoke about the economy, Qiao and Tian raised the Deng flag about "speeding up the pace of reform". A typical Qiao statement was: "In enterprise reform, one must be bolder; the pace should be quickened; and work should be more substantial."[111]

During his 1996 tour of Liaoning, Qiao warned that "time may not be on our side for long". "We must be fully determined and not worry too much," he added. "Reform must not remain on the lips of officials and in party documents."[112] This was, of course, another way of saying that some other cadres had been too timid, slow and waffling in the reform enterprise. By contrast, the neo-conservatives would only allow that they would "deepen reform" while taking into consideration the requirements of stability.

Tian sounded a similar message in 1997. While on a trip to Hunan in June that year, the NPC leader pointed out that the country faced a harsh challenge in the run-up to the new century. "Our thoughts must be further liberated," he told local cadres. "We must be bolder and our pace must be faster." A month after the 15th Party Congress, he visited Shanghai — the bastion of the Jiang Faction. Without mentioning Jiang, Tian credited Deng's *nanxun* talks with the fast progress of the East China metropolis. "There must be a big liberation in our thoughts, a big change in our concepts," he said. "Only with reform will there be accelerated development; and only with development will there be sustained, reliable stability." Tian's line was of course different from that of Jiang or Li Peng, who put stability before reform and development.[113]

The strategy of "localised warfare"

Just as Mao Zedong won his revolution through a strategy of "using [bases in] the countryside to surround the cities", reformers were hoping that the fast-growing private sector in pockets of liberalisation in the regions could nibble away at the "mainstay status" of the state sector. According to bankruptcy expert and leading reformer Cao Siyuan, the SOEs' share of national assets dropped from more than 97 per cent in 1978 to about 70 per cent in 1996. Cao said he hoped the state sector's share of total assets and resources would in 10 to 20 years plummet to 15 per cent, the same proportion as in developed countries such as the US and France. The liberal economist indicated, however, that in China "it would not do to hurry the pace unrealistically".

However, Cao was enthusiastic about the fact that without prompting from the authorities, cadres and entrepreneurs in the regions had made a go of forming private or collectively-owned firms. Apart from Guangdong, Cao cited provinces such as Shandong and Sichuan. Nationwide, non-state enterprises accounted for 70 per cent of the value of industrial production, even though they took up just 30 per cent of assets and resources.[114]

Avant-garde cadres and economists such as Yu Guangyuan argued that neither Marx nor Lenin had insisted that SOEs should dominate every province or city. There were no theoretical injunctions against regions and districts with the requisite resources and comparative advantage to put their emphasis on the collective or private economy. Not surprisingly, liberal cadres who had been edged out of the central decision-making process were privately encouraging local officials and businessmen to score big in the marketplace. As Qiao Shi put it while touring Jiangsu in early 1997: "Regional governments should take bolder and speedier steps in reform."[115]

Apart from the rich, coastal areas, Qiao and Tian also encouraged the central and western provinces to close the gap with the "Gold Coast" through bolder reforms. While touring Guizhou in mid-1996, Tian pointed out that cadres in poorer districts should go that extra mile in thought liberation. With particular reference to the reform of medium- and small-scale enterprises, Tian urged them to do away with constraints. "Liberalise [the economy] to the extent that is possible," Tian said. "Whatever forms [of production] that work should be adopted."[116]

Conclusion: Constraints on Reform

Even Deng Xiaoping was often criticised for the lack of a comprehensive approach to reform. After all, one of his most famous adages was "crossing the river while feeling out for the boulders". Jiang and his colleagues suffered even more direly from a "dearth of philosophy". Among the Jiang team, Zhu Rongji had the best grasp of economic issues; the premier also had a reputation for resolute action. However, the Great Rectifier was a lot more effective in *shou* — or imposing macro-economic order — in areas including the banking system and the stock market. He was hardly an innovative thinker or a risk-taker in reform and liberalisation.

Most of Jiang's statements on economic policy were exercises in strategic ambiguity: trying to work both sides of the fence. Take, for example, his remarks in an internal meeting in early 1996. "We shall continue to fully develop market mechanisms and to strengthen macro-economic controls and adjustments," the president said. "Both are basic requirements for building up a socialist market economy. Both are indispensable."[117]

Then vice-premier Zou Jiahua, also not known for his bush-whacking proclivities, put the best face on this state of drift when he proposed something like a "to each according to its characteristics" strategy for SOEs. He had this to say on turning around loss-making concerns while touring Tianjin in 1996: "Each factory should come up with its own solutions. For each particular problem, a suitable method should be adopted."[118] This seemed another way of saying that the *zhongyang* had run out of gimmicks.

Lack of clear-cut directions

The lack of direction was evident throughout Jiang's protracted struggle with the economy. In a major speech on SOE reform in mid-1996, Jiang for the first time cited Deng's edict on the "three favourables". This meant a policy should be affirmed if it boosted productivity, raised the people's livelihood, and promoted the country's overall strength. Jiang pledged his support for turning all types of enterprises, including SOEs, into "autonomously managed, financially self-sufficient entities that can compete in the marketplace". At the same time, however, the party chief cited orthodox values for assessing economic policies. They included strengthening the state-owned sector and boosting the "core status" of CCP cells in enterprises.[119]

As with other initiatives of Jiang, the need to conciliate all elements of the polity could make for policy paralysis — or at best, a slowing down of liberalisation. This was the underlying reason why Jiang did not have much to show in the economic-reform arena during the bulk of his tenure. Zigzags and delays were frequent. For example, then Vice-Minister for Economic Restructuring Hong Hu announced in mid-1996 that work on the modernisation of 100 key "pilot" enterprises would be delayed by one year. According to plans announced in 1994, the 100 guinea-pig state enterprises should by the end of 1996 have been transformed into autonomous, market-oriented business units. The deadline was extended to the end of 1997.[120]

Plans for reform announced in the run-up to the 15th Party Congress coincided with a need for Jiang to flash his reformist credentials. Analysts, however, cast doubt on his claims. Take Jiang's focus on building up *jituangongsi*. In 1997, there was a spate of media stories on the success stories of Chinese-style conglomerates such as the Baogang Steel Mill in Shanghai and the Daqing Oilfield. Cao Siyuan, for example, was less sanguine about amalgamating large SOEs into national enterprise groupings. "Unless there is a structural change, lumping together SOEs will only multiply inefficiency and the mentality of 'eating from the common wok' many times over," Cao said.[121]

Can a Chinese General Motors or Mitsubishi really come about? It is true that particularly in Japan and South Korea, there was a high degree of coordination between the state and the *zaibatsus* and *chaebols*. Yet there were also marked differences. In the Japan and South Korean models, the phenomenon of party and government officials or their children — the princelings — forming conglomerates and getting special favours through their political clout was less predominant. Corruption seemed more pervasive in China. Moreover, despite strong protectionist trends, the Japan or South Korean governments were more committed to market forces — and less burdened by ideological baggage.

As with other economic targets, part of the rationale behind *jituangongsi* was serving political ends. These included promoting cooperation between east and west China, "saving" inferior companies and absorbing excess labourers, and maintaining the supremacy of the socialist system and the party. Jiang himself was ready to admit that market forces could never be the be-all and end-all of the economy. "Competition in China is different from competition in the West," Jiang reportedly said. "Competition in the West is based on self-interest; it's a dog-eat-dog world. In China, we try to put emphasis on cooperation as well as competition."[122]

Need to preserve party supremacy

It was unlikely that in the foreseeable future, the neo-conservative leadership could smash through the taboo of "party leadership" of enterprises. After all, *gufenhua* and other experiments in quasi-privatisation could eventually lead to the atrophy of the power of the CCP committee in each enterprise. However, a key decision of the post-June 4, 1989 administration was to uphold the authority of the party boss by rolling back the factory director responsibility system introduced by Zhao Ziyang.

In most SOEs, the CCP committees or cells remained the highest authority responsible for setting the general direction of the concerns. The party secretary of, say, a steel factory was responsible to the party committee of the Ministry of Metallurgy. If a SOE was converted into a full-fledged shareholding company, the party cell and CCP functionaries would become redundant. Indeed, the Law on Companies specified that the general manager of an enterprise was the foremost authority; and that he was responsible to the board of directors. There was no mention of the role of the party cell.[123]

It was characteristic of Jiang that he wanted it both ways: a "modernised" SOE system and a revitalised party cell. In early 1997, party authorities passed a "circular on further strengthening and improving the work of party construction in SOEs". Organisation Department chief Zhang Qianjing pointed out that "the party's work in enterprises will be gradually strengthened". In the first half of 1997, the department and other party units such as the Central Party School ran special classes for more than 10,000 SOE managers. In such courses, market norms took second place to Marxist values.[124]

As Chinese University of Hong Kong political scientist Lee Nan-hsiung put it, enterprise reform would be hampered by the fact that Beijing still needed to let cadres — not professionals — run enterprises. "Not just know-how and ability were involved when party and government cadres tried to turn themselves into entrepreneurs," he wrote. "At stake were the chasms of culture and value systems." Lee added it would be difficult to conceive that the CCP would invite professional managers with little party affiliation to run big enterprises.[125] By contrast, "red-chip companies" in Hong Kong had by the mid-1990s begun to promote Hong Kong-Chinese professionals to top management positions. This latitude and open-mindedness could hardly take place in the mainland.

THE CHALLENGE OF THE CIVIL SOCIETY

By early 1998, a Chinese-style civil society — defined broadly as the world beyond the CCP's control — was growing at a heady pace. And this realm of colour and diversity was on collision course with a leadership that seemed bent on preserving Chairman Mao's "one-voice chamber". Groupings that were throwing their weight about in the civil society included non-party intellectuals, private businessmen, Christians and members of wild-cat trade unions. Their numbers and activities had increased in spite of the fact that the authorities had hardly relaxed political control since the Tiananmen Square crackdown. For example, the ban on non-official trade unions remained intact. Non-official organisations had to seek police approval for meetings of more than 20 people.[126]

At the same time, the CCP leadership had by the mid-1990s realised that it had to accept reality. There was some liberalisation towards denizens of the civil society at the social and cultural level. The regulation over the flow of information became difficult in the age of the Internet. Links between official and non-official units on the one hand, and foreign organisations on the other, grew in the wake of the progress of the open-door policy. Representatives of the private-business and middle classes were clamouring for a voice in politics. At least in the urban areas, new, heretical ideas circulated and took root in a world that the party could only tame at the expense of economic development.

The Itch to Organise

Nearly five decades of Communist-Chinese rule had not blunted the Chinese zeal to organise. For millennia, Chinese have formed groupings ranging from clans to a plethora of socio-political outfits. The triads — perhaps the most "pro-active" forms of clans — had since the Ming Dynasty (1368–1644) played a big role in the polity. Both Chiang Kai-shek and Mao Zedong had intimate dealings with these "black societies". Given its *l'état, c'est moi* mind-set, the CCP had since 1949 frowned on efforts by citizens to band together. And for the two years or so after the June 4, 1989 crackdown, practically all organisations were banned.

After Deng's *nanxun* ("southern tour"), however, there was a limited degree of relaxation by the Ministry of Civil Administration, the "mother-in-law unit" for non-official outfits. As of late 1995, the ministry had registered 1,810 "national social organisations". They boasted 90 million-odd individual members and more than 410,000 corporate and group members. At the same time, there were in excess of 200,000 county, municipal- and provincial-level organisations. Another Chinese source said the number of societies was much higher, with those whose names that began with the word "China" exceeding 170,000.[127]

Most of these organisations were professional, academic and business-oriented bodies such as research institutes, guilds and chambers of commerce. Consumer associations had sprung up in most large and medium-sized cities. Groupings to promote women's rights were equally popular. There were 6,800 grassroots-level women organisations in addition to 2,682 women's rights units in private companies. More offbeat outfits were also proliferating. After a period of suppression, associations affiliated with *qigong* and the occult arts had surfaced again. Students in the Shanghai Medical Science University founded the nation's first non-smokers' club in 1997.[128]

This zeal to form "people's associations" had not been dented by the party's decision in 1996 and 1997 to limit the growth of several categories of national-level organisations, including academic and research units. In early 1997, the Ministry of State Security administered checks to dozens of non-official research units that had received foreign funding.[129] The party also raised its guard against fast-growing underground entities ranging from wild-cat trade unions and clansmen's associations to the triads and cults. These, together with the house churches, were a time bomb that had not been defused by the deployment of more police and para-military units.

The Private Entrepreneurs, Professionals and *Gumin*

Of all the sectors in the civil society, the growing class of private entrepreneurs — including the middle class and the professionals — was most important because of their political clout. A fast-expanding body of citizens was no longer beholden to the party for their livelihood or their station in society. In opinion surveys on career choices among urbanites in the mid-1990s, jobs in the party and government had become less popular than ever. In the favourites were private entrepreneurs, "financiers", doctors and lawyers.[130]

As of late 1996, the owners and staff of private businesses numbered more than 61 million. *Getihu* ("individually-owned shops") and private

enterprises numbered respectively 27 million and 810,000. They had combined assets of nearly 600 billion yuan. These "red bosses" included the
thousands of young academics who returned to China to start businesses
after obtaining advanced degrees in the West. Then there were the 18
million-odd *gumin*, or citizens hooked on the stock markets. Stock brokers
and other related professionals had exceeded 100,000 by early 1997. They
included the burgeoning ranks of *jingji*, or commercial go-betweens who
survived on commissions and kick-backs. By 1997, more than 55,000 *jingji*
were registered by the authorities in 14 provinces and cities including
Sichuan, Shanghai, Shaanxi and Henan.[131]

Influential professional groupings had appeared in the cities by the
mid-1990s. The semi-official Hong Kong China News Agency reported that
lawyers would be China's first batch of self-employed professionals. More
and more of the country's estimated 80,000 legal personnel had started
their own practices. The next to follow could be doctors and accountants.
In the Hong Kong Special Administrative Region, professional groups or
"functional constituencies" were entitled to seats in the legislature. Similar
bodies in the mainland could soon be clamouring for such rights.[132]

By late 1997, there was no obvious way that private businessmen could
influence decision-making. After a spate of public relations in the early
1990s, the authorities stopped talking about reserving a "quota" of seats on
the NPC and CPPCC for private entrepreneurs. Perhaps the only exceptions
seemed to be "princelings" who had gone into business. However, businessmen had at least informal channels to lobby for policy changes. For example, a dozen-odd private entrepreneurs in Hunan huddled with party secretary Wang Maolin before he departed for Beijing to take part in the 15th
Party Congress of September 1997. These private bosses were anxious that
the party spell out more favourable policies for the private sector.[133]

Businessmen also gained influential positions through the backdoor. In
the eyes of leftists, Deng's "imperial tour" of Guangdong in 1992 was a
result of cadre-businessmen in the southeast "hijacking" the old man to the
south to make propaganda for the quasi-capitalist road. By the early 1990s,
nouveau riche private entrepreneurs had begun the direct purchase of official positions. They first began with grassroots-level seats on the legislative
and consultative organs. Later, positions as senior as county chief and
vice-mayor of medium-sized towns were within reach.

According to an internal document, 5,401 *nouveau riche* bosses had by
1994 become people's congress deputies at the level of county or above. The

comparable figure for consultative conference members was 8,558. In quasi-capitalist enclaves such as Shishi, Fujian Province, private entrepreneurs had fielded candidates for the position of mayor or its equivalent. Starting in 1995, the official media began revealing relatively minor cases as negative examples for cadres nationwide. For example, a mid-1996 issue of the official *Outlook* weekly reported that Zheng Yuansheng, a county party secretary in Jiangxi Province, had from 1991 to 1994 sold more than 40 positions to his cronies. Then came one of the biggest scandals in Guangdong Province in 1998. Private entrepreneur Cai Denghui was appointed to senior positions, including the head of the Finance and Trade Department of Puqiao District, after handing out 400,000-odd yuan in "black money".[134]

There were signs that one of the leadership's worst nightmares — the "collusion" between businessmen and dissidents — was becoming reality. In April 1997, Robiya Kodir, a successful Uighur entrepreneur and CPPCC member in Xinjiang, was detained by state security agents for providing financial help to the separatists. Her husband, a history professor with alleged sympathy to the splittist cause, had sought political asylum in the US. The party secretary of Xinjiang, Wang Lequan, confirmed in late 1997 that she would not be allowed to leave the country even though the businesswoman could still carry on her commercial activities.[135]

The Influence of the Internet

The net had caught on in China. There were an estimated 250,000 web surfers in China by the end of 1997, up from just 150,000 a year earlier. A lopsided proportion of enthusiasts was concentrated in a dozen-odd large cities, particularly those along the coast. Internet cafes had become the rage in Shanghai and Beijing, whose aficionados easily accounted for one-quarter of the national total. Fudan in Shanghai became the first university to offer courses using the Internet as a teaching aid.[136]

Like other authoritarian governments in Asia, China was aware of the destabilising influence of the Internet. It could be the conduit for another high tide of "bourgeois-liberal poison". Dissidents in China could hook up with the vast community of US-based activists. Propaganda chief Ding Guan'gen was quoted in 1996 as asking his experts whether the net system in China could be grounded for a day or so after the announcement of the death of Deng.[137]

Beijing took action in February 1996 by requiring all Internet users to register with the police. Net service would only be offered by government-run providers, including a subsidiary of the New China News Agency. In September 1996, these units blocked off 100 websites. Apart from pornographic material, they included sites run by the US government; foreign, Hong Kong and Taiwan newspapers; and those concerned with human rights.[138] In the same month, Beijing demanded that users of Microsoft's Chinese-language Windows 95 hand in their software to the authorities after the discovery of "subversive slogans". Styled in complicated characters, the offending clauses included "Communist bandits" and "Take back the mainland". Microsoft later came out with a sanitised version.[139]

By 1998, however, the authorities had by no means liquidated the poisonous electronic weeds. First of all, given the proliferation of websites, there was no way that the government-designated providers and other net nannies could screen out the politically incorrect ones. Chinese sources said dissidents and their relatives were able to download daily "subversive" material from sites in the US and other countries. One such site that was well-known in dissident circles in China was called "Tunnel". Moreover, objectionable material could always get into China the same way that VOA and Radio Free Asia beat the jamming: cracks were showing in the government's thought-policing apparatus.[140]

A sign of the times was the appearance of Internet versions of *dazibao*, or big-character posters. Such a novel form of expression — and protest — first came to public attention during the 1996 movement to wrest control of the Diaoyu or Senkaku islands from Japanese control. Electronic *dazibao* was used to good advantage by students on such elite campuses as Beijing University and Fudan University.[141]

Moreover, there were limits to the extent to which the authorities could crack down on the new media. After all, know-how related to the information superhighway represented tomorrow's technology. Blocking out the Internet would result in China missing the boat in the information age. In mid-1996, the official *China Daily* pointed out that "the value of the Internet so outweighs its potentially harmful aspects — pornography and politically destructive information — that the Chinese government has approved its opening to the public". Even though this view only represented that of more enlightened officials, it was an overall admission of the inevitability of progress.[142]

The Civil Society in Action

Democracy in most countries East and West developed when citizens began having money, owning property — and paying taxes to the government. They became more assertive in protecting their private wealth — and liberty. As discussed above, private entrepreneurs started buying political positions to lobby for more clout in policymaking. The growing "political independence" of ordinary folk could be gauged by the increasing amount of taxes Chinese were paying. In the first ten months of 1997, Guangdong residents forked out over three billion yuan in income taxes.[143] These taxpayers would feel entitled to a bigger say in socio-economic if not political affairs.

The "invisible hand" of the civil society was evident in the legal arena. In the five years since the promulgation of the 1991 Law on Administrative Litigation, courts of all levels had handled 141,949 cases. These were mostly citizens, companies or groups that took government departments to court over dereliction of duty or other alleged lapses. According to official statistics, the government lost 36.2 per cent of these cases. This percentage was considered high compared with the results of similar lawsuits in other countries.[144]

While the ideal of the rule of law was a long way off, citizens had become more enthusiastic in asserting themselves. Cases exposed in the official media ranged from Jiangsu peasants suing a polluting factory for damages to a Shandong high-school graduate taking a Beijing college to court for turning down his application "without justifiable reasons".[145] Consumers became more aggressive in taking on unscrupulous manufacturers. In the first half of 1996, Guangdong consumer organisations handled nearly 7,000 cases of complaints and court cases.[146]

In April 1997, 500 property-buyers converged at the municipal government office in Guangzhou to demand that the authorities take action against a real estate firm that had folded. The culprit, New East Property, had sold more than 100 million yuan worth of unfinished flats to 600-odd people from 1994 to 1997. Part of New East's gimmicks was showing off pictures that its bosses had taken with Guangdong leaders — and to ask local officials to write calligraphy for the names of buildings.[147]

In spite of the lid on non-sanctioned political activities, the growth of the civil society would engender the kind of activism that would at the very least embarrass the administration. In the wake of the stocks crisis in the autumn of 1996, small-scale rioting took place not just in large cities but rural areas. The offices of stockbrokers were vandalised and the premises of local administrations besieged. Most participants were small-time *gumin*, including farmers, who had lost heavily when the bubble burst.[148]

Then there were more politically motivated events over which the authorities found alarming. At the height of the campaign to "protect" the Diaoyu archipelago in the summer of 1996, a number of Diaoyu-related organisations sprouted in cities ranging from Beijing and Nanjing to Shenyang and Shenzhen. Units that played a big role included those that were offshoots of the national movement for seeking wartime damages from Tokyo. Also active were hitherto unknown associations of PLA veterans who wanted Beijing to teach the "Japanese devils" another lesson. These social forces swung into action again during Japanese Premier Ryutaro Hashimoto's visit to China in September 1997.[149]

THE CHALLENGE OF HONG KONG

In Chinese eyes, the return of Hong Kong to the motherland represented the "wiping away of 156 years of colonial humiliation". The relatively smooth handover gave a big boost to the administration of Jiang Zemin. It also added immeasurably to the "comprehensive strength" of the nation, which now had the largest foreign-exchange reserves in the world. However, the absorption of Hong Kong also posed one of the biggest challenges to CCP orthodoxy since 1949.

Hong Kong culture, including its political and economic systems, would have a sizeable impact on the motherland. While there was little possibility of David slaying Goliath, much cross-pollination would take place across the Shenzhen River. Whether the CCP administration would stoop to conquer — that is, swallow its pride as the sovereign power and learn from the Hong Kong success story — would be a good test of whether the party was capable of catching up with the times.

As Beijing futurologist Wang Shan pointed out in his book *Looking at Post-Deng China with a Third Eye*, however, the "one country, two systems" model could never be construed to mean that the mainland and Hong Kong were equals. The high degree of autonomy enjoyed by the Hong Kong Special Administrative Region (SAR) was dependent on Beijing's approval. This dispensation, Wang wrote, could change according to "the political situation and policy requirement of the mainland". Moreover, the theorist pointed out, even assuming that "Hong Kong culture" was more advanced than mainland culture, there was no guarantee that the former would not be crushed by the latter. "The party which has a higher level of civilisation but which is weaker often becomes the loser in a struggle," he wrote.[150]

There was a temptation for Beijing to take the most cynical — and shortsighted — view of Hong Kong: to milk all the economic advantage that could be squeezed out of the rich metropolis while screening out the bourgeois-liberal or colonial "poison" in the ideological or cultural arena. Looking at the crystal ball in early 1998, however, there was no cause for excessive pessimism. This section will examine areas where the tiny SAR could help make a difference in the vast hinterland.

Influence of Hong Kong Politics
The liberalising influence of the Hong Kong model

Post-1997 Hong Kong could provide an impetus to the mainland administration — or at least the forward-looking factions within the CCP — to speed up political reform. In spite of what in Beijing's eyes was its ugly colonial past, the SAR had the best qualifications for democracy: a per capita GNP higher than that of Britain and Canada; near universal education; and large middle and professional classes.

As Xu Jiatun, Beijing's one-time chief of mission in Hong Kong, put it, the very idea of "one country, two systems" meant Beijing not only acquiesced in but actively supported the further development of democracy in Hong Kong. Xu pointed out in an interview in 1997 that Beijing had in the mid- to late 1980s encouraged Hong Kong businessmen to form political parties. The former party secretary of Jiangsu Province indicated that the CCP leadership realised democracy was vital to Hong Kong's maintaining its success formula in economic matters.[151]

Less certain was whether cadres not so open-minded as Xu would consider the SAR's democratic model as an object of emulation for at least parts of China — or as a threat. Liberal cadres in the CCP had always been struck by Hong Kong's richness and vibrancy. They were humble enough to admit that parts of the British legacy were worth studying — and learning from. Zhao Ziyang was a well-known fan of the Independent Commission Against Corruption. In the mid-1980s, he showed public-relations films of the ICAC to cadres at the Zhongnanhai party headquarters as they explored ways to improve China's own anti-graft measures. Former Politburo mem-

ber Hu Qili was knowledgeable about the composition of Hong Kong's
Legislative Council. He once remarked that the Hong Kong system of having both elected and *ex officio* members could have reference value for the
mainland.[152]

Much as they had ruffled the features of Zhongnanhai, Chris Patten's
reforms had admirers galore in Beijing. For example, a number of former
associates and advisers of Zhao Ziyang and Hu Yaobang wished Patten's
reforms well. Such liberals lambasted the "small-mindedness" of officials
such as former premier Li Peng and former head of the Hong Kong and
Macau Affairs Office Lu Ping, who characterised Patten as "a sinner of a
thousand antiquities". The British governor also had quite a following
among Guangdong intellectuals. In spite — or because — of his long-
standing quarrels with the Beijing administration, public opinion surveys
in large cities in Guangdong showed Patten had a better name recognition
than the then Guangdong governor Zhu Senlin.[153]

Other cadres were of the opinion that Beijing should in any case preserve the full smorgasbord of the Hong Kong capitalist system, including its
political institutions and values. Former NCNA official Huang Wenfang
argued that not only Hong Kong's economic system but its political system,
culture and way of thinking should remain intact. "If Hong Kong's political
pluralism, democracy and liberties cannot be further developed, its capitalist economic system will be seriously hampered," he said. This warts-and-all
approach to safeguarding the Hong Kong tradition gained support from
CPPCC chief Li Ruihuan. Li compared Hong Kong to a priceless Yixing
teapot with thick residues of tea-rust accumulated through decades of use.
Some time in the Qing dynasty, it fell upon the hands of a foolish woman
who offered it for sale in the market. A connoisseur was willing to pay big
bucks. While waiting for him to return with the money, the woman
scrubbed the vassal clean. It became worthless.[154]

How will the Hong Kong model exert its influence? At least at the
initial phase, through a "demonstration effect". After gaining more knowledge about the SAR, mainlanders may be persuaded to ask themselves: if
Hong Kong Chinese can do it, why can't we? As Singapore-based political
commentator Ching Cheong indicated, Hong Kong had played a role in
each of the pro-democracy movements undertaken by the mainland since
the 1911 Revolution. For example, Dr Sun Yat-sen had a big base in Hong
Kong, and Hong Kong citizens contributed millions of dollars to the
Tiananmen Square demonstrators.[155] Or as Hong Kong-based political sci-

entist Zheng Yongnian put it: "If Hong Kong succeeds in building up a good democratic system, it will have a pacesetting effect for leaders and ordinary people in the mainland."[156]

The Hong Kong model and regionalism

Beijing's ability to live peacefully with a politically and culturally more advanced Hong Kong — to at least let the hundred flowers continue to bloom in the SAR — will have important implications for the *zhongyang*'s ability to resolve regional conflicts. Much was written about the "one country, two systems" as a model for Taiwan. After all, this formula was first conceived for Taiwan, not Hong Kong. And after July 1, 1997, Beijing's Taiwan propaganda machinery was dominated by this theme: Now that the "one country, two systems" formula has "triumphed" in Hong Kong, Taiwan should consider talking to the mainland on the same terms.[157] Semi-official emissaries from the mainland were also telling Taiwan that the island could enjoy much better terms than the SAR.

Since Taiwan unification remained illusory, of much more immediate significance was whether Beijing was tolerant enough to extend elements of Hong Kong-style autonomy to other parts of the country with heterogeneous traditions, principally Tibet, Xinjiang and Inner Mongolia. In the run-up to July 1, 1997, Beijing was bombarded by requests from ethnic-minority cadres in Xinjiang and Tibet for "Hong Kong-like" freedoms. The *zhongyang* was also under pressure to re-formulate the law on autonomous regions — with Hong Kong's Basic Law serving as a new standard (see Chapter 5).[158]

Seventeen days after the Hong Kong handover, the Dalai Lama said in an interview with the international press that Beijing should apply the "one country, two systems" scheme to Tibet. "The Hong Kong transition is a harbinger for Tibet's implementation of self-rule," the Lama said. "I am full of optimism about this." Both Beijing and Lhasa authorities, however, pointed out that the central government would not consider extending the Hong Kong formula to Tibet. Indeed, to discourage Tibet and Xinjiang from taking advantage of the July 1, 1997 ceremonies to agitate for more freedoms, Beijing slapped a tight regime of security over the two regions in June and detained dozens of the "ringleaders".[159]

It seemed certain that Beijing would after 1997 prevent other provinces and cities from fantasising that they could become like Hong Kong one day.

Restrictions on cadres, businessmen, academics and ordinary mainlanders going to Hong Kong were at least as severe as before July 1, 1997. It was possible, however, that a post-Jiang Zemin team might adopt a more liberal attitude — and see the wider application of the "one country, two systems" principle as a viable solution to the problem of ethnicity and diversity. After all, both before and after the *nanxun*, Deng had indicated that "tens of Hong Kongs" should be established in the mainland.[160]

Growing Chinese influence and the "Singapore model"

By early 1998, the contradictory nature of Beijing's Hong Kong policy had become clear. On the one hand, the *zhongyang* wanted SAR Chief Executive Tung Chee-hwa at least to be seen as wielding real power: the former shipping magnate was promised a free hand and given some substantial power. On the other, the control mechanisms were in place, and there were overt as well as subtle attempts to tamper with the Hong Kong way of life. This gave rise to criticisms that Beijing might want to turn Hong Kong into a Singapore-like entity. Should this come to pass, however, the "demonstration effect" of the SAR might be dealt a body blow.

On the positive side, Beijing made sure that there would be no rival power centre in the SAR. Thus, Xinhua, or the New China News Agency, which had been China's *de facto* mission in Hong Kong, was downgraded soon after the handover from a ministerial to a vice-ministerial organ. The CCP's mastercell in Hong Kong, known as the Hong Kong and Macau Work Committee, was also scaled down. Tung, whose ranking in the hierarchy was state councillor, or one rung above minister, was given reassurances by the Jiang Zemin Office that there would be minimal meddling from the mandarins from up north.[161]

At the same time, Beijing flexed its muscles to ensure control. A new power elite centred on pro-Chinese Hong Kong businessmen began running the town. After midnight on July 1, the Legislative Council (Legco) elected into place in 1995 under Patten's reforms was scrapped. It was replaced by a "provisional legislature" that was not provided for by the Basic Law — and that was elected into office by 400 Beijing appointees. Polls for a new legislature were promised for May 1998. However, the SAR administration soon introduced changes to the electoral laws — including proportional representation — with the apparent objective of marginalising the democratic coalition led by barrister Martin Lee. Election results on May 24, 1998 seemed to bear this out: the democrats won only 19 out of 60 seats.[162] Moreover, during the campaign period, the Chinese establishment in Hong Kong mobilised tremendous resources to boost pro-Chinese parties such as the Democratic Alliance for the Betterment of Hong Kong.

A concerted effort was made to de-politicise Hong Kong life — taking out the residue in the Yixing teapot. Noteworthy were the near-hysterical remarks by leaders including Li Peng, Qian Qichen and Lu Ping that Hong Kong would never be allowed to "degenerate" into a political city. A basic element of Hong Kong culture — freedom to hold assemblies and demonstrations — could be threatened by new regulations authorising the police to ban them on the nebulous ground of "national security".[163]

Conservative politicians in both Beijing and Hong Kong were by 1997 brandishing the so-called Singapore model. Contrary to Huang Wenfang's argument, these traditionalists thought Hong Kong's economic success and its pluralistic, "Westernised" political system could be put in separate compartments. They cited the so-called Singapore experience: "Western" norms in doing business on the one hand, and a quasi-Chinese system of authoritarian, one-party rule on the other.

Tung himself, an admirer of authoritarian figures such as Deng Xiaoping, Lee Kuan Yew, and Margaret Thatcher, did not hide the fact that he would rule in a patriarchal manner. He claimed that the "excessive politicisation" of Hong Kong life had led to a neglect of social problems — and the rise of irresponsible radicalism. "I lived in America in the 60s and I saw what happened: the slow erosion of authority and the society became less orderly than is desirable," he said.[164] Very few people in Hong Kong, however, would think that Tung's analogy was apt. While rallies and demonstrations had by the mid-1990s become almost daily occurrences in Hong Kong, there were minimal disruptions to law and order. The chief executive also called upon educational and cultural units to inculcate in the young the "rightful and patriotic" attitude to take towards the mainland.

Test Case: The Influence of Hong Kong Culture

By 1997, even critics in the mainland, known for their Middle Kingdom "sino-centricism", had given the thumbs up to Hong Kong culture, or at least the popular variety. A much-noted book on Hong Kong published by an official press pointed out that the territory had metamorphosed from a cultural desert to a cultural oasis, in the process becoming "the arts centre for popular culture for Chinese worldwide".[165] After all, Hong Kong movies, videos and other items of popular culture had won fans even among high-brow critics in the US. As Australian sinologist Geremie Barme put it in late 1996: "The Hong Kong style with its hip, modernised Shanghai decadence, worldly petit-bourgeois patina and consumer sheen, has profoundly shaped the face of mainland culture for the past 15 years."[166]

In culture as well as business, Hong Kong served as China's window on the outside world. One apparently insignificant phenomenon told the story well: on their trips to Hong Kong, mainland cadres and businessmen invariably snapped up books banned in China. They were mostly politically incorrect tomes published in Hong Kong, Taiwan or overseas such as *The Memoirs of Xu Jiatun* and *The Private Life of Chairman Mao* by Dr Li Zhisui.

Beijing had, of course, always erected barriers to screen out Hong Kong culture. Since the early 1980s, only cadres with the rank of head of bureau or above could peruse Hong Kong papers in the confidential reading rooms of party or government units. It was true that Hong Kong television could penetrate Guangdong — and that SAR TV stations were much more popular in the province than local offerings. However, provincial authorities invariably jammed sensitive TV programmes such as those about the June 4 massacre. Mainland propaganda and culture units had a strict quota system concerning Hong Kong singers or artists performing in Chinese cities.[167]

The most ambitious forays into the mainland cultural market was made by the now-inactive CIM Group in the 1993–1995 period. The Hong Kong-based conglomerate adopted an aggressive, all-encompassing strategy. They had plans to set up newspapers, magazines, TV stations, movie houses, multi-media production and distribution centres, even entire "culture complexes" of cinemas, bookstores, and other facilities. By 1995, some of these projects had been developed in cities ranging from Beijing to Lhasa.

This is how US-based culture writer Zha Jianying described the activities of CIM executives: "These Hong Kong businessmen are showing the Chinese a new way, a style of running cultural business. Along with their technology and staff, they've brought their vision and institution, and they are here to promote certain kinds of cultural tastes and trends, certain lifestyles and attitudes."[168] According to Chinese sources, CIM was initially considered a pacesetter by mainland cadres who wanted to adulterate the Maoist "one-voice chamber" imposed immediately after the Tiananmen Square crackdown.

The modus operandi of CIM, then owned by the mercurial Hong Kong entrepreneur Yu Pun-hoi, was joint ventures. This format allayed to some extent the suspicions of Chinese authorities. For example, in a cultural or journalistic venture, the Chinese partners had jurisdiction over editorial contents. Unsure of the blessing from the very top, the flamboyant Yu and his executives spent a lot of resources wooing mid-ranking cadres, many of whom became the Chinese partners of his joint ventures. Seeing the challenge and the profits, these medium-level officials — usually high-fliers in their 30s and 40s — had a vested interest in selling CIM's ideas to the senior cadres.[169]

By early 1994, CIM had made impressive headway in repackaging two influential papers: the Beijing-based *China Business Times* and the Guangzhou-based *Modern Mankind*. In theory, editorial materials were controlled by mainland cadres — and CIM staff from Hong Kong were only responsible for advertising, sales and other management areas. In actual fact, the Hong Kong way of doing things had "infiltrated" the papers. In a matter of months, they became two of the most lively and iconoclast publications in China. And CIM enjoyed the patronage and support of local cadres and intellectuals.

It did not take long, however, for Beijing to be alarmed. After all, the *zhongyang* had never given formal approval for a joint-venture newspaper or magazine. According to reports in Hong Kong and Taiwan, even as CIM went about its expansion blitz, the party Central Committee's Propaganda Department had issued a series of documents warning cultural units against cooperating with this Hong Kong company. Other unnamed Hong Kong parties were also accused by other party circulars of attempting "cultural infiltration".

The fate of *Modern Mankind*, which started as a weekly in Guangzhou in 1985, was illustrative. CIM was able to acquire the publication through forming a joint venture with the Guangdong Branch of the China Council for the Promotion of International Trade. The Hong Kong company had the support of local officials when the paper was turned into a daily. However, *Modern Mankind* was abruptly closed in December 1994 on orders of Politburo member Ding Guan'gen. By late 1995, practically all CIM enterprises on the mainland had been closed down. In 1996, Beijing gave permission to Hong Kong's Sing Tao Group to form a joint-venture newspaper with a Shenzhen unit. However, its circulation was restricted to the special economic zone.[170] By mid-1998, there were reports that partly for the sake of joining the WTO, Jiang was considering giving the green light to joint-venture publications — starting with non-political magazines. Yet no time-table was announced.

Conclusion: Will the Hong Kong Influence Last?

In the final analysis, whether Hong Kong can fulfil its historic value of expediting changes in China depends on the pace of development in China. There is a danger that to ward off challenges from the SAR, the Jiang administration — and the post-Jiang leadership — may try to battle the "colonial legacy" of Hong Kong. Thus Barme, the Australian sinologist, expressed fears that after July 1997, the vibrancy of Hong Kong culture could be choked off by an upsurge of "anti-Western sentiment" fostered by both China and the SAR administration.[171] Beijing might also opt for a "decolonisation" and patriotism campaign in Hong Kong as a means to further edge out the democrats. The latter could be portrayed as "traitors" who are in collusion with "hostile foreign forces".

By mid-1998, there were signs that the political culture from up north had "infiltrated" Hong Kong. A growing number of media began treating top cadres such as Jiang Zemin or Zhu Rongji in deferential terms. Public debate had become tamer, less pluralistic. In the longer term, however, there seems little question that the SAR would be at the cutting edge of Chinese reform — particularly in the area where Beijing is weakest, that is, new ideas and ways of doing things. Even a neo-conservative chieftain such as Jiang Zemin recognised that Hong Kong was heading towards "Western-style democracy". He said on July 1, 1997 that "Hong Kong will gradually develop democracy". "Eventually, the goal of the SAR chief executive and the legislative council being elected by universal suffrage will be achieved," he added.[172]

While the majority of the above-50 generation in Beijing might see in Hong Kong a mere goose that lays the golden egg, many among the younger — and more liberal — cadres appreciated the value of the SAR as a window on the non-socialist world. As of mid-1998, the Politburo and other *zhongyang* units were able to hold back medium-level or regional units from forming joint ventures with Hong Kong companies and institutions in fields including culture and the media.

However, Hong Kong had already emerged as a role model in areas such as democratisation. Cadres in more advanced cities in coastal China had at least in internal meetings discussed plans of introducing elements of

"Hong Kong-style democracy" including the election of officials and legislators through a mixture of consultation and direct elections. These included Tianjin, Guangzhou, Shenzhen and the Shenzhen zone of Shekou.[173] Moreover, the impact of Hong Kong on the fast-developing Chinese civil society (see previous section) would be incalculable. Apart from politics, the SAR had by the mid-1990s set the standard in areas ranging from architecture and accountancy to cuisine and cinema.

Perhaps the last word on mainland-Hong Kong dynamics should belong to the rabidly liberal Zhu Houze, who was head of propaganda during Hu Yaobang's tenure. In an early 1997 seminar on Hong Kong, he saluted its contribution to "an open, multi-faceted spirit of humanism". Zhu praised the SAR as "foremost in the world in the area of the free flow of information". On Beijing-SAR relationship, the retired cadre cited the famous 1950s play on the role of the PLA in Shanghai, *The Sentry under the Neon Lights*. China's duty, Zhu indicated, was to safeguard the SAR's sanctity, not to obliterate the glittering opulence. "The admirable quality of the sentry is that he stands every day 'under the neon lights'," he wrote. "If, by accident or design, the neon lights are blown out, the sentry will lose his special radiance."[174]

CONCLUSION: INTO THE 21ST CENTURY

The East Wind Versus the West Wind

As can perhaps be expected of the longest continuous civilisation in the world, it is often a case of *plus ça change* with China. The year 1998 marked the centenary of the great 1898 Reform Movement of the Qing Dynasty — as well as the 79th anniversary of the May Fourth Movement. Both crusades had a heavy element of Westernisation. Yet the powers-that-be still had not made a choice between the "Western" or the "Eastern" model.

By the mid-1990s, the mainstream factions of the CCP were edging closer to the "East Asiatic model" or its variants. Top cadres including Jiang Zemin and Li Peng empathised with the philosophy and statecraft of Singapore and Malaysian leaders. These "neo-authoritarian" figures believed in the co-existence of one-party dictatorship with "international" norms of doing business. As discussed earlier, Beijing's models for developing conglomerates were the state-owned corporations in ASEAN countries as well as the *zaibatsus* and *chaebols* of respectively Japan and South Korea. The leadership's faith in the Asian model did not seem to have been significantly shaken with the financial crisis of late 1997 and 1998 (see Chapter 8).

Moreover, the CCP leadership was convinced that by perhaps the 2020s and 2030s, China would lead an Asian bloc of countries that could rival America — and to a degree, Europe — in some form of a clash of civilisations. One pan-Asian theme could be resistance against the imposition of Western, mostly American norms. During a trip to Malaysia in August 1997, Li Peng expressed agreement with his hosts that the UN Universal Declaration of Human Rights should be redrawn to express Asian — not just Western — values. Li said he found Dr Mahathir Mohamad's proposal full of "vision and courage".[175]

Chinese leaders believed that by around 2025, China's economic clout would overtake that of the US. In a closed-door speech in 1997, Jiang mentioned a kind of a tripolar world: the Americas dominated by the US; the European Union; and an Asia led by China. The party chief believed that the country's economic might would fuel a revival of Chinese civilisation whose influence across the Asia-Pacific region would be as momentous as Confucianism.[176] Domestically, big play given to Chinese prowess would mesh in with the recurrent campaigns of nationalism that the CCP was expected to wage well into the new century.

There are problems galore with Jiang's worldview. First of all, this pan-Asian vision leaves out Japan, the economic powerhouse that has largely chosen Western, principally American values. Secondly, it is unlikely ASEAN's suspicion of China's "hegemonistic" tendencies will decrease in spite of celebrations of a set of revived Asia-wide values. ASEAN's misgivings about Chinese intentions can intensify following the growth of Chinese economic and military power in the coming decades. Most importantly, apart from some form of revised Confucianism, the CCP administration is hard put to offer the rest of Asia a new "ism" that is in tune with the new century.

The Western Model; The East European Model; "One Country, Many Systems"

One reason why Jiang's dream of a Great 21st Century Chinese Civilisation might not bear fruit was that China minus the CCP neo-conservatives was generally not hostile towards the US and other English-speaking countries. In spite of the relentless America bashing in the official media, some elements of the civil society could be described as fans of American culture and technology. This trend might be exacerbated given the fact that the US — and to a lesser extent Canada, Australia, and the UK — had become the recipient of the bulk of graduate students seeking advanced degrees abroad.

Ironically, the appeal of America and the West increased from 1996 to 1998 following the revaluation of the experience of Eastern Europe and Russia. The official line remained that the radical reformers in these countries committed fatal errors by following the advice of their American consultants and moving too precipitously down the capitalist road. By the mid-1990s, the authorities had practically slapped a ban on open discussion of the former Eastern bloc. The only exception were journals controlled by leftists, which carped on the sins of Gorbachev, Yeltsin, and their pro-West consorts.[177]

Truth, however, was being sought from facts. More neutral scholars and intellectuals had by 1997 and 1998 realised that several East European countries had made a quick recovery from the chaos induced by shock therapy — and they were well on their way to First-World status. "We have a highly positive appraisal of the Czech Republic, Hungary and Poland," said a CASS economist in mid-1997. "Russia has also managed to stabilise its currency and other aspects of its economy." He added that major problems in the former Soviet bloc did not stem from being "too Westernised"; they were due to the residual influence of the old system.[178]

The relative success of Eastern Europe lent credence to the argument that Zhao Ziyang — and Deng Xiaoping — was right in advocating that "short-term pain is better than long-term pain". "The failure of the Zhaoists in 1988 and 1989 did not necessarily mean that shock therapy is wrong," said a veteran party cadre. "There could have been tactical errors. Our perennial failure to crack the problem of SOEs shows there are big advantages to moving quickly on problems such as the common wok and the fusion between party, government and business."[179] By late 1997, academic institutions had begun holding unpublicised seminars on the experience of former Eastern-bloc nations. Should the economies in countries such as Poland and the Czech Republic continue to forge ahead, more Chinese may gravitate towards Eastern Europe as a model for how China should radically incorporate Western norms.

Of course, China need not go all out for either the Eastern or Western way. Following the incorporation of Hong Kong in 1997 and Macau in 1999 — and further studies on the federal system — it is conceivable that different ways of doing things can be allowed to co-exist in this huge country. The extent to which this is practicable depends on the success of economic and political reforms being waged in the late 1990s.

Indeed, in the coming two to three decades, the formula of "one country, two systems" or "one country, many systems" could show the way out for this heterogeneous, fast-developing land. This means in essence that apart from Hong Kong and Macau, other enclaves will be permitted to try out socio-economic systems that may deviate from the national norm. For example, a handful of cities deemed to have the economic and educational prerequisites can experiment with larger degrees of democracy. That this idea is not far-fetched can be seen from the fact that in the economic arena, the ideal of "one country, many systems" had already come to pass in the mid-1990s. Thus, in the northeast, it was still very much the publicly-owned sector being the mainstay of the economy. Along the coast, the non-state sector was beginning to hog the limelight.[180]

An interesting current of thought hitting Beijing in 1997 and 1998 was the idea of "the harmony and synthesis of cultures" raised by non-CCP politicians including Cheng Siyuan, Lei Jieqiong and Wu Jieping. In a 1997 article, Cheng wrote that the principles of harmony, synthesis and cooperation should be used to handle "inter-personal relations, and relations among political parties, nationalities and countries". Other proponents of the same school quoted the famous saying by the founder of Taoism, Laozi: "The sage should harmonise and fuse ten thousand things; this is the will of heaven to incorporate the yin and the yang." They pointed out that the value of Chinese civilisation resided in its ability to absorb and harmonise different value systems.[181] Cheng and his cohorts used Deng's "one country, two systems" ideal to support their theory of cultural tolerance. No less a figure than Vice-Premier Qian Qichen seemed to agree. In an internal speech that approved of Cheng's theories, Qian said: "The world is developing along multipolar lines. [Parties with] different ideas and cultures can engage in interchanges — and conflicts should be avoided."[182] The CCP, however, will have to forge ahead with real political reform and "thought liberation" before the goal of fusion and harmony can be attained.

7 The 15th Party Congress and China's Future

INTRODUCTION: NEW TRICKS FROM A THIRD-TERM PARTY CHIEF?

The momentous events of 1997 left Jiang Zemin with a golden opportunity to prove he was a real helmsman. The original helmsman Deng Xiaoping's departure, the Hong Kong handover, and the 15th Chinese Communist Party (CCP) Congress (September 12–18) provided Jiang with the platform for blazing new trails and introducing novel solutions. Jiang deserved some credit for trying. Beginning in late 1996, the president assembled a team of top advisers, think tank associates and social scientists to work on the political report to the 15th congress and allied proposals for the future. Technically Jiang began his third and probably final term as party chief on September 19, 1997 — and he knew that time was running short for a makeover.

Both in internal discussions and during meetings with foreigners, Jiang began holding forth on new ideas for economic if not political reform. In a talk with US Senator Max Baucus in May 1997, Jiang expressed admiration for Franklin D. Roosevelt. The president likened the reforms he was mulling to the New Deal, whose essence was to revive the economy — and to introduce free-market initiatives. After hearing Jiang talk about his fresh agendas, Baucus said: "It struck me as the thoughts of a man who is looking towards the future and trying to understand the modern world."[1]

Yet Jiang and his team faced a tall order. In the first eight years of his tenure, Jiang spent the bulk of his energy not on policy matters or problem-solving — but on backroom manoeuvres to consolidate power. While his clout kept expanding, there was little indication the head of the Shanghai Faction would devote more time and political capital to making weighty — and invariably risky — decisions affecting the party, the economy or society in general.

Moreover, 19 years after Deng kicked off his open-door policy in late 1978, the going was getting very rough. The easy reforms — those that did not involve power-sharing by the CCP — had already been tried out. To achieve further results — or to avoid a retrogression — Jiang and company had to tackle fundamental issues such as the ownership of enterprises and political reform. Since the 1990s, the putative Chief Engineer of Reform had largely been dragging his feet over these issues. At the same time, whatever reforms had been implemented had already made a substantial dent in the vested interests of major groupings in society including farmers, workers and intellectuals. As a senior cadre in the Policy Research Office of the Central Committee General Office, Liu Defu, put it, "The reformers have disappeared!" "Once you mention the word reform, the farmers think about more taxes, the workers unemployment, and intellectuals dwindling income," Liu said. "It seems the driving force for reform only comes from various levels of government."[2]

It remained to be seen how much Jiang and his colleagues were committed to ringing in the new. The hype and brouhaha notwithstanding, the 15th Party Congress showed that the Jiang team was forced by circumstances to tackle reform — rather than waging it through their own initiative or conviction. Moreover, these neo-conservative cadres made it clear that certain aspects of the *ancien regime* — for example, the 1,000-odd "key" state-owned enterprises and the party elite's monopoly on power — would not be touched by new forces such as market economics or political liberalisation. As we shall see, a major decision of the congress was to enshrine Deng Thought in the party charter. Yet what Jiang had in mind was basically conservative Dengism: enlivening the economy while upholding the "dictatorship of the proletariat".

This chapter will look at economic and political reforms introduced at the congress — as well as new ideas broached both in and out of the CCP in the crucial year of 1997. The new leadership line-up and the balance of power will be thoroughly analysed. The fate of not just Jiang and the mainstream faction but the entire party and country hinged on whether the new power elite could take quick and effective action to cure China's ills.

ECONOMIC REFORM AT THE 15TH PARTY CONGRESS
The Emperor Sheds His New Clothes

The major achievement of the 15th Party Congress was endorsing a multi-sector economy through giving up, on a *de facto* basis, the principle of the predominance of public ownership. The emperor was shedding his (Marxist) new clothes. Put another way, much of the fig-leaf called socialism was being removed. To all intents and purposes, the People's Republic remained a socialist or Communist country only in the following two aspects: politically, insistence upon Communist party monopoly on power and party control over the weapons of the "democratic proletarian dictatorship" such as the army and the police; and economically, party-and-state control over 1,000-odd "key enterprises" and the continued exercise of "macro-level controls and adjustments".

Much of the "new way of thinking" enshrined in the congress documents had been foreshadowed by the teachings of Deng and radical reformers such as Zhao Ziyang and Bao Tong. These included the theory of the "primary stage of socialism" — that for at least 100 years, the country should focus on economic growth through the co-development of the "wholly people-owned sector" as well as non-state and "mixed" sectors. In his political report to the congress, Jiang pointed out that China being a large Eastern country, "we are destined to go through a rather long primary stage of socialism". "This is a historical stage we cannot jump over," he said.[3]

While in many aspects Jiang and company were re-inventing the wheel, the congress report did make some new points. Firstly, Deng's teachings were enshrined in the party charter. These included a latter-day version of the black-and-white cats theory: that any policy was correct so long as it satisfied the criterion of the "three favourables" (raising productivity, boosting the comprehensive strength of the nation and improving living standards). Secondly, while the document gave public ownership pride of place, it pointed out that public ownership was not the same as state ownership and that it "can and should take diversified forms", including shareholding companies and cooperatives. As Jiang put it: "All management methods and organisational forms that mirror the laws governing socialised production can be utilised boldly." Such a relatively opened-minded approach was seen as the *sine qua non* for transforming ailing state-owned enterprises (SOEs), deemed the nation's No. 1 problem.[4]

Jiang and other leaders recommended disparate forms of production and mechanisms to restructure and improve SOEs: bankruptcies and mergers; clean sale of assets; "renting out" SOEs; operating the firms under the contract system; and above all, *gufenhua,* or turning business units into joint-stock companies and cooperatives. The congress report said the shareholding system was "advantageous towards separating ownership from management and raising efficiency". "*Gufenhua* enterprises can be used both under capitalism and under socialism," the document said. Added top ideologue Xing Bensi: "As long as an enterprise is owned by the people, it is still public."[5]

Of China's estimated 350,000-odd enterprises, 4,000 were classified as joint-stock companies and 160,000 as urban shareholding cooperatives in 1997.[6] Jiang and his colleagues hoped the pace of *gufenhua* would be expedited. The president pointed out that the state or government need not hold more than 50 per cent of those SOEs that had taken the *gufenhua* path. "Predominance of public holdings [in the entire economy] should manifest itself in quantitative terms, but more so in terms of improved quality," the report said, adding that the state sector need not hold sway in all industries or trades.

What forced the CCP to give up its monopoly on business and commerce was the rising sea of debt. The debt-to-assets ratio of SOEs was an astounding 83.3 per cent. The government's outstanding loans to enterprises equalled 84 per cent of GDP. Government economists estimated that two to three trillion yuan was required to "save" the lumbering SOEs. People's Bank of China Governor Dai Xianglong admitted that at least one trillion yuan was needed to render the debt-to-assets ratio of SOEs "to a reasonable level".[7] Theoretical casuistry was perpetuated by Jiang and the ideologues to justify Beijing's call to citizens, private firms and foreign companies to come to the aid of the dinosaurs.

Perhaps out of this practical consideration, the congress had the most positive things to say about foreign and private capital. Jiang pointed out: "We shall use foreign capital actively, rationally, and effectively." As then premier Li Peng put it in a talk to congress delegates, the fast-paced introduction of foreign capital would not harm native industry. "If we can uphold the principle of taking in and digesting [foreign capital and technology] and reinventing our own, Chinese industry will be able to go up market," he said.

To expedite accession to the World Trade Organisation, Beijing announced at the time of the congress that tariffs would be cut by a further 6 percentage points to 17 per cent. Areas including financial services and army-related production would be opened for foreign participation.[8]

The private sector was given much-needed legitimacy by the congress. "The non-public sector is an important component of China's socialist market economy," the congress document said. "We should continue to encourage and guide the non-public sector comprising self-employed and private businesses to facilitate its sound development." Previously, the CCP would only consider the non-state sector a "supplement" to the "wholly people's owned sector". As then Hubei party secretary Jia Zhijie pointed out, the party had progressed from thinking that "the public and private sectors are opposed to each other" to "the theory of co-development". In any case, non-state firms already accounted for 24 per cent of GDP in 1996 despite the fact that they still suffered discrimination in areas including securing bank loans.[9]

After Jiang read out his 30,000-character speech, a number of court scribes and apologists tried to protect the party chief's flank against leftists, or Maoists, by insisting that he was not advocating privatisation. "We will find the best way to improve public ownership, but privatisation is out of the question," said then vice-minister at the State Economic and Trade Commission Zhang Zhizhang. "Collective ownership, rather than private investors, will continue to dominate China's economy." Senior ideologue Xing Bensi went so far as to deny that the country would sell off most SOEs and keep a minority of big firms. "It is impossible for China to do so, because such a method will not work and will only lead to chaos," he said.[10]

To no avail. No sooner had the congress ended than practically every province and city mapped out fast-track programmes to auction off state assets or offload SOEs. Many provinces and municipalities appointed a vice-governor or vice-mayor to handle this task. According to economics guru Wu Jinglian, the congress gave a particularly strong impetus to the effort to "render small SOEs alive". Wu reckoned that 60 per cent of the restructured small-scale enterprises were functioning well.[11] However, unlike Zhao Ziyang and his avant-garde advisers — who recommended quasi-privatisation out of the belief that this was best for China — Jiang and company were propelled on to the same path by force of circumstance. The emperor had reluctantly shed his new clothes — and the consequences would be felt across the length and breadth of the country.

The CCP Severs its Special Link with Labour

So far as the congress's socio-economic ramifications were concerned, the largest impact was felt among workers. As sociologist Wang Shan pointed out, from this point onwards, the CCP parted ways with the workers. Labourers lost their role as the vanguard of the proletariat: they no longer counted as "masters of the state" or "masters of factories".[12]

During the gestation period of the congress documents, a few free-thinking theorists proposed that the party should admit formally that labour had become a commodity that could be bought and sold. One set of terminology suggested was that workers be labelled as "hired employees" whose status, salaries and perks would be determined by the forces of supply and demand. For obvious reasons, this was deemed politically incorrect. In the report, Jiang kept up with the fiction that the party would "uphold the goal of relying on the working class with all hearts and minds". The president admitted that in the course of the transformation of SOEs, large numbers of labourers would be fired or laid off. "Yet from the longer perspective, [reforms] are beneficial to economic development, and this tallies with the long-term interest of the workers," he said.

The congress pledged to build up a comprehensive social insurance system to help jobless labourers tide over this difficult period. Special funds were channelled for retraining programmes in all major cities. Entrepreneurs were told to take care of labour interests when selling off SOEs or transforming them into joint-stock companies. What this often meant, however, was just that laid-off workers were given severance fees amounting to at most ten months of their salaries. In many instances, employees were encouraged — and very often obliged — to become "bosses" through buying out their insolvent factories.[13]

All this, however, could not disguise the fact that a socio-economic revolution was in the offing — that all workers were forced to take a plunge into the proverbial sea of the marketplace. For the estimated 150 million or so unemployed, the state ceased to be a cradle-to-grave benefactor and they had to fend for themselves. Many found this hard to take. Starting in 1996, industrial incidents including demonstrations and other protests took place on a daily basis in provinces with high concentrations of old-style SOEs. As of mid-1998, however, the central government was able to prevent such local incidents of unrest from mushrooming into a nationwide crisis. Theorists insisted that the "labour as commodity" concept was a breakthrough that would help China reach a new threshold in market reform.[14]

A Third-wave of Liberation?

Jiang's allies and public relations men were bursting with enthusiasm that the "new thinking" incorporated in the congress report would herald the party's third wave of thought liberation. As Li Peng put it the day after the congress opened, there had been two thought-liberation movements before: jettisoning class struggle after the Cultural Revolution; and Deng's decision to build a socialist market economy during the 1992 *nanxun*. This time, Li said, the party smashed another taboo by declaring that public ownership could take diverse forms. Li Junru, a Deng Xiaoping scholar and vice-chief of the Theoretical Bureau of the Propaganda Department, claimed that Jiang had attained the "third thought liberation" through using the yard-stick of the "three favourables" to solve the problem of whether a policy was surnamed "public" or "private".[15]

Given the innate conservatism of the leadership, a more advanced theoretical breakthrough was achieved by the think tanks. First of all, Marxism and socialism went through a further "secularisation". These creeds lost their otherworldly halo — and now amounted to little more than tools to promote national development. For Jiang adviser and Chinese Academy of Social Sciences (CASS) vice-president Liu Ji, Marxism could be summed up by two principles: "The people's benefits are most important; and the party should serve the people wholeheartedly"; "Seek truth from facts; practice is the sole criterion of truth". Wu Jinglian, a Zhu Rongji adviser, disturbed the Communist-Chinese universe when he said socialism was no more than "social justice and market economics". Analysts said it was significant that Professor Wu did not even bother to put the qualifier "socialist" before market economics.[16]

A second thrust of the congress "new wave" was that no one single creed could be a panacea. This was in effect a development of Hu Yaobang's famous statement in 1985 that "Marxism cannot solve all the problems of today". Despite the quasi-deification of Deng Thought, cadres were bold enough to point out that the patriarch's teachings were hardly sacrosanct. As Shenzhen's radical party boss Li Youwei put it: "It is not possible for us to find, from what Deng Xiaoping said before, ready-made answers to all our questions." Following Deng blindly, he added, "would repeat the wrongs of dogmatism".[17]

If nothing was sacred anymore, a veritable can of heretical worms had been opened. The zeal for breaching forbidden zones could spill over to the most sensitive area: political liberalisation. For Central Party School lecturer Wang Jue, the key to achieving the congress objective of economic reform and SOE transformation was overhauling the management system of government. The liberal professor added that the reform of the political structure must be waged at the same pace as economic liberalisation.[18] As we shall see in a later section, there were radical calls for the Jiang regime to stop dragging its feet in this crucial area.

Carte Blanche for Regional Autonomy?

As with previous rightwards turns in policy, regional power barons were the first to jump on the economic-reform and thought-liberation bandwagon. This was for the simple reason that these movements contributed to local autonomy: the idea that the economy developed best when each area of the country had carte blanche to do its own thing.

Even before the congress, many regional "warlords" had paved the way for another season of liberalisation and devolution of power to the localities. Shandong's new party secretary Wu Guanzheng said the entire province should better sum up the experience of previous thought-liberation movements so that "thought liberation this time around will become more mature and more scientific". One of Wu's proposals was that Shandong should develop the private sector more. Likewise, Liaoning party boss Wen Shizhen said he and his colleagues should "make bolder explorations". "We must break through the fear that [new policies] would affect the status of public ownership or deviate from the socialist road."[19]

Representatives from the *zhongxibu* (central and western areas) took advantage of the occasion to lobby for more resources and autonomy for fast-paced development. The New China News Agency quoted delegates as saying that since the *zhongxibu* accounted for 86 per cent of the territory and 58 per cent of the population, "the time is now ripe for boosting development". They also laid out plans for a cluster of "new pillar industries" and "new economic growth areas". For example, Chongqing party boss Zhang Delin was quoted as mapping out a multi-pronged strategy to expedite economic growth in the whole of central and western China. Political analysts said by contrast, cadres from the rich coastal areas had indicated their willingness to comply with Beijing's strictures on fiscal prudence and non-inflationary growth.[20]

After the congress, most provinces and cities bombarded the *zhongyang* with plans on how they would "implement the 15th congress spirit". Focus was put on the transformation of SOEs. Cities in the vanguard such as Shenzhen lost no time in passing local regulations facilitating the *gufenhua* of state firms. One Shenzhen statute authorised SOEs to sell shares to their staffers — and to give the latter loans so they could afford to buy the issues. Only banks, telecommunications and insurance firms were barred from this new-fangled policy.[21]

Indeed, most of the post-congress statements of local leaders were about "seizing the day". The new party secretary of Guangxi Cao Bochun told the official media that provincial cadres must "implement the 15th congress spirit in a down-to-earth manner" and that they must "further liberate their thoughts and set their sights on bigger things". For Shaanxi Governor Cheng Andong, it was a question of provincial officials displaying more aggressiveness and chutzpah so as to catch up with the coast. "Some of our cadres still think in the old way and have no guts to reform when other people have already gone ahead," he complained. Very few "warlords" cited the need to remain in step with the central authorities.[22]

This was in spite of the fact that in numerous circulars to the regional chieftains in the congress period, Beijing warned them against indiscriminately off-loading loss-making firms, particularly those that had assets owned by the central government. The leadership was also worried about unqualified SOEs becoming joint-stock companies and the total lack of compensation for laid-off employees. Yet another headache was a new wave of unrealistic and redundant infrastructure projects. These caveats elicited some verbal pledges from selected warlords. For example, the NCNA quoted officials in the rich city of Suzhou as saying they would "make every effort to preserve and increase the value of state assets ... and to set up a social security system that covers every citizen".[23] Most regional cadres, however, were but going through the motions of saluting the principle of making sacrifices for the national good.

THE FACTIONAL BALANCE AND LEADERSHIP CRISIS

Jiang's Power Runneth Over

Jiang's power reached its zenith at the 15th Party Congress. In terms of prestige and charisma, the self-described Chief Engineer of Reform could probably never rival Mao or Deng. However, in terms of turf — the number of party, government and People's Liberation Army (PLA) departments over which Jiang had control — it could be argued that the head of the Shanghai Faction had surpassed the Chief Architect of Reform. At the height of Deng's powers in the mid-1980s, the patriarch's authority did not cover areas such as finance (the preserve of Chen Yun and his protégés such as the late vice-premier Yao Yilin) and ideology (the bastion of "underground party general secretary" Deng Liqun).

During his eight or so years in power, Jiang had managed to consolidate his hold over the party and army. After the congress, the party apparatus was under the thumb of Zeng Qinghong, his alter ego and head of the Central Committee General Office. The ideology and propaganda departments were stacked with Jiang loyalists including head of propaganda Ding Guan'gen, vice-propaganda chief Xu Guangchun, and speech-writer Teng Wensheng. With the retirement at the congress of Generals Liu Huaqing and Zhang Zhen, the two remaining Central Military Commission (CMC) vice-chairmen — Generals Zhang Wannian and Chi Haotian — were Jiang's men. The president also installed trusted aides in the PLA administration and in the party's security factions. For example, the vice-head of the CMC General Office, Jia Ting'an, was his former personal secretary. And General You Xigui, the commander of the Zhongnanhai guards, was a former police officer in Shanghai.[24]

From the mid-1990s, Jiang, who lacked economic expertise, was able to extend his tentacles into the economic decision-making process — and the State Council in general. Two senior members of the Central Committee's Leading Group on Finance and Economics were long-time protégés: Zeng Peiyan and Hua Jianmin. Zeng was once a colleague of Jiang's in the Ministry of Electronics. And Hua was a former Shanghai vice-mayor who was transferred to Beijing in 1996.[25]

By 1997, Jiang's influence in the State Council was also felt in the foreign policy sector. The president was grooming Shanghai-born protégé Tang Jiaxuan to succeed Qian Qichen as foreign minister. The new head of the Central Committee's International Liaison Department, Dai Bingguo, worked in the Eastern European Department of the Foreign Ministry when Jiang served in Romania in the 1950s. The year also saw the transfer of two Jiang associates to head central government ministries. They were former Shanghai vice-party secretary Chen Zhili, who was made party boss of the State Education Commission; and the new head of the Construction Ministry, Yu Zhengsheng. The son of Madam Jiang Qing's first husband, Yu had also worked with Jiang in the Ministry of Electronics.[26]

The night before the congress opened, Jiang made no secret of his great expectations for the Shanghai Faction by spending time in the Shanghai Pavilion of an exhibition on "major national achievements since the 14th Party Congress". There he exhorted cadres from the East China metropolis that "Shanghai can serve the entire nation better". After the conclave, the mood of the *Shanghaibang* hit the ceiling. Jiang's principal economic adviser Zeng Peiyan praised the president for having "scientifically summed up history and mapped out the future". The 15th congress, he claimed, "has inherited the past and opened up the future".[27]

Factional Balance in the Politburo and Its Standing Committee

After much wrangling and hand-wringing, the new leadership line-up was announced at the end of the 15th Party Congress on September 18 and at the half-day First Plenum of the 15th Central Committee a day later. The supreme Politburo Standing Committee (PSC) consisted of seven politicians: Jiang Zemin, 71; Premier Li Peng, 69; Executive Vice-Premier Zhu Rongji, 69; Chinese People's Political Consultative Conference Chairman Li Ruihuan, 63; organisation chief Hu Jintao, 55; head of the Central Commission for Disciplinary Inspection (CCDI) Wei Jianxing, 65; and Vice-Premier Li Lanqing, 66. The Politburo was expanded by two to 22 full and two alternate members.

In the Politburo, *bona fide* affiliates of the Jiang or Shanghai Faction included the following: Jiang Zemin, Vice-Premier Wu Bangguo, propaganda chief Ding Guan'gen, Shanghai party secretary Huang Ju, Beijing party boss Jia Qinglin, Generals Zhang Wannian and Chi Haotian, and alternate member Zeng Qinghong. The Li Peng faction, which was allied to Jiang, comprised the outgoing premier and State Council secretary-general Luo Gan. Politburo members who did not see eye to eye with Jiang were Wei Jianxing, NPC vice-chairman Tian Jiyun, Li Ruihuan, and, to a lesser extent, State Councillor Li Tieying.[28]

Other senior bureaucrats and regional leaders in the Politburo included Vice-Premiers Li Lanqing and Jiang Chunyun, Foreign Trade Minister Wu Yi, and the party bosses of Henan, Shandong and Guangdong, respectively Li Changchun, Wu Guanzheng, and Xie Fei. In general, these technocrats and local chieftains tended to side with Jiang rather than his opponents. However, it was also true that their views often reflected the needs and aspirations of their departments and localities rather than the dynamics of personalities.[29]

With the gradual decrease in the importance of the full Politburo — which usually met only once a month — it was the PSC that made the key decisions. Jiang's authority was undoubtedly augmented with the departure of bitter foes Qiao and General Liu. Yet a rough balance of power obtained in the seven-man PSC. The principle of collective leadership reigned, meaning votes still had to be cast to settle contentious issues. During rough times in 1995 and 1996 such as the Taiwan crisis, Jiang found himself on the defensive — and outgunned by a coalition of his opponents including Qiao, Li Ruihuan, and General Liu. In the post-15th congress PSC, would he always command a majority?

In the new Standing Committee, Jiang's most solid ally was still then premier Li Peng. If votes were cast, it could be a scenario of the two versus Wei and Li Ruihuan. Wei was Qiao's protégé. The CPPCC chairman had a record of siding with Qiao. This was despite unconfirmed reports that Li Ruihuan had supported Jiang's motion that Qiao be booted out of the PSC. Moreover, Li took umbrage at the fact that Jiang had designated Hu Jintao as his successor (see following section), which meant his own chances for becoming party chief at the 16th Party Congress in 2002 would be diminished.

The balance could be tipped by the three other PSC stalwarts: Zhu Rongji, Hu Jintao, and Li Lanqing. Here, Jiang enjoyed a clear advantage — but not necessarily all the time. The differences between Jiang and Zhu went back to their Shanghai days — and there were signs their rivalry had intensified after Zhu became premier in March 1998. Because of his sensitive portfolio of ideology and personnel, Hu usually affected neutrality when arguments erupted in the PSC. This was despite increasingly obvious signs that he would give his support to the president in return for having been designated his successor. Li Lanqing was friendly with Jiang, but he was also a man for all seasons. The executive vice-premier-designate might not go all the way with Jiang given the fact that the president had backed Wu Bangguo for that position.[30]

The upshot was that while Jiang would normally be able to command a majority of PSC votes, he often had, depending on the issues, to do aggressive lobbying to have his way. The day after the first plenum, practically all the international media proclaimed that "Jiang is in charge". What was not so obvious was that Jiang had suffered setbacks in different areas.

His nominees for the PSC — Vice-Premier Wu and General Zhang Wannian — were snubbed. General Zhang barely got the "consolation prize" of ordinary Politburo membership as well as membership in the Central Committee Secretariat. Analysts said General Zhang had been attacked on two scores: for his building up a personality cult for Jiang the way that Marshal Lin Biao did for Mao; and for his alleged links with a group of tainted PLA officers who served under him when he was head of the General Staff Department (see Chapter 4).[31]

Indeed, the Shanghai Faction hardly enjoyed unalloyed success at the congress. Ballots garnered by Vice-Premier Wu were low for both the Central Committee and the Politburo. Jiang failed in his two-year-old bid to move Huang Ju to Beijing to become head of the Central Commission for Disciplinary Inspection (CCDI). Zeng Qinghong barely secured enough votes to become an alternate Politburo member. There was widespread criticism among congress delegates and Central Committee members that Jiang even tried to elevate his bodyguard General You Xigui to the Central Committee. You was among the alternate members who garnered the least ballots.[32]

The Fate of the "Qiao Shi Faction"

The departure of long-standing Jiang foe Qiao Shi showed Chinese politics was still tinged with the rule of personality — and Byzantine bickering. He was forced to quit the Central Committee and therefore the PSC at a Politburo conclave that had been orchestrated by Jiang. The president convened an enlarged Politburo meeting the night of September 15, half way through the congress. He told his colleagues that owing to a divergence of views, the leadership was unable to present the 2,048 delegates a list of recommended candidates for the Central Committee. Before the fateful gathering, Jiang had quietly secured the support of party elders, particularly former vice-premier Bo Yibo.

Chinese sources said Jiang opened the session by saying senior cadres and delegates could not agree on a retirement age for a number of veteran comrades. Those present knew the 71-year-old Jiang was referring to himself, Qiao, 73, and Liu Huaqing, 81. "I respect the delegates' wish for rejuvenation," Jiang said. "I myself am ready to retire." Whereupon Bo interrupted him and said the party should opt for both rejuvenation and unity. Pointing to the fact that Jiang was due to meet US President Bill Clinton the next month, Bo said: "You should remain in office since you are the core of the third-generation leadership, and the authority of this leadership corps is not yet totally secure." Bo suggested, however, that all other septuagenarians resign to set an example for the party.[33]

Most of the "immortals" present, including former president Yang Shangkun, former NPC chairman Wan Li and Song Renqiong, did not dispute Bo's views. Qiao had no choice but to offer his resignation. This was despite the fact that the retire-at-70 regulation was riddled with contradictions. Hua Guofeng, 76, was re-elected to the Central Committee. When the list of recommended candidates for the Central Committee was ready the next day, delegates were shocked at not seeing Qiao's name. His non-candidacy notwithstanding, NPC chief Qiao received around 200 votes during the ballots. At the end of the session, Bo delivered an unscheduled speech asking all cadres to rally around "core" Jiang. The congress organisers, including Jiang's aides, forgot to deliver a eulogy to Qiao. They vowed to make amends for this at the NPC in March 1998.[34]

That Qiao had been the apparent victim of a palace coup showed the long way the CCP had to go in modernising its institutions. His retirement, however, did not mean that the influence of the so-called NPC Faction was finished. From early 1997 onwards, Qiao had already intimated his desire to call it quits. He just wanted to ensure that his protégés could remain in place. And the former security chief largely got his wish. As we saw earlier, Wei Jianxing was his representative on the PSC. And Wei retained the CCDI portfolio, which went with it control over the dossiers of all party members. Tian Jiyun managed against all odds to stay on in the Politburo. Before the congress, there was tremendous pressure on both Wei and Tian to quit.[35]

Immediately after the congress, Qiao also tried to block Li Peng from succeeding him as NPC chief. Instead, the veteran head of the security and legal establishment was throwing his support behind Tian. "Comrade Jiyun is capable and has a long experience in the NPC," Qiao reportedly told his intimates. "He has made a big contribution to legislative work." Qiao said his crony's lack of PSC status should not be a handicap. Previous NPC supremoes including Peng Zhen and Wan Li were also ordinary Politburo members. Qiao also hinted that Li lacked legislative experience and that there had been no precedent for a retired prime minister becoming parliamentary chief. At the Ninth NPC in March 1998, of course, Li became head of the legislature. Yet Qiao was able to ensure that Tian retain his position as NPC executive vice-chairman.[36]

In the last remaining months of his tenure, Qiao intensified efforts to build up *zhidu* ("systems and institutions"): for example, boosting the deputies' supervisory powers over government and legislative leaders. By mid-year, Qiao and Tian had set up ad hoc bodies to work out required institutions and mechanisms so that they would be well in place by the NPC chief's retirement in March 1998. "Qiao and Tian want deputies to have larger powers in writing new laws and in selecting their own leaders," an NPC source said. He said a committee had been studying the issue of "self-supervision" in the congress so that legislative leaders would also be subject to scrutiny. The committee said in a report that crimes committed by veteran legislators — including municipal deputies implicated in the affair of disgraced Beijing party boss Chen Xitong — had increased. "What this means is even if Li Peng and the protégés of Qiao's foes can secure top NPC positions, they will be subject to the scrutiny of Qiao's men," said a diplomatic analyst.[37]

In internal speeches after the congress, Qiao revisited his oft-repeated theme of boosting "inner-party democracy" through building up viable *zhidu* and abandoning the rule of personality. Perhaps referring to Jiang's self-lionisation, the NPC chief indicated that there should be a definite set of criteria for the retirement of cadres. Qiao said it was not normal for a senior cadre to hold too many titles, particularly if those titles were out of line with their actual jobs. He warned against building personality cults around individual leaders.[38] While Qiao was clearly taking a swipe at Jiang, his advice for institution-building struck a chord among party members.

Issues of Leadership and Political Reform
The quality of the new leaders

At least judging by superficial statistics, the new leadership represented a step forward for modernisation. The average age of the 193 Central Committee members was 55.9, about one year lower than that five years ago. Twenty-one were under the age of 45, compared with just 14 at the 14th congress. A total of 92.4 per cent had a college education, or 9 per cent better than last time. Fully 88 per cent of committee members held substantial posts at the level of vice-minister, vice-governor, vice-commander or above. There was a noticeable decrease in party apparatchiks, model workers or ethnic-minority showcases. The few exceptions included Hua Guofeng, the former chairman who was still popular with broad segments of the party. This led the Beijing press to crow about the party having attained the ideal of "experts running the country" or "technocrats running the country".[39]

The Jiang leadership also won brownie points by excluding the princelings. In early 1997, the Organisation Department was thinking of elevating up to 15 offspring of senior cadres to the Central Committee. However, it turned out that illustrious princelings including Deng Nan, Chen Yuan, He Pengfei, Liu Yuan and Bo Xilai were snubbed. Deng Pufang, the eldest son of patriarch Deng, and Xi Jinping, the son of elder Xi Zhongxun, ended up at the bottom of the list of alternate members to the Central Committee. Throughout the summer of 1997, Jiang had indicated agreement with Deng's opinion about the princelings. In internal meetings, he quoted this Deng instruction: "While we must care for the offspring of first-generation revolutionaries, there is no need to let them rise too fast."[40]

The Central Committee and Politburo line-up, however, was unsatisfactory on many counts. The degree of rejuvenation was disappointing. The average age of the Politburo Standing Committee was 65.4, compared with the 14th congress figure of 63.7. Factionalism was rife as Jiang took every opportunity to install his own men in the policy-setting core. Jiang's power urge had affected the programme for expanded regional representation on the Politburo. While the president had reiterated in internal meetings the need to induct politicians from the provinces and cities to the high council, his first priority was to look after his protégés.

Of the five "warlords" who made it to the supreme council, three hailed from areas which had already gained Politburo status at the 14th congress: Beijing, Shanghai and Guangdong. Newcomers included the party bosses of Shandong and Henan, respectively Wu Guanzheng and Li Changchun. The powers-that-be had a hard time explaining why Shandong and Henan should be favoured. Shandong had lost its Politburo representation when former party boss Jiang Chunyun became vice-premier in 1995. In a post-congress document the authorities pointed out that Henan was chosen as a representative of the *zhongxibu*, or central and western provinces. Moreover, its status had been lifted now that it had displaced Sichuan as the most populous province. (Sichuan "lost" nearly 20 million people to the directly administered city of Chongqing in early 1997.) Above all, Henan cadres were praised for toeing the line of the party leadership with Jiang as its core.[41]

While both had reformist reputations, Wu Guanzheng and Li

Changchun could have won out because of their Jiang connection. Li was known to have proffered his loyalty to Jiang. The Shenyang native suffered a setback in his career when he was transferred from industrialised Liaoning to backwater Henan in the early 1990s. Now he made a comeback to the big times apparently due to Jiang's patronage. In the run-up to the congress, there was fierce lobbying by provinces and cities including Sichuan, Xinjiang and Tianjin to have Politburo representation. (Li's subsequent transfer to Guangdong in March 1998 as party secretary meant effectively that the entire *zhongxibu* had again lost their Politburo representation.)

The principle of the "five lakes and four seas", to which Jiang paid lip service, was also flouted in other areas. For example, followers of Zhao Ziyang were, with the exception of Tian Jiyun, practically wiped off the stage. This was despite the fact that on the same day the congress opened, Zhao — or at least his followers — circulated a document calling for an early reversal of the Tiananmen Square verdict. "It is baseless to determine the nature of the 1989 pro-democracy movement as a counter-revolutionary rebellion," the missive said. "It is better to resolve this sooner rather than later." While the petition had no direct impact on the congress, it showed that Zhao still commanded respect among a sizeable sector of party cadres. After all, his supporters pointed out, much of the economic programme of the 15th congress stemmed from Zhao's ideas.[42]

Equally dubious were the qualifications of the neophytes. In theory, they satisfied the fourfold criteria of being "revolutionary, young, competent and professional". However, the scourge of factionalism ran deep. Many of the rising stars, particularly those from the provinces, were picked by a Jiang Faction-dominated Organisation Department because of their willingness to toe the party line, or more specifically, the instructions of the dominant clique. Jiang also took advantage of the new institution of the rotation of cadres (see Chapter 2) to place protégés in the provincial leadership.

A step forward for "inner party democracy"?

Whatever achievement in "inner party democracy" that was made at the congress was a function of the core leadership responding to socio-political changes and the growing demands of ordinary CCP members. This was most obvious in the electoral process: the 2,000-odd delegates choosing the Central Committee and the latter picking the Politburo. A large number of cadres opposed the old tradition of congress delegates rubberstamping final shortlists for the Central Committee that had been settled upon by party elders and other heavyweights. "Liberal cadres are saying, now that the patriarch is gone, congress delegates should exercise their constitutional rights and enjoy full autonomy in selecting future leaders," said a party source. "These liberals also complain that several arch-conservative veterans have been given too much power to draw up the shortlists for Central Committee members. These headhunters include former organisation chief Song Ping and the Mao Zedong relative and former party boss of Hunan Mao Zhiyong."[43]

Partly to satisfy these new demands, the top leadership decided to give the delegates a larger "margin of elimination" during *cha'erxuanju* ("elections where candidates outnumber the positions available") for the Central Committee. Thus, 10 per cent of those shortlisted for the committee were eliminated during elections on September 16, the fifth day of the congress. This was higher than the five per cent during the 14th and 13th congresses.[44]

Sources close to the congress said much lobbying was done over wine and moon cakes. As expected, the leftists or remnant Maoists suffered a Waterloo. Almost no representative of Deng Liqun made it to the Central Committee. However, free marketeers also met with a rebuff. Then Shenzhen party boss Li Youwei barely kept his status as an alternate member. And several Guangdong delegates including vice-governor Ou Guangyuan — who was praised by Deng during the 1992 *nanxun* — were among the ten least popular alternate members.[45]

There was a smaller degree of choice during the *cha'erxuanju* at the First Plenum of the 15th Central Committee on September 19, when the 193 committee members picked the Politburo members. While the results of the ballots were kept secret, Chinese sources said at least three nominees for the Politburo were snubbed: Xu Kuangdi of Shanghai, Zhang Lichang of Tianjin, and Zhang Delin of Chongqing. Both Xu and Zhang Delin could have suffered because of their close association with President Jiang. Moreover, Zeng Qinghong and Wu Yi had dismal performances, as a result of which they had to be contented with alternate member status.[46]

After the conclave, individual delegates privately expressed dissatisfaction with the degree of openness. Some of their more radical demands had been ignored or watered down. These included the possibility of delegates nominating their own candidates for the Central Committee, and Central

Committee members nominating candidates for the Politburo. However, a break with tradition was attained. In practically all previous congresses, the top-echelon line-up had been decided at least two months in advance by party elders as well as top cadres such as PSC members. This was not true for the 15th congress. With patriarchs such as Deng and Chen Yun no longer around, neither Jiang nor the PSC members could dictate their choices. Right up to the eve of the meeting, it was not even sure whether the PSC would be expanded to nine members — or whether Qiao Shi would be retiring.

THE FUTURE OF ECONOMIC REFORM

The Influence of Politics on Economics

In its 1997 report on the Chinese economy, the World Bank cited the following flashpoints: a fragile financial system, problematic rule of law, corruption and pollution. Issues of law and corruption obviously had to do with the CCP's unwillingness to implement genuine political reform. These lapses took on extra significance with the new wave of ownership changes and the offloading of state assets. Fraudulent and undervalued sale of state assets cost the government an estimated US$60 billion in the ten years ending 1997.[47]

What was less obvious was that financial and social problems also had political roots. The World Bank called China's financial institutions its "soft underbelly". In spite of Zhu Rongji's reforms, the four main state banks and 14 smaller banks were poorly managed. The World Bank's verdict on the four financial giants: "It is cause for concern that their financial performance is weakening, their accounting, risk management, and credit analysis systems are woefully inadequate, and the quality of their portfolio is unknown."[48]

Bureaucratic interference was evident at both the top and regional levels. It was stated government policy to give preferential lending to the 1,000 conglomerates and other favoured enterprises. At the local level, bankers were under pressure to throw money at social crises. For example, "emergency" payouts were often given to factories whose workers were bombarding the headquarters of local administrations. Political factors were also at work behind the staggering scourge of pollution, which, according to the World Bank, accounted for a three to eight per cent GDP loss annually.

Polluters with good connections or who were willing to pay hush money were often able to beat the system.

As Du Guang, a lecturer at the Central Party School, pointed out, political reform was "the guarantee of a healthy transformation of state firms". Without the reform of the political structure, he warned in an interview with the official *China Business Times*, SOEs risked "degenerating into bureaucratic enterprises".[49] As we shall see in the next section, nowhere was this risk more apparent than in *jituangongsi*, or conglomerates and multinationals that Jiang and Zhu were nurturing with gusto.

Great Expectations for the Conglomerates

At the 15th Party Congress, Zhu Rongji reaffirmed the central government's commitment to bolster the "big-league fleet" among SOEs. "We put our emphasis on nurturing 1,000 large and medium-sized SOEs, which account for 95 per cent of the profits and taxes [collected from all enterprises]," he told delegates from Shaanxi Province. "This testifies to the concentrated nature of Chinese industry and that it enjoys economies of scale." He added that once these 1,000 enterprises were rendered well, "there is hope for the nation". Echoed Zhang Guixing, the general manager of the mammoth Northeastern Electric Power Group: "Once large enterprises have been revitalised, the state sector and even the entire national economy will get a big lift."[50]

Beijing was painting fantastically rosy pictures about the *jituangongsi* or conglomerates. Plans were fixed by the central government and large cities for at least a dozen Chinese corporations to enter the ranks of the *Fortune* 500 by the early years of the 21st century. The most gung-ho ideas were floated by Shanghai. Three top companies, Shanghai Motor Industry, Shanghai Electric, and Shanghai Huayi expressed confidence of making the exalted ranks around 2000.[51]

However, by late 1997, the extent to which the conglomerates could function as free players in the marketplace was unclear. A common point raised by foreign investors was the role of party committees. Speaking at a press conference on the fringes of the 15th Party Congress, Shaanxi Governor Cheng Andong insisted that party cells were the "political fortresses of enterprises". "Since all Chinese realise that the country can only be prosperous under the leadership of the CCP, changes in the investment system will not alter the party's role as the political nucleus in enterprises," he said.[52]

Chinese officials said the 1,000-odd "blockbuster SOEs" would benefit from unprecedented government support. Then minister at the State Economic and Trade Commission Wang Zhongyu pointed out that these behemoths would be "financially armed" by the state. For example, they would have more autonomy to list shares, float convertible funds, and undertake institutional investment. The question arose, however, as to whether these privileged darlings were operating under market norms. Moreover, in return for the special dispensation, the bureaucrats in Beijing would be demanding more than a fair share of control.[53]

Less than ten days after the congress, the Anhui government announced that it was forming 15 conglomerates that would become the "dragonheads" of the provincial economy. "They would be the pillar and backbone for spearheading the Anhui economy," local cadres said. They added that by 2000, these firms would account for more than one-third of the sales and profits of all industrial companies in Anhui. Special privileges accorded the 15 companies included loans for technological development; rights to form quasi-banking institutions; and export rights without going through national import and export corporations.[54] But were these favours being granted totally according to market criteria?

The all-too-visible hand of the state was evident in the formation of many *jituangongsi*. A good example was the merger of the giant Yihua Group of Jiangsu with three other petrochemical factories in the province: Yangzi Petrochemical, Jinling Petrochemical and Nanjing Chemical Industry. Cadre-managers there proudly told visitors that the corporate marriage had the blessing of President Jiang, a Jiangsu native. "This idea gained momentum over the past two years," said Yihua Vice-Chairman Chen Jinfang. "President Jiang has shown great concern over the development of Jiangsu Province."[55]

Independent economists, however, had cast doubt on this "marriage arranged from on high" because the four units might be incompatible in terms of financial and output profiles. Economics professor Wu Jinglian pointed out that in many places, the urge to form *jituangongsi* had much to do with the local cadres' desire to become famous or to be promoted. He said in early 1998 that conglomerates that were formed as a result of state plans and executive fiats had had lacklustre performances. Wu added that only those *jituangongsi* that had experienced an improvement in the structure of ownership as well as overall efficiency could excel in the marketplace.[56]

The fear of executive interference in enterprise behaviour was raised at a meeting on the development of large SOEs held in Beijing in September 1997. Participants, including economists and entrepreneurs, had qualms about politically motivated "marriages" among enterprises. Petrochemical executive Dong Yulin said unwise mergers could lead to "strong firms becoming weak and weak ones failing to become strong". Others queried Beijing's desire that Chinese conglomerates win slots in the *Fortune* 500 list in the coming decade. They said enterprises with huge assets or sales did not mean they were necessarily competitive. Moreover, it was dangerous to encourage officials to reach out for unrealistic goals.[57]

"Half Market, Half Planning"

Hype about a new era of liberalisation notwithstanding, the commitment of the Jiang Zemin-Zhu Rongji team to the marketplace was dubious. This was despite the warning of the congress document against skipping the "early stage of socialism". In private, many cadres had again recycled the Zhaoists' famous slogan about taking "remedial lessons in capitalism". Policymakers such as Zhu, however, remained convinced that China could somehow pick and choose those aspects of market economics that suited the requirement of the party. As Zhu reportedly said in early 1997: "Within a relatively long period, China will have a comparatively independent economic system that is different from both market economics and a planned economy."[58]

One section of the congress report was entitled "giving full play to the role of market mechanisms and improving the macro-economic control system". Obviously, Jiang and Zhu saw no contradiction between the two goals. The congress made clear-cut stipulations that reforms introduced would be subject to macro-economic controls and adjustments (MECA). In early 1997, Zhu stunned the party's liberal wing by saying that the programme of controls and adjustments would be a long-term policy. This was despite the fact that MECA was first introduced in 1993 as a short-term mechanism to rectify the economy. There were expectations that the strict regime would be lifted once a soft landing had been attained in 1996.[59]

Much of the restructuring of SOEs would be done under strict government guidance and supervision — not via market forces. While travelling to the northeast a month before the 15th congress, Zhu told cadres he expected the battle with SOEs to be won in three years. The warlords and bureaucrats were surprised. But given the economic tsar's penchant for MECA, his underlings obliged. Officials in different provinces soon came up with matching programmes to "cure" SOEs under their jurisdiction in three years.[60]

Indeed, it was ironic that while the main message of the 15th congress was economic liberalisation, the first reaction of central and regional cadres was to boost macro-economic "guidance". This manifested itself in bureaucratic decisions on which companies should qualify for preferential treatment such as priority access to government loans. Other decisions involved forming conglomerates (see above section). For example, electronics-related departments decided soon after the congress that five computer companies out of the national total of 176 would be accorded "priority in governmental nurturing".[61]

Soon after the congress, the authorities went so far as to appeal to the *gumin* ("stocks-crazed citizens") to give up their pessimism: they were told to help speed up SOE reform through buying stocks. Official media such as the *China Securities News* and *Shanghai Securities News* upbraided *gumin* for thinking that since more SOEs would be listed on the stock markets, overall prices would fall. Stock-buyers were asked to maintain confidence in the market. The director of the Enterprises Department of the State Economic and Trade Commission, Jia Xiaolong, indicated in late 1997 that Beijing would only "choose enterprises that possess good track records for listing so as to alter the situation of markets being dominated by garbage stocks".[62]

The government's appeal to *gumin* to help prop up SOEs betrayed another aspect of the residual influence of the *ancien regime*: there was an element of the Maoist "mass movement" in the entire campaign to revive state firms. As veteran economist and NPC deputy Dong Fureng warned: "After the 15th congress, shareholding companies will sprout like bamboo shoots in the spring. There could be mass chaos. Bogus joint-stock firms may emerge and deal a blow to reform."[63]

Leaders including then executive vice-premier Zhu Rongji gave repeated warnings that officials and entrepreneurs must not "kick up a storm" in the *gufenhua* process. Unfortunately, the central authorities were to blame. The way that Jiang exhorted all and sundry to jump on the *gufenhua* bandwagon at the congress evoked unpleasant comparisons with Mao egging on the nation to take part in the Great Leap Forward. As economist Wei Xinghua of the People's University pointed out, turning SOEs into shareholding companies should become neither a fad nor a cure-all. "The Chinese people have this habit of going wild once leaders say a certain policy is to be promoted," he said. "This has happened so many times in the past decade of reform."[64]

Ideological and Social Hurdles

The future of reform also hinged on ideological and social currents many of which were anti-reformist. A key rationale behind Jiang's revival of the theory of the primary stage of socialism was to pre-empt opposition from the leftists, or neo-Maoists under the leadership of ideologues such as Deng Liqun ("Little Deng"). Since late 1995, the remnant Maoists had circulated dozens of petitions to the leadership and among political circles in Beijing attacking economic liberalisation. A typical complaint was that market reforms such as *gufenhua* would undercut the basis of socialism and lead to the demise of the CCP.[65]

In the "10,000-character petition" entitled "Certain Factors that Affect our National Security", the leftists linked the revival of quasi-capitalist practices to redoubled threats to the survival of the socialist state. The anonymous tract of late 1995 raised the spectre of "the substitution of the dictatorship of the proletariat with the direct and open dictatorship of the capitalist class". Likewise, writing in a leftist journal, ideologue Shi Zhonglai saw a Manichean struggle between socialism and capitalism. For Shi, market economics would "obliterate good morality and spawn corruption and decadence".[66]

The neo-Maoist petitions and articles laid directly into reformist cadres and Jiang advisers including then Shenzhen party boss Li Youwei and CASS vice-president Liu Ji. They also attacked Jiang by implication. Leftists compared Jiang's fine-tuning of the concept of public ownership and other reforms to "revisionist" policies perpetrated by Mikhail Gorbachev and Boris Yeltsin in the Soviet Union and Russia.[67] It was true that the leftists were largely spurned by the congress delegates. Apart from Hua Guofeng, no big-name Maoists made it to the Central Committee. Moreover, the quasi-Maoists faced a tremendous problem recruiting adherents among officials or intellectuals under 50.

This did not mean, however, that the ultra-radicals would just fade away. They got a new lease of life thanks to the worsening problem of unemployment, which was practically non-existent in the 1950s. While their theories sounded as specious as they were antediluvian, the Maoists struck a chord among laid-off workers. By early 1997, Little Deng's operatives started sending leaflets and other propaganda material to large SOEs, particularly those that were unable to pay their staff. Arguments such as the socialist state's obligations to the "vanguard of the revolution" provided the unemployed with the theoretical justification to demand a return of the common wok and the iron rice bowl.[68]

At a press conference held on the sidelines of the 15th congress, then Minister of Labour Li Boyong played down the dangers of social unrest stemming from the ranks of the unemployed. The official urban unemployment rate was three per cent while Chinese economists reckoned it was at least 7.5 per cent. An independent study put a five per cent unemployment rate as the most that Chinese society could cushion without massive disorder. In spite of Beijing's calls for restraint in the "special banner year" of 1997, wave upon wave of labour unrest hit regions with heavy concentrations of state industry such as Heilongjiang, Liaoning and Sichuan. It was estimated that each of these provinces had at least 500,000 laid-off workers. Yet even affluent provinces such as Guangdong were not immune.[69]

By mid-1998, the labour situation had deteriorated. This was despite Herculean efforts by the authorities to create jobs through multiple re-employment programmes. In large cities such as Wuhan and Chongqing, worker protests had become so routine that authorities ruled off large segments of the roads outside government offices as a venue for rallies and demonstrations. Given the gravity of the situation, the pace of SOE reform had noticeably slackened.[70]

Indeed, given the news blackout on such events, what came to be reported was just the tip of the iceberg. The labour problems were exacerbated by the archaic political system: there were no channels through which workers could air their grievances or engage in "collective bargaining" (see also Chapter 3). Unofficial trade unions were banned. There were no labour representatives in either government or legislative councils save for Lei Feng-like model workers. The upshot was the CCP had to pay the price of a retardation in economic reform. To keep workers off the street, SOEs had to keep idle or semi-employed work hands on the payroll. Banks continued pumping loans into firms that had no prospect of repayment. In many provinces and cities, factories were not allowed to transform themselves into shareholding units unless they had resolved the livelihood of laid-off workers.[71]

By mid-1998, even such a committed reformer as Zhu Rongji had to admit that the success of SOE reform hinged on how well the problem of unemployment could be solved. This was despite the fact that liberal economists such as Wu Jinglian kept arguing against slowing down the pace of reform to "match" the unemployment level. Moreover, cadres in charge of security such as Politburo Standing Committee member Wei Jianxing had raised alarms about unemployment threatening the party's ruling status. In his 1998 May Day message, Wei indicated that the unemployment issue was intimately related to "social stability and the viability of the socialist regime".[72] In other words, the party's mandate of heaven could be in tatters unless the scourge of joblessness could be eradicated.

THE PROSPECTS FOR POLITICAL CHANGE

A Real Thaw?

Suddenly, there was some kind of Beijing spring. Starting in May 1997, a handful of intellectuals began giving vent to bold ideas which could have far-reaching consequences for political development. Some said they were responding to Jiang's call for economic and political liberalisation in the run-up to the 15th Party Congress.

"Once the people have had enough to eat and their cultural level is raised, they want to have their say and to take part [in politics]," said Chinese Academy of Social Sciences (CASS) Vice-President Liu Ji. "If the CCP is an advanced party that is ahead of the times, it should come up with new measures to accommodate this demand of the people." The social scientist went so far as to say that elements of Western democracy should be incorporated. One example he cited was British philosopher Lord Acton's dictum that "absolute power corrupts absolutely" in the absence of checks and balances. "Democracy is a science, a kind of political science," he said. "And science has no international boundaries."[73]

Beijing University economics professor Shang Dewen envisaged a gradual march to democratic institutions — including universal suffrage — in 25 years. In early summer, he began circulating a political manifesto to the foreign media in Beijing — and his interviews on the Chinese services of VOA and BBC reached a large number of intellectuals in urban areas. "The head of state and the chief officials of all provinces and municipalities should be elected on the basis of national polls," he wrote. "We should elect our president through national elections with a term of four years and adopt a parliamentary system with all members elected." Shang insisted that non-Communist political parties be allowed to contest in the ballots, even though he thought the CCP would win.[74]

Veteran economist Yu Guangyuan chimed in with his vision that political modernisation should be accomplished by the 2030s. Yu, a one-time adviser to Hu Yaobang and Zhao Ziyang, indicated that Western-style reforms might be introduced after the country had achieved basic economic prosperity in a 30-year effort that started in 1979. Yu said that by 2008, a market system would be established and genuine popular participation in politics could begin in earnest. Like Shang, Yu prescribed familiar goals such as multi-party competition and polls.[75]

The professors were echoed by the few dissidents who had still not been put behind bars. For example, former secretary of Hu Yaobang, Lin Mu, wrote from his home in Xian that after the 15th Party Congress, the "time was ripe" for new-fangled institutions such as multi-party democracy. In a letter to the congress, he said China was saddled with problems including corruption, unemployment, and polarisation of incomes. "In order to surmount these obstacles, the only way is to apply democratic principles and to govern by law, not force," he wrote.[76]

As distinguished from earlier periods of thought liberalisation, however, it was mostly intellectuals working within the system — not dissidents or college students — who hogged the limelight in the three months or so before the congress. They put their support behind a kind of gradualist, party-initiated reform that would stretch over two or more decades. Like Professor Shang, most of these "establishment radicals" envisaged that the reforms would be conducted under CCP guidance. Moreover, there was the possibility that universal suffrage might actually help strengthen the CCP by getting rid of the black sheep.

Perhaps the cautious tone of Jiang's "political message" at the congress frustrated these thinkers, who kept a much lower profile after the conclave. However, this did not mean that their ideas would not function as a catalyst in the long tug-of-war called China's modernisation.

The 15th Party Congress and Political Reform
Jiang's cautious blueprint

In his congress report, Jiang devoted a large segment to the reform of the political structure. Yet practically no new ground was broken. The Jiang Faction was intent on preserving the prerogatives of the elite. In public, the neo-conservatives kept up with the shibboleth that political change would be implemented to break through the bottlenecks of economic reform. Yet they offered this "neo-authoritarian" pretext for foot-dragging: without socio-political stability and the concentration of power in the *zhongyang* ("central authorities"), economic reform could not be accomplished.

The president cited the following goals in what amounted to mere tinkering with the system: governmental streamlining; boosting the legal system; and "improving the system of democratic supervision". Of the three, the first — and least politically sensitive objective — might bear the most fruit. Government departments dealing with production and economic activities — such as ministries in charge of electronics, machine building, coal and chemical industries — would be turned into state corporations. Other units would be combined to promote efficiency. This goal was largely attained at the Ninth NPC of March 1998 (see Chapter 8).

Throughout 1997, much hype was given to the ideal of a kind of rule by law with Chinese characteristics. Up to 1996, Jiang and other leaders raised the slogan of "building up a country with a socialist legal system". This had since been changed to "building up a country with rule by law" (see also Chapter 6). Jiang made it clear in his congress report, however, that "ruling the country by law" would be done "under the leadership of the party". After all, he said, "the party has led the people in drawing up the constitution and the laws". "In ruling the country by law, we can unify [the goals of] adherence to party leadership, development of people's democracy and doing things in strict accordance with the law," he added. The underlying principle of legal reform could only be "ensuring that the party's basic line and basic policies are carried out ... that the party plays the role of the core leadership at all times".[77] In other words, the "rule by law" goal would still be subsumed under the long-standing ideal of party supremacy.

In talking about "improving the systems of democracy", Jiang repeated old pledges about seeking the views of non-party elements. "We shall gradually establish a mechanism that will help decision-makers go deep among the people ... so that decision-making will be more scientific, democratic and efficient," Jiang said. He mentioned "extending the scope of democracy at the grassroots level". However, the president did not even give vague promises that polls for the selection of heads of village committees — or county-level people's congress deputies — would be extended to higher levels. The party boss vowed to boost "supervision by public opinion". However, in the brief section on the press, emphasis was put on ensuring that the media would "adhere to the principle of upholding the party spirit" — and on "tightening control over the press and publishing".

Throughout the text, the over-riding principle of CCP suzerainty was cited repeatedly.[78]

Much of the congress report was devoted to quasi-Maoist themes about "party construction" — or boosting its combativeness in order to counter ideological invasion from the West. The CCP's 3.4 million grass-roots cells would be turned into fortresses against "peaceful evolution". And the 58 million members would become new Lei Fengs committed to the "leitmotifs of collectivism, patriotism and socialism". They should stay in unison with the party core "in thought, organisation, action and style".

Many urban intellectuals felt let down by the congress's failure to introduce new mechanisms to stamp out corruption. Jiang had adamantly turned down the views of moderate officials that checks and balances had to be introduced: corruption could never be curbed if wrongdoers, investigators and judges shared the same background and worked for the same boss — the party. In the report, however, the General Secretary stuck to the hackneyed theme that the key was not building up *zhidu* but rectifying the "personal philosophy" of party members. Jiang rehashed clichés about "ceaselessly raising the leadership and administrative level of cadres, and boosting their ability to withstand corruption". "Officials must act against the corrosion of corrupt thoughts and they must self-consciously accept supervision," he said.[79]

Spin control by Jiang's men

Perhaps to warn the party's bourgeois-liberal members — and Western observers — against entertaining illusions about political change, Jiang's aides were frank about the limited and conservative nature of the congress platform in this area. The vice-head of the Central Party School Wang Jiamiu said on the sidelines of the congress that no revolutions were being contemplated. "The reform of the political structure does not mean breaking up the [existing] system or dismantling the [political] framework," she said. "It must be gradually deepened and implemented."[80]

After the congress, Xing Bensi, another party-school don and one of Jiang's top gurus, said there was no question of the party embracing Western-style democracy. "China will draw on the good experience of Western democracy but it will not copy features such as the two-chamber [legislative] system and multi-party electoral race," said Xing.[81] Wang, Xing and other spin doctors confirmed that in the near future, political reform would be confined to administrative changes and the separation of government and business.

Apart from administrative streamlining, the media also played up the "success" of building up a Western-style civil-service system. The then Vice-Minister of Personnel Zhang Xuezhong claimed at the congress that in a relatively short four years, the country had established a modern civil service. This, he said, consisted of "the clear-cut categorisation of posts, recruiting through open exams, annual performance assessment, rotation of posts and dismissal of incompetent officials". In the four years ending 1997, central-level units signed up more than 1,700 cadre-level officials through open examinations. The figure for localities was nearly 20,000. In the same period, more than 5,000 civil servants nationwide were dismissed for incompetence. Sixteen thousand were forced to quit.[82]

Progress was also claimed for the related objective of "rendering decision-making scientific and democratic". At both the central and local levels, experts of diverse backgrounds were tapped for their views on policy. For example, Guangzhou authorities said they had accomplished the goal of "experts running the city". A "consultative committee" of 300 academics and professionals was engaged by municipal authorities as advisers. Guangzhou officials said they had "modernised" decision-making through a "three nos" policy: no decision would be made without thorough investigation, discussion with experts, and other kinds of "democratic consultation".[83] Top leaders such as Jiang and Zhu had also increased the size and sophistication of their think tanks to include scholars and professionals with more liberal leanings.

The chasm between Jiang's vision and that of liberals such as Zhao Ziyang was obvious when comparing the 15th with the 13th congress. Jiang lifted from the Zhaoists — without acknowledgement — the theory of the preliminary stage of socialism. However, most of the other ideals of Zhao were ignored. They included transparency of government, the separation of party and government, and other ways to remove Leninist claptrap from the party.

Can the "15th Congress Spirit" Last?

In spite of the aforementioned limitations, the party did inch forward in certain key areas. First of all, some of Deng's liberal teachings — "taking economics as the key link" and "combating leftism is the major task of the party" — were enshrined in the CCP charter. Jiang expressed agreement with such avant-garde cadres as the former Guangdong party boss Ren Zhongyi that it was leftism, not rightism, that had wreaked the most havoc on post-1949 China.[84] After the 15th congress, it would be that much more difficult for the ultra-conservatives to mount a campaign against "all-out Westernisation".

Moreover, either with or without Jiang's imprimatur, the more liberal among his think tank members had given vent to avant-garde proposals for political reform. Many of these ideas had been leaked to the Hong Kong, Taiwan and foreign press — and become known in political circles in Beijing and Shanghai. Take, for example, the hot issue of direct elections. In internal meetings, some Jiang aides raised the possibility of extending such elections from the level of *cun*, or village, to that of *xiang*, or aggregate villages, which is just one rung below counties in the Chinese administrative system. They thought direct polls for heads of counties should be considered round the time of the 10th NPC, to be held in 2003. According to this line of thinking, elections for municipal chiefs should be tried out by 2008, provincial chiefs by 2013, and national leaders by 2018, or 2023 at the latest.[85]

The 15th congress could also prod liberal cadres into ensuring that electoral reforms already carried out would be implemented without fail. For example, regional parliamentarians had from the early 1990s begun voting to select or confirm party nominees for positions up to provincial governor. Depending on individual cases, an element of *cha'erxuanju* was allowed. On the party side, nominees by the Organisation Department for positions up to provincial party secretaries had to be confirmed through convening a party congress at the relevant level. While *deng'erxuanju* (elections where only one candidate was put forward for one position) was the norm, unpopular candidates could be thrown out if they gained less than half the votes. Under the pretext of recentralisation, the neo-conservative leadership had tried to water down or tamper with these "elections".[86]

Steps taken at the 15th congress at relaxing state control over the economy were bound to have a liberalising impact on politics. As CASS political scientist Liu Junning put it, the result of *gufenhua* and other moves at quasi-privatisation would lead to the growth of individual wealth. "Out of an urge to protect their own wealth, people will demand the rule of law and supervision of the government," he said. Liu added that this demand for political change would be much more broad-based — and effective — than that raised by theorists and students in the 1980s.[87]

It was for this reason that not only leftists but mainstream politicians were worried about threats to the socialist orthodoxy. In an internal talk, out-going CMC vice-chairman Liu Huaqing expressed fears that the ideal of a "party army" would be jeopardised when the CCP — and the state in general — ceased to own the majority of the nation's enterprises. General Liu said if semi-privatisation were to run its course, national revenue — including the PLA budget — would be dependent on taxes generated by the non-state sector. The corollary could only be that the "private bosses" would become the ultimate bosses of the defence forces.[88]

WAITING FOR THE 16TH PARTY CONGRESS

A New Urgency for Something to Show

"The Chinese are the smartest people, one with the highest level of intelligence," said economic tsar Zhu Rongji at a function in Hong Kong in September 1997. The then vice-premier stressed that he was not advocating jingoism but he wanted to ensure that Chinese would have enough self-confidence. "In the past, owing to lack of education, their potential had not been developed," he said. "If our education and technology are well developed, we can solve any problem."[89] Zhu was, of course, voicing one version of Jiang Zemin's theory that "economic development plus science equals socialism".

But where was Mr *De*? It had been China's enduring tragedy that no solution had yet been found for the puzzle raised during the May Fourth Movement of 1919: how to properly introduce Mr *Sai* and Mr *De*, the Chinese translation for Science and Democracy. After the ravages of the 1950s and the Cultural Revolution, democracy had taken on the wider context of establishing viable institutions of governance that would allow popular participation — and provide for built-in mechanisms for rectifying policy errors.

In 1997, pressure was mounting for the 76-year-old party to have something to show. Once the CCP had shed its Marxist new clothes, the people would be asking these questions: why should we always stick to the Communist shop; why not let other political parties and forces have a go of developing the economy and satisfying people's aspirations? Moderate scholar Li Junru stated this issue clearly when he told the Beijing-based *China Economic Times* that "we should have a very deep sense of crisis".[90]

For Li, who headed the Shanghai-based Institute of Deng Xiaoping Thought before moving to Beijing in 1994, China was at a crossroads. "If we don't have a new breakthrough, there might be a retrogression and the fruits of reform could be nullified in an instant," he said. He cited the examples of Russia, Eastern Europe and other former Communist countries. "Once these countries had attained a relatively high level in the reform process, their faith in socialism was shaken."[91] Put in simple terms, Li's fear was that once people have enough to eat and have learnt to think independently, they may see the CCP as an obstacle rather than an aid to the goal of developing the economy and getting rich.

Similar alarms were sounded by the former vice-chief of propaganda Gong Yuzhi, a noted liberal. Gong expressed worries that the party might have missed the boat. "Owing to reasons including the regrouping of various [international] interest groups, the globalisation of economies and particularly the speed of technological breakthrough, it is difficult to catch up once we have lapsed," he told the NCNA at the time of the congress.[92] Gong's point: if the CCP did not move faster, it would be left behind by the times — and forsaken by the people.

The One Step Forward, Half-a-step Backwards Syndrome

At least on the surface, however, no such urgency informed the speeches or behaviour of mainstream politicians such as Jiang or Zhu. They remained convinced that the party could hold on to power through to the 16th congress — and thereafter — without making radical changes.

The 15th Party Congress demonstrated clearly that nearly 20 years into the era of the open door, the party remained torn by conflicting impulses of reform and retrogression, innovation and stagnation. Many of the "new ideas" adopted at the congress were a reinstatement of the central tenet of "Dengism": less is more. A major tactic adopted for SOEs was to chop and slash: to lop off the dead wood accumulated through decades of party and state mismanagement. This cutting and downsizing extended to the programme to streamline the bureaucracy and to demobilise 500,000 PLA soldiers.

The second prong of Jiang's save-the-party package was to reach out, to integrate and internationalise. Foreign capital was invited to buy into joint-stock companies. Tariffs were further lowered to help China's accession to the World Trade Organisation (WTO). The president stressed that during the primary stage of socialism, China should absorb not just Western technology but "the valuable fruits of foreign culture". Above all, the party made a commitment to keep up with the times through constant renewal. Aping the late Hu Yaobang, Jiang said that Marxism must never be studied in a "stagnant and isolationist environment".

This impulse to curtail state control, to embrace global norms and to blaze new trails was juxtaposed against an equally strong tendency found in the congress report and speeches by leaders at the time: to shore up outmoded institutions and to wallow and stagnate in a splendid isolation with Chinese characteristics.

In the economic arena, the propensity for bolstering the *ancien regime* was evident in the strategy to "take a firm grip on large SOEs" — the 1,000 key enterprises many of which were to be turned into world-class conglomerates. Senior cadres quoted Lenin on the need to "concentrate national resources on developing big-league industrial giants".[93] The preoccupation with resuscitating the Marxist canon was particularly evident in the congress report's section on party construction. Jiang told the faithful there had never been a political party "so densely and tightly organised" as the CCP. He urged members to develop further this "tremendous organisational superiority".

At the 13th Party Congress of 1987, Zhao sought to apply the "less is more" philosophy to party reform by chipping away at CCP omnipresence through means such as the separation of party and government. The Jiang leadership, however, ignored pleas by liberal intellectuals that the Leninist concept of an all-embracing party was self-defeating — and that the CCP must disengage its tentacles from areas including business, government and the army.

Unsurprisingly, the corollary of Jiang's call to "boost [party members'] ability to fight corrosion" was to banish Western culture and thoughts, which, his ideologues said, were replete with "individualism, hedonism and Mammonism". In stark contrast to the pro-West, internationalist strains of his economic message, the president practically relaunched a "campaign against bourgeois liberalisation" to fight infiltration by the "hostile foreign forces".

These strictures cast doubt on the Jiang team's fundamental approach to modernisation: while the neo-conservatives sought change for aspects of the "superstructure" such as the economy, they resisted change in things dearest to their hearts, such as the CCP's monopoly on power. The reform-ist patina notwithstanding, there was an element of stasis in the key theme of the congress: to enshrine Deng theory in the party charter. What Jiang wanted above all to preserve in perpetuity were Deng's conservative in-structions such as his "both hands be tough" doctrine of the late 1970s: the party must grasp economic development on the one hand, and grasp "re-gime building" and uphold the Four Cardinal Principles of Marxism on the other.[94]

China After the 16th Party Congress
Using old methods to cure new problems

In assessing the five years that had elapsed between the 14th and 15th congress, pro-establishment economist Hu Angang heaped praise on the Jiang leadership. He cited in particular the following three "achievements": reform of the taxation system to boost Beijing's income; macro-economic controls and adjustments; and shrinking the gap between rich and poor. "These are tasks that the first- and second-generation leaderships wanted to do but failed to accomplish," he said. "This testifies to the ability of the existing Chinese government."[95]

Hu's claims were suspect. As we saw in Chapter 5, Beijing was not successful in arresting the decline of central revenue, which dropped to just over 10 per cent of GDP in the mid-1990s. While the CCP leadership scored some success in helping the most destitute sector of the population, the overall problem of the polarisation of income had hardly been solved. According to the Beijing-based *Financial Times*, 0.1 per cent of the popu-lation owned 33 per cent of the bank deposits. By contrast, one per cent of the richest residents in the US controlled 40 per cent of its wealth.[96]

Yet even assuming that Professor Hu was correct on these scores, Jiang and company had let down his countrymen regarding a much longer list of major objectives: fighting corruption, improving SOE efficiency and mod-ernising a Leninist-Stalinist state system, to name a few. Even Western com-mentators gave Jiang some credit for trying to break new ground at the congress. However, owing to the neo-conservatives' background and train-ing — and the need to preserve the CCP Leviathan — the methods used to bring the reforms to fruition smacked too much of the *ancien regime*.

As discussed earlier, executive fiats and even Maoist-style mass movements were used to transform SOEs into modern enterprises. Independent economists cast doubt on the scientific basis of the promise made by Zhu Rongji in July 1997 that all state firms would be "turned around" in three years. They said this might have to do with the fact that the 69-year-old economic tsar was unlikely to stay on after his five-year tenure as premier was up. In any case, Zhu toned down his pledge in speeches later that year. By early 1998, the premier-designate was merely saying that in three years' time, the difficulties facing the 500 or so major SOEs would "basically be relieved".[97]

The same penchant for tackling 21st century problems with mid-20th century tactics manifested itself in other areas. For example, in the congress report, Jiang stuck to the Maoist viewpoint that "retooling the worldview of cadres" was the best way to eradicate corruption. Throughout 1997, Jiang dispatched a dozen-odd senior aides to Singapore and Malaysia to study anti-graft operations in countries with relatively authoritarian one-party rule. Obviously, the "Western" model of ensuring probity in government was still alien to his thinking.

It was true that with the introduction of the retire-at-65 rule for ministerial-ranked officials, the bulk of the cadres trained in the Soviet Union in the 1950s would leave the stage by 1998 or 1999. However, major changes might only come at the 16th Party Congress, when figures like Jiang, Zhu and Li Peng would finally bid adieu.

"New thinking men" for the 21st century

At a Politburo meeting soon after the 15th congress, Jiang underscored the need for rejuvenation. Pointing to the fact that the average age of Politburo Standing Committee (PSC) members was slightly higher than that of the 14th congress, Jiang reportedly said: "We are getting on in years and should delegate more authority to younger members [of the leadership]." Then Jiang pointed to Hu Jintao, who was first inducted to the PSC five years earlier. "Comrade Jintao, as well as other capable young cadres, will win new achievements for the party." The president added: "We of the third generation should do more in paving the way for the young and minimising their obstacles."[98]

Much, much more important than age was the new way of thinking. After all, the CCP had already set records in rejuvenation in the 1950s, when numerous cadres in their 40s such as Deng Xiaoping were calling the shots. The big question was whether so-called fourth-generation leaders could ring in the new. Hu would face tough competition. Would-be successors of Jiang included other high-fliers in their 50s such as Wu Bangguo, Wen Jiabao, Huang Ju and Zeng Qinghong. By late 1997, there was already talk of a Hu-Wu axis, with Hu becoming party boss and Wu premier in 2002 and 2003 respectively.

By CCP standards, the likes of Hu, Wu and Wen were late bloomers. By mid-1998 they had not had much chance of fully displaying their talents and idiosyncrasies. Yet it could be said they would be more "progressive" and open-minded than Jiang and his colleagues. Hu, best known for being the party boss of Guizhou and Tibet, was described as a "fragile flower vase" when inducted to the PSC in 1992. Since then, he had made no major errors in his portfolio of ideology and personnel. The organisation chief lent his support to fighting leftism; and he largely maintained his neutrality in the Jiang-Qiao slugfests.[99] Yet the former Communist Youth League star had hardly established himself as an original policymaker. To maintain his momentum, Hu had to quickly demonstrate that he had the wherewithal to rejuvenate the party and make it relevant.

Both Wu and Wen wisely kept a low profile in ideological matters. They were, however, instrumental in nudging economic policy slightly towards the right, that is, the marketplace. The consistently underrated Wu should be given credit for new ways of thinking such as the *zhuada fangxiao* approach to SOEs. It is possible that towards the end of the five years covered by the 15th congress, they will be able to come up with more initiatives.

Then there were the fast-rising young turks working for Zhu Rongji. By early 1998, the premier-designate had already assembled his kitchen cabinet. Quite a few members of Zhu's inner circle were technocrats in their mid- to late-40s who had ample exposure to Hong Kong and the West (see Chapter 8). Most of these officials had excelled in Zhu-style macro-management of the economy. Yet they had also benefited from the free-market teachings of Professor Wu Jinglian, the master guru of the Zhu camp. Given their familiarity with international norms, these rising stars could make a positive contribution to economic if not political reform.[100]

Younger affiliates from other political persuasions — loose cliques linked with liberal heavyweights such as Zhao Ziyang, Tian Jiyun, Qiao Shi and Wei Jianxing — could also make waves. This was despite the fact that owing to the success with which the Shanghai Faction had monopolised the media, outsiders were not sure about the identities of these "rival young turks". Some could be found within the NPC system, and others in the regions. Radical reformers who had been marginalised in the wake of the June 4 crackdown — and who had gone into business and other non-political pursuits — could re-enter the stage at the right juncture, for example, when the party was overwhelmed by the rigorous demands of the information age.[101]

Moreover, a new generation with exposure to the West could soon be calling the shots. This included the tens of thousands of elite college gradu-ates who studied in the US and other countries from the early 1980s on-wards. Among those allowed to settle in the West immediately after the June 4, 1989 massacre, a sizeable percentage had returned to China to take ad-vantage of the rapidly rising salaries and advancement prospects. Ninety per cent of the 1,107 scholars the Chinese government sent overseas from 1995 to 1997 returned on schedule.[102]

Most of these returnees worked in the commercial field, particularly joint ventures. But quite a few opted for party and government positions. In many instances, graduates from famous universities — particularly those with expertise in law, international trade and diplomacy whom the party could trust — were allowed to leapfrog to positions of heads of depart-ments just one or two years upon their return. Within limits, members of this elite were by 1998 able to bring new insights to decision-making proc-esses. And they could spell a difference towards the second half of the first decade of the new century.

Internationalisation and 21st century shocks

Since he came to power in mid-1989, Jiang had reacted to rather than anticipated events. By late 1997, the CCP had owing to more than eight years of procrastination lost much of the drive and dynamism once asso-ciated with Mao or Deng. The good news on the economic front up to mid-1997 might perhaps have given the leaders a false sense of confidence that the Jiang way — his interpretation of Deng's "both hands be tough" policy — was sufficient to see China through to the 21st century.

Then came the Asian financial crisis of late 1997 and 1998 (see Chapter 8). The "Asian flu" hit home the fact that the phenomenon of globalisation and China's transition to the Asia-Pacific century could pose the biggest challenge to the party since 1949. The great majority of the crises since mid-century had been domestically brewed: the Great Leap Forward, the

Cultural Revolution and the June 4 massacre. From the mid-1990s onwards, however, the shocks — delivered in the form of "sugar-coated bullets" or otherwise — would be coming from outside the party and outside the country.

On the economic, social and cultural fronts, the impact of internationalisation was getting more obvious by the day. Apart from the requirements of the WTO and other global trading arrangements, Jiang's ambition of nurturing world-class SOE conglomerates involved yielding substantial amounts of "economic sovereignty". The CCP leadership had yet to come to grips with the fact that thorough-going integration with the world economy would bring with it not just a re-definition of the concept of the traditional "sovereign state" but also ferocious challenges to party orthodoxy.

Domestically, the mentality of the people was undergoing unprecedentedly fast changes. With the formal disavowal of many tenets of socialism at the congress, the CCP's only legitimacy lay in its ability to deliver the goods. And not just in terms of economic performance. Chinese people's demands had become multifaceted and sophisticated. They wanted not just an improvement in the standard of living but also "self-fulfilment" in politics, culture and other arenas.

Since 1949, the CCP had effectively prevented other political organisations and forces from taking root. Yet a party committed to "stability" and stasis could not forever insulate the Middle Kingdom from cataclysmic changes. Even before the 17th Party Congress of 2007, a non-mainstream faction of the CCP could win over and refashion the party into a new entity — perhaps called the Chinese Social Democratic Party — that is more in sync with the *zeitgeist*. Moreover, the party could implode. Should the CCP or its variants continue to put party suzerainty before change, a coalition of socio-political forces armed with 21st century solutions to 21st century problems could come to the fore by the late 2000s or early 2010s.

Epilogue:
8 The Rise of Zhu Rongji and Beijing's Response to the Asian Financial Crisis

INTRODUCTION: GREAT EXPECTATIONS FOR THE JIANG-ZHU TEAM

The meteoric rise of Zhu Rongji added a new twist to the era of Jiang Zemin. Given the popularity of the economic tsar and his dynamism, the so-called "Jiang-Zhu axis" could provide a new impetus to solving the nation's ills such as economic inefficiency and political stagnation. However, owing to the size of the two egos, teaming Jiang with Zhu could engender questions of incompatibility. Yet if Jiang could swallow his pride and yield a measure of the limelight to his premier, this might work out to be a win-win scenario. Given the relatively narrow nature of Zhu's power base, it was improbable that the former Shanghai mayor could challenge the president's status of "quasi-helmsman". It was obvious that a novel — and much bolder — approach was needed to tackle the nation's problems, which had been rendered more intractable by the Asian financial turmoil.

How well 70-year-old Zhu handled the economic crisis could settle the question of whether — as he claimed — he deserved the Nobel Prize for Economics. After all, in internal meetings, Zhu and his aides had boasted that they had "forestalled" the turmoil when the economic tsar began to tackle China's bubble economy in 1993 — and that it was Zhu's success in bringing about a soft landing that enabled the country to be immune from the "Asian flu" in 1997 and 1998. As the following sections will explain, however, the picture was much more complicated and China's weakness — and susceptibility to an Asian-style meltdown — much more pronounced. Zhu's big test hinged on whether the iron-willed trouble-shooter could take on China's deep-seated economic and political malaise.

The same was true for Jiang — and perhaps on an even larger scale. Time was running out for the 72-year-old president to claim a place in the Communist-Chinese pantheon alongside Mao Zedong and Deng Xiaoping. He was expected to step down from his post of General Secretary by 2002. It was questionable whether Jiang could achieve anything solid on the unification of Taiwan, the one issue which, he hoped, would give him his place in the history books. More and more of his aides from Wang Daohan to Wang Huning, were urging him to try something out of the ordinary such as political reform.

As we shall see in the following sections, the Asian crisis was not just a matter of bad business decisions and poor management. It had its roots in "institutional" issues such as archaic political values and systems, which manifested themselves in ills with which most Chinese were familiar: corruption, cronyism, and the fusion of government, business, and even the army. This was despite the fact that the Chinese propaganda machinery was letting on that the Asian meltdown was but a new form of "economic hegemonism" perpetrated by fund managers and international speculators working in cahoots with Washington. This chapter examines the rise of Zhu, "power-sharing" between Zhu and Jiang, the post-1998 leadership, and the viability of the new team's strategies against the Asian crisis. It will also look at the possible impact of the financial turmoil on the legacy of President Jiang and on the fate of China in the 21st century.

THE RISE OF ZHU RONGJI

Zhu Rongji was never Jiang Zemin's first choice as premier. When the Politburo Standing Committee first deliberated on the candidates for head of government a year or so before the 15th Party Congress of September 1997, the names of Vice-Premiers Wu Bangguo and Li Lanqing, Chinese People's

Political Consultative Conference (CPPCC) chairman Li Ruihuan, and even Politburo stalwart Hu Jintao were raised. Zhu got the position virtually by default, thanks to the widespread perception that he alone possessed the qualifications for the job.[1]

The Hunan native's confirmation as premier by the NPC on March 18, 1998 had all the elements of a coronation: the margin of support of 98 per cent was much wider than people expected. Then came adulation from the Hong Kong, Taiwan and foreign media. One Hong Kong daily made much of the fact that he was the descendant of Zhu Yuanzhang the first emperor of the Ming Dynasty. Influential foreign media also heaped on the accolades, calling him a "no-nonsense technocrat", an "intrepid reformer", or simply "the boss".[2]

Power Sharing between Jiang and Zhu

A number of Chinese officials and commentators characterised the mid-1998 Chinese leadership as a "Jiang-Li-Zhu triumvirate". This was a reference to the fact that during the period covered by the 15th Party Congress (1997–2002), major decisions would be made by the Politburo Standing Committee led by President Jiang, NPC chairman Li Peng, and Premier Zhu. However, it would be more accurate to describe the political dynamics as power sharing between Jiang and Zhu. Li Peng's star was fading in spite of the fact that in the official pecking order, he still outranked Zhu as the No. 2 in the Politburo.[3]

Much of the stability in the leadership hinged on the division of labour between Jiang and Zhu — and questions such as whether the two could work out a satisfactory cohabitation. Jiang would still be in charge of the "overall situation" with particular emphasis on party affairs, personnel, the People's Liberation Army (PLA), foreign affairs, Taiwan and Hong Kong. Zhu had the run of the economy. However, the premier had to report major decisions to Jiang, who still retained his leadership of the party's Leading Group on Finance and Economics (see Chapter 2). After his confirmation as premier, Zhu was made one of two vice-chiefs of the party's Leading Group on Foreign Affairs headed by Jiang. This meant Zhu would have some say in diplomacy as well.[4]

The size of Zhu's power base vis-a-vis that of Jiang was demonstrated in the composition of Zhu's 38-member cabinet. While the premier was able to put a number of his protégés in the economic and financial departments (see following section), Jiang's cronies and associates in the State Council out-numbered Zhu's men by a comfortable margin.

Close to 20 ministers were either card-carrying members of Jiang's Shanghai Faction or were inclined towards Jiang. Twelve were born in the Shanghai and Jiangsu area. Among the more important of the president's men and women in Zhu's cabinet were Vice-Premiers Wu Bangguo and Wen Jiabao; Defence Minister General Chi Haotian; Foreign Minister Tang Jiaxuan; Minister at the Development Planning Commission Zeng Peiyan; Education Minister Chen Zhili; Construction Minister Yu Zhengsheng; State Security Minister Xu Yongyue; Minister of Information Industry Wu Jichuan; Railway Minister Fu Zhihuan; Procurator-General Han Zhubin; and Health Minister Zhang Wenkang.[5]

Jiang's prowess was also attested to by the fact that middle-of-the-road cadres or those acceptable to all factions such as Vice-Premiers Li Lanqing and Qian Qichen were seen as closer to Jiang than Zhu. Moreover, the premier's ability to promote his protégés was hampered by his lack of con-trol over the party's Organisation Department, which was under Jiang's thumb. Under long-standing rules, the premier could have a near-decisive influence in the appointment of cadres up to the vice-ministerial level. Full ministers had to be decided by the Politburo Standing Committee and formally seconded by the Organisation Department.

Zhu's New-look State Council

Superficially, Zhu's State Council was hardly a radical makeover from that of Li Peng. Four cabinet members were trained in the Eastern bloc in the 1950s. Li's main protégé and adviser, Luo Gan, retained the key position of state councillor. Overall, the cabinet carried a large number of holdovers from the *ancien regime*: there were six members who were serving their second terms; four who shifted portfolios and 13 promoted from vice-ministerial positions.[6]

From another perspective, however, change was in the offing. The av-erage age of the cabinet was 59.7, or four years younger than the previous one. Zhu was able to fill many critical economic portfolios with his men. The premier's influence was more evident at the level of vice-ministers and department heads. For the first time, computer-literate, numbers-crunching cadres who spoke good English would be running the central government. The first thing that Zhu and many of his colleagues did every morning was to peruse the charts provided by on-line financial services and to surf the Net for comments in the world's leading newspapers.[7]

In the cabinet, Zhu had control over most financial and macro-economic units. State Councillor Wang Zhongyu, concurrently State Council Secretary-General, was Zhu's overall trouble-shooter. And Dai Xianglong, the veteran Governor of the People's Bank of China (PBoC), was Zhu's point man for macro-level adjustments and controls. Other Zhu affiliates included the new Minister of Finance Xiang Huaicheng and the new taxation chief, Jin Renqing. Yet Dai's failure to win the concurrent appointment of state councillor showed Zhu had suffered resistance in pushing his protégés.[8]

The premier's team was strengthened by the first-time-ever induction of entrepreneurs. Sheng Huaren, a veteran chief of the China Petrochemical Corporation, headed the new super-ministry, the State Economic and Trade Commission. Another oil executive Zhou Yongkang was made Minister of Land and Natural Resources. Sheng had won Zhu's praise for building up a hugely successful conglomerate that was a model for the reform of state-owned enterprises (SOEs). Yet, analysts said, Sheng's patrons also included Li Lanqing and Wu Yi. Moreover, the oil executive probably had links with the Jiang Faction, particularly Jiang protégé and alternate Polit-buro member Zeng Qinghong, who worked in the petroleum field in the early 1980s.[9] A former model worker and cadre at the Daqing Oilfield, Zhou had links with both Zhu and former premier Li.

A more telling sign of Zhu's expanding clout was his elevation of a host of young turks to vice-ministerial positions. They included long-time asso-ciates and personal secretaries who worked under him at the now-defunct State Economic Commission and in Shanghai. For example, Lou Jiwei was promoted to Executive Vice-Minister of the Finance Ministry, Li Jian'ge, vice-head of the new Office for the Reform of the Economic Structure, and Guo Shuqing, Vice-Governor of Guizhou. These high-fliers were joined by rising stars in the regions. The latter included Wang Qishan, tipped to one day take over from Lu Ruihua as Governor of Guangdong; and Zhu Xiaohua, whose Everbright Holdings was fast becoming the premier "red-chip" concern in Hong Kong.[10]

The guru of "efficient planning", who still kept the title of dean of the Management School of Qinghua University, was determined to bring the spirit of "scientific problem-solving" to the new administration. Analysts said Zhu was trying to groom a generation of Qinghua graduates into like-minded technocrats. His association with the university remained deep despite the fact that he ceased taking doctoral students as of 1992.[11]

Zhu Rongji's Statecraft
Is Zhu a free-marketeer?

Almost immediately after the initial euphoria over Zhu's elevation, doubts began to surface about the qualities of the new premier. The big question for Chinese and foreign observers alike: was Zhu already past his prime? Put another way, was the economic tsar out of sync with the *zeitgeist*? Biological age was not an issue. Most of Deng's reforms were thrashed out when the patriarch was in his 80s. The concern was whether a cadre whose career was chiefly influenced by 1950s-vintage Soviet economics could lead a nation into the 21st century.

It was an open secret in Beijing that Zhu was often a reluctant fellow-traveller with respect to market reforms, including those endorsed at the 15th Party Congress such as the conversion of SOEs into *gufenhua* ("shareholding") companies. Many of the new-fangled ideas for reform, including *zhuada fangxiao*, were the brainchild of Wu Bangguo. In fact, Zhu did not even see a pressing need to tackle the ownership issue. As a senior Chinese Academy of Social Sciences economist put it: "Zhu does not think there is anything particularly wrong with the existing structure. He has been telling managers that the problem is more themselves — sloth, inefficiency, and corruption — than the system." Until the spring of 1997, Zhu had cited bankruptcies and mergers as tools to streamline SOE operations without tampering with ownership. He considered *gufenhua* unnecessarily destabilising.[12]

Zhu's reservations about stocks and shares was responsible for one of the major policy changes in the Jiang administration: while *gufenhua* was cited as a near-panacea for SOEs at the 15th Party Congress, the idea was practically shelved by early 1998. Zhu again poured cold water on the experiment in the weeks before he became premier.

While leftists, or remnant Maoists, decried stocks and shares as undermining the purity of socialism, Zhu's worry was pragmatic: that the shareholding system would undercut the central bureaucracy's control over industry and commerce. For if the *gufenhua* experiment ran its course, shareholders and board directors, not technocratic cadres, would be the arbiters of SOEs. In his speech to Liaoning officials two months before the 15th congress, Zhu listed three ways to turn around SOEs. Unsurprisingly, the first method was that Beijing must "make the right selection of factory directors and managers". The second consisted of non-radical changes such as mergers and bankruptcies. *Gufenhua* was mentioned not as a means to overhaul the ownership system but a way for SOEs to "directly raise funds in society", his third recommendation.[13]

In internal talks in 1997, Zhu cited a number of reasons for not taking the *gufenhua* alternative. Firstly, companies that had gone joint-stock had hardly become more efficient. Often, while cadre-mandarins from the *ancien regime* had donned new hats such as chairman of the board or managing director, they operated the new companies much the same as before. Particularly in poor areas, the shareholding format was often used to milk workers of their savings. Zhu and fellow neo-conservatives were worried that owing to lack of legislation, particularly concerning corruption and money laundering, *gufenhua* would allow the new bosses to engage in questionable practices, including reckless raising of funds.[14]

Efforts by the Great Rectifier to regulate the stock markets had fed the criticism that in China, it was neither a bull nor a bear — but a pig market. ("Zhu" and "pig" sound the same in *putonghua* Chinese.) This was despite the fact that Zhu was often forced to intervene in the market due to circumstances beyond his control. Take, for example, executive measures he took to douse the bourses in mid-December 1996, as a result of which millions of *gumin* were burnt. Zhu was blamed for failing to arrest the speculatory spiral — and for the fact that hundreds of well-connected brokers managed to sell at top prices before the announcement of Beijing's cooling-off measures.[15]

At least in the first half of his five-year term, Zhu was expected to balance market reforms with time-honoured macro-economic controls and adjustments. Particularly after the onset of the Asian currency crisis, the accent of the leadership was stability. After all, Zhu and practically all the vice-premiers and state councillors — Li Lanqing, Wu Bangguo, Qian Qichen and Wu Yi — were old-timers whose cardinal principles were gradualism and the Golden Mean. Real changes in the State Council could only come when some of Zhu's young turks assumed positions of state councillors or above.

Long-time Zhu watchers liked to point out that while he was classified a "rightist" in the 1950s for showing admiration for experiments in Hungary and Yugoslovia, the premier was — by inclination, education and experience — not opposed to planning *per se*. His only quarrel was with bad planning: Zhu left academic life and started working in the State Council in the early 1980s with a messianic zeal to bring about "efficient planning", which Western economists think is a contradiction in terms. The economic tsar was not immune to the siren song of Adam Smith. Yet compared with cadres ranging from Deng Xiaoping to Zhao Ziyang, he was obsessed with the imperative of using the state's all-too-visible hand to guide market forces.[16]

Cracks in Zhu's armour

While Zhu's ascent had caught world attention, it was also clear that his honeymoon might be short-lived. Even setting aside for the moment the huge challenges on the economic front, chinks in the armour of the economic tsar were evident to all. There was evidence aplenty to show that in style and substance, the premier was very much a politician of his generation, that is, cadres whose worldviews and methodologies were shaped in the 1950s.

Take the touchstone popularised by the patriarch: "seek truth from facts", meaning don't embellish reality. During his trip to London and Paris in late March and early April, 1998, the premier impressed Western media by not using prepared texts when making addresses and by allotting ample time for press queries. On numerous occasions, Zhu said: "I never tell lies or use empty words." While highlighting China's "excellent" investment climate in Paris, he asked Western businessmen to visit the country to find out the truth and "make their own decisions".[17]

Yet Zhu seemed to have made a *faux pas* or two when sensitive issues were involved. While attending a breakfast meeting in Paris, he was taken aback by a demonstration by French reporters who wanted Beijing to release dissident journalist Gao Yu. When asked by a Hong Kong TV reporter what he felt about this, Zhu shot back: "I saw nothing." Later, that reporter was soundly scolded by one of Zhu's aides, who threatened to "cut off all future cooperation" with the journalist.[18]

Earlier, during a banquet with leading British executives in London, Zhu won numerous fans by saying he had followed the advice of former premier Edward Heath: "Tell the world, tell the press." Yet some of the premier's remarks that day seemed to have flunked Deng's "seek truth from facts" standard. When asked about the plight of the unemployed, Zhu claimed the situation was under control. "We have confidence they [the jobless] will not lead to social unrest," he said. The economic tsar also raised eyebrows when he asserted that the country's bad debts only amounted to six per cent of total loans. These were seen as efforts at spin-doctoring the truth.[19]

According to Zhu watchers, apart from his somewhat idiosyncratic view of the truth, the premier shared with leaders of his generation a preference for a "neo-authoritarian" approach to governance: using executive fiats to accomplish goals, including stifling the voices of dissent. A Western diplomat said that as soon as the leadership decided in late 1997 not to devalue the yuan, Zhu asked the media to stop running "discussions of the pros and cons of the issue" (see following section). According to a new book on Zhu by Chinese economist Xiao Zhengqin, the economic tsar also sought to quash opposition to his now-famous "austerity programme" of 1993–1996. Xiao hinted that Zhu was furious about the views raised by liberal social scientists that he had "gone back on the old road" of the command economy. The result, he wrote, was an internal document saying "the news media should stop reflecting views that do not match those of the central authorities".[20]

Zhu specialists highlighted intriguing similarities between the premier and his equally famous Hunan native, Chairman Mao. Both had fiery tempers and a belief in the invincibility of the human spirit. In spite of his avowed commitment to strengthening legal systems and institutions, Zhu often showed a soft spot for "rule of personality". Author Xiao disclosed that on a trip to Heilongjiang in 1994, the then vice-premier became involved in a heated argument with party boss Sun Weiben — and decided to fire him on the spot. "This was the first time that a Chinese vice-premier fired a provincial party secretary," Xiao wrote. After all, Sun did not actually report to Zhu. And even if he had performed poorly in his job, he should have been cashiered by the party General Secretary or the Organisation Department.[21]

On policies ranging from reforming SOEs to fighting graft, Zhu put the emphasis on cultivating the "superior virtues" of an elite corps of manager-cadres.[22] This seemed to run counter to most modern theories of public administration, which cautioned against over-reliance on Lei Feng-like officials making saintly decisions. For partisans of modernisation, democratic institutions and market forces were more important than the perspicacious edicts of a helmsman-like figure, even if he happened to be Great Rectifier Zhu.

Zhu's advisers and disciples

In spite of his reputation for being headstrong and intolerant of dissent, Zhu could sometimes display flexibility — and an ability to move with the times. One of his important assets was a group of advisers many of whom were unabashed free-marketeers. Zhu often leaned on economists and technocrats in their 40s who had made a go of market forces. Most had won their spurs in State Council units over which Zhu had direct responsibility: the People's Bank of China, the Finance Ministry, and state watchdogs for securities. These moderate cadres and academics were led by master economist Wu Jinglian. In 1994, the Fudan University-trained academic almost single-handedly persuaded Zhu to throw caution to the wind and merge the country's two-tier foreign exchange regimes at a stroke.[23]

Many of Wu's ideas revolved around the goal of "small government, big society". To the extent that the 68-year-old professor had Zhu's ear, many of his recommendations could be implemented during the latter's term of office. In a wide-ranging interview with this author in May 1998, Professor Wu indicated in no uncertain terms that the state must beat a retreat before SOEs could be turned around. "The key is *chongzu* ['reorganising'] the ownership and management of enterprises," he said. "There are more than 300,000 SOEs in China. Without regrouping and restructuring their ownership and assets, it is difficult to overhaul them one by one."[24]

Wu never used the word privatisation, still considered taboo in official circles. And he toed Zhu's line that it was imperative that Beijing retain overall control over 500-odd "strategic" SOEs. Yet the thrust of his argument was the state must stage a wholesale retreat from most areas of the economy, so that all sectors, including privately and foreign owned enterprises, could "compete on level ground and jointly develop". As an example for retooling large-scale SOEs, Wu said some could be converted into "shareholding companies with multiple layers of ownership". Under this scheme, their stocks could be held by the state, other SOEs, non-state concerns, collectives, individuals and foreign firms.[25]

Wu was among a host of liberal economists who thought that *fangxiao* ("rendering the medium- and small-sized enterprises alive") could be more important than *zhuada* ("taking a firm grip on major SOEs"). He said that about 60 per cent of the tens of thousands of SOEs that had been given the *fangxiao* treatment were performing well in the marketplace. Apart from the efficiency argument, the influential Zhu adviser believed that the fast-paced development of medium and small firms in the non-state sector would solve major social problems including unemployment and the polarisation of income. He was at the forefront of the crusade to ensure that private firms could compete on a level playing field with huge SOEs.[26]

At least in the eyes of Western economists, however, Wu also had his "limitations". Like Zhu, he believed in the necessity of a high degree of centralisation of economic decision-making powers. Wu was insistent that new-fangled economic vehicles such as the stock market should develop at a cautious pace. The professor admitted that while his nickname was "Market Wu", he had been criticised by younger colleagues for being a "closet conservative". "I hear alarm bells when the stock market is lurching towards a speculative binge," he said. "I get worried when the price-earning ratio of a stock has hit 40 and is still going up. I don't agree with officials and economists who encourage jobless people to go into the stock market."[27]

THE ASIAN FINANCIAL CRISIS AND CHINA

"Crisis? What Crisis?"

The CCP administration was ill-prepared for the currency and economic crisis that gripped Southeast Asia, South Korea and Japan beginning in the second half of 1997. Jiang and company were from May to October of that year preoccupied with the Hong Kong transition, the 15th Party Congress and the president's visit to the US. The leadership did not at first see the relevance of the "Asian flu" to the Middle Kingdom.

Mainland papers were slow to report and analyse the drastic turn of events. When they eventually came out with commentaries in November and December, these were meant to reassure the public and the world community that China would be "exempt" from the crisis. Senior officials played up the "strong fundamentals" of the Chinese economy: foreign exchange reserves in excess of US$140 billion; a US$40 billion trade surplus; an 8.8 per cent growth rate in 1997; and foreign debt amounting to just 10 per cent of GDP.[28]

However, a major factor behind China's apparent immunity to the shocks was its relative lack of openness: the yuan was not fully convertible and the capital markets were close to foreign brokers and speculators. There were remarkable similarities between the Chinese and Asian economies. The most obvious instance was the intimate relationship between political power and business — and the lack of transparent legislation and supervisory mechanisms regarding commercial transactions. Common features abounded between the Chinese and, say South Korean, banking systems.[29]

Chinese banks fit Asia specialist Paul Krugman's description of Asian financial institutions, which "benefited from implicit government guarantees" and other politically based advantages. The banks and finance companies were encouraged to make risky and anti-market decisions to achieve what the MIT economist called "Pangloss values". Western estimates of bad loans sustained by Chinese banks ranged from 25 per cent to 35 per cent of their total credit portfolio, which was close to South Korean standards (see following section).[30]

Moreover, perhaps worse than Thailand and South Korea, China suffered from massive — and untraceable — capital flight. One internal report claimed that an amount equivalent to nearly 40 per cent of total foreign investments in the country had left China via the back door. Somewhat like Indonesia, the "princelings", or offspring of party elders, maintained huge holdings overseas under front companies.[31]

It was no secret that much of China's economic strategy was patterned after the so-called East Asiatic Model: to synthesise Western high technology and business norms on the one hand, and Confucianist, authoritarian political culture on the other. Since the mid-1980s, economic development had followed the examples of countries including Singapore, Malaysia, Japan and, in particular, South Korea. In 1996 and 1997, the leadership sent numerous delegations to these four countries to study areas including industrial policy, fighting corruption, housing and social welfare. One of the biggest economic reform initiatives of 1997 — merging SOEs and turning them into conglomerates — was based on the *chaebols* of South Korea.[32]

By mid-1998, Beijing was still patting itself on the back that it had emerged from the turmoil unscathed. Leaders stressed their spirit of "self-sacrifice" in not devaluing the yuan — as well as their considerable economic aid to affected countries such as Indonesia. Yet the impact on China was substantial. Both exports and foreign investment were expected to suffer. For example, while exports in 1997 grew by 20.9 per cent over 1996, the figure for 1998 could dip below 10 per cent. Direct foreign investment, which was US$45 billion in 1997, was expected to slip to less than US$30 billion in 1998. After all, some 40 per cent of China's exports in 1997 went to countries hit by the "Asian flu"; these countries and regions also contributed 80 per cent of investments into China. Black market activities were rampant — to the extent that some experts believed the yuan had already devalued by 10 per cent in non-official trading.[33]

Beijing's nervousness was shown by the fact that it had imposed a virtual news blackout on the growing pro-devaluation lobby. It comprised elements that had suffered worst in the turmoil. They included coastal provinces with a heavy dependence on foreign trade such as Guangdong and Fujian. About 70 per cent of firms engaged in foreign trade were losing money. Economists and politicians who favoured devaluation — including the well-known leader of one of the eight "democratic parties" — were unable to air their views in the media.[34]

The "Asian Flu" and the Clash of Civilisations

The Asian financial crisis had an impact on China that went much further than economic performance. Beijing's entire approach to modernisation was being challenged. The currency and banking woes highlighted what Harvard political science guru Samuel Huntington called the clash of civilisations: Western, principally American, values versus the East-Asiatic model of neo-authoritarianism in government, culture and economic policy.[35]

At least for Asia's critics, the "Asian bug" was symptomatic of the bankruptcy of a set of values championed — or at least condoned — by a host of "neo-authoritarian" Asian chieftains. They included "Confucianist" authoritarianism, "crony capitalism" and, in general, lack of transparency if not the absence of the rule of law in government and business. On a deeper level, these ills could be attributed to a culture and mind-set which despised democracy and institutions of checks and balances — and which suppressed the initiatives and rights of the individual. While President Jiang was much less vociferous in advocating "Asian values" than Malaysian Premier Dr Mahathir Mohamad, his general philosophy was in line with those of Asian leaders (see Chapter 2).[36]

Most galling to the Jiang leadership were arguments that it was deep-seated political imperfections such as the dearth of "Western-style democracy" that did Asia in. As the former South Korean ambassador to the US, Hyun Hong Choo, put it: "This financial crisis told us that the root cause of our problems had something to do with the political system. People in the street had had a revelation that their belief in Asian values is not well-founded." According to Hong Kong democratic legislator Martin Lee, the correlation between democracy and financial soundness was obvious.

"The countries that have weathered the Asian financial storm best are democracies — Taiwan, the Philippines and Japan," he wrote in the *New York Times*. "Those nations that are in the process of recovering, including South Korea and Thailand, have done so only after jettisoning their corrupt former regimes through a democratic process."[37]

The multiple currency fiascos coincided with — and to some extent galvanised — "people power-style" agitation in countries including South Korea and Indonesia. The election of long-time dissident Kim Dae-jung as South Korean president in December 1997 — and the demise of the Suharto regime in Indonesia in May 1998 — were watched closely by China's urban intellectuals. Few in China would as yet buy the argument of overseas dissidents such as Wei Jingsheng that after the triumph of movements led by Corazon Aquino in the Philippines, Vaclav Havel in the Czech Republic and Kim Dae-jung in South Korea, it would "soon be China's turn".[38]

Yet expectations were high in the cities that the Jiang administration would grasp the nettle and stop dragging its feet on reform. It was significant that fearful of a "revolution of rising expectations", the authorities told the media to play down reports of political developments in countries hard hit by the turmoil, in particular the downfall of the Suharto regime. The official Xinhua commentary on Suharto's fall focused on "social problems" such as polarisation of income but soft-pedalled the tyrant's symptoms of "oriental despotism" such as cronyism and refusal to share power. Yet sizeable numbers of urban intellectuals were keeping themselves abreast of the Indonesian situation through the Internet and other means. As dissident Qin Yongmin said, the Indonesian example showed "the falseness of the idea that Asian people are happy under a dictatorship that allows economic but not political growth".[39]

There were signs that the more moderate members of the think tanks of Jiang and Zhu were urging the leadership to take real steps to fine-tune the political structure. In a widely-noted article on the Asian crisis and China, economists Wu Jinglian and Wei Jianing said much had to do with the absence of scientific decision-making — perhaps the two official academics' euphemism for democratic politics. They drew attention to the fact that a number of countries that had succumbed to the Asian bug had practised a mixture of "authoritarian politics plus market economics". They also noted China might be worse off than its Asian counterparts in the quality of its "decision-making systems" and "systems underpinning decision-making" such as think tanks and consultative organs.[40]

ZHU RONGJI'S MASTER PLANS

It was typical of Jiang Zemin's statecraft that he left the responsibility for tackling the Asian crisis to Zhu Rongji. And devising ways to enable China to emerge unscathed from the "Asian flu" would be the economic tsar's first major challenge as premier.

From November 1997 to January 1998, Zhu held marathon meetings to craft counter-strategies, some of which were presented to the public soon after his confirmation as premier in March. The steps taken were a mixture of specific plans to boost the nation's "immunity" from the Asian bug and rectification measures that Zhu had implemented since he became vice-premier in 1991. These moves squared with his overall philosophy of balancing the needs of market forces and recentralisation.

"Small Government, Large Society"

Zhu's much-hyped game plan to downsize the central government apparatus was not originally conceived with the Asian financial meltdown in mind. Yet the premier's team realised that the goal of "small government, large society" was essential to enable China to avoid the mistakes that plunged its neighbours into financial crisis.

The small government ideal was first raised by Zhao Ziyang and tried out to some extent on Hainan Island.[41] What analysts called Beijing's "seventh revolution" also involved trimming the bureaucracy and separating business from government. Many Zhu advisers realised that much of the malaise of companies in countries ranging from Japan and South Korea to Indonesia had to do with excessive — and wrongheaded — government interference. According to government researchers, 30 Chinese were in 1997 supporting one cadre or civil servant. The ratio in the Qing Dynasty was 911 to one, the Tang Dynasty, 3,927 to one and the Han Dynasty, 7,945 to one. At his NPC press conference Zhu complained that funds for technology and education had been "eaten up" by civil servants. Food bills alone for government employees in 1997 came to a mind-boggling 360 billion yuan.[42]

Zhu decided to cut the Gordian knot. In one masterstroke at the Ninth NPC, 11 ministries were abolished. Four million civil servants were due to be laid off in less than three years. Several ministries and departments dealing with economic affairs and production — including the coal industry, metallurgy, machine-building, forestry, and chemical and petroleum industries — were downgraded into bureaux and subsumed under the "super-ministry", the State Economic and Trade Commission (SETC). The SETC would eventually become somewhat like Japan's Ministry of International Trade and Industry, an organ that both Jiang and Zhu admired for its ability to balance state control with market forces.[43]

The SETC would still be engaged in "macro-economic adjustments" of the economy — but executive fiats would be avoided. According to minister Sheng Huaren, the industrial and commercial bureaux under its umbrella would cease to be the proverbial "mother-in-law" units. "These bureaux will no longer engage in the direct management of enterprises," said Sheng after the NPC. "They will be drafting rules and regulations as well as formulating [long-term] strategies for different product lines."[44]

The State Council would shed many of its "direct subsidiary companies" such as the mammoth CITIC Corporation and Everbright Corporation. From March onwards, these high-profile behemoths would, at least in theory, be financially self-sufficient entities. There were early signs the market was taking Zhu's attempt to separate government and business seriously. The prices of several red-chip companies in Hong Kong, one of whose selling points was "special links with the PRC government" fell after announcement of the news.[45]

Equally significant, first steps were taken to slash the structure of units under the party Central Committee such as those handling organisation, propaganda and ideology. Personnel in various levels of party schools would be curtailed. The goal was that one-third of party apparatchiks would be lopped off. Some moderate cadres hoped this would eventually contribute to the separation of party and government.[46]

Retooling State-owned Enterprises

At his now-famous "inauguration" press conference at the NPC on March 19, 1998, Zhu again vowed to "turn around" loss-making SOEs in three years. "We are fully able to ensure that the majority of loss-making enterprises would be relieved of their difficulties in three years," Zhu said. He added that he was referring to the 10 per cent or so of the 500 "major" enterprises that Beijing was nurturing. However, the premier gave no new clue on how to render them productive or competitive. During a trip to the northeast in late March, he merely reiterated the time-tested method of "reforming, regrouping and restructuring [the SOEs] and strengthening their management".[47]

It was a time for soul-searching. At least in the short term, Beijing would play down the *gufenhua* or shareholding experiment that was billed as the panacea for SOEs at the 15th congress (see previous section). Another constraint for radical surgery was worsening unemployment — and rising labour unrest. Zhu was forced to admit in March 1998 that the success of SOE reform hinged on how well the issue of joblessness could be tackled.[48]

The biggest rethink in SOE strategy concerned the so-called East Asiatic, particularly South Korean, model for forming conglomerates. After all, Beijing was still following the principle of *zhuada fangxiao* ("taking a firm grip on the major ones and letting the minor ones go free") strategy. Many of the 500 to 800 SOEs accorded the *zhuada* treatment would be turned into *chaebol*-style enterprise groupings.[49]

According to sources close to Zhu's inner circles, the then vice-premier was shocked by the bursting of the South Korean bubble in late 1997. In December that year, he told senior aides in internal sessions they must thoroughly reassess the Korean experience. "Zhu and his aides are reappraising strategies such as pumping extra resources into 800 or more SOEs with a view to nurturing them into Chinese Samsungs or Hyundais," a source said. "Also to be re-examined are plans to convert a number of industrial ministries and departments into state corporations." Throughout 1998, Zhu dispatched a number of young aides on fact-finding missions to Seoul and other Asian capitals.[50]

Individual cadres and think tanks also cast doubt on South Korean-style industrial policy such as propagating government-aided *jituangongsi* ("conglomerates"). Senior economist Wu Jinglian warned that under the *zhuada* goal, many bureaucrats were forming conglomerates via executive fiats and not market mechanisms. "There have been cases of mismatches among the components of conglomerates — and most conglomerates borne out of government directives have not done well," he said. Likewise, State Development Planning Commission economist Yin Wenquan decried the following faults in *jituangongsi* that were cobbled together thanks to executive fiats: "poor internal management; lack of a rational relationship between headquarters and the units; and failure to achieve economy of scale".[51]

In a commentary in early 1998, the *People's Daily* questioned the wisdom of excessive speed in forming *jituangongsi*. Rushed mergers were "likely to drag core and good enterprises into collapse," it said. "Some enterprise groupings and government departments have asked certain *jituangongsi* to enter into the ranks of the world's top 500 companies at the turn of the century. We are doubtful about the feasibility of this." The newspaper urged cadres to exercise caution in "arranging marriages between firms or to turn an entire industry into a mega-company". "South Korean conglomerates have already set a [bad] precedent," the party mouthpiece said.[52]

A New Deal for the Private Sector

While privatisation remained in theory a forbidden zone, there was a growing consensus that the way to building a healthy market economy was expanding the non-state sector. According to Beijing-based economics professor Liu Wei, "economic growth in China is being pushed along mainly by the non-state sector". The so-called totally people's-owned sector only accounted for 30 per cent of industrial production in 1997. Latest statistics showed that private enterprises had the highest productivity. For every yuan of remuneration to staff, private firms were in 1996 able to create added value worth 5.97 yuan. The comparable figure for joint ventures was 5.72 yuan and for SOEs, only 3.35 yuan. And as liberal economist Cao Siyuan said in early 1998, while mainstream cadres still talked about "restoring the former glory of the SOEs", this could be a hopeless task. Cao favoured a more aggressive privatisation policy to ensure China did not succumb to a financial crisis.[53]

There were signs in early 1998 that some changes were finally taking place. A number of NPC and CPPCC members made proposals to revise the state constitution to legitimise both private companies and private property. Guangzhou promulgated China's first-ever body of legislation to protect the rights of non-state entrepreneurs.[54]

More importantly, under the prompting of liberals such as Wu Jinglian and Li Yining, the central government decided to ask the banks to treat private enterprises on more or less the same footing as SOEs. "There is a growing awareness that non-state enterprises, particularly the medium and small ones, are the most efficient generator of growth and jobs," said Professor Wu. In an April 1998 dispatch, the NCNA quoted People's Bank of China (PBoC) cadres as saying they would "support the development of medium and small enterprises through credit policy". The official news agency also said Beijing encouraged private firms and village and township enterprises to take over SOEs.[55]

By mid-1998, however, private enterprises still suffered considerable "discrimination". One glaring example was the possibility of being listed on the Shenzhen or Shanghai bourses. The authorities largely tended to give the green light to "key" SOEs. At the end of 1997, barely three per cent of the 745 listed companies were non-state owned. In March 1998, the All-China Federation of Industry and Commerce drafted a petition calling on the authorities to give more opportunity to private firms. Liu Yonghao, the owner of one of the successful listed private enterprises, the Hope Group, said investors preferred efficient non-state companies to run-of-the-mill SOEs.[56]

New Emphasis on Science and Technology

Building on Jiang's slogan, first coined in 1995, of "reviving the nation through science and technology" (see Chapter 2), Zhu raised the battle-cry of "catching up with the Americans by 2020". The premier said the task had new urgency given the Asian financial troubles. "Reviving the country through science and education is the most important task of this adminis-tration," he said soon after becoming premier.[57]

In an early 1998 internal meeting, Zhu cited the hi-tech achievement of the US as a major reason for the "world dominance of the US economy". "If the hi-tech content of a country's economy is up to an advanced level, the question of the bubble economy does not exist," he said. Zhu told his subordinates that the best way to avoid a bubble economy was to "raise the technological content of our economy and our products". He also wanted quicker industrial application of scientific research.[58]

Zhu and his advisers thrashed out a three-pronged game plan to go hi-tech. The first aim was the so-called "policy of north-to-south migration": well-established technology bases in northern China — in-cluding Beijing, Tianjin, Dalian and Shanghai — would move some of their facilities to commercially-vibrant areas such as Guangdong. Secondly, planning must give way to the marketplace in areas including the produc-tion and commercialisation of technological breakthroughs. Thirdly, the PLA should speed up the process of transferring know-how to civilian factories.[59]

The media was in the first half of 1998 full of success stories of science and technology in cutting-edge areas ranging from artificial intelligence to genetic engineering. Aeronautical departments unveiled plans to put a

Chinese in space in the "coming two years or so". The *Seventh Science and Technology White Paper,* published in April of that year, committed the nation to investing unprecedented funds and resources in hi-tech areas. Cadres of all levels were given semi-quotas for setting up new colleges, science laboratories and post-doctoral stations in industry.[60]

The new Minister of Science and Technology, Zhu Lilan, sought to combine fast-paced scientific development with the open-door policy. Beijing began lobbying foreign universities and research institutes to set up joint laboratories in China in areas ranging from the information superhighway to "21st century medicine". By mid-1998, European and American institutes, including Bell Lab, had agreed to set up branches in cities such as Shanghai. Both Intel and Microsoft also increased investments in their China plants.[61]

Fresh Impetus for Banking Reforms

With the bitter lesson of South Korea and Japan in mind, Zhu took action to overhaul the financial system beginning in December 1997. The central theme was to boost the authority of the PBoC as a supervisory organ — and to "marketise" the commercial banks. As the communique from a national banking conference pointed out: "Banks must be run like real banks. We must strengthen the financial supervisory powers of the PBoC. We must speed up the commercialisation of state commercial banks." Zhu later added: "We must not repeat the same mistake as Seoul."[62]

A key recommendation was to abolish the credit-related authority of regional administrations. Zhu aides indicated that the economic tsar had, as early as 1993, wanted to transform the unwieldy PBoC system — which had 200,000 employees in more than 2,000 branches nationwide — by using the model of the American Federal Reserve system. However, it was not until early 1998 that definite steps were taken. From then onwards, power over the allocation of state credit would only be vested with the headquarters of the PBoC and 10 to 15 regional branches to be set up in 1998. For example, a south China branch would cover the provinces of Guangdong, Guangxi, Jiangxi and Hainan (see also Chapter 5).[63]

Other "Western" norms would be observed. International standards would be adopted in making loans and monitoring bad debt. PBoC Governor Dai Xianglong said the Western model of loan classification would be adopted. New PBoC Vice-Governor Liu Mingkang noted that monetary tools such as interest rates would be used to determine money supply. Formerly, money supply was predicated upon the size of largely politically-motivated loans. More state commercial banks would be turned into autonomous, self-sufficient business units. Regional commercial banks would eventually be converted into shareholding units with stocks to be held by local governments, enterprises and citizens.[64]

A major factor behind the "bubble economy" in 1993 was banks becoming involved in speculative activities in the property and stock markets. Zhu was determined to delink banks and their subsidiaries and associate companies that were business enterprises. The latter included trust companies, stock brokerages, real estate and insurance companies. The State Council formally announced in May 1998 that banks would be severed from their commercial subsidiaries or adjuncts.[65]

Anecdotal and other evidence suggested that some improvements had been made by mid-1998. For example, more banks were using "Western" methods of risk assessment in evaluating loan applications. The official media reported that regional cadres including Guangdong officials, were largely willing to heed central demands that they surrender loan-making powers. However, Western experts still cast doubt on what counted most: transparency.

A case in point was the size of the bad debts — estimated at between two to three trillion yuan — which was never disclosed by the authorities. Senior officials including Zhu and Dai insisted that while non-performing loans of all types amounted to around 20 per cent of all loans, only six to eight per cent or so of the total credit portfolio was irrecoverable. Western estimates, including those by international rating agencies, said non-performing loans amounted to 25 per cent to 35 per cent of all loans and that at least 20 per cent of the entire credit exposure could be written off as irrecoverable.[66]

AN ASSESSMENT OF ZHU'S STRATEGY

Liberal economist Xiao Geng spoke for many when he called on the administration to speed up reforms in the wake of the Asian crisis. "Asian countries which have suffered most in the recent crisis will, under the pressure of the US, undergo drastic structural reform of their economic systems in the coming few years," he said in early 1998. "When such reforms are completed in three to five years, they will become very vibrant and may pose a serious threat to China." Xiao, who sometimes advised the central government, urged Beijing not only to reform the financial system but also to "strengthen legal services and cut corruption by increasing political transparency".[67]

While Zhu was praised by observers inside and outside of China for making timely moves to ensure that the country did not succumb to the "Asian flu", there were doubts as to whether the actions went far enough. The economic tsar's fire-fighting efforts were frequently bogged down by age-old problems in the areas of unemployment, corruption and, in particular, the party's quasi-feudalistic political set-up.

Refusal to Tackle the Fundamentals

Doubts galore were raised as to whether the Jiang-Zhu economic team would bite the bullet on a host of issues connected with the bottom line of Communist Party suzerainty. Take the reform of financial institutions. The restructuring of the PBoC system — including taking away the loan-making authority of regional cadres — would at best minimise misguidance from local officials. Yet insufficient efforts were made to lower the risk of top-level aberrations in credit and other banking policies. After all, how "scientific" were decisions made by the PBoC headquarters — and the party's Leading Group on Finance and Economics, to which it reported?[68]

The neo-conservative leadership continued to spurn demands from radical reformers for the creation of an "independent" central bank along Western lines. Suggestions that the NPC should have supervisory powers over banking continued to be suppressed (also see Chapter 3). As an economic cadre put it: "Like the People's Liberation Army, the banking apparatus would remain a preserve of the party and subject only to its control."[69]

By mid-1998, there was scant evidence that Beijing would fine-tune its policy of pumping prime resources into 800 to 1,000 key enterprises. As party insiders saw it, the only argument within the leadership was which SOEs should qualify for special treatment, not the basic principle of the state nurturing "elite" enterprises and conglomerates. Up to early 1998, Zhu and then premier Li Peng were fighting over rival sets of "priority SOEs". Li's list of 1,000 observed traditional considerations such as geographic distribution and a roughly equitable division of the spoils among different power blocs. For example, each province had at least a few SOEs on the list. A large quota was vouchsafed heavyweight sectors such as iron and steel. Zhu's so-called austerity list of 800 gave more weight to sectors and product lines deemed competitive in the marketplace. At least one province had no representation. And only two steel mills — Shougang and Baogang — were selected.[70]

The *chaebol*'s demise had no impact on Beijing's policy of "taking a firm grip on big SOEs". Zhu aide Chen Qingtai, then a vice-minister at the SETC, said the Korean example would not kill China's desire to form *jituangongsi*; government regulators would "learn their lessons" and pay more attention to the efficiency factor. "Unlike South Korea, Chinese regulators will make sure new conglomerates or large-scale enterprises stick to core businesses and keep liabilities down," he indicated. Chen added that conglomerates were still the answer for China as they would help weather competition from gigantic foreign multinationals. By mid-1998, South Korean-style *jituangongsi* were being formed daily. Local administrations were still scrambling to fulfil Beijing's "quotas" on the formation of regionally based conglomerates.[71]

For many cadres, the collapse of economies and factories in Asia was proof that central authorities must never let go. The fate of *chaebols* had the ironic effect of convincing Beijing that it should tighten its grip over the 800 or so elite enterprises. Many neo-conservative cadres believed the superiority of *jituangongsi* over *chaebols* was that the former were under stricter state guidance and supervision.

According to the head of Guangdong's Economic Bureau, Mao Kaili, judicious government control accounted for the fact that the debt-to-assets ratio for the 70 Guangdong-based conglomerates was 60 per cent, against 400 per cent for most Korean counterparts. He added that because the state held the majority of the assets and shares of *jituangongsi*, they would continue to "benefit" from a higher level of macro-economic control and adjustments.[72] Yet Mao did not mention what would happen if those control and adjustments turned out to be misguided.

A Partial Retreat from Reform and the Open Door?

The Asian financial disaster fuelled a debate in the leadership on whether Beijing should be more cautious in its open-door policy. After all, one reason China was shielded from the storms was that its currency was not fully convertible and the capital markets were still ruled by state fiats.

For top economist Wu Jinglian, Beijing should not slacken its drive for globalisation. "Don't think that because of the Asian financial crisis, there are advantages to rolling back the open-door policy," he told a meeting at

Qinghua University in mid-1998. Wu said it would be bad for the entire economy if the pace for opening up the capital markets was slowed. Then vice-governor of the PBoC, Chen Yuan denied that plans to make the yuan convertible by 2000 were postponed indefinitely. "China will move step by step towards full convertibility of its currency," Chen said. "The Asian crisis makes us realise we have to exert even greater effort in preparation for full convertibility of our currency."[73]

During his trip to Britain in March, Zhu indicated that China would continue to open up selected financial markets such as insurance. However, by and large, the views of the conservatives seemed to have prevailed. Despite Chen Yuan's statement, convertibility of the yuan was rolled back indefinitely. President Jiang repeated in an interview with a Western news agency in June 1998 that no date was set for the currency's full convertibility. Moreover, Zhu gravitated towards slowing down the pace with which foreign companies should be allowed into the banking and stock-brokerage business. The premier cited the graphic example of an "unequal boxing match". "How can China, a featherweight in the world financial market, compete with the heavyweights in the West?" he reportedly asked.[74]

A broad-based faction against the open-door policy had by early 1998 coalesced to lobby for a delay in China's accession to the World Trade Organisation — or at least to insist that the country would join only if guaranteed exemptions from some requirements on tariff reductions and market access. In late 1997, anti-WTO lobbyists sent Beijing a tough petition. Signatories comprised representatives of departments and areas that stood to lose the most from an escalation of the open-door policy. They included departments and SOEs in the areas of agriculture, automobile, electronics, telecommunications and the services — as well as central and western provinces. The anti-WTO brigade claimed that the best time for joining the world trading body was the late 2000s.[75] By mid-1998, there were signs that Beijing leaders were less aggressive in negotiations with the US and other Western powers regarding WTO accession.

The Bogey of the Neo-imperialist West (Again)

Another factor that predisposed the leadership against grasping the nettle was the perception that the Asian crisis was a "Western conspiracy". For Maoists as well as neo-conservative politicians, there was an element of "the East Wind versus the West Wind": the Western world, led by the US, was taking advantage of the fiscal chaos to impose its values on the East. They claimed that after vanquishing the Soviet "evil empire" and, to some extent, Islamic fundamentalism, Washington was out to tame Asia, the last impediment to its quest for world domination.[76] That this view might have been cited as a pretext for putting off genuine reform did not mean it did not find favour with a sizeable segment of cadres and intellectuals.

This mind-set manifested itself in a *People's Daily* commentary in early 1998. The piece accused Washington of using the IMF rescue package to pry open Asian markets — and to promote structural changes in these countries to facilitate further economic globalisation and even political reform. "The US is certainly not offering a new Marshall Plan to East Asia," the article said. "By giving help it is forcing East Asia into submission, promoting the US economic and political model, and easing East Asia's threat to the American economy."[77]

Individual cadres and scholars were even convinced that the US government had colluded with "international speculators" in conjuring up the currency crisis in the first place. This was reflected in a May 1998 commentary by the semi-official Hong Kong China News Agency. It attributed the financial turmoil to the activities of fund managers — mostly in the US and Europe — which had a US$7 trillion war chest. "If a financially powerful country directly or indirectly goads international *youzi* ['floating capital'] into attacking the currency of a particular country, a financial crisis will erupt," HKCNA said. "That country can then 'peacefully' control the financial lifeline [of its prey]." There was little doubt which "power" the agency was referring to. As precaution, top leaders including Jiang and Zhu repeatedly underscored the imperative of safeguarding China's "financial security", now lifted to the same plane as territorial integrity.[78]

Intriguingly, Beijing also accused Taiwan, viewed by some cadres as a "US lackey", of fishing in Asia's troubled waters. In internal speeches in early 1998, Zhu Rongji accused Taipei of letting its currency slide so as to aggravate the Asian meltdown. The premier said Taiwan, which had strong reserves, "had no need for a depreciation". "It was acting out of political considerations," Zhu said in an internal briefing. Beijing was convinced Taipei was again using "dollar diplomacy" and a "Look South strategy" to buy diplomatic influence in Asia. A spokesman for the Foreign Ministry said of Taipei's bid to buy influence through its "rescue missions" to Asian nations: "It is obviously a political plot carried on step by step in a planned way."[79]

There was also evidence that flashes of xenophobia arising out of the Asian crisis had fanned the theories of conspiracy artists who saw a new, anti-China containment policy perpetrated by a coalition led by the US, Japan and Taiwan. From Beijing's perspective, the diplomatic aspect of the "anti-China triangle" was highlighted by the 1996 US-Japan security arrangement, which put Taiwan within the sphere of common defence interests of the two Asia-Pacific giants. As Jiang adviser Wang Daohan put it in early 1998, the US-Japan scheme was an effort to include the Taiwan Strait in the two countries' sphere of influence. "This can absolutely not be accepted by the Chinese government and the Chinese people."[80]

THE QUANDARY OF REFORM

By mid-1998, the Jiang administration was torn by opposite impulses. Despite alarm bells on the economic front, senior leaders such as Jiang and Zhu could find ample reason to stay put. The leadership had its hands full with the target of an eight per cent GDP growth rate — and containing the spillover of labour unrest. There was tremendous inertia against opting for risky or radical measures. On the other hand, Jiang was aware of the need for change now that change had taken place in countries as diverse as South Korea and Indonesia. And it would seem to be much better for the CCP leadership to initiate changes rather than have these changes forced on it as in the case of the Suharto regime.

After all, during his trip to the US in late 1997, Jiang had vowed to a world audience to transform his ancient land into a strong, forthright, and culturally proud nation fit for the 21st century. "We are conducting comprehensive reform," he said in Massachusetts in November. "We'll realise the socialisation, marketisation and modernisation of the economy. Politically we will develop socialist democracy and govern the country according to law." While in the US and Mexico, Jiang even waxed eloquent about democracy, saying that "without democracy, there will be no socialism and no socialist modernisation".[81]

A Moratorium on Political Liberalisation?

Beefing up the police apparatus

Political reform could be an unexpected casualty of the Asian turmoil as the

Jiang leadership wanted all the muscle it could muster to prevent chaos. In an early 1998 editorial, the Chinese-run Hong Kong daily, *Wen Wei Po*, attributed China's ability to withstand the Asian crisis to its "efficient socialist system". "In China, political orders are carried out relatively smoothly, and the political system is highly efficient," the paper said. "The central government has enough authority."[82]

Was *Wei Wei Po* protesting too much? As we saw above, the Beijing leadership was in fact highly aware of the country's susceptibility to the "Asian flu". The semi-official mouthpiece, however, correctly reflected the CCP's mind-set: it must continue to concentrate power to forestall a possible outbreak of financial — and political — disorder.

Throughout 1998, internal security organs such as the Ministry of State Security (MSS) beefed up operations against "economics-based infiltration" instigated by the US. At a time of across-the-board administrative streamlining, the MSS, Ministry of Public Security or police, and the People's Armed Police (PAP) were the only units to have maintained their strengths. There were even reports that police forces in large cities such as Shanghai and Beijing had been swollen by tens of thousands of recruits. In a ceremony honouring the police and the PAP, top security cadre Ren Jianxin called the former "the iron-and-steel protectors of the people" and the latter "a corps capable of waging brave struggles".[83]

The leadership realised very well that a potent police apparatus was the final guarantee that the financial system would not implode. In late 1988, when the country was hit by an unprecedented outbreak of hyperinflation and panic buying, there were runs on banks in large cities including Shanghai. The police and PAP were deployed to keep nervous account holders away from banks. While the administration seemed confident that such a crisis would not recur in 1998 or 1999, it wanted to ensure the control mechanisms were in place.

Keeping the democratic forces at bay

Heightened gestation of democracy in South Korea, Indonesia and other countries and areas made the guardians of CCP dictatorship more aware of the dangers of a Chinese-style "people power" revolution. The onset of the Asian crisis coincided with local-level elections in Taiwan, which saw the opposition Democratic Progressive Party (DPP) win by a landslide. In polls for county and municipal chiefs held in November 1997, the DPP garnered

12 seats, against eight for the KMT. The advent of a "post-Lee Teng-hui era" meant the DPP had a good chance of clinching power at presidential elections in 2000.[84]

Highly significant was a meeting of retired elders in December 1997 to discuss the political situation in Asia, in which the veterans raised the spectre of the CCP losing power if elections were held. Participants included the just-retired vice-chairmen of the Central Military Commission, Generals Liu Huaqing and Zhang Zhen. They were disturbed by the DPP's sweep of the polls. Chinese sources quoted General Liu as saying: "If popular elections were held in China, the Communist Party would win the first and second polls without difficulty. Starting with the third election, the party's grip might slip. And it is conceivable that it could lose power by the fourth election."[85]

While Maoist leader Deng Liqun was absent from the conclave, some of his anti-reformist sayings were quoted. One Deng dictum cited was that China's national security would be threatened if the "new class" of entrepreneurs were to develop further and if Western-style political reforms were introduced. Analysts said fear of losing control could short-circuit even the limited reforms that the leadership had pledged to carry out at the 15th Party Congress.[86]

Then there was the refusal of the leadership to tackle corruption, which was integral to the "Asian bug" from Jakarta to Seoul. Soon after taking over the premiership, Zhu ordered a series of arrests of dozens of mid-level managers of SOEs, including a number of fat cats based in Hong Kong. Preparations were intensified for the trial of disgraced Politburo member Chen Xitong.[87] Yet the consensus among China watchers was that these moves were aimed at pacifying citizens affected by the worsening polarisation between the have-nots and the *nouveau riche*.

Perhaps to come up with a pretext not to implement a structural solution to corruption — such as setting up an "independent" anti-graft body — leaders continued to recycle theories about "transforming the worldview of cadres". President Jiang stuck to the Maoist teaching that the country would be a much better place if only every Chinese were to seek enlightenment through thorough studies of Marxist dogma. "Once we are armed with the correct theory, the level of our thoughts will be raised, our ability will increase, and we can easily meet our challenges," Jiang said on the eve of Chinese New Year in 1998.[88] Zhu had no quarrel with this view.

The Impulse of Change
First footsteps on the stairs

However, to use a Chinese proverb denoting signs of change, there were also sounds of footsteps on the stairs. The Asian woes came as President Jiang wanted to impose his stamp as the new helmsman. In early 1998, the neo-conservative leader signalled his desire for at least limited political liberalisation in a series of internal briefings for party leaders, top NPC members and prominent non-Communist Party politicians. Two factors were behind the party chief's new-found enthusiasm for tinkering with the political structure. One was his trip to the US in late 1997, during which he gained first-hand impressions of Western-style democracy. The other, more important, factor was soul-searching on the Asian situation — and the realisation that China was home to many ills that precipitated the crisis.

In these briefings, the president said that his discussions with American politicians such as Bill Clinton had convinced him of the urgency of rejuvenating the Chinese leadership and bringing in new ideas. In terms of age, Jiang said, he and Clinton were like "father and son". He hinted that his US experience was instrumental in his surprising decision in February 1998 to pick Hu Jintao as state Vice-President and heir apparent.[89]

Of perhaps more significance were Jiang's views on China's susceptibility to the "Asian flu". The president recalled how, during discussions with Asian leaders in the early 1990s, they had agreed that it was "neo-Confucianism" that had underpinned the economic miracle of the four Asian Dragons and the Asia-Pacific region in general. On those occasions, Jiang pledged to work for the further revival of pragmatic, "growth-oriented" Confucianism. Jiang pointed out, however, that he had a different perspective after the Asian meltdown. A major reason behind the crisis was systemic imperfections in the East Asian tradition, including corruption and "remnant feudalism". "We have hardly eradicated feudalism [in China]," he said. "We must aim for a transformation of our systems and institutions."[90]

Jiang's "liberal persona" was given eloquent expression by protégé Liu Ji, the Vice-President of the Chinese Academy of Social Sciences (CASS). In a late 1997 talk, Liu indicated that "popular participation in politics" was not only unavoidable but "a sign of the prosperity of the socialist enterprise". Liu also said there were certain elements of "bourgeois democratic values" that could be adopted by China.[91]

Liu went further in the spring of 1998. He was quoted as saying that in spite of Deng's injunctions against "all-out Westernisation", it was permissible to study Western models of institutional change. "Deng said China should not follow the example of the US and Britain where two parties take turns in forming the government," Liu reportedly said. "But he didn't say explicitly that it was not permissible to have a multi-party system." He added: "Deng also said he was opposed to the tripartite division of power, or state power divided amongst the executive [branch of government], the legislature and the judiciary. But he didn't say it was wrong to have checks and balances in the system."[92]

Tinkering with the political structure

In recommending change, Jiang made it clear that it would be political reform with Chinese characteristics. For example, he stuck to the building up of *zhidu* ("systems and institutions"), which had been stressed by former NPC chief Qiao Shi. Indeed, he often used the term "reform of *zhidu*" instead of political reform. The president also indicated that *zhidu* construction must be predicated upon "scientific and democratic principles".[93]

Some of the more moderate members of the Shanghai clique were in early 1998 given the task of looking for new ideas in institutional building. They in turn asked elite research units such as the Central Committee's Policy Research Office (CCPRO) and CASS to come up with papers on how the changes would be brought about. Such aides included Liu Ji and Wang Huning, who was promoted CCPRO deputy chief in mid-1998. The topics included allowing non-party elements to run newspapers and magazines, separation of party and government, even the *guojiahua* ("nationalisation") of the army. For example, a team under Liu was looking at the possibility of the country's first Law on Political Parties. The statute would lay down the relationship between the CCP and other elements of the polity including the government, the judiciary and the PLA.[94]

The most ambitious programme concerned expanding the scope of elections by universal suffrage — which was, up to 1998, restricted to the village level. In internal discussions, Jiang had given theoretical approval to "upgrade" democratic polls from the village to the level of aggregate villages and counties some time early in the 21st century.

An internal paper drafted under the Central Committee's General Office highlighted the need to narrow the gap on political development with Taiwan if unification were to be achieved in the time frame of 2020 to 2025. The paper recommended that universal-suffrage elections be expanded according to this projection: polls at the level of counties by 2003, cities by 2008, provinces by 2013, and the national level by 2018 or 2023. While Jiang, Zhu and other leaders refused to make a commitment on the details of the timetable, the principle of "narrowing the democracy gap" with Taiwan was mentioned in a national meeting on Taiwan in May 1998.[95]

At this stage, most of the discussions on elections and related issues were restricted to the arena of "theoretical exploration". For example, progress in direct elections depended on whether the CCP was ready to lift the long-standing ban on forming political parties. As a member of a quasi-official think tank put it: "It is very difficult for direct, universal-suffrage polls to be held at the county level or above if candidates and other activists cannot form their own political organisations to broadcast their views." Moreover, liberalisation continued to take a back seat to the need to maintain stability. By mid-1998, the leadership was again downplaying political reform. A CASS spokesman went so far as to deny that the academy had been asked by Zhongnanhai to map out blueprints on the subject.[96]

The Asian Crisis and the Future of China

The Asian crisis, then, was a case of dangers, challenges — and opportunities. Premier Zhu, forever the gung-ho economic impresario, encapsulated the upside in an internal speech in January 1998. Zhu told his aides that China should take advantage of the Asian crisis to boost its economic and political standing in the region. The then premier-designate said China's ability to withstand the pressure of speculators and protect the yuan's value showed its global stature had significantly improved. He raised the possibility of taking over selected banks and companies in Asia, particularly those which could compete with Chinese products in the world market. Zhu's advisers claimed that such an "economic rescue package" would also endear China to its cash-strapped neighbours.[97]

Protestations of self-confidence aside, Beijing had to live with the fact that one devastating impact of the "Asian flu" could be a loss of direction for reform, which had been patterned after the Asian experience. The vaunted East-Asiatic model turned out to be a giant with feet of clay. The

CCP faced the challenge of drawing the right lesson from the turmoil. Apart from idle boasts that China was a "safe haven" and a "model international citizen", Beijing had to make long overdue structural changes to its economic and political system. The Jiang leadership might be reminded that the last time when heaven seemed to collapse — the dissolution of the USSR — Deng Xiaoping saw the writing on the wall and initiated large-scale reforms during his tour of southern China in 1992.[98]

The Asian turmoil coincided with deep soul-searching by Jiang on how best to leave his mark in the annals. Shortly after dumping party chairman Hua Guofeng in 1979, Deng said: "Hua was merely a transitional figure. You can't say he represented a generation of comrades. He didn't have an independent way of thinking."[99] In the run-up to the 15th Party Congress, liberal Jiang aides such as Wang Huning had persuaded the "core of the third-generation leadership" to come up with a "Jiang Zemin Theory" to buttress his claim to be China's next helmsman and philosopher-king. As discussed earlier, the year 1998 saw a fairly broad array of tentative steps taken by the Jiang administration to ring in the new. These included the somewhat surprising gambit of borrowing elements of American ideas and institutions such as the Rooseveltian New Deal, the Federal Reserve central-banking system, the circuit court system, and even US-style command-and-control mechanisms for the army.[100]

By mid-1998, however, the president had yet to cut his Gordian knot. On the one hand, there were signs that Jiang the muddle-along artist was playing safe by sticking to old formulas — and the woeful strategy of artful procrastination. On the other, there was early evidence he might align himself with the forces of change. President Bill Clinton was certainly looking on the bright side when he gave this assessment of the Chinese supremo in July 1998: "He has a good imagination ... he can visualise and imagine a future that is different from the present." Jiang, however, had to do much, much more to prove that, in Clinton's terms, he was "on the right side of history".[101] The future of China — whether the great nation could avail itself of the exciting opportunities of the new century — hung in the balance.

Notes

CHAPTER 1

1. For a discussion of the significance of the October 1997 Sino-US summit, see, for example, Ou Yongxi, ed., *Trip of the Century* (Hong Kong: Hong Kong Culture and Education Publishing Ltd., 1998), pp. 39–45.
2. Cited in Ou Yongxi, op. cit., pp. 206–207.
3. Jiang also frequently used different Chinese dialects when talking with guests from Taiwan, Hong Kong and Chinese communities overseas. For a discussion of Jiang's musical talents, see He Ruohan, *Jiang Zemin and his Era* (Taipei: Yu Dan Press, 1995), p. 192.
4. Author's interviews with sources in Beijing and Shanghai.
5. In early 1998, Jiang took over from Li Peng as head of the party Central Committee's Leading Group on Foreign Affairs. However, the president had by late 1996 emerged as the principal policymaker on diplomacy as well as Taiwan and Hong Kong affairs.
6. *South China Morning Post* (SCMP) (Hong Kong), December 1, 1997; *Ming Pao* (a Hong Kong daily), December 1, 1997.
7. For a discussion of the contribution of Hu Yaobang and Zhao Ziyang to liberalisation, see Willy Wo-Lap Lam, *The Era of Zhao Ziyang* (Hong Kong: A.B. Books & Stationery International, 1989) pp. 19–44, 199–260.
8. Cited in SCMP, February 14, 1996.
9. Zhao foes including former premier Li Peng and ideologue Yuan Mu had in internal meetings accused him of condoning corruption.
10. Jiang largely shelved his plans to formally declare the birth of Jiang Thought or Jiang Zemin Theory. It was only in the People's Liberation Army that propaganda was made concerning Jiang's "military teachings", which were elevated to the same level as the edicts of Mao and Deng.
11. For a discussion of Jiang's views on "common prosperity", see Weng Jieming *et al.*, eds., *A Heart-to-heart Talk with the*

General Secretary (Beijing: China Social Sciences Press, 1996), pp. 100–118.
12. Cited in SCMP, May 27, 1998.
13. Most of Jiang's "theories" were put together by a group of Shanghai-affiliated aides such as Wang Daohan and Wang Huning. For a discussion of the contributions of these advisers, see, Gao Xin, *Jiang Zemin's Counselors* (Toronto & Hong Kong: Mirror Books, 1996).
14. Agence France-Presse, January 9, 1998.
15. For a discussion of Jiang's views on SOE reforms, see Weng Jieming, op. cit., pp. 142–165.
16. The issue of *qiuzhi* was first raised by the *World Economic Herald* in 1986; author's interviews with *Herald* editors Zhang Weiguo and Zhu Xingqing.
17. New China News Agency, December 24, 1997; Associated Press, November 2, 1997; *People's Daily*, January 25, 1998.

CHAPTER 2

1. A widely circulated saying in Beijing and other large cities beginning in early 1997.
2. Author's interview with Wu Guoguang.
3. For a discussion of Jiang's challenges after the 15th Party Congress, see, for example, Wu Guoguang, *Power Game in China* (Hong Kong: Pacific Century Institute, 1997), pp. 66–89; Ma Licheng and Ling Zhijun, *Cross Swords* (Beijing: Today's China Press, 1998), pp. 388–424.
4. The "Chinese learning as essence" theory was propagated by Qing ministers such as Zhang Zhidong and Li Hongzhang. It found echoes in statements by Jiang and other neo-conservative leaders that Chinese culture must never become the "vassal" of that of the West.
5. Jiang was the first senior Chinese leader (the second one was Zhu Rongji) to have mastered the art of using the modern media, particularly television, to enhance his prestige. He also employed a sizeable team of public relations aides. For example, Wang Huning was widely known as a "consultant in political cosmetics".
6. Jiang was also adept at winning over Hong Kong reporters. For example, while touring Mexico in late 1997, he volunteered to Hong Kong journalists he would like to go to Hong Kong and swim in its waters. See, for example, *Ming Pao* (a Hong Kong daily), December 1, 1997.
7. *Ming Pao*, March 10, 1995.
8. CNN, May 9, 1997.
9. *The Mirror* (a pro-Beijing Hong Kong monthly), July 1995; April 1994.
10. Author's interviews with sources in Shanghai and Beijing.
11. Jiang's largesse and personal favours, however, were seldom extended to elements beyond members of his narrow Shanghai Faction. This was a far cry from former leaders such as Hu Yaobang or Zhou Enlai, even though Jiang wanted very much to cultivate the image of a Zhou Enlai-like "people's politician".
12. For a discussion of the career of Hu Guangbao, see Yang Zhongmei, *The Biography of Jiang Zemin* (Taipei: China Times Book, 1996), p. 292.

13. Author's interviews with sources in Shenzhen.
14. For a discussion of the fate of Bao Tong, see Wei Guo, "From Political Reformer to Political Prisoner", in Xiao Chong, ed., *Zhongnanhai's New Think Tanks* (Hong Kong: Xia Fei Er International Press, 1997), pp. 343–351.
15. Author's interviews with Chinese sources in Hong Kong.
16. *South China Morning Post* (SCMP) (Hong Kong), February 27, 1995.
17. New China News Agency (NCNA), July 6, 1995.
18. Other geographically and professionally based factions that enjoyed a close working relationship with Jiang included the Shandong Faction and the Petroleum Clique.
19. For a discussion of the differences between Deng and Jiang prior to and immediately after the *nanxun*, see Willy Wo-Lap Lam, *China after Deng Xiaoping* (Singapore & New York: John Wiley & Sons, 1995), pp. 17–23.
20. For a discussion of the fate of the Deng children, see, for example, "Deng Children Find Somewhere to Hide", *Newsweek* (Asia Edition), November 3, 1996.
21. For a discussion of the political significance of the Deng children, see, for example, Gao Xin and He Pin, *The Power of Papa* (Toronto & Hong Kong: Mirror Books, 1995).
22. SCMP, November 4, 1995.
23. *Open* (a Hong Kong monthly), January 1997.
24. SCMP, March 12, 1997.
25. For a discussion of Jiang's Shanghai-affiliated aides, see Gao Xin, *Jiang Zemin's Counselors* (Toronto & Hong Kong: Mirror Books, 1996).
26. *Hong Kong Economic Journal* (HKEJ) (a Hong Kong daily), February 11, 1998.
27. For a discussion of the career of Zeng Qinghong, see Gao Xin, op. cit., pp. 71–196.
28. SCMP, January 7, 1998.
29. *Hong Kong United Daily News*, July 31, 1995; *Wen Wei Po*, June 19, 1996.
30. Author's interviews with Chinese sources in New York.
31. SCMP, August 9, 1996.
32. For a discussion of the career of Xu Kuangdi, see *Wen Wei Po*, June 26, 1995; *Cheng Ming* (a Hong Kong monthly), July 1996.
33. SCMP, July 12, 1995; *Ming Pao*, October 28, 1996.
34. SCMP, October 30, 1996.
35. *Ming Pao*, October 28, 1996.
36. Jiang succeeded in transferring Chen Zhili to Beijing in 1998. From the early 1990s, the party chief had tried several times to move Chen, a key protégé, to central-level positions including vice-head of the Propaganda Department.
37. SCMP, November 3, 1996.
38. Ibid.
39. Author's interviews with sources in Shanghai.
40. For a discussion of the aides and associates of Zhu Rongji, see, Yang Zhongmei, *The Biography of Zhu Rongji* (Taipei: China Times Press, 1998), pp. 203–224.
41. *Frontline* (Hong Kong), April 1998.
42. Cited in Xiao Zhengqin, *The Coming Challenges of Zhu Rongji* (Hong Kong: Pacific Century Institute, 1998), p. 237.

43. Cited in SCMP, January 15, 1997.

44. Ibid.

45. NCNA, September 19, 1997.

46. For a discussion of Zhu's relationship with Deng Xiaoping and other elders, see Xiao Zhengqin, op. cit., pp. 155–169.

47. For a discussion of Jiang's ideas on personnel issues, see, for example, Office of the CCP Organisation Department, ed., *Documents of the National Organisation Work Conferences* (Beijing: Party Construction Literature Press, 1998), pp. 1–14.

48. For a discussion of the traits of Shanghai Faction affiliates, see Willy Wo-Lap Lam, op. cit., pp. 332–341.

49. *Sing Tao Daily News* (Hong Kong), April 4, 1996.

50. *Sing Tao Daily News*, October 19, 1995.

51. Author's interviews with sources in Beijing.

52. *Wen Wei Po*, March 15, 1995.

53. *Wen Wei Po*, March 8, 1996.

54. *Sing Tao Daily News*, June 27, 1995.

55. *Frontline*, December 1996.

56. *People's Daily*, October 16, 1996.

57. SCMP, September 20, 1995.

58. SCMP, November 20, 1995.

59. For a discussion of the phenomenon of factionalism in Chinese politics, see, for example, Lucian W. Pye, "Factions and the Politics of *Guanxi*" and Tsou Tang, "Chinese Politics at the Top: Factionalism or Informal Politics", *China Journal* (Canberra), July 1995, pp. 35–54 and pp. 95–156.

60. SCMP, February 27, 1995.

61. SCMP, July 7, 1996.

62. SCMP, November 20, 1995.

63. Author's interviews with sources in Beijing.

64. Largely owing to opposition from the "anti-*Shanghaibang* coalition", Zeng failed to become a full member of the Politburo at the 15th Party Congress. He became instead an alternate member of the elite body.

65. The powers of these two party offices were not hurt by the effort to streamline party Central Committee units which began in March 1998.

66. SCMP, October 19, 1995.

67. SCMP, February 8, 1995.

68. SCMP, June 26, 1995.

69. Author's interviews with sources in *People's Daily*.

70. SCMP, July 7, 1996.

71. For a discussion of the background of Zhao's advisers, see Willy Wo-Lap Lam, *The Era of Zhao Ziyang* (Hong Kong: A.B. Books & Stationery, 1989), pp. 132–137.

72. The power of the Beijing faction petered out after the 15th Party Congress with numerous cadres from disparate backgrounds being transferred to senior municipal positions. They included Jia Qingling and Jin Renqing.

73. For a discussion of the relationship between Deng's children and the business world, see Reuters, September 3, 1997; SCMP, March 23, 1997.

74. Wei Jianxing was largely a compromise candidate as the replacement of Chen

Xitong because there was considerable opposition to Huang Ju's transfer to Beijing.

75. SCMP, November 15, 1995; September 16, 1997.

76. HKEJ, November 29, 1996.

77. For a discussion of Zhao Ziyang's statecraft, see Yuan Hui Zhang, *Zhao Ziyang's Last Chance* (Toronto & Hong Kong: Mirror Books, 1997), pp. 37–56.

78. Deng Xiaoping had to share power with fellow elders such as Chen Yun, Li Xiannian and Peng Zhen, who had a lot of say in matters including ideology, finance, personnel, and legal affairs.

79. *United Daily News* (Taipei), November 10, 1996.

80. For a discussion of Qiao Shi's power base, see Gao Xin, *Qiao Shi, The Chinese Communist Party's Heavyweight Politician* (Taipei: The World Bookstore, 1995), pp. 237–276.

81. SCMP, October 23, 1996.

82. Author's interviews with Beijing sources.

83. Like other communist countries, China had overlapping intelligence operations under different party, government, and army units. The Central Committee General Office (CCGO) had had intelligence-gathering functions since the early 1950s. Yang Shangkun, who used to be CCGO director, was hounded by Red Guards during the Cultural Revolution for "spying" on Chairman Mao.

84. SCMP, October 16, 1995.

85. The Central Committee General Office also had some military functions during the Cultural Revolution. This ceased to be the case under party general secretaries Hu Yaobang and Zhao Ziyang.

86. SCMP, February 8, 1995.

87. *People's Daily*, January 21, 1996.

88. For a discussion of the *biaotai* craze during the debate on "practice as the sole criterion of truth", see Shen Baoxiang, *The Story of the Discussion of the Criterion of Truth Issue* (Beijing: China Youth Press, 1997), pp. 217–253.

89. *Wen Wei Po*, October 13, 1995.

90. SCMP, December 6, 1994.

91. *People's Daily*, January 21, 1996.

92. Ibid.

93. Author's interviews with Beijing sources.

94. *People's Daily*, July 7, 1996.

95. Jiang was careful to ensure that the PLA would be at the forefront of propagating the "politically correct" ideology and propaganda. For example, in a talk to cadres in the National Defence University, Jiang called on them to pay more attention to ideological and political work. See China News Service, November 28, 1995.

96. CCTV news, August 2, 1996.

97. Author's interviews with Chinese sources.

98. Agence France-Presse (AFP), November 5, 1996.

99. *Wen Wei Po*, December 12, 1996.

100. *Economic Daily* (Beijing), July 1, 1995.

101. *People's Daily*, October 30, 1995.

102. *People's Daily*, October 16, 1996.

103. NCNA, September 26, 1996.

104. AFP, October 29, 1996.

105. *Media* (a Hong Kong biweekly magazine), January 21, 1996.

106. SCMP, January 20, 1995.

107. Cited in SCMP, July 2, 1996.

108. The official view on Radio Free Asia was expressed by *China Daily* in its October 2, 1997 issue: "The US is attempting to impose its values and so-called democracy on people in Asia."

109. *Sing Tao Daily News*, June 16, 1997.

110. *Sing Tao Daily News*, April 20, 1995; *Ming Pao*, May 8, 1995.

111. AFP, July 19, 1997; *Ming Pao*, October 20, 1996.

112. *Sing Tao Daily News*, June 16, 1997.

113. *Ming Pao*, October 23, 1996.

114. *People's Daily*, April 1, 1996.

115. For a comparison between Mao's "eight contradictions" and Jiang's "12 contradictions", see *Hong Kong United Daily News*, October 15, 1995.

116. For a discussion of Deng's *nanxun* message, see, for example, Tang Youlun, ed., *1992: A New Starting Point* (Beijing: The China Encyclopaedia Press, 1992), pp. 25–68.

117. *Wen Wei Po*, July 14, 1995.

118. *Ming Pao*, March 10, 1995; SCMP, March 10, 1995.

119. Ibid.

120. NCNA, March 7, 1996.

121. NCNA, December 26, 1995.

122. *People's Daily*, October 9, 1995.

123. Ibid.

124. NCNA, June 30, 1996.

125. NCNA, April 2, 1996; *Sing Tao Daily News*, April 3, 1996.

126. Cited in *The Mirror*, June 1996.

127. Ibid.

128. *Liberation Army Daily*, April 1, 1996.

129. For a discussion of Deng's views on "economic work as the centre" and economic reform in general, see, for example, Li Ping, ed., *The Era of the Thaw* (Beijing: Economic Daily Press, 1997), pp. 124–188.

130. Ibid.

131. Cited in China News Service, June 30, 1996.

132. See Willy Wo-Lap Lam, *China after Deng Xiaoping* (Singapore & New York: John Wiley & Sons, 1995), p. 240.

133. NCNA, June 30, 1995.

134. *Wen Wei Po*, March 15, 1995.

135. NCNA, June 30, 1995.

136. NCNA, January 17, 1996.

137. *Sing Tao Daily News*, June 27, 1995.

138. HKEJ, May 29, 1997.

139. China News Service, November 28, 1995.

140. NCNA, December 27, 1995; *People's Daily*, March 2, 1995.

141. NCNA, October 10, 1996.

142. NCNA, July 15, 1997.

143. For a discussion of the relationship between "spiritual civilisation" and Marxist orthodoxy, see Reuters, May 26, 1997.

144. NCNA, May 26, 1997.

145. *People's Daily*, May 12, 1995

146. *People's Daily*, October 11, 1996.

147. China News Service, October 21, 1996; *Liberation Army Daily*, October 23, 1996.

148. NCNA, December 26, 1995.

149. For a discussion of popular reaction to Jiang's Taiwan gambit, see Ho Pin, ed., *The PLA Attacking Taiwan* (Toronto & Hong Kong: Mirror Books, 1996), pp. 319–333.

150. NCNA, December 31, 1996; *People's Daily*, July 2, 1997.

151. SCMP, July 2, 1997.

152. For a discussion of the rise of Chinese nationalism and anti-American feelings, see, Song Qiang *et al.*, *China Can Say No* (Beijing: China Industry and Commerce Joint Press, 1996), pp. 61–70, 82–93.

153. In the early 1990s, Deng posited the dictum "keep a low profile and never take the lead" on relations with the West, particularly the US. Jiang inherited this policy in his own instructions on relations with Washington: "avoid trouble and lessen confrontation".

154. *Titanic* was shown in 200 Chinese cinemas. After seeing it, Jiang said: "We shouldn't think that capitalism has no ideas to exchange." See Associated Press, March 13, 1998.

155. SCMP, March 21, 1995.

156. *Hong Kong United Daily News*, October 9, 1995.

157. NCNA, December 27, 1996.

158. *People's Daily*, June 28, 1995.

159. NCNA, December 26, 1995.

160. AFP, November 5, 1996.

161. NCNA, September 22, 1996.

162. NCNA, November 4, 1996.

163. For a contemporary discussion of the ideals of the May Fourth Movement, see Fan Xing, "The Emotional Ties of the May Fourth Movement", in Yang Shuzi, ed., *Thoughts on the Humanities in Chinese Universities* (Wuchang, China: Huazhong University of Science and Engineering, 1996), pp. 197–208.

164. NCNA, January 18, 1996.

165. NCNA, May 27, 1996.

166. *Sing Tao Daily News*, May 28, 1996.

167. NCNA, May 26, 1995.

168. *Wen Wei Po*, May 28, 1996.

169. *People's Daily*, July 13, 1995.

170. For a discussion of China and the "Asian model", see, for example, Xiao Zhengqin, op. cit., pp. 361–376.

171. *Sing Tao Daily News*, December 11, 1995.

172. *Sing Tao Daily News*, October 2, 1995; *The Mirror*, May 97.

173. For a discussion of the development of Chinese conglomerates, see, for exam-

ple, Ying Wenquan, "Seize the Opportunity to Develop Large-scale Enterprise Groupings", *Reform* (a Chongqing-based monthly), January 1998, pp. 52–53.

174. *Sing Tao Daily News*, October 2, 1995.
175. AFP, July 12, 1995; *People's Daily*, July 13, 1995.
176. *People's Daily*, July 13, 1995.
177. Author's interviews with Chinese sources in Beijing.
178. *Sing Tao Daily News*, November 27, 1995; SCMP, January 16, 1996.
179. Ibid.
180. *Sing Tao Daily News*, January 16, 1996.
181. *Ming Pao*, May 23, 1996.
182. See *Chosun Daily* (Seoul), December 9, 1995, for a discussion of Jiang's assessment of the *chaebols* during the president's trip to South Korea in late 1994.
183. NCNA, June 27, 1995.
184. *People's Daily*, July 13, 1995.
185. NCNA, June 27, 1995.
186. NCNA, September 25, 1995.
187. *Asian Wall Street Journal*, September 5, 1994.
188. *People's Daily*, October 9, 1995.
189. For a discussion of Tian Jiyun's ideas on SOE reform, including the reform of village and township enterprises, see Tian Jiyun, *China's Situation, Challenges and Responsibilities* (Beijing: Central Party School Press, 1996), pp. 425–443.
190. Cited in *Wen Wei Po*, May 21, 1995.
191. *People's Daily*, October 9, 1995.
192. NCNA, April 29, 1998; China News Service, April 17, 1998.
193. HKEJ, February 7, 1995.
194. NCNA, June 8, 1996.
195. NCNA, June 7, 1996.
196. *People's Daily*, June 7, 1996; HKEJ, July 7, 1995.
197. NCNA, June 7, 1996.
198. HKEJ, February 7, 1995; NCNA, June 8, 1996.
199. NCNA, March 28, 1995.
200. HKEJ, July 17, 1996.
201. *People's Daily*, June 7, 1996.
202. NCNA, February 26, 1996.
203. *Wen Wei Po*, March 8, 1996; China News Service, March 7, 1995.
204. For a discussion of the peasants' plight, see *People's Daily*, November 8, 1995; *China Times Weekly*, April 10, 1994.
205. *Ming Pao*, August 30, 1996.
206. *People's Daily*, March 8, 1996.
207. SCMP, December 18, 1996.
208. HKEJ, March 18, 1997.
209. SCMP, May 6, 1998.
210. *Ming Pao*, May 20, 1996.
211. Cited in *Ming Pao*, April 3, 1996.
212. *Liberation Army Daily*, May 19, 1996; *Shenzhen Special Zone Daily*, January 17, 1997.

213. Cited in SCMP, June 4, 1996.
214. *Seeking after Truth* (a Beijing monthly), January 1997.
215. Author's interview with Wang Shan.
216. Part of Jiang's two-facedness manifested itself in the fact that while he sometimes highlighted "Chinese-style democracy", the focus at other times was on "democratic centralism". See for example, *Ming Pao*, July 15, 1995, on Jiang's theory that "even in a socialist market economy, 'democratic centralism' should not be weakened". This Maoist ideal was the antithesis of "people power".
217. *Ming Pao*, October 7, 1996.
218. SCMP, July 14, 1995.
219. It was former NPC chairman Wan Li who first championed the ideal of "rendering decision-making more scientific and democratic", a goal that was approved by Jiang Zemin. See Wan Li, *Selected Works of Wan Li* (Beijing: People's Press, 1996), pp. 514–532.
220. *Wide Angle*, September 1996; November 1996.
221. *Ming Pao*, March 19, 1996.
222. Beijing also agreed in early 1998 to sign the United Nations' covenant on political and civil rights, a move that was applauded by the US government, see *Newsweek*, May 11, 1998.
223. *Ming Pao*, October 22, 1996.
224. SCMP, October 18, 1996.
225. SCMP, October 5, 1996.
226. *Liberation Army Daily*, October 16, 1995; NCNA, January 29, 1997.
227. Author's interviews with sources in Beijing.
228. SCMP, March 1, 1995.
229. Author's interviews with sources in Shanghai.
230. *Liberation Army Daily*, October 14, 1995.
231. SCMP, March 10, 1995.
232. SCMP, May 22, 1996.
233. *Wen Wei Po*, March 8, 1996.
234. NCNA, January 18, 1997.
235. *Ming Pao*, May 25, 1996.
236. NCNA, March 16, 1995.
237. Cited in SCMP, March 12, 1997.
238. Weng Jieming *et al.*, eds., *A Heart-To-Heart Talk with the General Secretary* (Beijing: China Social Sciences Press, 1996), p. 262.
239. NCNA, January 5, 1997.
240. Author's interviews with sources in Beijing.
241. See Willy Wo-Lap Lam, op. cit., p. 19.

CHAPTER 3

1. For a discussion of Jiang's reform initiatives in 1997 and 1998, see Liu Zhifeng, *The Seventh Revolution* (Beijing: Economic Daily Press, 1998), pp. 26–42.
2. *South China Morning Post* (SCMP) (Hong Kong), March 5, 1996.
3. For a discussion of Jiang's views on party supremacy, see Willy Wo-Lap Lam,

China after Deng Xiaoping (Singapore & New York: John Wiley & Sons, 1995), pp. 244–248.

4. *Frontline* (a Hong Kong monthly), January 1992.

5. For a discussion of Jiang's statecraft, see Wu Guoguang, *Power Game in China* (Hong Kong: Pacific Century Institute, 1997), pp. 29–33.

6. The formation of leading groups and other special offices within the Central Committee was unaffected by efforts beginning in early 1998 to streamline the party structure, see SCMP, March 12, 1998.

7. *Hong Kong Economic Journal* (HKEJ) (a Hong Kong daily), June 22, 1996.

8. SCMP, February 9, 1995.

9. *Ming Pao Monthly* (a Hong Kong journal), September 1997.

10. Cited in Willy Wo-Lap Lam, "Leadership Changes in China", in Joseph Yu-shek Cheng, ed., *China in the Post-Deng Era* (Hong Kong: Chinese University Press, 1997), p. 35.

11. *People's Daily* (Beijing), December 13, 1995.

12. Ibid.

13. For a discussion of Jiang Zemin's efforts to consolidate his control over the PLA, see *Wide Angle* (a pro-Chinese Hong Kong monthly), August 1994.

14. *Ming Pao Monthly*, September 1997.

15. *Ming Pao* (a Hong Kong daily), June 28, 1995.

16. SCMP, July 5, 1995.

17. Ibid.

18. Author's interview with sources in Shenzhen and Guangzhou.

19. For a discussion of the potential role of *gaoganzidi* and Chinese cadres in post-1997 Hong Kong, see, for example, Willy Wo-Lap Lam, "The Chinese Government's Post-1997 Strategies", in Ian Scott, ed., *Institutional Change and the Political Transition in Hong Kong* (Hounmills, UK: Macmillan Press, 1998), pp. 192–200.

20. Premier Zhu Rongji's promotion of his former secretaries Li Jiange and Lou Jiwei to vice-ministerial level positions in mid-1998 provided the latest examples of the *mishubang* in action.

21. For a discussion of the background of the Beijing faction, see Chen Fang, *The Wrath of Heaven* (Hong Kong: Pacific Century Institute, 1997).

22. It was, however, true that in the wake of Zeng Qinghong's transfer to Beijing in 1989, dozens of Jiang associates were moved to the capital through the 1990s. Moreover, some of the "first-generation" Jiang aides such as Huang Ju also began promoting their own protégés to central-level units.

23. *Ta Kung Pao* (a pro-Beijing Hong Kong daily), July 1, 1995.

24. For an official biography of Xu Yongyue, see New China News Agency (NCNA), March 18, 1998; see also Xiao Zhengqin, *The New Administrative Strategy of Zhu Rongji's Cabinet* (Hong Kong: Pacific Century Institute, 1998), pp. 355–359.

25. HKEJ, July 15, 1996.

26. Other power blocs whose bases were outside Beijing included politicians from the northeast, principally Liaoning Province. Their influence in Guangdong politics began to grow in the early 1990s.

27. SCMP, March 13, 1995.

28. China News Service (a semi-official news agency), February 12, 1993.

29. SCMP, July 12, 1995.

30. SCMP, March 15, 1998.

31. Another "profession-based" power bloc was made up of cadres with experience in the machine-building and electronics ministries. It was led by none other than Jiang Zemin.

32. People's Daily, December 11, 1995; United Daily News (Taipei), October 21, 1995.

33. NCNA, November 20, 1996; November 29, 1996.

34. United Press International, April 14, 1996; Agence France-Presse (AFP), April 15, 1996.

35. For Jiang's views on personnel, see his speech to a high-level meeting of the Organisation Department, cited in Documents of the National Meetings on Organisation Work (Beijing: General Office of the Central Committee Organisation Department, 1998), pp. 1–13.

36. China News Service, November 30, 1994.

37. People's Daily, September 13, 1997.

38. AFP, June 16, 1996.

39. Ming Pao, June 12, 1996.

40. United Daily News (Taipei), October 21, 1995.

41. For a discussion of the neo-conservative princelings, see SCMP, October 19, 1994.

42. SCMP, March 22, 1995.

43. China Times Weekly (Taipei), March 19, 1995; November 19, 1995. For a discussion of the background of regional leaders installed in 1995, see Ho Pin, The New Lords of the People's Republic of China (Toronto & Hong Kong: Mirror Press, 1996), pp. 23–33.

44. Ming Pao, July 22, 1996.

45. NCNA, September 8, 1994; SCMP, September 9, 1994.

46. For a discussion of the career of Liu Zhengwei, see, for example, Reuters, May 2, 1995; SCMP, May 4, 1995.

47. NCNA, June 23, 1996.

48. NCNA, June 12, 1996; June 8, 1996; July 19, 1996.

49. China News Service, April 11, 1996.

50. NCNA, December 29, 1995; China News Service, October 19, 1995.

51. China Daily (Beijing), July 23, 1996.

52. SCMP, November 1, 1997.

53. NCNA, April 29, 1995.

54. As of early 1998, the phenomenon of regional party secretaries doubling as governors and mayors — or as heads of people's congresses — had not been put to a stop.

55. The ranks of the PAP grew from around 600,000 in the early 1990s to more than 1 million in 1998.

56. For a discussion of the history of regionalism, see Liu Guoguang and Zheng Yongnian, On the Relationship between the Centre and the Regions (Hong Kong: Oxford University Press, 1996), pp. 19–32.

57. SCMP, October 5, 1995; Wen Wei Po, December 22, 1995.

58. SCMP, May 15, 1996; China News Service, May 1, 1996.

59. Hong Kong China News Agency (a semi-official news agency), July 31, 1996.

60. NCNA, June 19, 1995.

61. Beginning in 1996, the propaganda machinery showcased new Lei Feng-like "paragon" figures almost on a monthly basis.

62. NCNA, July 6, 1996.

63. China News Service, May 1, 1996.

64. NCNA, July 30, 1996.

65. Hong Kong China News Agency, July 31, 1996. For a discussion of the dismissal of Sun Weiben, see Xiao Zhengqin, *The Coming Challenges of Premier Zhu Rongji* (Hong Kong: Pacific Century Institute, 1998), p. 223.

66. Cited in SCMP, May 8, 1996.

67. Protégés of Premier Zhu Rongji such as Zhu Xiaohua and Wang Qishan also led teams to check on the conduct of officials in Guangdong, particularly allegations of breach of financial discipline. Author's interview with Zhu Xiaohua.

68. *Ming Pao*, October 26, 1996; July 18, 1995.

69. Liaoning was also the first province visited by Zhu Rongji after he became premier in March 1998.

70. Governance by mass movements had been a hallmark of the Chinese-Communist administration since 1949. Beginning in 1998, however, there were more calls for institutional building. See, for example, *Newsweek* (Asia Edition), April 13, 1998.

71. *China Daily*, May 14, 1996; Reuters, May 14, 1996.

72. *Wen Wei Po* (a pro-Beijing Hong Kong daily), September 16, 1995.

73. NCNA, November 12, 1997.

74. For a discussion of Jiang's trip to the US, see Ou Yongxi, ed., *Trip of the Century* (Hong Kong: Hong Kong Culture and Education Publishing Ltd., 1998).

75. The SCRES was downgraded during the administrative restructuring of March 1998 into an Office for Restructuring the Economic System. There were plans for its conversion into a purely research unit before the 10th NPC in 2003.

76. Turf wars between the business empires of the police, the MSS and the PLA, were frequently reported in the southern provinces, particularly Guangdong and Hainan. By 1998, there were indications the internecine bickering might spread to Macau after its reversion to Chinese control in 1999.

77. The Ministry of Foreign Affairs clawed back some territory when vice-minister Tang Jiaxuan edged out Liu Huaqiu to become minister in March 1998. Tang was put in charge of preparations for the June 1998 visit of US President Bill Clinton.

78. At the height of the Taiwan Strait crisis in 1995 and 1996, Taiwan policy was mainly formulated by Jiang in conjunction with a host of senior generals such as General Zhang Wannian. For a discussion of the role of the top brass, see, for example, John Garver, "The PLA as an Interest Group in Chinese Foreign Policy", in Dennison Lane *et al.*, eds., *Chinese Military Modernization* (Washington: AEI Press, 1996), pp. 246–281.

79. SCMP, May 8, 1996.
80. China News Service, May 8, 1995.
81. Reuters, May 23, 1996.
82. NCNA, December 11, 1996.
83. SCMP, January 15, 1997.
84. Author's interview with NPC members in Beijing.
85. Cited in Willy Wo-Lap Lam, *China after Deng Xiaoping*, op cit., pp. 317–318.
86. NCNA, December 14, 1996.
87. Ibid.
88. NCNA, March 17, 1996.
89. HKEJ, March 14, 1996; *Handelsblatt* (a German financial paper), September 4, 1996.
90. NCNA, April 3, 1996.
91. NCNA, March 30, 1996.
92. SCMP, June 23, 1995.
93. Ibid.
94. China News Service, March 11, 1995.
95. SCMP, September 11, 1996.
96. NCNA, March 16, 1996.
97. NCNA, March 2, 1996; AFP, March 3, 1996.
98. *Legal Daily* (Beijing), December 12, 1995.
99. *Sing Tao Daily News* (Hong Kong), February 29, 1996.
100. SCMP, April 13, 1996.
101. HKEJ, September 6, 1995.
102. *Ming Pao*, March 11, 1994.
103. *Sing Tao Daily News*, March 8, 1995.
104. *Ming Pao*, November 20, 1996.
105. China News Service, March 4, 1996; HKEJ, March 15, 1996.
106. China News Service, March 11, 1995.
107. NCNA, October 30, 1995.
108. NCNA, July 17, 1995.
109. NCNA, August 29, 1995.
110. Hong Kong China News Agency, June 9, 1995.
111. *Sing Tao Daily News*, March 7, 1996.
112. *Sing Tao Daily News*, March 7, 1996; *Ming Pao*, March 7, 1996.
113. SCMP, March 18, 1996.
114. *Ming Pao*, August 2, 1996.
115. SCMP, June 26, 1996.
116. It was mainly for fear of disapproval by NPC members that the authorities decided in 1998 not to recommend Jiang Chunyun for another term as vice-premier. This was despite the overall good results in the agriculture sector, which was Jiang's portfolio.
117. SCMP, March 13, 1995.
118. Author's interview with Beijing sources.
119. SCMP, May 20, 1995; *Ming Pao*, May 21, 1995.
120. SCMP, May 23, 1995.
121. Ibid.

122. *Ming Pao*, April 19, 1995.
123. NCNA, March 1, 1996.
124. NCNA, September 20, 1995.
125. *Ming Pao*, May 31, 1996.
126. SCMP, May 20, 1995; NCNA, May 19, 1995.
127. *Ming Pao*, April 21, 1996.
128. *People's Daily*, December 21, 1995.
129. China News Service, May 19, 1995.
130. SCMP, November 19, 1997.
131. For a discussion of the powers of the village committees, see, for example, Kyodo news service, August 29, 1996.
132. Reuters, February 24, 1995.
133. *Hong Kong United Daily News*, July 16, 1995.
134. *Yazhou Zhoukan* (a Hong Kong weekly), March 3, 1997.
135. *Hong Kong United Daily News*, July 16, 1995.
136. Reuters, February 24, 1995.
137. AFP, February 28, 1997.
138. *Yazhou Zhoukan*, March 3, 1997.
139. Ibid.
140. HKEJ, September 18, 1995; June 6, 1995.
141. NCNA, October 9, 1995; November 21, 1995.
142. NCNA, June 3, 1996; HKEJ, June 4, 1996.
143. The Ministry of State Security was among the central-level units that were given a big role in collecting a wide range of information. Apart from "classic" intelligence-gathering, the MSS was interested in topics including economic development and public opinion on domestic and foreign-policy issues.
144. Hong Kong China News Agency, September 8, 1995.
145. *Wen Wei Po*, June 2, 1996.
146. NCNA, April 4, 1996.
147. *Wen Wei Po*, March 15, 1995; Hong Kong China News Agency, March 7, 1996.
148. *Wen Wei Po*, August 20, 1995.
149. *Wide Angle*, July 1996.
150. *Ming Pao*, June 19, 1996; November 28, 1996.
151. Hong Kong China News Agency, March 7, 1996.
152. Regular media such as the *CPPCC Paper* had tough rules against the dissemination of "bourgeois-liberal" views.
153. China News Service, June 14, 1996.
154. Cited in *People's Daily*, September 13, 1997.
155. For a discussion of Judge Bao and his relevance for today, see SCMP, March 23, 1994.
156. China News Service, March 16, 1996.
157. Hong Kong China News Agency, July 3, 1996; HKEJ, May 10, 1995.
158. NCNA, June 25, 1996; SCMP, July 9, 1996.
159. NCNA, June 7, 1996.
160. China News Service, March 16, 1996.
161. *Ming Pao*, October 9, 1995.
162. NCNA, April 18, 1996.

163. Hong Kong China News Agency, March 7, 1996.
164. The "interchangeability" of the Ministry of Supervision and the CCDI was confirmed by *Wen Wei Po*, April 14, 1998.
165. The excesses of the *yanda* campaign were repeatedly denounced by international watchdog organs such as Amnesty International and Human Rights Watch.
166. NCNA, July 31, 1998; Reuters, July 31, 1998.
167. Senior officials with close affiliation with the Beijing faction also included Li Peng and Li Ruihuan.
168. SCMP, May 21, 1997; September 23, 1997.
169. Ibid.
170. NCNA, July 31, 1998; Reuters, July 31, 1998.
171. SCMP, July 10, 1996.
172. *Ming Pao*, January 20, 1996.
173. Author's interviews with sources in Guangdong.
174. For a discussion of the factors behind corruption, see, for example, He Qinglian, *The Traps of Modernisation* (Beijing: Today's China Press, 1998), pp. 263–270.
175. Reuters, October 11, 1996.
176. For a discussion of the tax burden on farmers, see *Wen Wei Po*, April 1, 1997; SCMP, June 16, 1993; *Yazhou Zhoukan*, April 10, 1994.
177. *Ming Pao*, July 6, 1996.
178. Author's interview with Wang Shan.
179. AFP, January 9, 1996.
180. NCNA, November 7, 1995.
181. NCNA, December 7, 1996.
182. *People's Daily*, July 16, 1995.
183. HKEJ, June 6, 1995.
184. *Sing Tao Daily News*, July 8, 1996.
185. China News Service, March 28, 1995.
186. *Hong Kong United Daily News*, October 31, 1995.
187. NCNA, June 11, 1996.
188. SCMP, June 12, 1996.
189. Cited in Lawrence Sullivan, ed., *China since Tiananmen* (New York: M.E. Sharpe, 1995), pp. 202–205.
190. *Ming Pao*, August 31, 1995.
191. *Ming Pao*, May 19, 1995.
192. HKEJ, June 6, 1995.
193. *Ming Pao*, October 12, 1997; April 10, 1998.
194. SCMP, January 27, 1997; *Ming Pao*, April 17, 1996.
195. *Workers' Daily* (Beijing), July 3, 1997.
196. Associated Press, September 4, 1997; Reuters, August 31, 1997; AFP, October 12, 1997.
197. NCNA, August 14, 1996; *Sing Tao Daily News*, August 15, 1996.
198. *Ming Pao*, December 4, 1996.
199. Associated Press, April 3, 1995; *Ming Pao*, April 4, 1995.
200. NCNA, April 8, 1996.

201. NCNA, January 9, 1997; Reuters, January 1, 1997; NCNA, December 31, 1996.
202. *Wen Wei Po*, November 5, 1997.
203. NCNA, October 29, 1996; October 31, 1996.
204. Hong Kong China News Agency, November 9, 1997.
205. AFP, April 19, 1996.
206. HKEJ, February 11, 1997.
207. HKEJ, July 25, 1996.
208. NCNA, March 14, 1995; Associated Press, March 14, 1995.
209. China News Service, June 14, 1996.
210. *Ming Pao*, October 31, 1997.
211. HKEJ, February 11, 1997; February 27, 1997.
212. Ibid.
213. *Sing Tao Daily News*, July 12, 1995; *Ming Pao*, July 13, 1995.
214. For a discussion of the reformist ideals of Hu Qili and others, see Wu Guoguang, *Political Reform under Zhao Ziyang* (Hong Kong: Pacific Century Institute, 1998), pp. 87–89, 137–140.
215. Ibid.
216. SCMP, August 10, 1996.
217. Kyodo news service, April 16, 1996; *China Labour Bulletin* (Hong Kong), November 1995.
218. For examples of "alms-giving" by the ACFTU, see NCNA, November 28, 1996; November 23, 1996.
219. *Ming Pao*, April 10, 1997.
220. NCNA, April 16, 1996.
221. *Sing Tao Daily News*, September 7, 1995.
222. *Ming Pao*, July 22, 1997.
223. Cited in Shi Liuji, ed., *The 10,000-character Petition and Other Underground Writings in Beijing* (Toronto & Hong Kong: Mirror Books, 1997), p. 31.
224. See, for example, China's *White Paper on Human Rights*, cited in *China Daily*, November 4, 1991.
225. SCMP, June 17, 1997.

CHAPTER 4

1. For a discussion of the "China threat" theory, see, for example, Richard Bernstein and Ross Munro, *The Coming Conflict with China* (New York: Knopf, 1997). An "internal" Chinese translation of the book was widely read by cadres in the military and foreign policy establishment.
2. For a discussion of Deng's PLA-related reform ideas, see Willy Wo-Lap Lam, *China after Deng Xiaoping* (Singapore & New York: John Wiley & Sons, 1995), pp. 233–235.
3. Cited in New China News Agency (NCNA), July 31, 1997.
4. Cited in *Hong Kong Economic Journal* (HKEJ) (a Hong Kong daily), August 3, 1996.
5. *Ming Pao* (a Hong Kong daily), March 9, 1996; China News Service (a semi-official news agency), March 17, 1996.
6. NCNA, November 16, 1995.

7. NCNA, October 11, 1995.
8. HKEJ, December 10, 1995.
9. *Liberation Army Daily* (Beijing), October 11, 1995.
10. For a discussion of the fall of the Yang brothers, see Willy Wo-Lap Lam, op. cit., pp. 211–213.
11. *Liberation Army Daily*, September 1, 1996; NCNA, January 23, 1996.
12. *Liberation Army Daily*, January 22, 1996.
13. *Sing Tao Daily News* (a Hong Kong daily), July 18, 1995.
14. *People's Daily* (Beijing), December 11, 1995.
15. *Liberation Army Daily*, August 13, 1995; September 1, 1996.
16. NCNA, May 8, 1996.
17. NCNA, March 17, 1996.
18. *Wen Wei Po*, March 15, 1995; China News Service, November 28, 1995.
19. NCNA, December 26, 1995.
20. NCNA, July 8, 1996.
21. HKEJ, September 27, 1995.
22. *Liberation Army Daily*, April 1, 1996.
23. *Liberation Army Daily*, April 15, 1996.
24. *South China Morning Post* (SCMP) (a Hong Kong daily), January 9, 1997.
25. Cited in SCMP, January 1, 1997.
26. *Shenzhen Special Zone Daily* (Shenzhen), December 28, 1996.
27. NCNA, July 31, 1997.
28. *China Youth Daily* (Beijing), March 18, 1995.
29. *Wen Wei Po* (a pro-Beijing Hong Kong daily), August 26, 1995.
30. NCNA, March 19, 1996.
31. China News Service, March 14, 1995.
32. NCNA, July 10, 1995.
33. NCNA, November 16, 1996.
34. Hong Kong China News Agency (a semi-official news agency), November 16, 1996.
35. Ibid.
36. An internal paper put out by the Chinese military and foreign policy establishment said the authorities hoped the Diaoyu issue could be "resolved" by 2020 or so, when China's economic and military strength would have overtaken Japan.
37. *Far Eastern Economic Review* (Hong Kong), May 14, 1998.
38. *Sing Tao Daily News*, December 9, 1995.
39. *Wide Angle* (a pro-Beijing Hong Kong monthly), February 1997.
40. *Ming Pao*, January 3, 1997.
41. NCNA, March 14, 1996.
42. NCNA, October 19, 1995; March 19, 1996.
43. *China Youth Daily*, March 18, 1995; United Press International, March 18, 1995.
44. SCMP, September 14, 1997.
45. SCMP, March 19, 1996.
46. NCNA, July 30, 1995.
47. Cited in SCMP, August 2, 1995.

48. NCNA, October 19, 1995.
49. NCNA, May 14, 1995.
50. *People's Daily*, March 10, 1996.
51. *Shenzhen Special Zone Daily*, July 30, 1997.
52. *Liberation Army Daily*, August 4, 1996.
53. Ibid.
54. SCMP, June 27, 1996.
55. *Sing Tao Daily News*, March 7, 1998; *Ming Pao*, March 7, 1998.
56. NCNA, November 16, 1995.
57. Ibid.
58. *Ming Pao*, March 3, 1997.
59. Reuters, March 1, 1997.
60. Agence France-Presse (AFP), October 10, 1995.
61. For a discussion of the PLA's hi-tech aspirations, see, for example, William Kazer, "China Eyes Hi-tech Weaponry", Reuters, July 14, 1997.
62. AFP, December 25, 1996; *Wide Angle*, February 1997.
63. For a discussion of the PLA's capabilities and plans for modernisation of armaments, see, for example, Zhang Shan and Xiao Weizhong, *China Will Not Pledge to Give Up the Military Option* (Beijing: China Society Press, 1996), pp. 185–232.
64. For a discussion of the PLA's role in foreign affairs, see, for example, Michael D. Swaine, *The Role of the Chinese Military in National Security Policymaking* (Santa Monica, California: Rand Corp., 1996), pp. 74–76.
65. Associated Press, December 13, 1997.
66. NCNA, December 19, 1996.
67. *People's Daily*, January 31, 1995.
68. Wang Daohan remained Jiang's key adviser on Taiwan as of mid-1998. It was Wang who, during several talks with Taiwan politicians in 1998, said that the "one China" to be accomplished through reunification needed not be the PRC; it could be a "new China" to be worked out by both sides.
69. Author's interviews with sources in Beijing. For a discussion of the background of the generals' views on the Taiwan and US issues, see, for example, John Garver, "The PLA as an Interest Group in Chinese Foreign Policy", in Dennison Lane *et al.*, eds., *Chinese Military Modernization* (Washington: AEI Press, 1996), pp. 260–272.
70. Cited in SCMP, July 27, 1995.
71. *Ming Pao*, June 8, 1995.
72. HKEJ, December 22, 1995.
73. For a discussion of General Xiong's beliefs, see "General Reaffirms Rights to Use Force", Reuters, May 17, 1996.
74. For example, in its March 20, 1996 issue, the Chinese-run Hong Kong daily, *Wen Wei Po*, interviewed an "authoritative" military figure who sketched a rough plan for "taking over" Taiwan. The figure said the Taiwan Strait was "not impregnable".
75. Cited in SCMP, March 14, 1996.
76. In a speech in the Taiwan National Assembly, Lee Teng-hui disclosed that Taiwan had had plans to develop nuclear capabilities, even though those plans were shelved. See *United Daily News* (Taipei), June 27, 1995.

77. Cited in Hai Ke, "Cross-Straits Relations after the Communist Party's Fifth Plenum", *Hong Kong United Daily News*, October 1, 1995.

78. SCMP, November 30, 1995. For a discussion of the background of "liberation warfare" against Taiwan, see, for example, Ho Pin, ed., *The PLA Attacking Taiwan* (Toronto & Hong Kong: Mirror Books, 1996), pp. 258–294.

79. Author's interviews with Chinese sources in Beijing and Hong Kong.

80. *New York Times*, January 24, 1996.

81. *Sing Tao Daily News*, November 21, 1995.

82. *New York Times*, November 11, 1995.

83. Author's interviews with Chinese sources in Beijing and Hong Kong.

84. *Sing Tao Daily News*, November 21, 1995.

85. *Wen Wei Po*, November 28, 1995.

86. China News Service, August 6, 1995.

87. Author's interviews with sources in Fujian Province.

88. *Ming Pao*, March 9, 1996.

89. SCMP, March 14, 1996.

90. SCMP, March 27, 1996.

91. *Sing Tao Daily News*, March 6, 1996.

92. SCMP, April 12, 1996. For a discussion of the development of the air force, see Kenneth W. Allen *et al.*, *China's Air Force Enters the 21st Century* (Santa Monica, California: Rand Corp., 1995), pp. 184–189.

93. *Liberation Army Daily*, April 7, 1996; *Ming Pao*, April 9, 1996.

94. Wang Huning, who was promoted to Vice-Director of the Policy Research Office of the party Central Committee in mid-1998, was a key military adviser to Jiang. Wang drafted important papers on the "civilianisation" of the army and on the separation of party and army.

95. Deng's "five lakes" theory was essentially a continuation of Mao's teachings against "mountain strongholds" in the army. The "five lakes" dictum was also repeated by Long March veterans such as Generals Liu Huaqing and Zhang Zhen.

96. *Wide Angle*, September 1995; April 1994.

97. Wang Ruilin (born 1929) was another general past retirement age who was engaged by Jiang for Machiavellian reasons. The former head of the Deng Xiaoping Office was retained as a symbol of Jiang's special connection with the late patriarch.

98. *Sing Tao Daily News*, April 23, 1996; September 13, 1995.

99. SCMP, December 24, 1997; NCNA, February 5, 1997.

100. SCMP, October 23, 1995.

101. SCMP, September 19, 1995.

102. *Liberation Army Daily*, October 15, 1995.

103. Author's interviews with sources in Beijing.

104. For biographic details of General Chi, see NCNA, March 18, 1998; HKEJ, November 17, 1995.

105. For an official account of Wang Ke's achievements, see NCNA, March 17, 1998.

106. *Frontline* (a Hong Kong monthly), February 1996; HKEJ, January 19, 1996.

107. *Ming Pao*, February 14, 1996.

108. SCMP, February 28, 1996.

109. General You was nominated for Central Committee membership at the 15th Party Congress but he was snubbed by the delegates. The congress witnessed a groundswell of discontent against the Shanghai Faction in general.

110. NCNA, May 7, 1996.

111. *Wide Angle*, February 1997.

112. *Liberation Army Daily*, October 11, 1995.

113. *Liberation Army Daily*, August 13, 1996.

114. For a discussion of the residual strength of retired generals including Zhang Aiping, see Dennison Lane *et al.*, op. cit., p. 254. As of 1996, there were more than 3,000 Long March veterans said to be still in good health. See HKEJ, November 6, 1996.

115. On the one hand, the generals wanted to boost ties with the US and Russia to gain military know-how; on the other, they were wary of various kinds of infiltration allegedly perpetrated by the two powers. The top brass showed reservations about Jiang Zemin's effort to cement a "constructive, strategic partnership" with these two countries in 1997 and 1998.

116. NCNA, October 15, 1995.

117. *Liberation Army Daily*, October 16, 1995.

118. HKEJ, October 13, 1995.

119. SCMP, July 11, 1995.

120. For a discussion of the powers of the Fourth Field alumni, see Willy Wo-Lap Lam, op. cit., p. 400.

121. More and more officers aged 45 or below have had exposure to Western training and military theories. This is one reason why Jiang put so much stress on political and ideological work. See *Wide Angle*, May 1998; SCMP, June 27, 1998.

122. HKEJ, January 19, 1996.

123. *Sing Tao Daily News*, August 7, 1995.

124. *Frontline*, April 1996.

125. A number of PLA-affiliated princelings who had gone into business were implicated in a major anti-corruption swoop in 1998.

126. *Wide Angle*, February 1997.

127. HKEJ, December 10, 1995; SCMP, November 28, 1995.

128. SCMP, May 27, 1995.

129. SCMP, October 4, 1995.

130. In the run-up to the 15th Party Congress, there was intense competition between Generals Zhang Wannian and Chi Haotian for membership of the Politburo Standing Committee. The rivalry was in a way resolved after Zhang was forced to cut his workload after cancer surgery in early 1998.

131. Author's interviews with Chinese sources in Beijing.

132. NCNA, January 27, 1996.

133. *Liberation Army Daily*, January 7, 1996.

134. *Sing Tao Daily News*, December 17, 1995.

135. *Liberation Army Daily*, January 22, 1996.

136. *Ming Pao*, November 12, 1995; November 16, 1995.

137. *Sing Tao Daily News*, May 22, 1996.

138. SCMP, October 19, 1996.

139. China News Service, November 28, 1995.

140. NCNA, April 14, 1996.

141. *Liberation Army Daily*, August 1, 1997; SCMP, August 6, 1997; *Liberation Army Daily*, December 4, 1997.

142. Kyodo news service, September 30, 1997.

143. Author's interview with Wang Shaoguang.

144. *Ming Pao*, December 22, 1995; *Hong Kong United Daily News*, August 18, 1994.

145. *Sing Tao Daily News*, March 2, 1998.

146. NCNA, April 15, 1996; AFP, March 11, 1998.

147. NCNA, July 22, 1998; Associated Press, July 23, 1998; SCMP, August 3, 1998.

148. NCNA, November 3, 1995.

149. Qiao Shi retained substantial clout in the security establishment after his retirement in March 1998. Qiao protégé Jia Chunwang was appointed Minister of Public Security the same month.

150. NCNA, January 11, 1996.

151. SCMP, July 24, 1996.

152. *Inside China Mainland* (Financial Times Asia Intelligence Wire), November 1, 1996.

153. *Sing Tao Daily News*, March 19, 1996; AFP, March 19, 1996.

154. China News Service, March 17, 1996.

155. *Inside China Mainland*, November 1, 1996.

156. SCMP, January 27, 1997.

157. *Sing Tao Daily News*, January 10, 1996; *People's Daily*, July 30, 1997.

158. *Ming Pao*, July 17, 1996.

159. NCNA, September 1, 1997.

160. NCNA, December 21, 1995; *Ming Pao*, December 22, 1995.

161. *Liberation Army Daily*, October 9, 1997.

162. NCNA, September 14, 1997; *Wen Wei Po*, September 15, 1997.

163. NCNA, November 17, 1997.

164. *People's Daily*, January 28, 1996.

165. NCNA, March 30, 1996; HKEJ, April 16, 1996.

166. Anti-corruption work in the PLA was heavily politicised. The CMC chairman always made sure that his men were in charge of the General Political Department (which controlled all the dossiers) and the PLA Disciplinary Inspection Commission.

167. *Ming Pao*, August 2, 1996.

168. NCNA, August 23, 1996.

169. NCNA, March 2, 1997.

170. Ibid.

171. *Ming Pao*, March 3, 1997; SCMP, March 3, 1997.

172. AFP, March 7, 1997.

173. *Ming Pao*, March 6, 1996.

174. *Sing Tao Daily News*, March 7, 1996.

175. SCMP, March 19, 1996; March 12, 1996.

176. For a discussion of Sino-US military ties, see, for example, Jim Mann, "US Seeking to Strengthen Defense Ties with China", *Los Angeles Times*, June 3, 1994.

177. At the third anniversary of his eight-point initiative of January 30, 1995, President Jiang reiterated his peace offensive; see *Wen Wei Po*, January 31, 1998. Much-delayed talks between negotiators from Beijing and Taipei, Wang Daohan and Koo Chen-fu respectively, were resumed in October 1998.
178. SCMP, December 31, 1997.
179. Cited in SCMP, January 9, 1997.
180. *China Times* (Taipei), December 12, 1997; SCMP, December 31, 1997.
181. Reuters, October 28, 1997; *Ming Pao*, October 30, 1997.
182. Reuters, May 21, 1997.
183. NCNA, September 13, 1997; *Wen Wei Po*, September 9, 1997.
184. NCNA, August 25, 1995.
185. NCNA, March 1, 1997.
186. *Ta Kung Pao*, April 7, 1998; *Sing Tao Daily News*, April 14, 1998; SCMP, June 30, 1998.
187. SCMP, June 3, 1998.
188. Ibid.

CHAPTER 5

1. Reuters, March 14, 1996.
2. Cited in *The Mirror* (a pro-Beijing Hong Kong monthly), June 1994.
3. For a discussion of Jiang's views on the relationship between Beijing and the regions, see, for example, Weng Jieming *et al.*, eds., *A Heart-to-heart Talk with the Party General Secretary* (Beijing: China Social Sciences Press, 1996), pp. 213–223.
4. Chongqing party secretary Zhang Delin, a Jiang protégé, was an unsuccessful candidate for the Politburo at the 15th Party Congress of 1997.
5. In their private capacities, former Hu and Zhao aides such as Zhu Houze continued to make their views known. For example, they criticised Zhu Rongji's "austerity programme" of 1993–1996. See *South China Morning Post* (SCMP) (Hong Kong), October 26, 1993.
6. For a discussion of the "personnel card", see Wu Guoguang and Zheng Yongnian, *On the Relationship between the Centre and the Regions* (Hong Kong: Oxford University Press, 1995), pp. 186–187.
7. For a discussion of the more independently-minded regional leaders in the early 1990s, see, for example, Willy Wo-Lap Lam, *China after Deng Xiaoping* (Singapore & New York: John Wiley & Sons, 1995), pp. 366–371.
8. *China Times Weekly Magazine* (Taipei), November 19, 1995.
9. New China News Agency (NCNA), June 23, 1994.
10. For a discussion of Li Youwei's career, see, for example, Xiao Zhengqin, *The Coming Challenges of Zhu Rongji* (Hong Kong: Pacific Century Institute, 1998), p. 267.
11. *The Mirror*, January 1998.
12. China News Service (a semi-official news agency), January 27, 1996.
13. SCMP, April 21, 1996.
14. Author's interviews with sources in Guangdong.
15. China News Service, December 7, 1995.

16. *Sing Tao Daily News* (a Hong Kong daily), July 17, 1995.
17. *Wen Wei Po* (a pro-Chinese Hong Kong daily), January 18, 1996.
18. *Ming Pao* (a Hong Kong daily), November 13, 1996.
19. *Ming Pao*, March 2, 1996; *Hong Kong Economic Journal* (HKEJ) (a Hong Kong daily), February 27, 1998.
20. SCMP, January 14, 1998.
21. *Ming Pao*, March 2, 1996; NCNA, April 16, 1996.
22. NCNA, February 16, 1995; *Hong Kong Economic Times* (a Hong Kong daily), February 16, 1995.
23. *The Mirror*, January 1998; *China Daily* (Beijing), January 17, 1998.
24. *Wen Wei Po*, January 17, 1996.
25. *Ming Pao*, March 21, 1996.
26. HKEJ, April 15, 1998.
27. SCMP, July 7, 1995; China News Service, July 3, 1995.
28. *Asia Times* (a Bangkok newspaper), April 25, 1997.
29. *The Mirror*, January 1998.
30. NCNA, December 11, 1996; *Wen Wei Po*, January 9, 1998.
31. NCNA, December 27, 1995; January 21, 1998.
32. *Ming Pao*, March 6, 1996.
33. SCMP, July 15, 1995.
34. NCNA, April 17, 1998; *Ming Pao*, April 4, 1998.
35. NCNA, January 17, 1998.
36. NCNA, January 20, 1998.
37. China News Service, December 25, 1995.
38. NCNA, June 22, 1996.
39. NCNA, November 30, 1996.
40. SCMP, January 14, 1998.
41. SCMP, April 10, 1996.
42. China News Service, December 7, 1995.
43. SCMP, January 17, 1996; August 15, 1994.
44. China News Service, March 16, 1996.
45. SCMP, September 20, 1995.
46. Cited in *Ta Kung Pao* (a pro-Beijing Hong Kong daily), January 14, 1996.
47. China News Service, December 20, 1995.
48. SCMP, January 11, 1996.
49. *Wen Wei Po*, April 28, 1996; SCMP, April 16, 1997.
50. *Ming Pao*, March 15, 1996; March 6, 1996.
51. NCNA, June 29, 1996; July 25, 1996.
52. Reuters, August 11, 1986.
53. For a discussion of aid provided by Guangdong and other rich provinces to the interior, see *Newsweek*, October 9, 1995.
54. NCNA, March 16, 1996.
55. Agence France-Presse (AFP), March 5, 1996.
56. *Sing Tao Daily News*, March 8, 1996; NCNA, July 29, 1996.
57. *Ming Pao*, September 11, 1996; HKEJ, October 18, 1995.
58. Author's interviews with Chinese sources.
59. SCMP, March 6, 1996.

60. NCNA, March 16, 1996.

61. NCNA, June 29, 1996.

62. For a discussion of Xinjiang's border trade, see AFP, April 16, 1997; December 1, 1997.

63. The suggestion that members of ethnic minorities be appointed party bosses of regions such as Xinjiang and Tibet was shelved indefinitely after the 15th Party Congress.

64. Author's interviews with Chinese sources in Beijing and Hong Kong.

65. For a discussion of the unstable situation in Xinjiang, see, for example, Reuters, January 8, 1998; March 28, 1997.

66. SCMP, January 12, 1998; *Shenzhen Special Zone Daily* (SSZD) (a Shenzhen daily), December 13, 1995; *Wen Wei Po*, December 14, 1995.

67. *Sing Tao Daily News*, March 6, 1996.

68. SCMP, March 6, 1996.

69. *People's Daily* (Beijing), April 19, 1996.

70. SSZD, December 15, 1995.

71. China News Service, December 25, 1995.

72. NCNA, March 14, 1996.

73. Cited in Hu Angang, *Challenges Facing China* (Taipei: The Journalist Press, 1995), pp. 135–140.

74. NCNA, December 31, 1995.

75. NCNA, December 9, 1995; December 31, 1995.

76. *Ming Pao*, January 18, 1996; NCNA, February 21, 1996; SCMP, February 22, 1996.

77. SSZD, December 13, 1995; *Sing Tao Daily News*, December 12, 1995.

78. SCMP, September 20, 1995.

79. *Ming Pao*, March 6, 1996.

80. SCMP, April 10, 1996.

81. Cited in SCMP, January 29, 1997.

82. *Wen Wei Po*, November 15, 1995; SSZD, December 15, 1995.

83. *Wen Wei Po*, November 15, 1995.

84. SSZD, December 20, 1996; January 24, 1997.

85. SCMP, January 29, 1997.

86. SSZD, January 22, 1997.

87. SSZD, February 27, 1997.

88. SSZD, November 15, 1995.

89. *Wen Wei Po*, March 2, 1997.

90. Beijing's reservations about an excessively intimate relationship between Hong Kong and Guangdong was evidenced by the fact that it was not until the end of March 1998 that the two areas formalised a "Cooperation Joint Conference" to promote symbiotic ties on a regular basis. See *Ming Pao*, March 31, 1998; *Sing Tao Daily News*, March 31, 1998.

91. For a discussion of the relationship between Shenzhen and Hong Kong, see, for example, Roger C.K. Chan, "The Prospect of Special Economic Zones Policy", in Joseph Y.S. Cheng, ed., *China in the Post-Deng Era* (Hong Kong: Chinese University Press, 1998), pp. 440–442.

92. SCMP, June 28, 1994.

93. Despite the abolition of the State Council SEZ Office, Shenzhen was still seen as a national pacesetter in areas including the introduction of foreign capital. See SSZD, May 7, 1998.
94. *Ming Pao*, November 27, 1996.
95. NCNA, December 25, 1995; SCMP, April 10, 1995.
96. *Ming Pao*, November 18, 1996.
97. SCMP, January 14, 1998; *Ming Pao*, January 17, 1998.
98. SCMP, January 16, 1998.
99. SCMP, January 9, 1998; NCNA, March 8, 1998.
100. SCMP, February 7, 1996.
101. NCNA, June 22, 1996; *Ming Pao*, August 15, 1996; December 21, 1996.
102. *Ming Pao*, March 2, 1996; *Guangzhou Daily* (Guangzhou), December 21, 1996.
103. NCNA, February 10, 1998.
104. SCMP, September 7, 1995.
105. *Wen Wei Po*, February 6, 1996; China News Service, November 22, 1996.
106. *Sing Tao Daily News*, January 27, 1996; *Wen Wei Po*, February 27, 1995.
107. SCMP, January 14, 1998.
108. Ibid.
109. Upon arrival in Guangdong in February 1998, Li Changchun met a lot of resistance from local cadres. Central authorities had to dispatch Organisation Department chief Zhang Quanjing to persuade Guangdong officials to accept his appointment. Li told local cadres he would like to stay in Guangdong "for a long period"; see *Wen Wei Po*, March 26, 1998.
110. *Sing Tao Daily News*, January 8, 1998; *Ming Pao*, January 9, 1998.
111. China News Service, January 8, 1998.
112. Author's interviews with experts on Guangdong including Professor Ezra Vogel.
113. SCMP, February 3, 1996.
114. Hong Kong China News Agency (a semi-official news agency), November 18, 1996.
115. Ibid.
116. SCMP, February 4, 1996; *Wen Wei Po*, August 16, 1996.
117. China News Service, January 13, 1998; NCNA, March 2, 1998.
118. Author's interview with Chen Kaizhi.
119. NCNA, February 4, 1996; SCMP, February 5, 1996.
120. Hong Kong China News Agency, January 23, 1998; SCMP, June 16, 1996.
121. HKEJ, January 12, 1998.
122. *Ming Pao*, July 29, 1996.
123. SCMP, September 20, 1995.
124. *Ming Pao*, March 27, 1997; SCMP, January 3, 1997.
125. *United Daily News* (Taipei), July 26, 1995.
126. *Ming Pao*, January 6, 1997.
127. *Outlook Weekly* (Beijing), June 4, 1996.
128. NCNA, October 18, 1995.
129. Cited in *The Mirror*, November 1994.
130. *Outlook Weekly*, April 28, 1997; AFP, April 29, 1997.
131. Reuters, September 19, 1995.

132. Author's interviews with sources in Beijing and Wuhan.
133. SCMP, November 24, 1993.
134. *Ming Pao*, March 15, 1997.
135. Analysts cited as a good example of regional protectionism efforts by the automobile-producing cities of Shanghai, Tianjin, and Wuhan to virtually force companies and individuals within their jurisdictions to buy locally-made cars. The glut in the car market in 1997 and 1998 led to vicious price wars among the manufacturers.
136. By the mid-1990s, regional blocs such as those in southwest and northwest China had put immense pressure on Beijing for a more equitable distribution of resources nationwide.
137. *Ming Pao*, March 1, 1995.
138. *Sing Tao Daily News*, March 10, 1995.
139. China News Service, March 28, 1998; HKEJ, April 2, 1998.
140. China News Service, April 27, 1998; HKEJ, April 27, 1998.
141. Cited in *China Constitutionalism Newsletter* (a San Francisco-based monthly), January 1995, p. 34.
142. *Sing Tao Daily News*, November 28, 1995.
143. *Ming Pao*, March 15, 1996.
144. Author's interviews with Chinese sources in Beijing and Hong Kong.
145. China News Service, March 16, 1996.
146. *The Mirror*, May 1996.
147. For a discussion of pioneering efforts by different provinces to "render small SOEs alive", see, for example, Department of Foreign Affairs and Trade (Australia), ed., *China Embraces the World* (Canberra: Australian Government, 1997), pp. 334–336.
148. China News Service, February 4, 1996.
149. SCMP, September 9, 1995.
150. China News Service, January 10, 1997; January 7, 1998; *Guangzhou Daily*, April 1, 1998.
151. NCNA, April 2, 1997.
152. *Ming Pao*, March 17, 1993.
153. SCMP, April 3, 1997.
154. *Wen Wei Po*, March 9, 1996.
155. *Ming Pao*, March 6, 1996.
156. Ibid.
157. SCMP, March 6, 1996.
158. Cited in *Ming Pao*, March 24, 1997. The idea of regionalism was discussed at the central level in the late 1970s. Then Guangdong party chief Xi Zhongxun tried to persuade Beijing to grant his province autonomous powers equivalent to those of an American state. See Ezra Vogel, *One Step Ahead in China: Guangdong under Reforms* (Cambridge, Massachusetts: Harvard University Press, 1989), p. 85.
159. Cited in Wu Guoguang and Zheng Yongnian, *On the Relationship between the Centre and the Regions* (Hong Kong: Oxford University Press, 1995), p. 33.
160. Author's interview with Wang Shaoguang.
161. SCMP, September 26, 1995; January 11, 1996.

CHAPTER 6

1. For example, Jiang said in his White House press conference in October 1997 that it was a "splendid, colourful" world in terms of the co-existence of different creeds and ideologies. Cited in Ou Yongxi, ed., *Trip of the Century* (Hong Kong: Hong Kong Culture and Education Publishing Ltd., 1998), p. 111.
2. China News Service (a semi-official Chinese news agency), October 22, 1996.
3. In its October 10, 1996 issue, the official *China Daily* (Beijing) accused the Western media of deliberately confusing "patriotism" with "nationalism", saying that more often than not, Chinese authorities were merely celebrating patriotism, not nationalism.
4. New China News Agency (NCNA), November 6, 1996.
5. Agence France-Presse (AFP); September 24, 1997; October 10, 1997.
6. Reuters, November 15, 1996.
7. For a Chinese view of Chris Patten's machinations, see, for example, Guo Shiping, *The Stable Transition and Future Prosperity of the Hong Kong Economy* (Shenzhen, China: Haitian Press, 1997), pp. 79–88.
8. AFP, April 29, 1997; NCNA, April 29, 1997.
9. For a discussion of Beijing's xenophobic tendencies, see, for example, Xiao Pang, ed., *How China Faces the West* (Toronto & Hong Kong: Mirror Books, 1997), pp. 273–283.
10. NCNA, October 13, 1996.
11. *China Daily*, April 15, 1996.
12. *Ming Pao* (a Hong Kong daily), June 20, 1996.
13. *Hong Kong Economic Journal* (HKEJ) (a Hong Kong daily), May 29, 1996.
14. China News Service, June 3, 1996.
15. AFP, July 17, 1996.
16. China News Service, August 4, 1996.
17. Hong Kong China News Agency (a semi-official news agency), June 16, 1996.
18. *Ming Pao*, August 7, 1996.
19. Author's interviews with Chinese sources in Beijing.
20. Cited in Willy Wo-Lap Lam, *China after Deng Xiaoping* (Singapore & New York: John Wiley & Sons, 1995), p. 176.
21. *South China Morning Post* (SCMP) (Hong Kong), August 4, 1996; *China Daily*, August 4, 1996.
22. *Wen Wei Po* (a pro-Chinese Hong Kong daily), May 17, 1996; *Ming Pao*, May 17, 1996.
23. Associated Press, August 12, 1996; HKEJ, June 27, 1996.
24. Hong Kong China News Agency, August 4, 1996.
25. SCMP, September 23, 1996.
26. Reuters, October 3, 1996.
27. SCMP, September 29, 1996; *China Business Weekly* (a Beijing business paper), September 28, 1996.
28. Hong Kong China News Agency, August 4, 1996.
29. *Ming Pao*, August 14, 1996.
30. *People's Daily*, August 12, 1996.
31. HKEJ, May 23, 1996.
32. *Ming Pao*, August 23, 1996.

33. HKEJ, August 22, 1996; *Ming Pao*, August 21, 1996.

34. Author's interview with Yu Haocheng.

35. SCMP, August 28, 1997.

36. The outburst of anti-Japanese feelings included the heightened campaign to seek reparations from Japan regarding World War II atrocities. Author's interviews with activists in China.

37. Cited in HKEJ, October 29, 1996. See Song Qiang *et al.*, *China Can Still Say No* (Hong Kong: Ming Pao Press, 1997), pp. 68–84, for a more detailed description of Sino-Japanese relations.

38. SCMP, January 31, 1997.

39. It was well known among urban intellectuals that at least half of Politburo members had children who had either studied overseas or gained foreign citizenship. Moreover, many "princelings" were working for foreign corporations. After the July 1 handover of Hong Kong, a large number of princelings set up consultancy and other businesses in the Special Administrative Region.

40. Reuters, August 26, 1996.

41. SCMP, April 24, 1996.

42. Ibid.

43. Cited in NCNA, October 11, 1996.

44. NCNA, May 22, 1995.

45. NCNA, May 8, 1995.

46. AFP, September 2, 1996.

47. For a discussion of the revival of Asian values, see, for example, Anwar Ibrahim, *The Asian Renaissance* (Singapore: Times Books International, 1997), pp. 98–99.

48. *People's Daily*, August 13, 1996.

49. NCNA, May 8, 1995.

50. *Wen Wei Po*, October 29, 1996.

51. SCMP, May 9, 1995.

52. SCMP, December 20, 1995.

53. China News Service, December 20, 1995.

54. Cited in SCMP, December 28, 1995.

55. Shanghai and its Pudong district were first conceived as "socialist special economic zones" in the early 1990s. The same was true of the "model" city of Zhangjiagang in Jiangsu.

56. Cited in AFP, August 27, 1997.

57. For a discussion of the limits of Deng-style reforms, see, for example, SCMP, April 22, 1998.

58. For a discussion of political reform initiatives by the third-generation leadership, see Liu Zhifeng, ed., *The Seventh Revolution* (Beijing: Economic Daily Press, 1998), pp. 26–59.

59. Author's interviews with sources in Beijing.

60. Cited in SCMP, September 3, 1997.

61. Cited in HKEJ, March 6, 1998.

62. See, for example, *People's Daily*, March 4, 1998, for Jiang Zemin's views on the development of science and technology.

63. Cited in HKEJ, March 21, 1997.

64. For a discussion of the background of Zhao's "petitions", see, for example, Yuan Hui Zhang, *Zhao Ziyang's Last Chance* (Toronto & Hong Kong: Mirror Books, 1997), pp. 37–56.

65. Author's interviews with sources in Beijing and Hong Kong.

66. SCMP, March 18, 1997; HKEJ, March 18, 1997.

67. Wu Guoguang, a former member of the Central Committee Research Office on Political Reform, published a book in Hong Kong based on the notes he had taken during internal discussion of the subject from 1986 to 1988. See Wu Guoguang, *Political Reform under Zhao Ziyang* (Hong Kong: Pacific Century Institute, 1998). The book had a large circulation in Beijing even though it was officially banned.

68. HKEJ, April 22, 1997.

69. HKEJ, April 3, 1997.

70. See Wu Guoguang, op. cit., pp. 150–151, 161–162.

71. HKEJ, February 25, 1997.

72. HKEJ, April 1, 1997.

73. HKEJ, April 22, 1997.

74. HKEJ, February 4, 1997.

75. Author's interviews with diplomats and foreign businessmen who have met Qiao.

76. Cited in SCMP, April 2, 1997.

77. Ibid.

78. HKEJ, December 28, 1996.

79. *Ming Pao*, April 19, 1995.

80. SCMP, June 26, 1996.

81. NCNA, January 4, 1996.

82. Author's interviews with Chinese sources in Beijing and Hong Kong.

83. For a discussion of Jiang's effort to revive the party chairmanship, see Wu Guoguang, *Power Game in China* (Hong Kong: Pacific Century Institute, 1997), pp. 97–98.

84. Senior cadres with children who had settled or worked in North America included Deng Xiaoping, Liu Huaqing, Zhu Rongji, Huang Ju and Lu Ping.

85. *The Nineties* (a Hong Kong monthly), September 1997.

86. Cited in SCMP, May 27, 1998.

87. Associated Press, July 7, 1996; Kyodo news service, July 23, 1996.

88. HKEJ, August 17, 1996.

89. For a discussion of leftists' opposition to market reforms, see, for example, Shi Liuji, *The 10,000-character Petition and Other Underground Writings in Beijing* (Toronto & Hong Kong: Mirror Books, 1997), pp. 147–169.

90. *The Mirror* (a pro-Chinese Hong Kong journal), April 1997.

91. Ibid.

92. NCNA, May 29, 1997.

93. NCNA, July 30, 1997.

94. For a discussion of the ownership system in the run-up to the 15th Party Congress, see, for example, Li Ping, ed., *The Age of the Thaw* (Beijing: Economic Daily Press, 1997), pp. 341–353.

95. NCNA, November 8, 1996.

96. Kyodo news service, January 10, 1998; SCMP, January 9, 1998.

97. Cited in *Wen Wei Po*, August 13, 1996.

98. NCNA, August 26, 1996.

99. NCNA, July 16, 1997; *China Daily*, July 27, 1996.

100. China News Service, April 30, 1997; HKEJ, May 1, 1997.

101. NCNA, February 7, 1997.

102. NCNA, June 30, 1997.

103. NCNA, December 28, 1996; *Wen Wei Po*, August 4, 1996.

104. NCNA, November 13, 1996.

105. SCMP, January 15, 1996; NCNA, January 14, 1996.

106. *Ming Pao*, July 24, 1996; SCMP, August 25, 1996.

107. SCMP, August 25, 1996.

108. *Wen Wei Po*, July 29, 1996; SCMP, July 30, 1996.

109. Ibid.

110. NCNA, January 10, 1996.

111. NCNA, March 7, 1996.

112. NCNA, July 27, 1996.

113. SCMP, November 16, 1997.

114. SCMP, February 19, 1997.

115. NCNA, January 13, 1997.

116. *People's Daily*, June 21, 1996.

117. Cited in *Shenzhen Special Zone Daily* (a Shenzhen daily), February 21, 1997.

118. SCMP, July 30, 1996.

119. NCNA, July 3, 1996; *Ming Pao*, July 4, 1996.

120. SCMP, July 31, 1996.

121. SCMP, February 19, 1997.

122. *The Mirror*, May 1997.

123. *Ming Pao*, November 16, 1996.

124. NCNA, July 6, 1997.

125. *Sing Tao Daily News* (a Hong Kong daily), August 13, 1997.

126. SCMP, August 1, 1997.

127. NCNA, September 18, 1995; SCMP, August 1, 1997.

128. NCNA, June 20, 1996; April 3, 1997.

129. SCMP, August 1, 1997.

130. *Ming Pao*, July 14, 1996; NCNA, June 19, 1996.

131. NCNA, October 8, 1997; Hong Kong China News Agency, August 16, 1997.

132. NCNA, November 15, 1995; Hong Kong China News Agency, August 1, 1996.

133. Hong Kong China News Agency, September 15, 1997.

134. Cited in Shi Liuji, op. cit., pp. 31–32; China News Service, May 12, 1998.

135. *Ming Pao*, April 5, 1997; Associated Press, September 17, 1997.

136. NCNA, November 20, 1996; *Ming Pao*, October 14, 1996; AFP, April 30, 1997.

137. Cited in SCMP, October 2, 1996.

138. AFP, August 15, 1996; Associated Press, September 9, 1996; SCMP, September 10, 1996.

139. Bloomberg news agency, September 27, 1996.

140. *The Economist* (London), February 7, 1998.

141. Author's interviews with academics at Fudan University.

142. *China Daily*, August 15, 1996.
143. *Ming Pao*, November 7, 1997.
144. *Ming Pao*, October 14, 1995.
145. *Ming Pao*, August 16, 1996; August 2, 1996.
146. China News Service, July 31, 1996.
147. *Ming Pao*, April 30, 1997.
148. Author's interviews with sources in Shanghai.
149. *Oriental Daily News* (a Hong Kong daily), September 6, 1997.
150. See Wang Shan, *Looking at Post-Deng China with a Third Eye* (Hong Kong: China Political and Economic Research Centre, 1998), p. 6.
151. *The Nineties*, May 1997.
152. Cited in HKEJ, May 5, 1997.
153. SCMP, March 21, 1993.
154. HKEJ, May 1, 1997; for a discussion of the "sinicisation" of Hong Kong's political and cultural life, see Willy Wo-Lap Lam, "Beijing's Hong Kong Policy in the First Year of Transition", in Chris Yeung, ed., *Hong Kong China, the Red Dawn* (Sydney: Prentice Hall, 1998), pp. 23–45.
155. HKEJ, April 30, 1997.
156. HKEJ, July 14, 1997.
157. NCNA, July 24, 1997.
158. The example of the Hong Kong Special Administrative Region — and other models for Taiwan's reintegration under the "one country, two systems" formula — also gave a new impetus to the research on federalism, which was undertaken by a couple of think tanks under the Jiang administration.
159. AFP, September 6, 1997.
160. Author's interviews with Chinese sources in Beijing.
161. SCMP, June 4, 1997.
162. Only 20 out of the 60 seats of the Legislature Council were open for elections by universal suffrage. The others were conducted via indirect elections. For example, "functional constituencies" were entitled to 30 seats — and they were dominated by business organisations. The Democratic Party scored a total of 13 seats at the May 1998 elections, making it the largest party in the legislature. However, the entire democratic coalition, including smaller parties such as the Frontline, controlled only 19 seats. See *Ming Pao*, May 25, 1998.
163. SCMP, April 14, 1998.
164. *New York Times*, May 6, 1997.
165. Cited in China News Service, April 30, 1997.
166. See Geremie Barme, "Hong Kong, the Floating City", in *Hong Kong Goes Back* (London: Index on Censorship, 1997), p. 154.
167. *Media* (a Hong Kong biweekly), July 25, 1997.
168. Cited in Jianying Zha, *China Pop* (New York: The New Press, 1995), p. 168.
169. For a discussion of the CIM enterprise, see Zha, op. cit., pp. 165–199.
170. SCMP, December 31, 1994; January 26, 1997.
171. Cited in Barme, op. cit., p. 160.
172. NCNA, July 1, 1997.
173. Special zones such as Tianjin and the Shekou district within Shenzhen were in the mid-1980s allowed to experiment with a limited degree of free elections.

174. Cited in *The Way* (a Beijing magazine), July–August 1997.
175. AFP, August 22, 1997.
176. Author's interviews with Beijing sources. In the wake of the Asian financial crisis, however, Jiang and his aides pretty much stopped talking about Confucianism. There was much more emphasis on "forward-looking" ideas such as "reviving the nation through science and technology".
177. For a discussion of leftists' diatribe against Gorbachev and Yeltsin, see, for example, *In Search of Truth* (a Beijing monthly), June and July 1996.
178. Author's interview with a senior Beijing economist.
179. Author's interviews with Chinese sources in Beijing.
180. HKEJ, June 6, 1996.
181. Cited in SCMP, February 18, 1998; Hong Kong China News Agency, February 20, 1998.
182. Ibid.

CHAPTER 7

1. Cited in *South China Morning Post* (SCMP) (Hong Kong), May 30, 1997.
2. *Ming Pao* (a Hong Kong daily), August 26, 1997.
3. New China News Agency (NCNA), September 12, 1997.
4. Ibid.
5. Reuters, August 31, 1997.
6. Kyodo news service, July 14, 1997.
7. Reuters, September 14, 1997; SCMP, September 23, 1997.
8. China News Service (a semi-official news agency), September 17, 1997.
9. China News Service, September 18, 1997; Associated Press, September 14, 1997.
10. Agence France-Presse (AFP), September 17, 1997; Reuters, September 15, 1997.
11. Author's interview with Wu Jinglian.
12. SCMP, October 16, 1996.
13. Ibid.
14. Associated Press, September 14, 1997.
15. NCNA, September 13, 1997; *China Economic Times* (Beijing), August 12, 1997.
16. China News Service, August 31, 1997; China News Service, August 23, 1997; Reuters, August 5, 1997.
17. Reuters, September 14, 1997.
18. *Wen Wei Po* (a pro-Beijing Hong Kong daily), August 16, 1997.
19. China News Service, July 13, 1997; *Wen Wei Po*, July 13, 1997.
20. NCNA, September 17, 1997.
21. NCNA, October 6, 1997.
22. NCNA, October 1, 1997; China News Service, September 3, 1997.
23. SCMP, October 4, 1997.
24. *Ming Pao*, July 15, 1997.
25. *Sing Tao Daily News* (Hong Kong), September 14, 1997.
26. The official biography of Yu gave him high marks as a reformer. See NCNA, March 18, 1998.

27. *People's Daily*, September 11, 1996; *Wen Wei Po*, September 23, 1997.

28. Jiang tried his very best to build bridges to Wei Jianxing and Li Ruihuan — mostly through the dispensation of favours — and by mid-1998 there were signs that his relationship with the two had improved.

29. Author's interviews with Chinese sources in Beijing and Hong Kong.

30. For a discussion of Li Lanqing's career, see *The Mirror* (a pro-Beijing Hong Kong monthly), October 1997.

31. For a discussion of the career of Zhang Wannian, see *Wide Angle* (a pro-Chinese Hong Kong monthly), September 1995 and February 1997.

32. Jiang met the same problem at the Ninth NPC of March 1998, when several of his favourites — all members of the Shanghai Faction — received substantial negative votes or abstentions during confirmation formalities. They included the candidates for procurator-general and education minister, Han Zhubin and Chen Zhili respectively.

33. For a discussion of Qiao's sudden departure from high-level politics, see *Open* (a Hong Kong monthly), October 1997; *Sing Tao Daily News*, March 5, 1998.

34. *Cheng Ming* (a Hong Kong monthly), October 1997.

35. The promotion of Wei Jianxing to the Politburo Standing Committee and the retention of Tian Jiyun's Politburo position were widely seen as Qiao Shi's conditions for stepping down.

36. Tian retained his position as NPC executive vice-chairman; however, Li Peng apparently decided to give the weightier legislative portfolios to other vice-chairmen such as Xie Fei and Peng Peiyun.

37. SCMP, October 15, 1997.

38. SCMP, October 9, 1997.

39. *Wen Wei Po*, September 20, 1997.

40. *Hong Kong Economic Journal* (HKEJ) (Hong Kong), September 9, 1997; SCMP, August 16, 1997.

41. SCMP, September 4, 1997.

42. Reuters, September 15, 1997; *Apple Daily* (Hong Kong), September 15, 1997; *Ming Pao Monthly* (Hong Kong), October 1997.

43. Cited in SCMP, August 20, 1997.

44. SCMP, September 17, 1997.

45. According to sources close to the 15th Congress, Li Youwei and other Guangdong delegates were criticised for prematurely introducing "capitalist policies" and for widening the gap between the coast and the heartland.

46. Wu Yi was savaged by the "anti-WTO" lobby for sacrificing the interests of native Chinese industry in her aggressive bid to join the world body.

47. AFP, September 16, 1997.

48. *New York Times*, September 19, 1997.

49. AFP, September 9, 1997; *China Business Times*, September 8, 1997.

50. NCNA, September 17, 1997.

51. NCNA, September 19, 1997; *Express* (a Hong Kong daily), April 19, 1997.

52. SCMP, September 18, 1997.

53. SCMP, October 14, 1997.

54. HKEJ, September 25, 1997.

55. Reuters, September 18, 1997.

56. See Wu Jinglian, "On the Reform and Reorganisation of State-owned Enterprises", paper delivered at the Conference on Contemporary Economic Reform and Social Development, Baptist University, Hong Kong, May 11, 1998.
57. HKEJ, September 28, 1997.
58. SCMP, August 27, 1997.
59. It was not until December 1997 that Zhu Rongji reluctantly decided to expand the money supply. Given signs of deflation in 1998, he was criticised that year for holding on to the austerity programme for too long.
60. NCNA, October 6, 1997; SCMP, October 7, 1997.
61. HKEJ, September 27, 1997.
62. NCNA, September 29, 1997.
63. *Ming Pao*, September 15, 1997.
64. Cited in SCMP, September 18, 1997.
65. For a discussion of the leftists' fusillades against reform, see Ma Licheng and Ling Zhijun, *Cross Swords* (Beijing: Today's China Press, 1998), pp. 239–251, 276–281.
66. *Searching After Truth* (a Beijing journal), July 1997.
67. For a discussion of the leftists' views on the Soviet and Russian experience, see Shi Liuji, ed., *The 10,000-character Petition and Other Underground Writings in Beijing* (Toronto & Hong Kong: Mirror Books, 1997), pp. 295–317.
68. SCMP, May 6, 1998.
69. AFP, September 14, 1997; Associated Press, September 14, 1997.
70. SCMP, July 15, 1998.
71. *Open*, May 1998.
72. NCNA, May 29, 1998.
73. China News Service, September 1, 1997.
74. SCMP, August 10, 1997; *Chicago Tribune*, August 17, 1997.
75. SCMP, August 8, 1997.
76. Associated Press, September 6, 1997.
77. HKEJ, October 24, 1997.
78. *People's Daily*, September 13, 1997.
79. Ibid.
80. NCNA, September 7, 1997.
81. Reuters, September 14, 1997.
82. NCNA, September 14, 1997; September 7, 1997.
83. NCNA, August 16, 1997.
84. *Ming Pao*, September 15, 1997.
85. SCMP, July 27, 1997.
86. Author's interviews with Chinese sources in Beijing.
87. *Apple Daily*, September 15, 1997.
88. Author's interviews with Chinese sources in Beijing.
89. *Wen Wei Po*, September 24, 1997.
90. *China Economic Times*, August 12, 1997.
91. Ibid.
92. NCNA, September 17, 1997.
93. Cited in SCMP, September 17, 1997.
94. Cited in SCMP, May 6, 1998.

95. NCNA, August 31, 1997.

96. Hong Kong China News Agency, January 11, 1998.

97. *Open*, February 1998.

98. SCMP, October 2, 1997.

99. For a discussion of the career of Hu Jintao, see *The Mirror*, February 1996.

100. SCMP, January 21, 1998.

101. A good proportion of the young followers of Zhao Ziyang have gone into business and might exert their influence in politics in the 2000s as representatives of the "new class" of private entrepreneurs.

102. NCNA, November 21, 1997.

CHAPTER 8

1. For a discussion of Zhu Rongji's "nomination" as premier, see Xiao Zhengqin, *The Coming Challenges of Premier Zhu Rongji* (Hong Kong: Pacific Century Institute, 1998), pp. 32–36.

2. Cited in Associated Press, March 17, 1998; Reuters, March 17, 1998; *Open* (a Hong Kong monthly), April 1998.

3. Li Peng continued to have much say in areas including legal and security matters. However, he was unable to shed his reputation as the "butcher" of Tiananmen Square and he was widely seen as much less effective a premier than Zhu.

4. *South China Morning Post* (SCMP) (Hong Kong), May 2, 1998. While Zhu was given more authority on foreign affairs, Jiang made sure that the premier would not threaten his dominance over policy towards Taiwan and Hong Kong. For example, Zhu was excluded from the Leading Group on Taiwan Affairs.

5. SCMP, March 18, 1998.

6. *Hong Kong Economic Journal* (HKEJ) (a Hong Kong daily), May 19, 1998; May 21, 1998.

7. *Wen Wei Po* (a pro-Chinese Hong Kong daily), March 20, 1998; SCMP, January 21, 1998.

8. HKEJ, May 5, 1998; May 20, 1998.

9. HKEJ, May 14, 1998; China News Service (a semi-official news agency), April 9, 1998.

10. *Ming Pao* (a Hong Kong daily), April 2, 1998; SCMP, January 1, 1998.

11. For a discussion of Zhu's relationship with Qinghua University and the "Qinghua Faction", see He Ruohan and Shi Tian, *The Biography of China's New Premier Zhu Rongji* (Hong Kong: Ming Pao Press, 1998), pp. 46–54.

12. Cited in SCMP, February 25, 1998. For a discussion of Zhu's ideas on SOE reform, see, for example, Yang Zhongmei, *A Biography of Zhu Rongji* (Taipei: China Times Press, 1998), pp. 225–248.

13. New China News Agency (NCNA), July 26, 1997.

14. SCMP, February 25, 1998.

15. SCMP, October 9, 1997.

16. Cited in SCMP, August 27, 1997.

17. *Ming Pao*, April 7, 1998; *Wen Wei Po*, April 7, 1998.

18. Associated Press, April 7, 1998; *Ming Pao*, April 8, 1998.

19. *Wen Wei Po*, April 3, 1998; *Ming Pao*, April 3, 1998.

20. Cited in Xiao Zhengqin, op. cit., p. 223.

21. Xiao Zhengqin, op. cit., p. 205.

22. Like fellow neo-conservative leaders such as Jiang Zemin, Zhu had a quasi-Maoist belief in the ideal of the "moral superiority" of "new socialist men". He thought that improving the moral quality of cadres was a prerequisite to solving problems ranging from corruption to SOE efficiency.

23. SCMP, May 13, 1998; *Far Eastern Economic Review* (Hong Kong), May 21, 1998.

24. Author's interview with Wu Jinglian.

25. Ibid.

26. SCMP, May 12, 1998.

27. SCMP, May 13, 1998.

28. NCNA, March 19, 1998; March 7, 1998.

29. For a comparison between the Chinese *jituangongsi* and Korean *chaebols*, see Fred Hu, "Should China Grow *Chaebol*", *Asian Wall Street Journal*, December 18, 1997.

30. HKEJ, January 12, 1998; *The Economist* (London), January 10, 1998.

31. For a discussion of Chinese- and Indonesian-style nepotism, see, for example, Su Shaozhi, "On Nepotistic Capitalism", HKEJ, May 21, 1998.

32. For a discussion of Chinese-style *chaebols*, see Pamela Yatsko, "The Bigger, the Better", *Far Eastern Economic Review*, May 21, 1998.

33. *Ming Pao*, March 8, 1998; *Asian Wall Street Journal*, March 8, 1998.

34. One of the rare economists who publicly said the yuan should devalue was Fan Gang, who gave his views to a small audience in Shenzhen. See *Ta Kung Pao* (a pro-Chinese Hong Kong daily), April 12, 1998. However, Fan's ideas were not reported in the Chinese media.

35. Samuel Huntington, *The Clash of Civilizations and the Re-making of the World Order* (New York: Simon & Schuster, 1996). Huntington's views were widely discussed in academic circles in China.

36. There was a general belief among liberal intellectuals in China that the Asian crisis exposed the deficiency of the feudal-Confucianist culture. For example, philosophy professor Ding Zilin, who spearheaded the campaign to overturn the Tiananmen Square verdict, thought that the fall of the Suharto dynasty in Indonesia was indicative of the bankruptcy of "Asian values". See AFP, June 3, 1998.

37. *International Herald Tribune*, May 22, 1998; *New York Times*, January 18, 1998; Reuters, January 21, 1998.

38. AFP, April 10, 1997.

39. *Ming Pao*, May 16, 1998; NCNA, May 21, 1998; AFP, June 3, 1998.

40. *Reform* magazine (Chongqing), April 1998, p. 18.

41. For a discussion of the Hainan experience, see Ru Xin, ed., *The Theory And Practice of "Small Government, Big Society"* (Beijing: Social Sciences Documents Press, 1998), pp. 52–79.

42. *Ming Pao*, February 28, 1998; AFP, April 2, 1998.

43. HKEJ, March 4, 1998.

44. *People's Daily*, April 27, 1998.
45. The value of "red-chip" stocks in Hong Kong fell by huge margins in the first half of 1998. Apart from separation of government and business, other factors behind the downturn included stepped-up efforts by the Zhu administration to crack down on corruption and other questionable deals by SOEs. The latter included those that had close ties with publicly-listed Hong Kong companies.
46. SCMP, March 12, 1998.
47. NCNA, March 27, 1998.
48. *People's Daily* (Beijing), February 16, 1998.
49. Associated Press, March 8, 1998.
50. SCMP, December 26, 1997.
51. SCMP, May 13, 1998; *Reform*, February 1998, p. 52.
52. Kyodo news service, January 10, 1998.
53. *Wen Wei Po*, January 23, 1998.
54. *Wen Wei Po*, April 29, 1998.
55. NCNA, April 28, 1998.
56. China News Service, March 12, 1998.
57. Cited in SCMP, April 15, 1998.
58. SCMP, February 9, 1998.
59. SCMP, February 11, 1998.
60. NCNA, April 7, 1998.
61. NCNA, April 2, 1998; SCMP, April 15, 1998.
62. Hong Kong China News Agency (a semi-official news service), January 10, 1998.
63. Hong Kong China News Agency, January 11, 1998.
64. *Wen Wei Po*, May 17, 1998.
65. Ibid.
66. HKEJ, April 7, 1998.
67. SCMP, January 15, 1998.
68. Liberal legislators had for years lobbied for the establishment of a monetary committee within the NPC which could "supervise" financial and banking policy initiated by the PBoC and other ministries. It was unlikely that the Ninth NPC (1998–2003) could win such powers, particularly given the conservative nature of NPC chairman Li Peng.
69. Author's interviews with sources in Beijing.
70. Cited in SCMP, February 25, 1998.
71. Associated Press, March 8, 1998; SCMP, December 17, 1997.
72. *Ming Pao*, January 11, 1998.
73. NCNA, April 28, 1998.
74. AFP, June 3, 1998; author's interviews with sources in Beijing.
75. SCMP, November 26, 1997.
76. Beijing leaders largely kept their views about "Western conspiracies" to themselves. In public, they sought the help of the West in relieving Asia's plight. For example, in his trip to London in April 1998, Zhu Rongji called on the European Union to adopt a "pro-active" stance in helping countries affected by the meltdown. See *Wen Wei Po*, April 4, 1998; NCNA, April 3, 1998.
77. *People's Daily*, January 6, 1998.

78. Hong Kong China News Agency, May 15, 1998.

79. AFP, April 27, 1998.

80. *Ming Pao*, January 21, 1998.

81. Associated Press, November 2, 1997; *Wen Wei Po*, December 3, 1997.

82. *Wen Wei Po*, January 23, 1998.

83. NCNA, January 21, 1998.

84. *United Daily News* (Taipei), November 23, 1997.

85. SCMP, December 21, 1997.

86. *Sing Tao Daily News* (Hong Kong), May 30, 1998.

87. *Next* (a Hong Kong newsweekly), May 21, 1998; AFP, May 20, 1998.

88. NCNA, January 24, 1998.

89. Cited in SCMP, April 22, 1998.

90. Ibid.

91. *Yunnan Daily* (Kunming), November 13, 1997.

92. Cited in SCMP, May 18, 1998.

93. "Institutional building" was first proposed by Qiao Shi. For a discussion of his reform ideas, see, for example, Gao Xin, *Qiao Shi, The Chinese Communist Party's Heavyweight Politician* (Taipei: World Bookstore, 1995), pp. 269–275.

94. SCMP, April 29, 1998; *Newsweek* (Asia Edition), April 13, 1998; Associated Press, May 2, 1998.

95. SCMP, May 20, 1998.

96. SCMP, April 22, 1998; July 11, 1998.

97. Author's interviews with Chinese sources in Beijing.

98. For a discussion of the significance of Deng's *nanxun*, see Willy Wo-Lap Lam, *China after Deng Xiaoping* (Singapore & New York: John Wiley & Sons, 1995), pp. 17–25.

99. Cited in *Open*, February 1998.

100. For a discussion of the "Americanisation" of Chinese values and systems, see Willy Wo-Lap Lam, "US Packs a Punch as Clinton Flies in", SCMP, June 17, 1998.

101. Associated Press, July 3, 1998.

Abbreviations and Glossary

ASEAN ■ Association of Southeast Asian Nations

biaotai ■ "airing of views" (by cadres in a political campaign)

bingshang ■ army businesses

CASS ■ Chinese Academy of Social Sciences

CCDI ■ Central Commission for Disciplinary Inspection

CCP ■ Chinese Communist Party

chaebol ■ a South Korean conglomerate

CMC ■ Central Military Commission

CPLA ■ Commission for Political and Legal Affairs

CPPCC ■ Chinese People's Political Consultative Conference

CYL ■ Communist Youth League

diktat **economy,** also **command economy** ■ an economy driven by state planning

fupin ■ save the poor

gaoganzidi, also **princelings** ■ sons and daughters of senior officials

getihu ■ "individually" run enterprises

guanxi ■ connections

gufenhua ■ a reference to turning SOEs into shareholding or joint-stock companies

gumin ■ "stocks-crazed" citizens

IPW ■ ideological and political work

jituangongsi ■ a conglomerate (sometimes called Chinese-style *chaebol*)

June 4 ■ often, a shorthand for the June 4, 1989 massacre

mu ■ a unit of measurement that is equal to 0.0667 hectare

nanxun ■ Deng Xiaoping's "imperial tour" of southern China in early 1992

NCNA, also **Xinhua** ■ the official New China News Agency

NPC ■ National People's Congress

PAP ■ People's Armed Police

PBoC ■ People's Bank of China

PLA ■ People's Liberation Army

PSB ■ Public Security Bureau, or the police

PSC ■ Politburo Standing Committee

renminbi or **yuan** ■ the Chinese currency

SAR ■ The Special Administrative Region (of Hong Kong)

Shanghaibang ■ the Shanghai Faction led by Jiang Zemin

SOE ■ state-owned enterprise

Tiananmen or **Tiananmen Square** ■ often, a shorthand for the June 4, 1989 crackdown

VTE ■ village and township enterprise

WTO ■ World Trade Organisation

xiahai ■ "diving into the sea of business"

Xinhua ■ see NCNA

yanda ■ the "strike hard" campaign against crime

yifazhiguo ■ running the country according to law; rule by law *yifazhisheng* ■ running a province according to law

Zhaoists ■ followers of ousted party chief Zhao Ziyang

zhidu ■ "systems and institutions" of governance

Zhongnanhai ■ the site of party and government headquarters in central Beijing

zhongxibu ■ the central and western provinces

zhongyang ■ the "central authorities"

zhuada fangxiao ■ the industrial strategy of "taking a firm grip on large-scale enterprises and letting the small ones go free"

Index